Publishing Contemporary Foreign Poetry

Transnational Exchange in the Italian Publishing Field, 1939–1977

Transnational Italian Cultures 8

Transnational Italian Cultures

Series editors:
Dr Emma Bond, University of St Andrews
Professor Derek Duncan, University of St Andrews

Transnational Italian Cultures publishes the best research in the expanding and increasingly diverse field of transnational Italian studies, thus setting new agendas for critical thinking on Italian culture. Interdisciplinary in nature, the series brings together innovative work investigating human mobility and cultural circulation in all their forms. With a strong list of publications in literary and visual cultures, the editors now see the series extending into other disciplinary fields such as the creative, environmental, digital and medical humanities which lend themselves to the kind of transnational methodologies the series promotes.

Publishing Contemporary Foreign Poetry

Transnational Exchange in the Italian Publishing Field, 1939–1977

Mila Milani

LIVERPOOL UNIVERSITY PRESS

First published 2023 by
Liverpool University Press
4 Cambridge Street
Liverpool
L69 7ZU

This paperback edition published 2025

Copyright © 2025 Mila Milani

Mila Milani has asserted the right to be identified as the author of this book in accordance with the Copyright, Designs and Patents Act 1988.

All rights reserved. No part of this book may be reproduced, stored in a retrieval system, or transmitted, in any form or by any means, electronic, mechanical, photocopying, recording, or otherwise, without the prior written permission of the publisher.

British Library Cataloguing-in-Publication data
A British Library CIP record is available

ISBN 978-1-83764-440-7 (hardback)
ISBN 978-1-83624-549-0 (paperback)

Typeset by Carnegie Book Production, Lancaster

Contents

Acknowledgements	vii
Introduction: Publishing and Poetry Translation: A Methodological Introduction	1
1 Publishing, Culture, and Poetry: A Field Investigation	11
2 Editors, Habitus, and Translation: Publishing Strategies in Poetry Translation	55
3 Contemporary Foreign Poetry Anthologies for New Cultural and Publishing Horizons	155
4 Towards Globalisation, by Way of a Conclusion	205
Appendix One: Numbers of contemporary poetry titles published in Italy, 1939–77	217
Appendix Two: Catalogue of contemporary Italian and foreign poetry titles published by Einaudi, Mondadori, and Scheiwiller, 1939–77	225
Works Cited	241
Index	257

Acknowledgements

The writing of this book coincided with a very significant period of research and personal development for me, which took a bit longer than expected due in part to the Covid-19 pandemic and the lack of access to archival fieldwork. I would like here to thank all those people who, in different ways, have sustained me throughout this 'journey'.

Special thanks are due to Francesca Billiani, who since my PhD years has always encouraged me, and provided me with generous advice at the start of my academic career. Thanks very much to Jenny Burns for her support throughout, and for reading some of the chapters. Thanks also to those who have read earlier versions of this work, in different languages and forms, from Francesco Maria Ciconte, Spencer Pearce, and Nigel Vincent, to Loredana Polezzi and Anastasia Valassopoulos. And thanks to those scholars with whom I have discussed my research over the years, alongside matters of translation, publishing, and sociology, at many conferences or in relation to other publications, including Giuliana Benvenuti, Daria Biagi, Jacob Blakesley, Anna Boschetti, Stefania De Lucia, Irene Fantappiè, Anna Lanfranchi, Daniela La Penna, Carol O'Sullivan, Kalliopi Pasmatzi, Chris Rundle, Michele Sisto, Sara Sullam, and Blaise Wilfert.

My gratitude goes to the staff at archives in Italy, who helped me to carry out such fascinating research: Anna Lisa Cavazzuti and Tiziano Chiesa (Fondazione Arnoldo e Alberto Mondadori di Milano); Raffaella Gobbo and Gaia Riitano (Centro APICE – Università di Milano); Valentina Bocchi (Archivio di Stato di Parma) and Chiara Tincati (Biblioteca Guanda di Parma); Federica Paglieri (Archivio di Stato di Torino). I would also like to thank all the copyright holders and estates for permission to quote from unpublished material in this book, particularly Walter Barberis and late president Roberto Cerati at Einaudi, and Alina Kalczyńska. Every effort was made to seek permission where copyright could be identified.

At Liverpool University Press, I would like to thank the series editors for giving me this opportunity, Chloe Johnson and the editorial team for their invaluable help, and the two anonymous readers who assessed the manuscript. I also wish to thank Georgia Wall for her help with proofreading earlier drafts of this work, and Amanda Recupero for her final check before submission.

Thanks to current and former colleagues at the University of Warwick, particularly Valentina Abbatelli and Caterina Sinibaldi, who have always helped to keep my spirits up. Special thanks go to Linda Shortt, for her friendship, precious support, and fun and laughter. Last but not least, I am grateful to my friends across the world, to my family, and especially to my parents for their unfaltering support. And to Irvin, to whom this book is dedicated: *grazie di tutto, semplicemente*.

Introduction: Publishing and Poetry Translation: A Methodological Introduction

The years following the Second World War saw an exponential increase in the translation of contemporary foreign poetry in Italy. The practice was at its most prevalent in the 1950s and 1960s, when publishing houses across the board almost doubled the number of foreign poetry titles in their catalogues. This remarkable phenomenon has, however, received scant critical attention. Poetry translations have largely been analysed from an aesthetic perspective, perhaps disregarded by more interdisciplinary approaches for their generally elite reception sphere. While poetry may not have a mainstream audience, by reaching out to elites, educators, and students, it has a fundamental role in shaping literary taste as a whole (Piazzoni, 2021: 180); when it comes to poetry *in translation*, we contend, it also has a pivotal function in orienting power relationships both within and beyond national borders. *Publishing Contemporary Foreign Poetry: Transnational Exchange in the Italian Publishing Field, 1939–1977* examines the sociological significance of publishing poetry translations by looking at patterns of cultural exchange vis-à-vis the internal dynamics and conflicts within key publishing houses. It explores the internal reconfiguration of Italian culture in the period following the Second World War, and how Italy sought to position itself in the world, without neglecting the contradictions of national and transnational cultural networks and movements.

This book investigates the role of poetry translation, both as a process and as a product, in the Italian publishing field from 1939 to 1977. These roughly forty years chart the increase in poetry translations, from the establishment of the first series devoted to contemporary foreign poetry, 'La Fenice' [The Phoenix], in 1939 by the Parma-based small-scale publishing house

Guanda, to the launch of the 'Libri Scheiwiller' [Scheiwiller Books] series by the independent Milan-based publisher Scheiwiller in 1977, an initiative supported by Italian banks which paved the way for a more globalised distribution system. Within this timeframe, we pay particular attention to the 1950s and 1960s. These decades could be dubbed a second 'decennio delle traduzioni' [decade of translations], following the first increase of translated novels that Italy experienced in the interwar period (Pavese, 1951: 247). What provoked this poetry translation 'boom'? What function did poetry in translation have in supporting, challenging, or subverting the cultural and literary fields of post-war Italy? To what extent and how did specific publishers employ translation strategically to (re)shape their role within the sector? How did translation help to reconfigure the position of Italy and Italian cultural operators in the wider, transnational context? Responding to these questions, we argue that translation was a means of modifying power relationships within the field of poetry publishing and the contemporary literary arena; this ultimately changed the map of Italian cultural production and its transnational networks, thus preparing the ground for the further developments provoked by globalisation in the 1980s.

Publishing Contemporary Foreign Poetry is not a history of poetry translation in Italy. Rather, it provides readers with a *histoire croisée* ('entangled history', Werner and Zimmermann, 2006) of publishing dynamics in post-Second World War Italy and the sociological praxis of translation. This means taking a 'relational, interactive and process-oriented perspective' (Werner and Zimmermann, 2006: 39), whereby points of intersection – in our case contemporary foreign poetry in translation – can produce change depending on the degree of permeability or resistance of the research object – the Italian literary and publishing fields. We therefore focus on why and how, through the publication of foreign poetry, Italian publishers developed transnational exchanges that informed internal and external power dynamics.

Drawing on the concept of *histoire croisée*, we employ the term 'transnational' to indicate a form of interconnection across nations that is not superimposed on to the national, but interacts with the latter to produce a more meaningful historical and cultural account of our object of study. In this sense, the term 'transnational' differs from both 'international', which might imply a hierarchy over local, regional, and national levels, and 'cosmopolitan', whose pejorative use would see it as a predominantly elite 'taste for cultural artefacts from around the world' (Vertovec and Cohen, 2002: 5). If one of the criticisms is that 'transnational' reinforces the concept of 'national' (Vertovec, 2009: 17), we agree that it 'recognizes the significance of national frameworks alongside the potential of cultural production both to reinforce and to transcend them' (De Cesari and Rigney, 2014: 4). In other words, we acknowledge the specificity of the national and its dynamic interconnectedness with the transnational to illuminate the tensions between culture and institutions – including, in our case, publishing houses – in a given historical context. This places the present study within recent developments in Italian Studies that outline the need to take a 'transnational turn' in the discipline which does not just stretch the borders of the nation-state as unit of cultural analysis, but also aims to highligh its porosity and its transnational character (Bond, 2014). It is not a question of uncritically 'globalising' the discipline but of conceiving Italian culture as 'constructed in and through the tension between the national [...] and transnational modes of production, circulation and fruition' (Burdett, Havely, and Polezzi, 2020: 232).

If transnational interactions have a particular focus on people, 'the social space that they inhabit, the networks they form and the ideas they exchange' (Clavin, 2005: 422), cultural products, including notably translations, are equally important. Translation holds for us a key position as an analytical category: the study of culture has to investigate its 'involvement [...] in the ways the translation market is composed, and in political-cultural fields of power' (Bachmann-Medick, 2014: 7), but also, we argue, the ways in which translation *shapes* these political-cultural fields. In this book, we employ the term 'translation' in its broadest sense, from the process of cultural exchange to textual practice. This enables us to use translations as hermeneutic tools and sites for negotiation where transnational presences and national discourses interweave. It also means shifting the perspective by looking at how the shape of the 'national' history of publishing is interconnected with transnational movements, networks, and texts. As such, we can complement (or question) domestic historical accounts (Ferretti, 2004; 2012), whose established and richly detailed investigations of Italian cultural production generally disregard translation perspectives.

Our entangled history intends to make evident how the value of studying poetry translation goes beyond an aesthetic study and offers a means of understanding the way translation shapes culture and politics. To this end, we adopt an interdisciplinary approach that productively integrates theoretical tools from Italian History of Culture and Publishing, Sociology of Cultural Production, and Translation Studies. In Italian Studies, investigations into the relationship between publishing and translation to date have focused primarily on key issues related to the Fascist regime, such as censorship and systems of cultural control (Billiani, 2007a; Rundle, 2010; Rundle and Sturge,

2010). Less systematic attention has been paid to the post-war republic, with the exception of studies focusing on the exchanges between Italy and the British and US poetic traditions (Caselli and La Penna, 2008), or sociological explorations of German literature in translation (Baldini et al., 2018; Sisto, 2019). This leaves a notable gap in our knowledge of the history of publishing and translation history in Italy and, crucially, a lack of understanding of the cultural and literary dynamics of post-Second World War Italian history from a transnational perspective. The current study addresses precisely this gap.

In Translation Studies, aesthetic, often empirical, analyses of poetry have been typical for decades.[1] To contest this unhelpful practice, scholars (Jones, 2011a; Blakesley, 2018a; 2018b) have recently engaged with the sociology of poetry translation, alluding to the fact that poetry translation, on account of being relatively less economically driven, is 'more likely to encourage experimental strategies that can reveal what is unique about translation as a linguistic and cultural practice' (Venuti, 2013: 174). It is necessary nonetheless to recognise the *historical* specificities of a certain publishing sector. Our investigation of poetry translation draws on an extensive range of previously unpublished correspondence between editors, translators, and publishers held in the archives of three key Italian publishing houses.[2] The three publishers have been chosen as representatives of small-, medium-, and large-scale publishers, which produced dedicated poetry series in the years under investigation. They are the elitist Milan-based Scheiwiller, founded in 1951 by Vanni Scheiwiller, who developed his father Giovanni's interwar publishing ventures; the left-wing publishing house Giulio Einaudi Editore, founded in 1933 in Turin by anti-fascist Giulio Einaudi; and the leading

---

1 This, starting from Holmes (1988), was probably due to the complexity of the meaning–form link. To move away from the dichotomy between form and meaning, other scholars focus on rhythm (Meschonnic, 1973), see poetry translation as a creative process (Robinson, 2010; Reynolds, 2011), or an act of reading and interpretation (Scott, 2000; Folkart, 2007); others draw on cognitive frameworks and focus on 'style' as an expression of the poet's mind (Boase-Beier, 2006).

2 In our more focused approach on editorial roles, we do not analyse at length other key players such as literary agents. Their pragmatic importance, in terms of making transnational exchanges and translations possible through the acquisition of translation rights, is not neglected, and we welcome in this sense recent studies such as Cécile Cottenet, *Literary Agents in the Transatlantic Book Trade: American Fiction, French Rights, and the Hoffman Agency* (New York: Routledge, 2017); Anna Ferrando, *Cacciatori di libri: gli agenti letterari durante il fascismo* (Milan: FrancoAngeli, 2019); and Anna Lanfranchi's PhD thesis, 'Contacts and Relationships between Italian and British Publishing Houses at the Beginning of the 20th Century' (University of Manchester, 2021).

and more traditionally canonical Milan-based Arnoldo Mondadori editore, founded in 1907. While substantial accounts drawing on the relevant archival data of each of these publishers already exist (Ferretti, 2009, for Scheiwiller; Turi, 1992, and Mangoni, 1999, for Einaudi; Decleva, 2007, for Mondadori), they tend to relegate poetry as well as translation to a marginal site.

The use of primary sources is instrumental in accessing working processes to produce a microhistory (Munday, 2014) that contributes to re-evaluating lesser-known agents and unveiling the materiality of literary processes.[3] In the following chapters, we explore the editorial discourse revealed by archival research as individual as well as collective sociological 'narratives' (Baker, 2006), which publishing agents elaborate in relation to their own literary, professional, social, or political trajectories, and which intersect with broader narratives developed by institutions such as publishing houses, literary, cultural or political movements.

To fully grasp how the dynamics of cultural production relate to sociocultural factors, in the critical analysis of these narratives we use Bourdieu's conceptual tools, such as field, symbolic capital, and habitus. Translation Studies scholars have engaged extensively with these concepts in the last two decades (e.g., Inghilleri, 2007; Wolf and Fukari, 2007; Vorderobermeier, 2014; Hanna, 2016); the debate has nevertheless prioritised the history of translators, while looking at how translation and publishing interact is crucial for our analysis. The field is a historical, *relatively* autonomous site of negotiating diverse capitals – economic, cultural, social, and more crucially symbolic, as source of honour and prestige – where agents undertake a fluid struggle over the appropriation of these capitals (Bourdieu, 1993; 1996). Based on these coordinates, some agents can be considered 'new' entrants to the field, who may draw on sources of symbolic capital (such as literary innovation) to position themselves against more established 'old' entrants, bearers of cultural capital. This applies particularly well to the artisanal character of the Italian sector of poetry publishing in the 1950s and 1960s, whereby agents were 'letterati editori' [literati publishers] (Cadioli,

---

3 Archival materials include mostly editorial correspondence, and, where available, drafts – or endogenetic *avant-textes* (Cordingley and Montini, 2015: 2) – and manuscripts with editorial notes. Though not objective and legitimated by institutional power (Foucault, 2002), these materials have been privileged as opposed to other ethnographical tools such as interviews (with those few agents still alive); as more overtly mediated sources (Munday, 2014: 68), interviews would also risk shifting the overall perspective in allowing post-hoc accounts and more subjective narratives to emerge.

2003), meaning that literary authors also acted as professional figures such as editors, publishers, and reviewers. The dynamics of the literary field, and the evolution of literary movements, thus decidedly interwove with those of the publishing field.

Agents adopt specific practices, or in Bourdieusian terms, 'position-takings', according to their values, dispositions, personal tastes, family inclinations, cultural background, as well as social trajectories, especially important for those 'letterati editori'. This is what Bourdieu defines as habitus, a 'system of durable, transposable dispositions, structured structures predisposed to function as structuring structures' (Bourdieu, 1977: 53), in which agents are simultaneously influencing and influenced by social structures, including their status or their publishers' status within the field. For instance, agents may lean towards a more 'heretical' position that is less orthodox, canonical, or traditional. Not the result of rational calculations but of dispositions internalised through socialisation, the concept of habitus avoids in part a deterministic reading of the agents' practice while debunking the misconception that agents are entirely indifferent to the negotiation of capitals. This is notably helpful in moving away from a merely aesthetic appreciation of poetry translation and small-scale publishing, an enduring perspective also in twenty-first-century Italian editors' public discourses (Pareschi and Lusiani, 2020).

The strategies for the publication of foreign poetry, conceived as a multiphase publishing process that moves from the initial selection of a foreign author to the textual practice of translation, are influenced by factors operating both within and externally to publishing houses and the agents that form them. But when speaking of translation, these strategies entail an explicitly transnational exchange, informed by the pressures and priorities of global cultural and political movements as well as the transnational network of influence. The national and transnational levels are shaped by one another, and this cross-fertilisation can be traced in the micro-dynamics of publishing strategies. The decision to publish a specific foreign author might be influenced by transnational connections (literary or broader political affinities) and reflect intellectual engagement within and beyond national borders. As a result, the publishing strategies related to contemporary foreign poetry in translation are a lens through which we can observe the transnational Italian history of culture.

Field analysis alone, however, fails to reflect the empirical aspects of the process of translation and its degree of heterogeneity and unpredictability. Although the present work does not systematically apply Social Network

Analysis (SNA) tools (i.e. graphs), it does take into account the articulate network of national and translational agents within and beyond the field, and considers the concrete interactions that emerge from the publishing correspondence examined. This includes the network of interactions between the translator and the other agents involved in the process of translation, including the translated text (Buzelin, 2005; 2007). Inspired by Bruno Latour's Actor Network Theory, which maintains that non-human as well as human actors can provoke change, translations are seen as texts, and translation drafts can be considered 'actors' in that they trigger responses on the part of translators, reviewers, and publishers. While we do not engage with the aesthetics of reception at large, we critically review hitherto unpublished editorial correspondence alongside examples of textual practice. These materials are textual (such as the specific translation choices, in terms of style and language, of some of the most significant poetry translations) – though limited to the languages we can read (English, French, Italian, some Spanish); paratextual (book covers, prefaces, footnotes), intertextual (journal reviews); and extratextual (actual print runs and sales, where available), in order to look at the very shape of the translation process in its materiality also. This unveils the network of relations behind the translation process, through which the agents – with their own specific habitus – negotiated the final product. In this sense, our textual analysis reaffirms translation as a fundamentally social practice.

Within this composite sociological framework, translation is reconceptualised as a means for publishers and intellectuals to gain the necessary 'symbolic capital' to reconfigure their position within the publishing and cultural fields (Heilbron and Sapiro, 2002: 7). This shifts the focus from a purely aesthetic consideration of poetry translation as an elite, cosmopolitan practice to a meaningful account of its historical function in developing transnational intellectual identities. Foreign poetry is generally considered a niche cultural product in comparison with national literature. Yet, despite its marginality in generic terms, foreign poetry as a source of prestige was a marked element of the cultural production of Italian publishers during this period. It became a key site in the struggle for intellectual prestige and publishing dominance and in reshaping the identity of Italian intellectuals within both national and transnational networks.

In this book, we therefore see poetry translation both as a publishing process, in which cultural agents' social positioning within the Italian as well as the (trans)European cultural fields strategically influences the selection of foreign poets, and as a publishing product, for its editing reflects contingent social, cultural, and historical dynamics that extend beyond national borders. The book follows three main lines of inquiry at a macro, meso, and micro level of social analysis, developed in the three main chapters. In Chapter 1, we provide the first sociological investigation to date of the role of translation in the poetry publishing field, spanning the years from the Second World War until the 1960s. The chapter examines the reasons for the increase in contemporary poetry published in translation in post-war Italy, and explores how this transnational turn in publishing modified the functions and dispositions of literary and cultural figures in Italy. We discuss how small- and larger-scale publishers sought, through translation, editorial paths to gain centrality in the national context and to position themselves in a wider transnational circuit. In tracing the publishing movements towards translation, we bring into question the perceived marginality of elitist publishing houses.

This largely unexplored change in publishing dynamics had a significant impact on the literary field of the time: editors, often poets and translators themselves, negotiated their social, cultural, and literary status through the publication of contemporary foreign poetry. Chapter 2 analyses the publishing strategies of each of the three publishers under investigation; a subsection is dedicated to each publisher, offering exhaustive reviews, but simultaneously placing the focus on the interrelated publishing strategies exhibited by the three publishing houses. The chapter maps the publishers' transnational exchanges, not only outlining geographical spaces but also exploring the passage from more elite, cosmopolitan dispositions (as in the case of Scheiwiller) to the accrual of transnational intellectual capital for Italian publishers and editors (as with Einaudi). The turn to translation also generated unexpected allegiances between publishing institutions and poetry movements within and across national borders. The chapter pays attention to the oft-neglected translating activities of some key Italian poets (including Camillo Pennati and Rodolfo Wilcock) and women translators (including Joyce Lussu and Mariolina Meliadò) of the period, as well as to the contemporary reception of the published poems.

Chapter 3 is concerned with how textual typologies, and particularly foreign poetry anthologies – fundamental to the formation of national and transnational literary canons as promoters of specific poetry models – evolved in relation to these publishing and editorial needs, and in relation to national and transnational historical and cultural processes informing the decades under consideration. Through our close reading of these texts in relation to contemporary poetry trends, as well as the habitus of the publishers under consideration, we observe the changing role of poet-translators and look at how new cultural perspectives and politically oriented forms of foreign poetry informed the intellectual function of Italian editors. The concluding and shorter Chapter 4 offers some initial reflections on the paradoxical situation established after 1969, in which the leading publishers regained strength through the publication of foreign poetry, while the small publishers, conversely, tried to resist marginality by drawing on contemporary Italian poetry. Negotiation of power relations in the field, we argue, eventually changed the map of Italian cultural production, stirring contradictory tensions that would be exacerbated by globalisation in the 1980s.

By focusing on the practice and production of translation, *Publishing Contemporary Foreign Poetry* offers new insights into the shifting dynamics of the publishing field, the micro-history of its translation agents, and their (at times controversial and surprising) relationships to the wider historical and cultural panorama of post-Second World War Italy in the context of Europe and beyond. The following pages will unfold a *trans*disciplinary analysis of the mechanisms at work when publishing foreign poetry: this will lay the foundations for a new way of studying the history of publishing by placing it into more explicit dialogue with transnational approaches, thus ultimately contributing to the development of current research in both Italian and Translation Studies.

CHAPTER ONE

Publishing, Culture, and Poetry: A Field Investigation

In the 1950s and 1960s the number of contemporary foreign poetry titles in the catalogues of both small- and large-scale Italian publishing houses increased systematically, indicating a dramatic transnational opening of the Italian publishing field: as the data collected in Appendix 1 show, figures increased from only one translation in 1951 to 24 new titles in 1969. This trend saw an average of six new titles published per year between 1951 and 1959, an average that tripled between 1960 and 1969. Poetry translations, previously published either sporadically by small publishing houses or occasionally in specialised literary magazines, also carved out a less fickle space in the publishing catalogues and were regularly published in ad hoc poetry series, such as Guanda's 'La Fenice' (1939–), Mondadori's 'Lo Specchio' [The Mirror] (1940–), Vanni Scheiwiller's 'All'insegna del pesce d'oro' [Under the Banner of the Goldfish] (1951–), and Einaudi's 'Collezione di poesia' [Poetry Collection] (1964–).

In the same period, Hermeticism, the national poetic tradition of the 1930s and 1940s focused on lyrical subjectivity and evocative imagery, passed its peak and came to its sunset (Bàrberi Squarotti and Golfieri, 1984). The closed and obscure Hermetic forms now felt stagnant, and a demand for stylistic and ideological realism, seeking a down-to-earth portrait of reality and societal issues, emerged more firmly. The 'polycentric' Italian poetry that developed in the first half of the twentieth century alongside Hermeticism would respond to this demand in more accomplished terms only in the second half (Crocco, 2015: 80). The negligible poetry translation activity in the first half of the 1940s – arguably also related to the more stringent censorship of the period (Rundle, 2010) and the close relationship between some key publishers and Fascism (Billiani, 2007a) – had not fully responded to this demand either (Lorenzini, 2005: 102). This shift would culminate in the immediate aftermath of the Second World War in the controversial productions of neorealism.

The concurrence of these two events – an increase in contemporary poetry translation and a move away from older forms of national poetry, one apparently linked to publishing logics, the other connected to literary dynamics – is highly significant for our analysis of the role that translation played, as both cultural product and process, in the history of Italian publishing. What were the reasons for this more systematic insertion of contemporary foreign poetry into the reading material of the Italian public? This raises other questions. In what ways does this reflect the interaction between, on one side, the aesthetic needs of a literary field out of Hermetic breath and desirous of new poetic forms, and, on the other, the pressing issues of a publishing world that, emerging from the Second World War, was undergoing radical internal development and moving towards industrialisation? Which were the modalities of this 'turn' to translation and its effects on Italian publishing? And ultimately, how did transnational directions interact with national dynamics?

A sociological perspective enables us to respond productively to these key questions. We see the Italian poetry publishing of the time as a Bourdieusian 'field', a space of interactive forces where diverse capitals – mainly but not exclusively symbolic – are sought after, thus generating reciprocal negotiations between the participating cultural agents, such as publishers, editors, poets, and translators. For literary and publishing agents who lack either cultural or economic capital, translation can be a means of legitimising symbolic capital (Heilbron and Sapiro, 2002). In addition, in a context relatively less focused on economic profit such as the poetry sector, the concepts of 'centre' and 'periphery', as defined by Wallerstein (2011) in relation to economic capital, and applied by de Swaan (2001) to world languages, are particularly effective; they make it possible for us to maintain a spatial metaphor of greater fluidity compared to the more static binary of 'dominant' and 'dominated' typical of Bourdieusian analysis. The distinction between centre and periphery does not involve a hegemonic subordination of one of the poles, thus avoiding a sterile geometry of relations that would be unable to synthesise the complex dynamics between the agents (Boschetti, 2010: 13). Rather, the peripheral and central positions can enter into dialogue and negotiate with each other, thus modifying the lay of the field itself. From this angle, we can provide a different vision of the role assumed by small publishers in particular, and overturn the stereotype of their functional marginality compared with the supposedly overwhelming power of the larger publishers.

Following these methodological lines, in this chapter we offer a chronological examination of the interaction between key cultural, publishing, and literary events from the end of the 1940s to the 1960s, with a particular focus on the 1950s. Looking at these wider phenomena through the lens of translation facilitates a more accurate understanding of the role of both small and larger-scale publishing houses and of alternative power relationships in the specific field of poetry. This contributes to a reassessment of the Italian history of publishing. From the static nature of both poetry and publishing at the end of the 1940s, coupled with the predominance of larger publishing houses, in the 1950s we see small publishers gaining a more central position thanks to translation projects. Such a change pushed the medium- to large-scale publishers to turn to translation, a move that redefined publishing production in Italy. The specific focus on foreign poetry also allows us to illuminate more effectively the new transnational perspective of Italian poets, translators, and editors in the decades under consideration, and how they shifted their interests, as well as the modalities of their engagement, from modernism to post-war realism and later to experimentalism. The result is a more critical, and less idealistic, appraisal of how transnational appeals interact with economic, publishing, and intellectual discourses.

Although we cannot deny the importance of other agents spread across the country and their regional peculiarities, our discussion here focuses on the key publishing centres, and crucial nodes of cultural production, of Turin and Milan, in order to keep this overview relatively brief and allow us to concentrate more strictly on poetry translation. This will strategically shed light on the main interlocutors that are the subject of Chapter 2, namely Scheiwiller, Mondadori, and Einaudi.

1.1 From interwar Hermeticism to post-war neorealism: the poetry publishing field being 'normalised'

In the first years of the Fascist regime and during the Second World War, specialised poetry publishers had already published translations, but with a more limited focus: Appendix 1 reveals that the overall number of titles was scant, with an average of 1.5 titles per year between 1939 and 1950. We contend that the publications were informed by a specific aesthetic trend, which linked professionally eclectic translators, generally belonging to the Hermetic movement, to a transnational modernist perspective that had been developing in Europe in the first part of the twentieth century, introducing elements of formal innovation such as precision as a means of linguistic expression.¹ A brief overview of the foreign poets published in the 1940s by the small publishers spread across the national domain, such as Giovanni Scheiwiller and Guanda, will illustrate this pattern more clearly.²

Although specialised in the arts, Scheiwiller showed a varied approach to poetry translation, ranging from controversial to more canonical authors. In 1938 he published the Russian Imagist poet Sergei Yesenin, translated by Dutch specialist Giacomo Prampolini, as part of the *Canto liturgico* [Liturgical Chant] collection. Scheiwiller's publication demonstrated the wider freedom that poetry enjoyed in relation to Fascist censorship when compared with other genres: Yenesin's blasphemous themes would have marked the book as 'un'opera ad alto grado sismico, se la censura di regime ne avesse considerato i contenuti' [a highly revolutionary work, if the regime's censors had looked into its content] (Mainardi, 1995: 778). Italian readers had already been exposed to Yesenin through the Symbolism-inspired Hermetic voice of Giuseppe Ungaretti, whose translations (via French) of two poems, 'Requiem [Sorokoust]' and 'Le navi delle cavalle [The Ships of the Mares, Kobylj korabji]' had been published in 1936 by the Rome-based publisher Novissima. For political reasons, interest in Yesenin would re-emerge only in

---

1   It should be noted, through Anna Dolfi (2008), that Florentine Hermetic poets of the third generation, such as Oreste Macrí and Piero Bigongiari, were particularly fascinated with French and Spanish Symbolism, and valued their translations produced in the 1930s and 1940s also as resistance tools against the Fascist regime. The present analysis does not intend to downplay their political intentions, but to outline the *publishing* reception of modernism between 1939 and 1945.

2   On Giovanni Scheiwiller, see *Una bicicletta in mezzo ai libri: Giovanni Scheiwiller libraio, editore, critico d'arte, 1889–1965*, ed. by Alina Kalczyńska (Milan: Libri Scheiwiller, 1990), and *Giovanni and Vanni Scheiwiller: Seventy Years of Publishing (1925–1995): Italy as a Publishing Bridge between East and West* (Milan: Libri Scheiwiller, 1996); on Guanda, see *Guanda, Delfini e la cultura modenese*, ed. by Giorgio Montecchi and Anna Rosa Venturi (Modena: Artestampa, 2012), and Aroldo Benini, *Ugo Guanda, editore negli anni difficili, 1932–1950* (Pescarenico di Lecco: Beretta, 1982). In addition, a rather short-lived small publisher Cederna (Ferretti and Iannuzzi, 2014: 115–18) was active in Milan between 1946 and 1950; run by Enrico Cederna and Gianni Antonini, Cederna published poetry books with parallel translations, with a specific focus on German literature (and particularly Hugo von Hoffmannsthal, Georg Trakl, alongside Rainer Maria Rilke and Stefan George), as well as poems by W.B. Yeats and James Joyce. Further publishing projects that Cederna and Antonini were not able to complete were subsequently featured in the 'Cederna' series published by the Florentine publisher Vallecchi.

the post-war period.³ The following year, Scheiwiller strengthened his links with the Hermetic circles through the publication of W.B. Yeats, translated by Germanist Leone Traverso. Traverso started his translation career in Florence with Hermetic theorists Carlo Bo and Oreste Macrí and literary critic Renato Poggioli, specialising in French, Spanish, and Russian literature respectively. In 1942 the collection *Liriche tedesche* [German Poems], edited by French Studies scholar Diego Valeri, included the Romantic Hölderlin and the decadent and already canonical Rainer Maria Rilke.

In 1939 Guanda started publishing 'La Fenice', the first series devoted to foreign poetry. Overseen by poet Attilio Bertolucci, the series published a range of modernist poets between 1939 and 1942. Although Bertolucci did not belong to Hermeticism, foregrounding in his poetry a less lyrical, more immediate tone, the series consolidated the bridge between Hermetic-inspired translators and modernist movements at the transnational level. It featured, in particular, the German poet Stefan George – who had already been translated by the anti-fascist Piero Gobetti's literary journal *Il Baretti* in the 1920s but who, unlike Rilke, had remained a more marginal voice in the German avant-garde in Italy – translated by Traverso; Katherine Mansfield's *Poemetti* [Short Poems], edited by journalist Gilberto Altichieri; T.S. Eliot's poems, translated by writer Luigi Berti; and Russian poet Alexander Blok, translated by Poggioli. It is worth mentioning that both Berti and Poggioli founded the journal *Inventario* in 1946, which also published T.S. Eliot, Vladimir Nabokov, and Pedro Salinas among others; similarly to 'La Fenice', their intention was to renew national literature through a more systematic exposure to foreign trends (Luti and Rossi, 1976: 167–68). As well as the poets mentioned above, we should devote specific attention to Federico García Lorca, translated by Bo and published by Guanda in 1940. Lorca's work had a particularly wide appeal in the post-war period, characterised by a more biographical, and political, curiosity on the part of left-wing intellectuals in relation to his shooting (Chiappini, 2002: 226); Guanda's publication showed instead more of an aesthetic interest on the part of Hermetic poets and translators, thus signalling how the Hermetic tradition had not only informed Italian poetry for several decades but also forged the approach to foreign poetry at a national level.

3   Yesenin was translated by poet and journalist Franco Matacotta for Guanda in 1946, by Slavicists Renato Poggioli and Angelo Maria Ripellino respectively for Einaudi in 1949 (*Il fiore del verso russo* [The Best of Russian Poetry]), and for Guanda in 1954 (*Poesia russa del Novecento* [Twentieth-Century Russian Poetry]) (Caproni, 2014: 136–38).

These trends shifted after 1945. While we cannot talk of neat caesurae in the history of publishing, as cultural periods tend to be fluid, as evidenced in the ambivalent relationships with Fascism (Piazzoni, 2021: 141), the political changes of this year contributed to shaping various, though short-lived, publishing, intellectual, and cultural projects. The end of the Second World War coincided in Italy with a period of intense publishing activity, with a significant 50% increase in book production (Santoro, 2008: 400). It also marked a period of pronounced intellectual ferment that pervaded European intellectuals more generally, in whom the Resistance experience had inspired a shared 'sense of moral mission' (Wilkinson, 1981: 1). For Italian intellectuals, after the fall of the Fascist regime, in the context of greater general freedom, the civic passion of the Resistance movement stimulated among other things a more profound urgency for cultural renewal linked to the neorealist movement; the latter to be seen as a hybrid, artistically varied, and 'expansive' cultural discourse in which Italian intellectuals collectively engaged (Leavitt, 2020). The attempt to define a different cultural role for intellectuals – one that was not limited to a cultural and aesthetic function but required a social and political commitment – questioned primarily the aesthetic and ideological paradigms of the recent past.[4] The elitist conception of literature that focused on the intellectuals' own subjectivity, outlined by Hermeticism in the 1930s, was now criticised, while more structured forms of political commitment were sought.

Among the many post-war journal ventures, *Il Politecnico* (1945–47), edited by anti-fascist writer Elio Vittorini (Ferretti, 1992: 69–114), was certainly one of the most influential and innovative, especially in terms of visual aspects (Lupo, 2011; Pontillo, 2020), and showcased most explicitly the tense relationship between culture and politics in the aftermath of the Second World War. The journal was part of the Turinese publisher Giulio Einaudi's broader aim of creating a 'fronte culturale' [cultural front] of democratic forces, as Einaudi himself suggested in a letter to Renata Aldrovandi on 16 May 1945 (Mangoni, 1999: 209; Turi, 1990: 171–72), and demonstrated a general effort to overcome the separation between the 'due culture' [two cultures] (Ferretti, 1994: 5–11) of the elite and the popular that had pervaded the interwar period. Remarkably, with its attention to translations, it also

---

4 For an overview of the function of the intellectual in the post-war period, see Massimo Romano, *Gli stregoni della fantacultura: la funzione dell'intellettuale nella letteratura italiana del dopoguerra (1945–1975)* (Turin: Paravia, 1977).

intended to project Italian intellectuals beyond national borders (Milani, 2016).

Il Politecnico's relationship with social and political institutions – first and foremost the Italian Communist Party (PCI) – was nonetheless complex. Exemplary was certainly the polemic between Vittorini and the PCI leader Palmiro Togliatti in 1947 (Ajello, 1979: 113–38), which anticipated the journal's subsequent closure for wider economic and publishing reasons (Zancan, 1984). The predominance that this polemic assumed contributed to the idea of a division between politics and culture, thus preventing the Party from becoming a productive agent of popular culture (Forgacs, 1990).[5] In general, the political commitment assumed by intellectuals in the aftermath of the Second World War tended to be grounded on an ideological rather than a sociological basis. From a Marxist perspective, Asor Rosa (1966) in particular criticised the populism and the *impegno* – or militant political commitment – of reforming Italian culture and society after Fascism that characterised Italian literature in the immediate post-war period[6] as based on a mythical vision of the people, completely disconnected from sociocultural analyses of the Italian working class.

The new post-war intellectual activities rapidly lost their momentum. More generally in Europe, the moral revolution sought by the Resistance intellectuals remained unfulfilled, and the 1950s veered towards a period of political 'restoration' (Wilkinson, 1981: 261). In Italy, beyond the political process of 'normalizzazione' [normalisation] (Ferretti, 2004: 81) that in 1947 saw the expulsion of leftist political forces from the De Gasperi government (Ginsborg, 2003: 145–48), the failure of intellectual activities was also caused by the intrinsic limitations of the publishing field. Still informed by artisanal methods, with the prevalence of family-run businesses that relied

---

5 On the history of the Italian Communist Party more broadly, see Paolo Spriano, *Storia del Partito comunista italiano: La resistenza Togliatti e il partito nuovo* (Turin: Einaudi, 1975), and Giovanni Gozzini and Renzo Martinelli, *Storia del Partito comunista italiano: Dall'attentato a Togliatti all' ottavo Congresso* (Turin: Einaudi, 1998) for the years of the Resistance and the first years of the Republic, respectively.

6 In the post-war period, the concept of *impegno* has been often charged with ideological connotations. Bobbio (1993) saw intellectual rigour as an explicitly political duty against dogmatic powers; Burns provides a more dialogic definition according to which the notion 'presupposes a relationship; and a relationship charged with moral significance', and 'dictates that the writer has some responsibility for the response she produces in the reader and that this respondent treats responsibly the commitment thus made by the writer' (Burns, 2001: 15).

on 'letterati editori', the Italian publishing sector appeared at that moment unable to effectively broaden the elite spectrum of its readership and to deliver culturally innovative projects. The limits of book distribution further worsened this situation and in the 1950s provoked a return to the traditional book market, the exclusive prerogative of intellectuals belonging to an educated middle class and of the few students enrolled in Italian universities (Cadioli, 1981: 37–40).

The scarce financial means of the small publishers left considerable freedom for established larger-scale houses to continue operating in more traditional terms. In this context, Arnoldo Mondadori was able to strengthen the central position of his own large-scale publishing house. Mondadori was the 'editore protagonista' [publisher protagonist] (Ferretti, 2004: 3) *par excellence*, who enjoyed a direct relationship with his collaborators and authors and could rely on a broad transnational network.[7] The compromises previously struck with the Fascist regime were now substituted by Mondadori's backing of the political forces in government in addition to astute strategies to satisfy market demand, spanning shrewd diplomacy and a wise balance between innovation and tradition (Ferretti, 2004: 13). Mondadori was the leader of the Italian publishing field, particularly the sub-field of the novel, which was the undisputed king of the market.

How did contemporary Italian poetry fare in this desired yet unaccomplished post-war cultural renewal? Unlike the novel, it struggled to affirm its place. The emergence of neorealist poetry demonstrated its inability to respond to the new cultural enthusiasm with an innovative style and language as opposed to Hermetic solipsism. Starting from the journal *Mercurio* (1944–48), but especially *La Strada* (1946–47) and *Momenti* (1951–53), the rejection – in mainly ethical and not critically aesthetic terms – of pre-war Hermetic poetry gave voice to a neorealist movement, thanks to poetic works by Elio Filippo Accrocca, Franco Matacotta, and Rocco Scotellaro. On a linguistic level, the poets tended to adopt 'una lingua povera e dimessa, il parlato, l'espressione mimetica e gergale, il voluto stile basso' [a poor and unassuming language, a colloquial style, mimetic and slang expressions, a deliberately rough style] (Turconi, 1977: 166), at times moving towards a mix of poetic genres and plurilinguism (Luperini, 1981: 665);[8] on a thematic

---

7   On the figure of Arnoldo Mondadori, see Decleva, 2007.
8   For a more thorough analysis of neorealist poetry, see Walter Siti, *Il neorealismo nella poesia italiana: 1941–1956* (Turin: Einaudi, 1980).

level, the push towards reality rapidly assumed the chronicle tone of a generic political commitment or even political propaganda.

Though the neorealist experience marked a pervasive desire to drive national poetry away from the stagnant forms of post-Hermeticism, neorealist poets, in particular the minor ones, lacked the critical means – in terms of creative experience, literary background, and cultural capital – to trigger an effective revolution of poetic language, and were therefore unable to obtain significant results. The elite nature of the genre further added to its limited appeal; neorealist poetry would not enjoy the same success as the neorealist novel and cinema in the same period (Turconi, 1977: 60–71). In Verbaro's analysis, neorealist poetry suffered from 'una duplice forza di penalizzazione: da una parte lo strapotere delle forme ermetiche, dall'altra una paralizzante concorrenzialità con una narrativa – ma più ancora, con una diffusa esigenza di narratività, di racconto, di comunicazione' [a two-pronged attack: on one side, the strength of the Hermetic tradition, on the other, the paralysing competition with the novel, but even more a general need for narrativity, storytelling, communication] (1995: 53). These circumstances gave rise to a wholly insufficient poetry production whose lingering lyrical traces were ill-matched with its new themes: the desired amalgamation of the elite genre with militant initiatives did not come to pass, and even the works produced by established poets seemed irrelevant, such as *Con il piede straniero sopra il cuore* [With the Foreign Foot Over the Heart] (Milan: Costume, 1946) by one of the foremost Hermetic poets of the interwar period, Salvatore Quasimodo.

The cultural renewal that intellectuals sought in the aftermath of the Second World War therefore did not materialise in poetry. However, from a transnational perspective, the experience of neorealist poetry arguably carried some significance for subsequent developments in poetry translation in Italy. Despite their simplistic appropriation of foreign literary models, the neorealist poets' use of foreign sources deepened the detachment from the French axis in favour of further exploration of anglophone production – an opening already enacted by the novel, through Vittorini and writer and Einaudi editor Cesare Pavese, and their 'mito dell'America' [American myth].[9] Stimulatingly, Leavitt (2013) talks of an 'impegno nero' [black *impegno*] developing in the early post-war period, derived from that American myth, that saw Italian intellectuals engaging with the African-American experience and struggling for equal rights in both societies. This resulted in an interest

---

9 See Claudio Antonelli, *Pavese, Vittorini e gli americanisti. Il mito dell'America* (Florence: Edarc Edizioni, 2008).

in African-American writers. African-American poets were not neglected, especially in post-war journals, but the attention paid to them in the poetry publishing field was more limited and probably less politically committed. Titles included edited anthologies by Hermetic figures such as Luigi Berti – *Canti negri* [Black Songs] (Florence: Fussi, 1949) – or Carlo Izzo – *Poesia americana contemporanea e poesia negra* [Contemporary American Poetry and Black Poetry] (Parma: Guanda, 1949). In broader terms, the interest moved beyond American poets already known in Italy, such as Edgar Lee Masters and Walt Whitman, and embraced, although only superficially, militant German poetry through Bertolt Brecht; Spanish poetry, as represented by Lorca and the politically engaged poet and member of the Spanish Generation of '27 Rafael Alberti; and the politically committed Turkish poet Nazim Hikmet (Turconi, 1977: 182–83).

More interestingly for our argument, these new trends began to break the traditional link between Italian Hermeticism and modernism, paving the way for new transnational connections for Italian translators, editors, and publishers. A case in point is the publishing house Edizioni della Meridiana [Sundial Editions]. Founded in 1947 by Giuseppe Eugenio Luraghi, and active until 1956, it featured, with parallel translations, the work of the aforementioned Alberti (*Poesie '44–'48*), translated by Luraghi himself in 1949, and French poet Jean Paulhan, translated by writer Gianna Manzini in 1952 (Iannuzzi, 2016: 9). The publication of Paulhan is crucial, as it signals a passage to new poetic forms and the introduction of new cultural mediators in Italian poetry. After introducing French modernism in the influential journal *La Nouvelle Revue Française* (*NRF*) which he edited, Paulhan opened the *NRF* to political debates and ultimately assumed an explicitly anti-fascist stance; in his 1941 *Les Fleurs de Tarbes ou La terreur dans les Lettres* [The Flowers of Tarbes, Or, Terror in Literature], the French intellectual criticised modernist poetry for a radicalism which, he suggested, distanced itself from a wider readership and diminished its political role (Bru, 2014: 109).

The same detachment of radical forms of expression from reality that Paulhan had disparaged in relation to French modernism had, we can argue, invested contemporary Italian poetry. Significantly, in the Italian translation, the introduction to Paulhan's poetry collection was penned by Luciano Anceschi, whose theories helped to move Italian poetry aesthetics beyond Hermeticism; in 1952 Anceschi edited the *Linea lombarda* [Lombard Line] poetry anthology, with such poets as Vittorio Sereni, Nelo Risi, and Luciano Erba, still within the Hermetic tradition but already projected towards a wider European poetics of the object; he would then edit the journal *il verri* (1956–), close to the experimental *neoavanguardia* which will be discussed later. Two years after Paulhan's translation, in 1954 Sereni was charged with the task of editing a new Edizioni della Meridiana series, 'I Quaderni della Poesia' [Poetry Notebooks], which featured some of the new and most notable Italian poets, such as Pier Paolo Pasolini and Andrea Zanzotto, who in different terms both refuted purist lyrical expression, thus enlarging considerably the reach of Italian poetry beyond Hermeticism.

But from a strictly domestic perspective, the dynamics of the poetry publishing field synthesised the poetic – and more broadly editorial – coordinates described above, and brought back the image of a 'normalised' field. Drawing on their greater financial solidity, large-scale publishers were able to secure the most established poets. Mondadori managed to consolidate the poetry venture that it had started in 1940 with the poetry series 'Lo Specchio' by resurrecting poets already active before the Second World War: Leonardo Sinisgalli (*I nuovi campi elisi*, The New Elysian Fields, 1947); Libero de Libero (*Banchetto*, Banquet, 1949); and Giorgio Vigolo (*La linea della vita*, The Line of Life, 1950). The publication of post-Hermetic poets enriched the catalogue of 'Lo Specchio' according to a canonical line that, in the structural void of a contemporary Italian poetry still stuck within a Hermetic lineage, permitted the Milanese publisher to acquire significant cultural capital and establish its central position in the field of poetry. The specialised small-scale publishing houses that were active in the 1940s also through translations, suffered from the post-war reconstruction. As late as 1947, Ugo Guandalini, owner of Guanda, which had been bombed in 1944, wrote to the literary agent Erich Linder: 'Vedrò volentieri il bollettino, ma il guaio è la crisi, che, si voglia o no, c'è e non si vede schiarire l'orizzonte' [I will see the bulletin with pleasure, but the problem is that the crisis, whether one likes it or not, does exist and the horizon isn't looking any clearer].[10] Financial reasons reduced the number of the small publishers' publications, and often forced them to recuperate the foreign modernist models from before the Second World War.

1.1.1 Einaudi: the poets' venture for a 'cultura militante'

Medium-scale publishers such as Einaudi staggered along in a peripheral position, looking for a politically committed identity which was not viable because of both the limits of Italian poetry and the economic issues

---

10 Fondazione Arnoldo e Alberto Mondadori [hereafter FAAM], Erich Linder archive, file Guanda, 11 November 1947.

experienced by post-war publishing. The failure of Einaudi's poetry series 'Poeti' was in this sense emblematic. In 1939 Einaudi released *Le Occasioni* [The Occasions] by one of the most important contemporary Italian poets, future Nobel prize winner Eugenio Montale, whose poetics were often aligned with Hermeticism and with T.S. Eliot's technique of 'objective correlative'. This publication was not followed by a substantial number of other titles, as Appendix 2 shows: over twenty-one years, only eleven books were published in the series 'Poeti', and other poetry books were moved to the more generic series devoted to theatre and literary production. Out of those eleven titles, eight were published in the 1940s – with more than 60% of them before 1945 – and only three in the 1950s. Alongside the peculiar publication of Ligurian dialect poet Edoardo Firpo (*O grillo cantadò* [The Singing Cricket]) in 1960, the books came mostly either from established Italian poets, including two titles from Montale (both in 1939, *Le Occasioni* and *Ossi di seppia* [Cuttlefish Bones]), one each from Umberto Saba (*Il Canzoniere* [Songbook], 1945) – Bertolucci's inspiration for a poetry of everyday experience – and Piero Jahier (*Con me e con gli alpini* [With Me and with the Alpine Troops], 1943), or Einaudi editors, with two books from Pavese (*Lavorare stanca* [Hard Labour], 1943, and *Verrà la morte e avrà i tuoi occhi* [Death Will Come and Have your Eyes], 1951), and one from left-wing intellectual Franco Fortini (*Foglio di via* [Marching Orders], 1946). There were only three translations: the already canonical Rilke, translated by Fortini; the more politically committed French poet Paul Éluard, translated in 1947 once again by Fortini; and the militant Chilean poet Pablo Neruda, translated in 1952 by Quasimodo, who, now a PCI member, had left Hermeticism to engage more closely with realism and who would be awarded the Nobel Prize in 1959. The translations of Éluard's and Neruda's poems would then merge into the 1950s 'Poeti stranieri tradotti da poeti italiani' [Foreign Poets Translated by Italian Poets] series.

The 'Poeti' series failed for two main reasons: Italian poets worthy of publication were lacking, as was the editors' interest in the series. As we can read in the correspondence exchanged between renowned writer and Einaudi editor Italo Calvino and the editor-in-chief of the series, Carlo Muscetta (Mangoni, 1999: 670n), although in 1949 two poets – neorealist Rocco Scotellaro and Saba-inspired poet Sandro Penna – were selected to re-initiate the series under new auspices, they were not published for various reasons, with Scotellaro (whose work would mostly be published posthumously after 1953) being rejected by both Pavese and Vittorini. Besides, a 1943 letter by the anti-fascist Giaime Pintor to Pavese – who had both contributed to the project of the publishing house since its infancy – indicates that the Einaudi editors had not been keen on a poetry series from the outset:

> Esprimo parere contrario all'iniziativa dei Poeti. So benissimo che quest'idea vagola da tempo nella testa del padrone il quale ritiene che sia suo dovere assumere il patrocinio della cultura militante, ma ho molti dubbi sulla validità di questi poeti a rappresentare la cultura militante (soprattutto quella del dopoguerra a cui dovrà essere legato il nome della nostra casa).[11]

> [I am against the poet series initiative. I know very well that our employer has been thinking about this for a while as he believes it is his duty to assume the patronage of militant culture, but I have some doubts as to the validity of these poets in representing this militant culture (especially that of the post-war which our publishing house intends to relate to).]

In theory, this 'poet series initiative' placed poetry publishing within Einaudi's wider project of leading the development of an Italian 'militant culture'. By giving poets the authority to intervene in current cultural and political debates in Italy, and more widely in Europe, this venture would confer upon these poets the status of 'public intellectuals'. Historian Stefan Collini (2006: 52) defines a public intellectual as a cultural authority coming out of the intersection of four dimensions: the success obtained in a specific intellectual activity; the availability in terms of media exposure to reach a public beyond their specialism; the expression of their opinion on general themes, and the consolidation of a reputation. In Bourdieu's words, the status of public intellectual is determined by their ability to transfer capitals across the different cultural fields, insofar as the intellectuals' symbolic capital derived from their established reputation provides them with the opportunity to surpass the limits of their specialised field and join the wider cultural and political debate (Bourdieu, 1993: 161–75).[12]

---

11 Archivio Einaudi [hereafter AE], file Giaime Pintor, to Cesare Pavese, Vichy, 24 April 1943. Also in Mangoni, 1999: 145.

12 Collini (2006: 57) does not accept Bourdieu's metaphor of struggle over cultural capital, since it might introduce overly restrictive notions of economic competition or strategies of positioning. While the latter is certainly a concern, we concur with Sapiro's reading (2009a) of symbolic capital in relation to the transnational intellectual space, which accurately highlights how this is not merely an economic interpretation and instead gives a sense of the prestige that these intellectuals have within the literary field.

The transfer of cultural capital follows a precise mechanism, however, which is not always operable, due to intrinsic issues of creating symbolic capital in the specific literary field and the wider cultural space. Hence, while the Einaudi poetry project aimed to reassess the modernist limits of the poet's function, the obstacles to this transfer of capitals were multiple, and we can distinctly identify them both on a literary and a wider economic level. It is Pintor himself, in the aforementioned letter, who seemingly defines these traits:

> Siccome prevedo che la cosa si farà aggiungo i miei giudizi personali con la preghiera di tenerne conto. <u>Saba</u>. Magari, ma in ogni modo non l'opera *omnia*. Cosa sono queste manie mondadoriane? L'opera omnia va bene per poeti che siano storicamente accettati; quella di Saba non significa nulla. Molto meglio una rigorosa scelta fatta dall'autore e con carattere definitivo. <u>Sinisgalli</u>. È nei suoi limiti il più riuscito dei giovani e quello che vedrei più favorevolmente. Ha anche il vantaggio di non essere mai stato pubblicato insieme. <u>Grande</u> assolutamente no, è un relitto. <u>Vigolo</u>. Direi di no. Anche lui rappresenta un momento superato. <u>Solmi</u>. Buono, ma troppo debole. <u>Betocchi</u> è assolutamente informe, non si può pubblicare. <u>Luzi</u> ha molte qualità, ma ancora non si capisce dove voglia andare a finire. <u>Penna</u> con Sinisgalli quello che sarebbe più ragionevole pubblicare. Anche qui una scelta rigorosa. <u>Sereni</u>. Benché abbia molti fautori mi pare ancora indeterminato. <u>Dal Fabbro</u>. Intelligente e stimabile, ma per ora non è un poeta.[13]

> [Since I foresee that this thing will go ahead, please find below my personal judgements I would be grateful if you could take them into account. <u>Saba</u>. Maybe, but in any case not his *opera omnia*. What is this Mondadori-style mania? The *opera omnia* is OK for poets who have been historically accepted, in the case of Saba, that does not mean anything. It would be better to ask the author to make his own rigorous selection, with definitive character. <u>Sinisgalli</u>. Within his limits, he is the most effective among the young poets and the one that I would view/regard more favourably. He has also the advantage that his works have never been published together. <u>Grande</u> absolutely no, he is a relic. <u>Vigolo</u>. I would say no. He also represents a season that has already passed. <u>Solmi</u>. Good,

---

13 AE, file Giaime Pintor, to Cesare Pavese, Vichy, 24 April 1943. In Ferrero, 2005: 208.

but too weak. Betocchi has absolutely no shape, he cannot be published. Luzi has many qualities, but it is not clear yet where he wants to go. Along with Sinisgalli, Penna is the one that would make more sense to publish. A rigorous selection, here too. Sereni. Though he has many supporters, I think he is still undefined. Dal Fabbro. Smart and appraisable, but he is not a poet yet.]

Beyond the appreciation for Sinisgalli, whose poems had been published by Scheiwiller in the 1930s and encountered a favourable reception, Pintor's negative judgement was directed in the first instance towards the choice of publishing format, the *opera omnia* [complete works] which Mondadori's 'Lo Specchio' had started utilising three years earlier in 1940. This format seemed too weighty, given the embryonic state of the new Italian poets ('has absolutely no shape', 'it is not clear where he wants to go', 'undefined'). Secondly, Pintor questioned the selection of the poets to be published. Though the poets quoted (other than Grande and Vigolo, both belonging to a previous time) would consolidate their poetic voices in the following years, at that time they had not achieved the platform necessary to lead the new culture that Einaudi wanted to promote.

Pavese stressed a similar point in a letter to poet Camillo Sbarbaro, whose poetry shunned the aulic tradition to welcome a crepuscular tone; the editor tried to persuade the latter to publish with Einaudi in order to turn the 'Poeti' initiative into a 'raccolta di quei libri che nell'ultimo ventennio segnarono un momento importante nella storia stilistica e poetica' [collection of books that in the last twenty years signalled a significant moment in stylistic and poetic history] (Mangoni, 1999: 141–42). From a strictly literary viewpoint, contemporary Italian poetry followed a more gradual path: in the immediate post-war period, the poetic subject had not yet achieved a collective dimension but underwent only slow development (Lorenzini, 2005: 145).

Apart from the obstacles to publishing Italian poetry which had not entirely rejected Hermeticism nor elaborated a firm response to the contemporary cultural and historical demands, the more stringent issue at that time was arguably economic. The reduced economic capital of poetry as an elite section of the publishing industry limited its potential to be shaped into a driving force for the desired cultural renewal, and would not help Einaudi's account books to navigate out of the dire straits caused by the war years. In a letter to Fortini, long-standing editor Natalia Ginzburg pointed out how the 'poet series initiative' ran aground because of these economic problems: 'Quel progetto di una nuova collana di poeti italiani è fermo, per ora: nel futuro, chissà?' [That project of a new series of Italian poets is at a standstill now: in the future, who knows?].[14] Probably for similar reasons, in 1951 Einaudi also refused an opportunity to act as distributor for the poetry-focused journal *Botteghe Oscure*, a publishing agreement that could have brought at least two poetry titles per year to the publishing house.

The uncertainty with regard to the new poetic trends triggered, we conclude, a structural void in the publication of contemporary Italian poetry, which was only haphazardly represented in the catalogues of the Turinese publisher. Einaudi's crisis was counterposed by the success of Mondadori's 'Lo Specchio', with the print runs of Salvatore Quasimodo reaching 15,000 (Ferretti, 2004: 57). Aided by backward publishing structures, the large-scale publishers in the late 1940s resisted small and medium entities simply by publishing stagnant Italian poetry that still circulated around Hermeticism. This strategy could not continue unchanged forever, and would in fact soon come to a halt.

1.2 The turn to translation in the 1950s: the small publishers seeking a central position in the field

In the early 1950s the status of the poetry publishing field reflected vividly the impasse experienced by contemporary Italian poetry, caught in the grip of an increasingly wheezy Hermeticism as well as the sterility of neorealist poetry. The lack of a dynamic contemporary national canon not only created issues for the medium-scale publishers such as Einaudi, but ultimately provoked the inertia of the publishers which had thus far dealt in the genre. Having enjoyed a favourable start, Mondadori's 'Lo Specchio' was stagnating, urgently in need of an aesthetic renewal that would detach it from Hermeticism (Ferretti, 2004: 133). The poetic crisis affected even more acutely the production of the small-scale poetry publishers, which were unable to acquire the copyrights of the more canonical poets – which belonged to large publishers such as Mondadori – and were too specialised and elitist for those contemporary poets whose literary value was not yet satisfactory.

Precisely in this moment of stagnation, poetry translation assumed a decisive role in altering the dynamics of the field. It was, we suggest, a way to satisfy the aesthetic and cultural desires described above, while simultaneously

---

14   AE, file Franco Fortini, Natalia Ginzburg, 24 February 1951.

increasing the prestige of the publishers that engaged in this practice. Foreign poems were considered innovative, not only because they were distinct from the domestic poetic canon, but also because they effectively brought some of the vanguard ferment that poetry was experiencing in these decades within and beyond Europe, particularly with Ezra Pound's *Pisan Cantos*, published in 1948. This opening inserted Italy into the transnational space, connecting the peninsula to contemporary foreign poetry and thereby changing the face of Italian culture and publishing.

With their more flexible publishing structures, the small publishers were the first to try to regain a more central position in the poetry sector, as the emergence of new or nearly new enterprises such as Vanni Scheiwiller (1951–), Schwarz (1952–), and Lerici (1956–) showed (Ferretti, 2004: 124–30). Most of them invested promptly and extensively in translation. Appendix 2 reveals that between 1953 and 1959, in the domain of contemporary poetry, Scheiwiller published 59 books of foreign poetry, which corresponded to one third of the overall poetic production. He also created ad hoc series for foreign poetry, namely 'Poeti stranieri tradotti da poeti italiani' [Foreign Poets Translated by Italian Poets] (1958–80), 'Pagine di letterature straniere antiche e moderne' [Pages of Ancient and Modern Foreign Literatures] (1954–78), and the 'Oltremare' [Overseas] series (1951–66), which, despite a relatively low number of titles, typical of Scheiwiller's practice, would all keep their distinctive character. Similarly, when in 1956 Roberto Lerici, with anti-fascist Aldo Rosselli's help, turned his own publishing house to literature, he would soon enough veer towards the publication of foreign poetry with the series 'Poeti europei' [European Poets]; there, authors associated with modernism such as Antonio Machado, representative of the Spanish generation of '98 committed to cultural and aesthetic renewal, as well as Ezra Pound found their place, all published in parallel versions and edited by relevant literary specialists (Ferretti, 2004: 128–29). 'European', according to the publisher, did not refer to the poets' geographical origin but to their role in building an European awareness, thus connecting the publisher's ambitions with the then current transnational discourses of European integration which culminated in the foundation of the European Economic Community in 1957 (Marchetti, 2016).

The bet on publishing contemporary foreign poetry was successful not only from a cultural perspective, in terms of the symbolic capital brought by translation, but also from a business perspective. It allowed small publishers to save on copyright obligations and to open a breach in Mondadori's monopoly by reaching a largely unexplored section of the literary market, as Vanni Scheiwiller outlined in lucid terms in a letter to Ezra Pound. In

1959 the elitist publisher painted a portrait of contemporary Italian poets who were dominated by the already canonical triad Montale–Ungaretti–Quasimodo and unable to achieve the stature of European poets due to their lack of 'poetic' bravery. Scheiwiller's words, reproduced below, are particularly interesting as they reveal the tensions in contemporary Italian poetry between national status and transnational ambitions, in dialogue with one of the most representative poets of the twentieth century worldwide.

The Milanese publisher's analysis recognised the beloved Montale as the only poet of fully established value, who nonetheless lacked self-esteem. This seemed to be a recurrent problem also with other emerging figures, such as Sereni, who reflected a higher level of poetry, but did not have the necessary audacity to assume an innovative role. What Italy was left with was an assortment of poets who were unable to rise to a further level. In particular, these minor poets did not seem able to equip themselves with adequate poetic baggage to move more soundly towards new horizons. According to Scheiwiller, a combination of two elements bestowed literary value on contemporary Italian poets: an unprejudiced, innovative attitude, and a poetry practice informed by relevant reading. In other words, innovation in dialogue with transnational poetic tradition was the necessary formula to attain 'European' status – to be properly conceived in terms of their ability to inform transnational cultural discourses – and to be read therefore outside national borders.

> Una lista di dieci scrittori d'oggi? È difficile. Dei viventi, tra i poeti, c'è solo MONTALE, se non avesse paura di se stesso e non fosse rovinato dal giornalismo (e con un po' più di spina dorsale). È l'unico di livello europeo. Come già certo UNGARETTI. SBARBARO ha dato tutto: una dozzina di liriche bellissime e delle belle prose, scarne e incisive. SERENI può essere il poeta di domani: sempre che vinca la paura di se stesso (e dei critici) [...] Tra i giovani quarantenni trentenni cinquantenni: ce ne sono troppi e tutti bravissimi, una specie di "mezzo secolo stilnovista", cioè abbiamo tanti bravi poeti MINORI. C'è in Italia 10 milioni di poeti (esclusi i neonati): su 49 milioni di abitanti – perché molti scrivono con 3 o 5 pseudonimi. Tutti che scrivono (e pubblicano) MA non leggono. Poeti ANALFABETI dunque. I pochissimi leggibili hanno dunque paura di scrivere. C'è da salvare il poco leggibile (io intendo sempre su di un piano europeo). 4 gatti.[15]

---

15 APICE, Archivio Vanni Scheiwiller [hereafter VS], file correspondence Ezra Pound, Vanni Scheiwiller, 19 March 1959. See also Milani, 2012: 102.

[A list of ten writers today? It's difficult. Of the living ones, there is only MONTALE, if he wasn't afraid of himself, and wasn't ruined by journalism (and had a bit more backbone). He is the only one at European level. As certainly also UNGARETTI. SBARBARO has already given everything: a dozen very beautiful lyrics and some beautiful prose, bare and vivid. SERENI could be the poet of tomorrow, if he overcame his fear of himself (and of the critics) [...] Among the young forty/thirty/fifty-year-old poets: there are too many and all very good, a sort of 'post-war stilnovo', that is, we have many good MINOR poets. In Italy there are 10 million poets (if we exclude the newborns): out of 49 million citizens, as many write with either three or five pseudonyms. They all write (and publish) BUT they do not read. ILLITERATE poets, therefore. The very few who can be read are afraid of writing. We have to save the very few who can be read (I mean, again, at European level). A handful.]

Scheiwiller's overview in this correspondence exposes the double preclusion faced by the publisher: contemporary Italian poetry did not satisfy the specialised publishers' wishes, and the national poetic canon with a fully transnational stature had already been acquired by the large-scale publishers. When, in 1953, Scheiwiller decided to focus more systematically on translation, this was arguably because publishing contemporary foreign poets would allow him not only to offer a different type of poetry, but also to gain a prestigious position within the national publishing field. We contend that, to a certain extent, Scheiwiller behaved as he wanted his poets to do, with an innovative spirit but also with a strategic reappraisal of the transnational poetic tradition. To overcome the crisis into which the centrality of Mondadori's 'Lo Specchio' had plunged the small publishers, Scheiwiller indeed 'imbocca una strada di importanza culturalmente peraltro decisiva, in questo forse sollecitato dallo stesso Pound: quella di *rileggere* il passato recente del Novecento, la sua tradizione (le sue tradizioni) "in ombra"' [undertook a culturally decisive path, perhaps elicited by Pound himself: that of *re-reading* the recent past of the twentieth century, its tradition (its traditions) 'in the shadow'] (Giovannetti, 2009: 160).

Yet it was not only Scheiwiller who moved decidedly towards contemporary foreign poetry. Over the course of the 1950s, Guanda also published translations of foreign poets more systematically: Pound, Dylan Thomas, Guillaume Apollinaire, but also, interestingly, Neruda. The publishing strategy was clearly outlined by Guandalini himself:

ho due libri che vanno molto bene (le poesie di Lorca e di Prévert) i quali pagano le spese del resto... [...] lo specializzarsi è certo [...] l'unica possibilità di sopravvivere che resta al piccolo editore: crearsi un settore ove la propria attività non sia seconda a nessuno. (Ferretti, 2004: 119)

[I have two books which are selling well (Lorca and Prévert's poems) which pay the taxes of the rest... [...] to specialise is certainly [...] the only possible way for a small publisher to survive: to create a sector where his own activity is not second to anyone else.]

A handful of poets – interestingly here *popular* poets too: one of the most representative Spanish poets for his role in the Spanish Civil War and an eclectic *chansonnier* – provided the Parma-based publishing house with the necessary economic capital, as opposed to contemporary Italian poets whose role was much more ephemeral. Such a translation strategy empowered Guanda to continue to offer readers a degree of specialisation that the bigger publishers could not, and that the small publisher could benefit from in terms of general prestige. However, in selecting the more popular Lorca and Prévert, and in continuing to work closely with cultural agents connected with Hermeticism who translated contemporary foreign poetry (*Poesia ispano-americana del '900* [Twentieth-Century South American Poetry], 1957, edited by Francesco Tentori, and *Nuova poesia francese* [New French Poetry], 1952, by Carlo Bo), Guanda appears overall less daring than Scheiwiller, and therefore gains slightly less literary value in terms of formal innovation.

1.2.2 The transnational opening of the medium-scale publishers: Einaudi's 'Poeti stranieri tradotti'

While in the 1950s foreign poetry acquired a significant position in the catalogues of the small publishing houses, it remained absent from those of the larger-scale publishers. The medium-scale publishing houses, such as Einaudi, felt the urgency to look beyond national borders but were not able to do so systematically when it came to poetry. The reasons for this were numerous, and we can once again identify them within the intrinsic limits of the publishing structure as well as in the weak status of national poetry. Relatively more strictly bound to the market outcome of cultural products and usually more cautious in the selection of authors, the medium-scale publishers were less agile in developing new publishing ventures and thus missed out on the opportunity to exploit the newly created market section.

The failure of Einaudi's series 'Poeti stranieri tradotti da poeti italiani' confirms the unfeasibility at this stage of a politically committed poetry project on a transnational scale and, at the same time, incurred an inevitable further loss of centrality for Einaudi in the field of poetry publishing.

Einaudi turned to the practice of translating foreign poetry in the early 1950s: it was a way to fill an aesthetic and ideological gap to overcome both literary and practical obstacles connected with the publication of contemporary Italian poetry. 1951 saw the inauguration of the 'Poeti stranieri tradotti da poeti italiani', a continuation of the 'Poeti' initiative, inscribed within the post-war militant perspective that Giulio Einaudi intended to assume. In effect, the series was intended as part of a wider transnational project of the Turinese publishing house, which not only aimed to publish translations but to use them strategically to develop transnational networks and to nurture an intellectual dialogue between Italian culture and the rest of the world:

> Dobbiamo, per quanto possibile, valerci delle migliori e più avanzate iniziative straniere (russe, francesi: 'Que Sais-je?' [Presses universitaires de France], [Armand] Collins, Hier et Aujourd'hui etc; americane: Mentor Books, Everyday Library etc; inglesi: Pelican Books, Sigma Books, 'Home University Library' [Oxford University Press], 'Teach Yourself History' [Hodder & Stoughton]; German: Recam, ecc), sollecitando e legando però la collaborazione italiana quanto più largamente è possibile.[16]

> [We should, as much as we can, draw on the best and more advanced foreign initiatives (Russian, French: 'Que Sais-je?' [Presses universitaires de France], [Armand] Colin, Hier et Aujourd'hui etc; American: Mentor Books, Everyday Library etc; English: Pelican Books, Sigma Books, 'Home University Library' [Oxford University Press], 'Teach Yourself History' [Hodder & Stoughton]; German: Recam, etc.), and especially on the works of the most well-known foreign authors in this field [...] but also, as widely as possible, elicit and cement Italian collaboration.]

We should not forget that, in the post-war search for a more profitable interaction with foreign cultural forces, Italy occupied a peripheral position when compared to the cultural innovations of such countries as France, where intellectuals were able to consolidate their public status in order to

---

16 AE, *verbali* [subsequently omitted], minutes of the editorial meeting on 12–13 January 1949. Also in Munari, 2011: 69.

lead a wider European cultural and political renewal (Boschetti, 2009: 177). This is the reason why the appeal to these 'foreign initiatives' represented a necessary cultural operation: by broadening the limited horizons of national culture in a political and cultural sense, Italy would no longer be considered 'marginal'.

From this perspective, the project 'Poeti stranieri tradotti da poeti italiani' had allegedly a dual purpose. On the one hand, it made it possible for Einaudi to directly acquire symbolic capital by publishing foreign poets who had already been recognised at world level as consolidated 'poetic voices'. Hence, the series would privilege authors who enjoyed a central position in the literary field, in line with a strategy of 'consolidamento delle proposte dei classici' [consolidating the classics] (Mangoni, 1999: 650) that characterised the Turinese publisher more generally in the early 1950s. As a result, Einaudi required renowned authors to establish itself, and more peripheral voices at the transnational level had to be rejected, such as Baroque French poet Jean de Sponde, proposed by translator Ariodante Marianni.[17] On the other hand, the foreign poets selected could not simply be established figures of the literary canon. Rather, they needed to have a more ideological position in the cultural field; the publishing house aimed for poets who could function as 'public intellectuals' and could start a dialogue with Italian cultural agents who understood the need to enhance their sociopolitical function.

Among the potential titles for the series, we find the politically committed poet Bertolt Brecht, who could 'rappresentare nella situazione della poesia contemporanea, in Italia e fuori, un richiamo straordinario e un esempio alto di classicità, di ricerca, di una (nuova) classicità' [represent, in the situation of contemporary poetry, both within and outside Italy, an extraordinary appeal and highly refined example of classicism, of innovation, of (new) classicism].[18] Brecht's work was eventually published in larger series, while the 'Poeti stranieri tradotti da poeti italiani' series would feature again the political force of Éluard, translated by Fortini. In other words, Einaudi sought a bond between national and foreign public intellectuals; a goal that would find its most accomplished example in the translation of Neruda's poems by Quasimodo.

The selection process was nonetheless difficult. Einaudi had to find relatively well-established foreign poets and Italian poet-translators who could aptly embody examples of public intellectuals who were well-regarded

---

17 AE, file Ariodante Marianni, Luciano Foà, 9 December 1959.
18 AE, file Paolo Chiarini, to Renato Solmi, 26 January 1956.

figures in their sector and were able to reach wider audiences and fields. The scarce results of neorealist poetry in terms of effective, politically committed works did not help. The case of Miguel Hernández, a Spanish militant poet of the 1927 generation, is illustrative. Hernández, jailed during the 1930s for his anti-fascist sympathies, was received in Italy as an emblem of the resistance movement against Franco's dictatorship (Darconza, 2006: 47). In correspondence with Giulio Einaudi, translator and Hispanist Vittorio Bodini explained that the original publication of Hernández's book *Viento del pueblo* [The People's Wind] relied more on empathy for the political destiny of the author than on his poetic value. At the same time, Bodini was unsure of whom to suggest as a translator; more than a Hispanic Studies specialist, the publisher would require a militant poet who could repeat the successful intellectual synergy between Quasimodo and Neruda.[19]

The issue was in the end a publishing one. Einaudi intended to be recognised as an 'editore di cultura' [culture-driven publisher] with a sociopolitical function, as its cultural products were aimed at forming the new intellectuals who were supposed to have a more direct link with society. Therefore, Einaudi wanted not only to reach out to the limited elite of specialists and critics, but to enter into contact with a broader intellectual community that could identify with younger energies, particularly university students. The wish to create 'bestselling' products – still framed within a more restricted cultural horizon than purely market-driven publishing productions, or in Bourdieu's terms, driven by the heteronomous principle of cultural production (Bourdieu, 1993)[20] – pushed Einaudi towards investing its economic and cultural capitals in novels and essays. The publication of poetry was temporarily put aside, and would merge into the general literary series 'Coralli' [Corals] in order to avoid the symbolic as well as economic responsibility of a specialised poetry series.[21]

The series 'Poeti stranieri tradotti da poeti italiani' was axed in 1959, with an insignificant number of titles. Beyond classical poets of the likes of Shakespeare, titles included works by American poets, such as the modernist Wallace Stevens, translated in 1954 by Poggioli, who benefited from a close relationship with the American author, and William

---

19   AE, file Vittorio Bodini, to Giulio Einaudi [hereafter GE], 19 January 1957.
20   As outlined by Alexander (2018: 28), Bourdieu tends to see 'heteronomy' as more explicitly related to commercial factors, partly neglecting political (including state) influence.
21   AE, editorial minutes of 22 May 1963, Franco Fortini. Also in Munari, 2013: 738.

Carlos Williams in 1961, a reprint of Vittorio Sereni and Cristina Campo's translation published by Scheiwiller in 1958. Besides the already mentioned Éluard, there was only Boris Pasternak, translated by Slavicist Angelo Maria Ripellino in 1957, to attract attention, possibly on the back of *Doctor Zhivago*'s publication in the same year by Feltrinelli (*Catalogo Einaudi*, 1999: 600). Instead of finding their place in this series, poetry translations, as well as occasional new Italian poetry, were published in more generic series, thus losing their high profile and ultimately failing to make Giulio Einaudi's name in poetry publishing. The poetry debate would surface again only in the mid-1960s, when Einaudi's headquarters on Turin's via Biancamano was enlivened with new agents and perspectives. It was a shift in literary and publishing dynamics in the latter half of the 1950s that at last enabled foreign poetry to affirm its place in the catalogues of the large- and then medium-scale publishing houses.

1.3 New entrants and publishing dynamism in the second half of the 1950s

The second half of the 1950s was characterised by substantial changes in poetry publishing dynamics, with a general aesthetic redefinition beyond Hermetic and neorealist poetry in favour of more experimental features, and with the entry of many new agents into the publishing field. This deepened the crisis of the more canonical national poetry, already suffering from repetition of titles and general stagnation. Notably, in the mid-1950s, the post-war poetic debate further questioned the role of the national poetic canon and, crucially, contemporary translation practices. A sense of discomfort and disorientation was perceived by the main poetic figures of the period, who in their writings condemned in particular the apparent Hermetic neglect of sociopolitical developments, as well as the limits of the neorealist *impegno* insofar as it only offered a perfunctory representation of and an uncritical relationship with society.

Once a key Hermetic figure, poet Mario Luzi's article 'I dubbi sul realismo poetico' [Doubts on Poetic Realism] (*La Chimera*, July 1954; Luzi, 1965: 25–27) argued that the recourse to chronicle, dialect and slang, typical of neorealist poetry, was not a synthetic way of representing reality – as poetry should be – but a superficial way to capture only a fragment of reality. In other words, Luzi dismissed the value of neorealist poetry in engaging with and meaningfully representing post-war reality. Poet and critic, and later Mondadori editor, Marco Forti's analysis is also representative. In 'Giovane poesia e poesia della Resistenza' [Young Poetry and Poetry of the Resistance] (*Paragone*, October 1956; Forti, 1971: 296–301), reviewing the anthology of contemporary Italian poetry *La nuova poesia* [New Poetry], edited by Enrico Falqui (Colombo, 1956), Forti stated that he would have liked to see a more rigorous editorial selection in order to prioritise only those expressions worthy of praise in terms of poetic value. Closer attention to stylistic experimentation, maintained Forti, would have eliminated many of the one hundred poets who were included purely on the basis of their sociopolitical commitment (Forti, 1971: 297). Interestingly for our analysis, when discussing another anthology, *L'antologia poetica della resistenza italiana* [Poetry Anthology of the Italian Resistance], edited by Elio Filippo Accrocca and Valerio Volpini (Landi, 1955), Forti noticed how in the Resistance years many poets had produced only 'deteriori' [shoddy] effects, a poetry based on the superficial imitation of the translations of Whitman, Lorca, Mayakovsky or Neruda (Forti, 1971: 301), those foreign authors that we have seen as particularly popular with some small and medium-scale publishers.

It was finally Calvino's 'Il midollo del leone' [The Lion's Marrow], published in the journal *Paragone* (66, June 1955; Calvino, 1980: 3–18), which pronounced most vividly the current distance from neorealism, calling for a more rigorous use of language that refused romantic lingering; the latter is seen as an antidote to a dry, intellectualistic approach or, on the contrary, an enthusiastic but irrational attitude, which in both cases misses the integration between literary and social reality. One year later, the Hungarian Revolution changed radically the relationships between culture and politics, and marked an increasing disaffection between left-wing intellectuals and the Italian Communist Party: the years of the post-war *impegno* were long gone, as were those of neorealism.

Italian intellectuals therefore began to discuss and conceive new aesthetics. In February 1956, in the journal *Officina* (1955–59),[22] Pasolini published an article entitled 'Il neosperimentalismo' [neo-experimentalism], in which he defined in disparaging terms the toxic combination of neorealism

---

22 For an in-depth study of the internal dynamics of the journal and the role assumed in the literary debate of the time, see Gian Carlo Ferretti, *'Officina': Cultura, letteratura e politica negli anni cinquanta* (Turin: Einaudi, 1975); for a discussion of *Officina*'s post-neorealist articulation of a form of historicist *impegno* that would connect the journal to transnational Marxist debates, see Francesca Billiani, '*Officina*: Experiments in Engagements in the Arts', *Modern Italy*, 21:2 (2016), 199–214.

and post-Hermeticism. Specifically, Pasolini complained about the limits of a merely linguistic experimentalism that was ineffective for a deeper re-evaluation and development of a new poetics. Of particular interest here is Pasolini's analysis of the still unaccomplished use and influence of foreign poetry, whose styles and forms were accentuated for provocative purposes, or simply remained close to the surface:

> i neo-sperimentali operano spesso dilettantescamente, di seconda mano, spesso sotto l'influenza delle traduzioni: con conseguente costante metrica caratterizzata dal verso libero, amorfo, gli ictus pericolosamente rampanti o sordidamente allineati, la punteggiatura abolita o abnorme, le trovate tipografiche ritrovate a épater les bourgeois, del resto da tempo vaccinati contro simili traumi. (Pasolini, 1994: 1214)

> [the neo-experimentals often operate unprofessionally, in a second-hand fashion, habitually under the influence of translations: as a result, their metrics are constantly characterised by free, shapeless verse, by dangerously jumping or sordidly aligned ictus, the punctuation is either abolished or abnormal, the typographical expedients intend to stick two fingers up to the establishment (*épater les bourgeois*), who have long been vaccinated against these traumas.]

Pasolini's 1957 article 'La libertà stilistica' [Stylistic Freedom] continued the debate, pronouncing the need for an innovative intellectual operation at a formal level (Levato, 2002: 25–55), which would draw on pre-twentieth-century models of poet Giovanni Pascoli, or on the 'anti-Novecento' line linking Saba and Bertolucci. This was conceived not as a return to the tradition but, on the contrary, as a necessary renewal of traditional forms to distance oneself from the free verse used by Hermeticism (Fioretti, 2017: 54). Pasolini's approach, and the emphasis on the poet's subjectivity, was ill-matched with the reduction to objectivity and the more radical formal experimentalism that poets and critics started to develop in these years on the pages of the journal *il verri*, inspired by transnational movements such as Surrealism, the Frankfurt School, and the French *nouveau roman*. The subsequent publication of the *Novissimi* anthology (1961), edited by Alfredo Giuliani, the founding of Gruppo 63, and the *neoavanguardia* movement dismantled for good the Hermetic tradition by means of linguistic experimentation informed by syntax and semantic dissonance, and represented a decisive element in orienting the dynamics of poetry production in a less canonical direction, within and beyond national borders.[23]

Such a poetry debate – here briefly summarised – is not ancillary to the history of Italian publishing if we consider the interweaving of the publishing world and poetic circles, a web also strengthened by the publishers' links with the main literary journals of those years: *il verri* was published first by Scheiwiller and then by Feltrinelli (Luti and Rossi, 1976: 251); *Paragone* changed publisher from Sansoni to Mondadori in the mid-1960s (Luti and Rossi, 1976: 194). The new Italian poets collaborating with Italian publishing houses would steadily assume a more prominent role, both in quantitative and qualitative terms; this laid the foundations for the osmosis between intellectuals and publishing that would take shape in the 1960s, shifting power relationships and aesthetic orientations accordingly, not least in terms of contemporary foreign poetry.

The changing aesthetic dynamics coincided with the entrance of new and distinctly provocative entrepreneurial figures who started to invest the profits of other industries in the publishing sector and who made the publishing field more dynamic. In 1952 Livio Garzanti entered the publishing scene in Milan. Dealing with popular and school books, his father Aldo had already been active since 1938, but it was with Livio that the publishing house moved more systematically towards literature. Garzanti's most noteworthy collaborators included Pasolini, Bertolucci, as well as the experimental writer Carlo Emilio Gadda.[24] The collaboration with these poets moved Garzanti's domestic poetry series away from Mondadori's Hermetic-related triad (Montale–Ungaretti–Quasimodo) to welcome Bertolucci's poetry companions, Sandro Penna and Giorgio Caproni, as well as the Crepuscular Camillo Sbarbaro and Clemente Rebora (Ferretti, 2020: 16) after they were rediscovered by Vanni Scheiwiller.

In 1954 it was Giangiacomo Feltrinelli's turn to enter the stage of the Milanese publishing sector. Until his death in 1972, the anarchic Feltrinelli became a protagonist of literary innovations, both in terms of titles (from Boris Pasternak's *Doctor Zhivago* – for this publication, Feltrinelli was expelled from the Italian Communist Party – to Giuseppe Tomasi di Lampedusa's *Gattopardo* [The Leopard]), and marketing strategies (his well-known

---

23 More broadly on Gruppo 63, see John Picchione, *The New Avant-garde in Italy: Theoretical Debate and Poetic Practices* (Toronto: Toronto University Press, 2004).

24 On Garzanti, see Ferretti, 2020; Tranfaglia and Vittoria, 2000: 420–21; and Ferretti, 2004: 200–11.

bookshops), thus acquiring a crucial role in Italian culture in the second half of the 1950s and through the 1960s. Feltrinelli was a highly original cultural agent in Italian publishing, as were his many collaborators, such as – to remain in the 1950s – Raffaele Crovi, Luciano Bianciardi, and Giorgio Bassani.[25] In the early 1960s Nanni Balestrini and other representatives of Gruppo 63 would enter the doors of Feltrinelli.[26]

The medium-scale publishers such as Einaudi and Bompiani,[27] which had mainly devoted their efforts to novels and non-fiction, became characterised by the union of a culturally refined afflatus, typical of a specialised publisher, and the aspiration to become recognised nationally as well as internationally. Einaudi drew on collaborations with new intellectual and literary figures: Daniele Ponchiroli, Giulio Bollati, Germanist Cesare Cases, Fortini, and in particular Calvino.[28] In so doing, the Turinese publisher overcame the crisis that it had experienced in the first half of the 1950s following political tensions with the PCI over cautious and astute editorial strategies, particularly in relation to poetry (Mangoni, 1999: 540–610, 611–873). Following a more radical line of experimentation than that of the larger-scale publishers, Einaudi developed numerous series in this period, including 'Narratori stranieri tradotti' [Foreign Novelists in Translation] (1938–62), as well as

---

25 On Raffaele Crovi as editor, see *Il mestiere di fare libri: Raffaele Crovi intellettuale e scrittore*, ed. by Giuseppe Lupo and Silvia Cavalli (Brescia: Morcelliana, 2018). On the intellectual figure of Bianciardi, see Gian Carlo Ferretti, *La morte irridente: ritratto critico di Luciano Bianciardi uomo giornalista traduttore scrittore* (Lecce: Manni, 2000). For an organic study of Bassani's work as editor, see Gian Carlo Ferretti and Stefano Guerriero, *Bassani editore letterato* (Lecce: Manni, 2011).
26 More generally on the Feltrinelli publishing house, see Feltrinelli, 1999; Roberta Cesana, *Libri necessari: le edizioni letterarie Feltrinelli (1955–1965)* (Milan: Unicopli, 2010); Tranfaglia and Vittoria, 2000: 455–58; and Ferretti, 2004: 199–204, 211–16.
27 On the Bompiani publishing house, see *Valentino Bompiani: il percorso di un editore artigiano*, ed. by Lodovica Braida (Milan: Sylvestre Bonnard, 2003); Irene Piazzoni, *Valentino Bompiani: un editore italiano tra fascismo e dopoguerra* (Milan: LED, 2007); Ferretti, 2004: 24–30, 142–46.
28 On Giulio Bollati and his editorial role, see Ernesto Ferrero, 'L'altro Giulio. Bollati e lo "struzzo"', in *Giulio Einaudi nell'editoria di cultura nel Novecento italiano: atti del Convegno della Fondazione Giulio Einaudi e della Fondazione Luigi Einaudi onlus (Torino, 25–26 ottobre 2012)*, ed. by Paolo Soddu (Florence: Leo S. Olschki, 2015), pp. 299–310. On Cesare Cases, see *Per Cesare Cases*, ed. by Anna Chiarloni, Luigi Forte, and Ursula Isselstein (Alessandria: Edizioni dell'Orso, 2010), and *Scegliendo e scartando: pareri di lettura*, ed. by Michele Sisto (Turin: Aragno, 2013). On Calvino as editor, see *Calvino e l'editoria*, ed. by Luca Clerici and Bruno Falcetto (Milan: Marcos y Marcos, 1993); and Cadioli and Vigini, 2004: 165–93.

the Vittorini-led 'I Gettoni' [Tokens], where innovative novels spanning Surrealism to sociopolitical commentaries affirmed their place.

At the beginning, however, especially in the case of the larger-scale publishers, some continuity was maintained in terms of the main publishing agents involved: Mondadori relied on the collaboration of established editors such as Vittorini and writer, literary critic, editor, and journalist Giuseppe Ravegnani, and drew on the literary agent Erich Linder for the driving sector of foreign novels, which became the protagonists of new ('Urania', in 1952) or old ('Omnibus') series. The national literary sector was affected by excessive inertia (Decleva, 2007: 397–461; Tranfaglia and Vittoria, 2000: 409–14; Ferretti, 2004: 10–13, 135–37); this would soon cause the large-scale publishing houses such as Mondadori to look elsewhere.

1.3.1 Beyond Hermeticism: revitalising Mondadori's 'Lo Specchio' by opening to translation

The presence of new and old cultural agents operating simultaneously in the field created tensions, both in terms of aesthetic perceptions, particularly in relation to the Hermetic tradition, and in terms of publishing intents in the more canonical institutions. In addition to the concurrent aesthetic redefinition, these tensions made the domain of national poetry slippery and risked questioning traditional bonds and social networks at national level. Emblematic was the case of Mondadori, which started paving the slow way for a greater receptiveness of transnational inspirations on the part of the publisher.

The need for aesthetic renewal notwithstanding – a need recognised by the intellectuals working for the Milanese publishing house – Mondadori was bound to the programmatic constraints of a poetry series which had canonising purposes. But when the loss of prestige was so profound, a publishing reorganisation was triggered: only in the second half of the 1950s did Mondadori start to feel an increasing uneasiness with regard to the poetic works published in 'Lo Specchio', which were all inscribed within the Italian literary space and unable to sustain the prestigious literary level intended for the series. At the same time, contemporary poets did not offer valid alternatives. At the end of the 1950s, the introduction of more innovative editors to Mondadori's editorial board, such as Vittorio Sereni, and the increasingly fierce competition with small-scale publishers led the publishing house to reconsider the publishing strategy of 'Lo Specchio', and consequently to insert foreign titles into its traditionally autarkic catalogue.

Translation thus also became for the larger companies a necessary means to reacquire prestige and compete with the now more central forces of the field, albeit normally in a more institutionalised manner and limited by more rigid planning.

Run by Arturo Tofanelli and Alberto Mondadori, and later by Ravegnani, 'Lo Specchio' had been structured around the cultural capital offered by the most established poets in the national tradition since its creation in the 1940s. Decleva maintains that there was nonetheless a 'discrepanza' [discrepancy] between the level of poetic value in the 1960s and 'l'immagine complessiva che della collana si cercava sin da allora di proporre' [the overall image that the series intended to promote] (2007: 250); this was due to the excessive corporatism in the early years of the series, a factor that had led Tofanelli and Mondadori to accommodate some intellectuals who had already collaborated with their journal *Primato* in the catalogue. The series traditionally only considered poets who had reached an accomplished stage of their career,[29] and thus even in 1957 the publication of new, younger poets was perceived as a destabilising element which would diminish its long-term prestige:

> È bene dir subito che io non posso declassare 'Lo Specchio' a collana sperimentale, di giovani di belle speranze, e per ciò qualsivoglia firma inedita dev'essere già valida in sé, quando figuri nello 'Specchio' per non diminuirne il tono e il significato.[30]
>
> [It is worth saying immediately that I cannot downgrade 'Lo Specchio' to an experimental series, of young poets full of hopes; therefore any unpublished authors should already be established if they are to be published in 'Lo Specchio', so as not to diminish its tone and significance.]

At the end of the 1950s, however, the recurrence of the same names in the catalogue started to become an issue. Quantitative analysis presented in Appendix 2 shows that between 1940 and 1956, when the first contemporary foreign poet was translated, 'Lo Specchio' published 138 books, half of them poetry collections. The authors published more than once were Saba (10) Ungaretti (7), Cardarelli (6), Quasimodo (5), Sinisgalli (4), De Libero,

---

29 FAAM, Alberto Mondadori [hereafter AM], file Giuseppe Ravegnani, to Arnoldo Mondadori, 'casa' [home], 2 December 1957.
30 FAAM, *Segreteria Editoriale Autori Italiani* [hereafter *SEAI*], file Giuseppe Ravegnani, 17 July 1957.

Montale, Gatto, Valeri, and Raffaele Carrieri (2), all of whom were associated with Hermeticism to varying degrees.

A close look at the readers' reports on the poetry manuscripts proposed by Italian poets – some of whom were already featured in 'Lo Specchio' – shows even more clearly how consolidated aesthetic formulas were greeted increasingly negatively, in line with the phase of re-evaluation of poetics informing the literary field and Italian culture more broadly. The rejection of mannerist aesthetics led Mondadori editors to criticise both the themes of the elegy and conventional closed forms, now felt to be stale. A new, fluid poetic form, distant from the traditional influence of Montale, was required, in conjunction with the search for more realistic content. This is precisely what poet and critic Giovanni Raboni suggested while reviewing poet Mario Cicognani: a break from traditional metrics and syntax in order to address in more skilful ways the urgency of reality.[31] Cicognani's first collection suggested themes pertaining to Florentine Hermeticism but with such a rigidity and elevated tone that the reader would desire 'un ritmo più fresco, più libero, una sintassi meno canonica' [a much fresher, freer, rhythm, a less canonical syntax].[32] In his analysis, Raboni identifies the solution to this issue when Cicognani shapes urban images into a more effectively dry metric rhythm. This way, according to Raboni, it would be possible to establish a more effective representation of the outer world and its objects.

Particularly blunt, furthermore, were the judgements against the work *Stato di cose* [State of Things] by poet and critic Piero Bigongiari, and his Hermetic-inspired manneristic style. It was again Raboni who saw the limits of Bigongiari's poetic testament in comparison with the greatest representatives of Florentine Hermeticism, such as Luzi.[33] Specifically, Raboni lamented in the incredibly long collection *Stato di cose* Bigongiari's 'naturale manierismo' [natural mannerism], with his constant and all-consuming amplification of poetic images.[34] This interfered with the quality of the poems and their

---

31   More generally on the figure of Giovanni Raboni as poetry critic, see Anna Chella, *Giovanni Raboni poeta e lettore di poesia (1953–1966)* (Florence: Florence University Press, 2017).
32   FAAM, *SEAI*, file Mario Cicognani, reader's report by Giovanni Raboni on *Alle assorti regioni* (To the Intent Regions, Guanda), *Anna a Milano* (Anna in Milan, Rebellato) and *Ritratti e racconti* (Portraits and Short Stories, unpublished), 24 January 1962.
33   FAAM, *SEAI*, file Piero Bigongiari, reader's report by Giovanni Raboni on *Stato di cose (poesie 1934–1962)*, 14 March 1963.
34   Ibid.

potential historical interest as a representation of the specific poetic school of Florentine Hermeticism: a more 'leggibile, arioso' [readable, airy] form would do the book infinitely more justice.[35]

Less harshly, Forti – who would become editor-in-chief at 'Lo Specchio' in 1966 – also acknowledged the echoes of the Florentine Hermetic environment that he himself knew very well and appreciated, having considered Bigongiari as one of his reference points in terms of literary criticism (Villano, 2020). More interestingly, though, Forti stressed the echoes of foreign models that had nourished the movement. Such a transnational perspective reveals that, in line with the translation trends of the pre-war period, the echo of French Symbolism was redundant, as was that of T.S. Eliot, while the influence of Éluard moved Bigongiari's work closer to the less filtered perception of reality characteristic of the post-war era. It was precisely this poetic mixture, imbued with transnational literary myths – only superficially digested – as well as highly literary tones,[36] which reflected the stagnation of poetic forms experienced by Italian post-Hermeticism. Forti concluded by reaffirming the syncretic role of this publication, which could function only as a review of a bygone poetic season and would be unable to attract attention beyond that of a specialist audience.

Indeed, beyond specialised circles, readers no longer seemed attracted by these 'second' voices of Hermeticism, and the reviews of literary journals in relation to 'Lo Specchio' were not flattering. In the early 1960s, for instance, in *Poesia e Critica*, Luciano Cerchi (1961: 84) identified Mondadori's only merit in 'aver saputo incapsulare il fondo inquieto della poesia ermetica, non accettata dalla formula del Croce, in un'atmosfera dignitosamente classica' [being able to encapsulate the restless soul of Hermetic poetry, rejected by Croce's formula, in a respectably classical atmosphere]. The publication of more obscure Hermetic mannerism had consequences not only in terms of editorial judgements but, more importantly, book sales, since of the 2,000 copies of Bigongiari's *Le mura di Pistoia* [Pistoia's Walls] printed in August 1958, 1,200 remained unsold at the end of March 1963. The print runs of other works by Bigongiari were even less substantial and limited to one sole edition: 1,448 for *Torre di Arnolfo* (1964), which all the same did receive the

---

35   Ibid. The same sense of fatigue, even discomfort, in reading Bigongiari's works was stressed by editor Raffaele Crovi in his reader's report dated 27 February 1964.
36   FAAM, SEAI, file Piero Bigongiari, reader's report by Marco Forti on *Stato di cose*, 30 November 1965.

Premio Città di Alghero in 1965, and 1,565 for *Stato di cose*.[37] We are thus a far cry from Ungaretti's publishing successes, whose print runs rapidly sold out (Decleva, 2007: 264).

Publishing choices were, however, influenced by broader cultural and power relationships. As early as 1957 Vittorini had repeatedly stressed the lack of innovation in Bigongiari's first work. Above all, Vittorini identified, and underlined repeatedly with a pencil, the risk for 'Lo Specchio' of 'inaridirsi' [stagnating] by offering readers a sterile poetic production, which would be detrimental to the literary status of the series and its marketing potential.[38] This was counterposed, nonetheless, by the strategic desire to keep an author who was 'degno d'attenzione' [worthy of attention] (Curi, 1999: 228) among the representatives of the Florentine Hermetic school. *Stato di cose* was published in 1968, probably not only due to Bigongiari's status as an established author in 'Lo Specchio' and an active translator (*Il vento d'ottobre* [October Wind], 1961), but also as a renowned French Studies scholar. Bigongiari in fact edited the French literature column in *L'Approdo letterario* and his collaboration enabled Mondadori to interweave relationships with such poets as Francis Ponge and René Char.

In a similar way, in 1956, poems written by Tuscan poet and translator Antonio Rinaldi, a close friend of Oreste Macrí, received a rather cold welcome from editor Raffaele Crovi, who deprecated their excessive lyricism and detachment from any historical developments or narratives.[39] The reading given by Sereni was not enthusiastic either, but it was more acute, as it recognised Rinaldi's authentic and accomplished poetic voice; Sereni saw as a positive that the work was detached from the influences of other literatures, especially the 'pervicace sperimentalismo' [obstinate experimentalism] characteristic of the second half of the 1950s.[40] The editor Raffaele Cantini concluded at the bottom of this judgement that the publication of Rinaldi's work would neither add to nor subtract value from 'Lo Specchio', but that it should go ahead 'per riguardo a Raimondi' [out of respect for Raimondi], who promised to write the preface. Aware of the negligible literary and market value of Rinaldi's manuscript, in 1958 the publishing house nevertheless agreed to its publication in the name of the delicate balance of

---

37 Ibid.
38 FAAM, *SEAI*, file Piero Bigongiari, Elio Vittorini, 18 May 1957.
39 FAAM, *SEAI*, file Antonio Rinaldi, Raffaele Crovi's reader's report on *Poesie*, 14 January 1956.
40 Ibid., reader's report by Vittorio Sereni, 10 April 1956.

power relationships with other poets, in this case with the Bologna-based Giuseppe Raimondi, a Mondadori author since 1949.

These dubious publishing choices, informed by a clear caution in maintaining the publishing house's relationships with its established poets, were unable to meet the literary demands of both editors and readers, as a growing stock of unsold books confirmed. This engendered a substantial loss for Mondadori not only in economic terms, but also in terms of symbolic capital, which risked invalidating the prestige of 'Lo Specchio'. Arnoldo Mondadori began to worry and, as early as late October 1957, invited Ravegnani to assume a more rigorous approach ('giudizio estremamente rigido e severo' [extremely rigorous and severe judgement]) with regard to the selection criteria for the series. 'Lo Specchio' had to include only poets of the highest calibre, and to exclude the mediocre poetic productions that for diverse, and not necessarily literary, reasons had previously found a place in the catalogue. Mondadori's main objective was to reclaim the prestigious 'tono' [tone] that the poetry series had always enjoyed in the Italian publishing field, and this involved the necessary 'sacrificio di alcuni pochi' [sacrifice of a few].[41]

This prerogative was part of a new publishing phase for Mondadori, characterised by 'un cospicuo sforzo di aggiornamento e potenziamento' [a substantial effort to update and strengthen its offer] (Decleva, 2007: 481). With the help of new editors (Sereni and Niccolò Gallo,[42] among others) the publishing house as a whole invested in this shift. As Decleva also pointed out, the risk was that of:

> restare confinati e appiattiti in un ruolo di rappresentanti di un certo numero di autori noti, ma che avevano già dato da tempo il meglio di sé, lasciando la via libera a strutture editoriali più agili e intraprendenti, più sensibili alle nuove mode e tendenze. (Decleva 2007: 482)

[remaining limited and flattened in the role of representing a certain number of well-known authors who had already given their best, thus leaving space for the more agile and dynamic publishing houses, more sensitive to the new trends and fashions]

---

41   FAAM, *SEAI*, file Giuseppe Ravegnani, Arnoldo Mondadori, 31 October 1957.
42   On Niccolò Gallo, see Giancarlo Ferretti, *Storia di un editor. Niccolò Gallo* (Milan: Fondazione Arnoldo e Alberto Mondadori, 2015).

The issue now moved to the validity of the Italian poets whom Mondadori had focused on in the past, and Sereni's report pointed out bluntly the monotony of Mondadori's current offer, comprising only established (or already published) Italian authors and a couple of foreign poets, who did represent some innovation:

> Forse non sarebbe il caso, e non ne vale la pena, ma sai quanti poeti nuovi escono nello 'Specchio' a partire da questo momento? Luciano Erba e basta. Gli altri sono: Pound, tutto Quasimodo in volume, Lucio Piccolo (ristampa del precedente volume più cose nuove), Giacomo Noventa (deceduto l'altro giorno), Ungaretti (le prose), Cavafis, un'altra parte del canzoniere di Saba, le poesie di Gatto che una volta uscirono da Vallecchi, ecc. Se ti pare che questa poesia italiana del dopoguerra...[43]

> [Perhaps I shouldn't, and it is not worth it, but do you know how many new poets will be published in 'Lo Specchio' starting from now? Luciano Erba, and that's all. The others are: Pound, all Quasimodo's works in one book, Lucio Piccolo (a reprint of his previous book plus some new things), Giacomo Noventa (who died the other day), Ungaretti (his prose writings), Cavafy, another section of Saba's *Canzoniere*, Gatto's poems that were once published by Vallecchi, etc. If you think that this contemporary Italian poetry...]

While such poets as Bertolucci, Pasolini, Penna, or Caproni were now irremediably in the hands of other large-scale publishers such as Garzanti, the remaining Italian poetry did not seem able to catch up, as a glance at the case of Vittorio Bodini's poems illustrates. Bodini embodied an alternative to the Hermetic lesson, thanks to the interweaving of his southern vitalism with images borrowed from his Spanish-speaking tutelary deities, but his works were not considered distinctive enough for the series.[44]

To overcome this impasse, Sereni decided to welcome contemporary foreign poetry in translation into the series. As he stressed in a letter to Pound's daughter, translator Mary de Rachewiltz, the pioneering action of such a

---

43 FAAM, *SEAI*, file Vittorio Bodini, Vittorio Sereni, 6 July 1960.
44 FAAM, *SEAI*, file Vittorio Bodini, reader's report by Della Corte, 24 May 1960. The poet did in the end find a place in the catalogue, despite an unflattering reader's report which compared his poems to those of Elio Filippo Accrocca, another contemporary poet viewed as being imbued with Ungaretti's models as well as neorealist content.

small-scale publishing house with regard to foreign poetry had inevitable consequences for the overall structure of the poetry publishing field.[45] With the small publishers obtaining a central position, Mondadori finally turned to translation in order to regain centrality and give 'Lo Specchio' back the prestige that was one of the series' core aims. It was 1956 when Guido Errante translated Emily Dickinson, paving the way for a more systematic publication of foreign poets. As data in Appendix 2 reveal, in less than twenty-five years translated poetry titles would account for a quarter of the overall poetry production of 'Lo Specchio', with 34 titles out of the 138 published between 1956 and 1977 being by contemporary foreign poets (25.4%), a dramatic move that would permit the Milanese publishing house to reassume a central position within the changing dynamics of the poetry publishing field of the 1960s.

1.4 The 1960s, the *neoavanguardia*, and the economic boom: a space for poetry in the Italian large-scale publishing houses?

With the turn to the 1960s, economic, social, as well as cultural movements shook the Western middle classes, which started to benefit from greater economic prosperity and to experience the growth of mass culture. In the second half of the decade, counterculture movements and student protests triggered revolutionary changes in social norms, civil rights, and cultural habits, while popular culture flourished. The 1960s brought very significant changes across Italian culture and society too, in particular in relation to the object of this inquiry: new aesthetic models emerged in the field of poetry and the economic boom opened new markets and readerships for the Italian publishing houses. Overall, these dissident years questioned traditional cultural modes and privileged a more critical approach (Piazzoni, 2021: 258). Notwithstanding some contradictions, these poetic and publishing developments would be strong enough to invert the dynamics of the poetry publishing field and create space for the potential repositioning of the medium- and large-scale publishing houses, which began with the production of foreign poetry in translation.

In responding to the phenomenon of mass culture and industrialisation, in similar terms to the French literary movement of the *nouveau*

---

45 FAAM, *Segreteria Editoriale Estero* – C [hereafter *SEE* – C], file Ezra Pound, Vittorio Sereni to Mary de Rachewiltz, 28 December 1961.

roman, the *neoavanguardia* configured a different relationship between the subject and the object in favour of a new, radical use of language that could portray the loss of subjectivity and the social changes wrought by industrial developments, while fighting the traditional, bourgeois linguistic tools. The mass-culture phenomenon, however, not only changed the literary modalities of representing society and reality, but questioned the function of intellectuals. Their role appeared still to be strongly anchored to the illusion of the cultural prestige of their activity; with their vehement proposals, the new entrants of Gruppo 63 polarised the publishing establishment at first, between their supporters – Scheiwiller, Feltrinelli, and partly Einaudi, as we will see in the following chapters – and those more sceptical – Mondadori, with Sereni, and Garzanti, with Pasolini. But their apparently greater freedom was deceptive, as Fortini outlined in his pivotal essay, 'Verifica dei poteri' [Check of Powers] (1974: 41–63), in which he acutely anticipated the transformation of roles.[46] Intellectuals were yet to reject the mass-culture system; many were entangled within the institutions which promoted it, occupying strategic positions on the editorial boards of the large-scale publishers or, later, in universities, according to the well-known dichotomy of 'apocalittici' [apocalyptic] and 'integrati' [integrated] coined by Umberto Eco (1964). The consequent long-term risk was conformity to this same system, which would mark the failure of the *neoavanguardia*.

The 1960s saw, moreover, the emergence of a potential new readership, thanks to social changes related, in part, to the economic miracle. With the Codignola reform of secondary education in 1963 – followed by the active opening, through the working-class and student struggles of 1968, of access to universities in accordance with the 910 law approved in July 1969 – there had been an increase in literacy rates, and a growing proportion of the population wanted to enjoy literature. From 1956 to 1960, the number of titles targeting a 'mass-culture' readership increased by about 43% (Ferretti, 2004: 160). Poetry did not remain static and reported a proportionally higher increase when compared to the novel genre, with a percentage of about 36% (Santoro, 2008: 405). This situation was a result of the large-scale publishers' more coherent interest in poetry in the 1960s. A quick overview is sufficient to give a sense of this increased engagement: Feltrinelli devoted a specific series to Italian poetry from 1958, focused mainly on Gruppo 63 authors; in 1964 Einaudi returned to poetry with its 'Collezione di poesia'; Mondadori

---

46 On the relationship between intellectuals and cultural production, see Ferretti, 1995.

reinvigorated 'Lo Specchio', with, as we have seen already, the arrival of Sereni first (1958) and Forti later (1966).

The fact that poetry, which is not strictly speaking a cultural product for a wider readership, became a more systematic and large-scale element of Italian publishing production might be seen as undermining the cultural directives of the economic boom, generally in search of a mass-culture audience. Yet the renewed interest in poetry demonstrated much broader structural requirements. We have to take into account the way that the delayed development of the cultural industries in Italy had engendered a separation between a section of educated readers and a 'mass' that was less interested in books but was fascinated with new media such as cinema and television. This is why the publishers' ideal readership was generally more cultivated than that usually associated with the phenomenon of consumerism (Ferretti, 2004: 48). We should also recall that the spread of the paperback format was intended to overcome the distinction between elite and popular, a further attempt to make poetry production more accessible. In this context, poetry assumed a key role, as it complemented the needs of a varied audience, usually with elite desires as a sign of sociological distinction in Bourdieusian terms. In this sense, Mondadori's 'Oscar' series is indicative:

> nel quadro generale degli 'Oscar', e anche di altre collane di tascabili, il prodotto-poesia non è più qualcosa di puramente esornativo, un mero blasone culturale (e non è neppure, come nella primissima fase, un'appendice dell''Oscar'-romanzo); esso è già una pedina ben definita della nuova strategia dell'industria culturale. Se è vero che questa strategia si articola e funzionalizza ogni livello di consumo culturale, secondo una gamma completa di offerte, allora nell'ideale supermercato del libro il prodotto poetico non può mancare (così come, si potrebbe dire con un esempio certo grossolano ma non impertinente, nel supermercato degli alimentari non manca il raro prodotto esotico). Anche se l'economico' di poesia spesso da solo non rende (almeno a quanto affermano i portavoce aziendali in questa fase) esso *copre* il suo settore di mercato, *fa blocco* con gli altri prodotti, assolve alla sua funzione di completamento della scala consumistica. (Ferretti, 2004: 49–50)

[As part of a bigger picture, with the 'Oscar' series, as with other paperback series, the poetry-product is no longer something purely ornamental, a mere cultural blazon (and it is not even, as in the very first phase, an appendix to the 'Oscar'-novel); this is already a well-defined element of the new strategy of the cultural industry. If it is true that this strategy is articulated on and sets functions for each level of cultural consumerism, according to a complete range of offers, then in the ideal bookshop the poetry book should feature (as much as, we could say with a crude example but not an irrelevant one, rare exotic products should feature in the supermarket). Although pocket-sized poetry series do not often generate income (as far as the publishers' spokesmen say at this stage), they *cover* their own market sector, to work as a whole with the other products, fulfilling the function of completing the scale of consumerism.]

While publishing houses struggled in the immediate post-war period to find financial support for their poetry series, in the 1960s poetry fully entered this new circuit of publishing production thanks to its symbolic capital, the emergence of a wider but still educated readership, and a more synergetic relationship between poets and agents of cultural production. But what was the role of translation in this changed context, and the function that publishing houses therein assumed?

1.5 The periphery becomes centre: is small publishing really 'useless'?

Quantitative analysis makes us appreciate the extent to which contemporary foreign poetry gained a central place: as data in Appendix 1 show, the average yearly publications of poetry in translation more than tripled in less than ten years (from 7 in 1961 to 24 in 1969), while those of contemporary Italian poetry failed to keep pace (from 9 in 1961 to 17 in 1969). Polarised by the Cold War, throughout the 1960s independence movements emerged across the globe; if anti-colonial aspirations often turned into civil wars, they sparked political and cultural interests for intellectuals and younger generations that expanded well beyond European borders. Italy in particular showed a theoretical interest and engaged with internationalist practices (Srivastava, 2018). The political developments of the 1960s explain in part a generally more marked interest in foreign products, but this also must be read against the specific dynamics at national level. As we have seen, a more systematic interest in translation had emerged since the 1950s, but had encountered some structural limitations and had been in part limited to specific agents. The response to changing aesthetics, and to the increasing prestige of the small publishers, alongside new sociocultural conditions, bespoke a more decisive transnational opening of the field, which, we argue, provoked a shift in the dynamics of poetry publishing. While the smaller publishers – traditionally the sector specialists – consolidated their hold, they were joined by the investment of the medium- and large-scale publishing houses trying to regain their centrality through translation.

Einaudi's 'Collezione di poesia' is the most typical example: following the failures of the 1940s and 1950s, the new series was an undeniable success, with 94 titles of contemporary poetry, 66 (70%) of them in translation. The normally more autarkic Mondadori devoted 25% of 'Lo Specchio' titles to foreign poetry, in the hope of increasing its competitiveness with both the small publishers and Einaudi. The translation practice of these publishers will be discussed in the following chapters, but the significance of the publishing events triggered by the translation of foreign poetry within the post-war Italian cultural framework becomes clearer if we draw them up according to the principles of 'centre' and 'periphery'. At the end of the 1940s, the small publishing houses, given their limited financial means which restricted their room for manoeuvre in terms of cultural products offered, were situated in a peripheral area of the poetry publishing field, while the centre was firmly occupied by the larger publishers, whose catalogues featured the most established Italian poets. In the early 1950s, however, by focusing on the publication of contemporary foreign poetry, the small-scale publishers – particularly Scheiwiller – acquired remarkable quantities of symbolic capital and were able to obtain a more solid position. The moves of the specialised publishers were not entirely isolated but, in the early 1960s, they engaged in a simultaneous competition and synergy with the larger publishing houses. The turn to translation influenced the strategies of the large-scale publishers, encouraged to pay attention to poetry production beyond national borders in order to enter into direct competition with the small publishers. As the latter, exploiting a marginal position which gave them more freedom, introduced new contributions in the field of poetry, these elements of novelty were then seized by a unifying centre. The role occupied by a large-scale publishing house such as Mondadori was one of integrating the innovation produced by the peripheral forces into its own canonical catalogue, thus affirming their value and granting them a wider circulation.

The metaphor suggested by Vanni Scheiwiller with regard to his father's editions aptly describes this dynamic: 'pesci pilota approdati al grande mare mondadoriano' [pilot fish dropped in the big Mondadori sea] (Ghidinelli, 2009: 150). Scheiwiller's books were elegant, small-format editions of select poems. This was due to the refined aesthetic taste of this publisher but also to the publishing context. In the case of canonical poets, Scheiwiller had to settle for the limited choices that remained beyond the primary editions published by Mondadori's 'Lo Specchio'. He also ought to take into account turnaround times, as his narrow financial means did not accommodate lengthy editions. Scheiwiller's *plaquettes* in their minimalist dimensions offered a taste of contemporary foreign poets, and they thus became a first point of access to new styles and poetic content in the Italian literary space. Far from being merely a 'plaquette-pearl' for its own sake, these micro-texts represent a pioneering aim and at the same time a 'libro di transito' [transit book] towards a macro-textual dimension more typical of large-scale publishing.

This does not mean that the innovative role of small publishers was simply incorporated within the tangles of larger publishing houses. Instead, we maintain that, via its explicit impact on the dynamics of the publishing field, translation indirectly assumed a key role in the national literary field. Starting from the mid-1950s, contemporary Italian poetry – in its more dynamic and innovative forms – found its greatest champions in the small-scale publishers. Able to adopt more flexible and inventive strategies, the publishing micro-structures could allow themselves the luxury of taking their chances with unpublished authors, thus anticipating textual productions that would be collected at a later stage in the catalogues of the large-scale publishing houses.

Drawing on the prestige they obtained through a transnational opening, the small publishers could function not just as brave, though economically limited, pioneers, but as effective consecrators of poetic innovation. To be published by specific small publishers meant being included in a prestigious catalogue, being placed side by side with high-level contemporary foreign poets, entering an elite and refined poetic circle. In the new field dynamics that translation had helped create, publication by a small publisher meant not simply the acquisition of a 'niche' audience but the assumption of a strategic and highly relevant position. Small-scale publishing houses thus had a significant impact on national poetry, contributing to the innovation of the Italian tradition itself. We should therefore not underestimate the role that a small publisher such as Scheiwiller had in the circulation of the *neoavanguardia*, from the publication of the journal *il verri* to the poets of Gruppo 63.[47] The small Milanese publisher's initial recognition of the poetry

---

47   On the role of Scheiwiller in relation to the *neoavanguardia*, in both the poetic and especially artistic context, and on the mixture of these two modalities as also evident in the materiality of publishing formats, see Isotta Piazza, 'Vanni Scheiwiller e la rivista "Il Verri": un contributo originale (e ambiguo) alla Neoavanguardia italiana', in *Memoria*

movement was crucial in enabling its entry into the wider circulation offered by Feltrinelli in the early 1960s.

The small publishers' pioneering role in terms of new literary contributions in the Italian context was also perceived by the literary agents themselves, who legitimised the significance of their position. In the case of Vanni Scheiwiller, it was poet and translator Claudio Magris who praised the activity of the publisher, confirming the image of a key and influential presence in Italian publishing:

> Vanni è stato un poeta dell'editoria, un editore piccolo e grande. Piccolo per le dimensioni della sua casa editrice e grande non solo per il genio e respiro culturale, ma perché – è questo l'aspetto singolare, eccezionale e indimenticabile della sua attività – era un editore che, con pochissimi mezzi, era una presenza nazionale, contribuiva in maniera eminente a determinare il clima culturale del nostro paese, come i grandi editori. Pubblicare da Scheiwiller era giustamente una grande ambizione per uno scrittore, perché significava non essere già incluso in una aristocratica ma appartata e isolata schiera, bensì entrare nel circuito letterario nazionale. (Magris, 2000: 186)

> [Vanni was a poet of publishing, a small but big publisher. Small for the dimensions of his publishing house and big not only for his genius and his cultural open-mindedness, but also because – and this is the peculiar, exceptional, and unforgettable aspect of his activity – he was a publisher who, with very limited means, had a national presence, contributed immensely to determining the cultural climate of our country, just like the large-scale publishers. To be published by Scheiwiller was with good reason a great ambition for a writer, since it meant, rather than [simply] being included in an aristocratic but private and isolated crowd, becoming part of the national literary circuit.]

The actions of Bertolucci testify to truth of the words of Magris. Although his *Viaggio d'inverno* [Winter Journey] had been published by Garzanti, Bertolucci gave Scheiwiller a book with the following dedication: 'A Vanni Scheiwiller, editore di poeti con la speranza di entrare fra i suoi poeti' [To

della modernità. Archivi ideali e archivi reali. Atti del XIII Convegno Internazionale della MOD, ed. by Clara Borrelli, Elena Candela, and Angelo R. Pupino (Pisa: ETS, 2013), pp. 257–66.

Vanni Schieiwiller, publisher of poets, with the hope of becoming one of his poets] (Pulsoni, 2011: vii). Still in the early 1960s, the translator Pontani used similar words and emphasised the weight and relevance of Scheiwiller's catalogue as a remarkable contribution to culture: 'Non si lamenti di essere un pesce piccolissimo: basta il suo Catalogo a dimostrare la validità della Sua presenza nella cultura italiana del nostro tempo' [Do not complain of being a very small fish: your catalogue is enough to demonstrate the validity of your presence within contemporary Italian culture].[48]

In these terms, the oxymoronic definition that Giuseppe Guglielmi gave of Scheiwiller as a 'editore periferico al centro della letteratura' [peripheral publisher at the centre of literature] (Guglielmi, 1986: 15) makes perfect sense, given the role that the publisher had in not only including, but consecrating, 'marginal' stimuli within the Italian literary field thanks to the prestige acquired through his translation-publishing strategies. Hence, the 'uselessness' of his activity, as Scheiwiller himself ironically suggested, must be reconsidered. Ferretti defines Scheiwiller's strategy as 'senza utili' [without profit] (2009: 19). Yet what the publisher lacked in short-term economic profit was balanced precisely by the symbolic capital that the marque 'Pesce d'oro' acquired over the years, first and foremost thanks to foreign poetry.[49]

By using contemporary foreign poetry production as a lens to critically engage with both the dynamics of the literary field and those of the wider publishing and cultural context in post-war Italy, in this chapter we have written a more articulate history of Italian publishing, which not only debunks the idea of a simply ingenuous and elite practice of poetry publishing, but also crucially takes into account the function of transnational phenomena in orienting the domestic context. We have demonstrated the inaccuracy of speaking of a simplistic domination of larger publishers over smaller, or of a detachment between the strategies of major publishers and minor ones; on the contrary, we have seen shifting patterns of behaviour caused by translation. At a macroscopic level of analysis, translation had a profound impact on the structure of the publishing field: when in the 1950s contemporary Italian poetry was redefining its own aesthetics, and Italian publishers sought new spaces and audiences, translation represented an opportunity to overcome the impasse of a stagnant national offer and satisfy the need for publishers to attain a key position in the field of poetry publishing. In

48 APICE, VS, Filippo Maria Pontani, 11 July 1962, ms.
49 These conclusions have been in part discussed in Milani, 2012: 105.

doing so, it prompted mobility and change for Italian culture at large: in the span of two decades or so, Italian publishers as well as editors and translators negotiated their perception of, and engagement with, transnational movements in more or less accomplished and productive ways – from the strict bond between Hermeticism and modernism, through neorealism and militant poetic experiences, to experimentalism. Having discussed *why* publishers introduced contemporary foreign poetry into their catalogues, we now move to a mesoscopic level of inquiry, to examine in detail *how* each specific publishing enterprise interacted with translation practice.

CHAPTER TWO

Editors, Habitus, and Translation: Publishing Strategies in Poetry Translation

In this chapter, we look at how the interactions between the objectives of three publishers, their editors' habitus, and the dynamics of the field, extending beyond the national, are implicated in translation selection and practice. The three publishers considered here are Scheiwiller, Mondadori and Einaudi, chosen as representatives of small-, large-, and medium-scale publishing houses respectively. We ask to what extent the choice of foreign poets and the (para)textual elements were strategies employed by the publishers in order to affirm their positioning in the field of poetry publishing, as well as by individual editors in establishing their status in the national and transnational literary field. Through a sociological analysis of the meta-discourse emerging from the publishing correspondence as well as from the reading of the published texts and paratexts, we shall shed light on how, in the general search for a source of symbolic capital that translation represents, the practice of publishing contemporary foreign poetry differs according to the aims and trajectories of a specific publishing house. As each publisher sought to appeal to a certain readership, the identification of how the publisher–audience relationship comes into play – how the editing of the translation adapts to a certain typology of reader – is a key element of our inquiry. This fosters a productive potential for a reassessment of transnational engagement in terms of elite and (more) popular cultural production. The value of translational relationships extends from an arguably cosmopolitan afflatus – which is both linked to, and critical of, the Hermetic aesthetic horizon – to a negotiation of position within the intellectual debate in more politically committed terms, within and beyond national borders.

In the following subsections – one devoted to each of the three publishers under investigation – we will demonstrate that the approach to foreign poetry of large-scale publishers, fixed within a more rigid market structure, was a constant attempt to strike a balance between the expectations of a less specialised readership and the need to avoid canonical solutions that might appear sterile. Translation was a vital aspect of capitalising on their catalogue and of maintaining a more central position in the publishing field. The editorial decisions of medium-sized publishers with regard to translation, generally politically motivated, tended towards innovations in both form and content. As such, they could simultaneously attract younger readers such as students and resignify in a transnational context the very identity of Italian literary figures, thus accomplishing a more wide-ranging cultural project. For small publishers, relatively free from external conditioning but not lacking in contradictions, the publication of foreign poetry was inserted within a wider project of distinction that addressed the strict circles of publishing insiders, as the case of Scheiwiller exemplifies.

2.1 Scheiwiller: elitist foreign poetry for the elite

At the beginning of the 1950s, Vanni Scheiwiller undertook a publishing path more decidedly marked by the publication of contemporary foreign poetry. Albeit in part influenced by the cogent dynamics of the Italian publishing field, this choice confirmed and amplified the elite cultural and family dispositions of the small-scale publisher. Scheiwiller entered the Milanese culture of the time by positioning himself in a site of 'distinction' (Bourdieu, 1994), thus embracing those cultural practices that express a search for social refinement. The revolutionary range of the notion of 'distinction' is that culture is not entirely uninterested in social function but, as shown by Bourdieu in his discussion of 1960s France, tastes and consumption models can be conceived as lifestyles able to orient social hierarchies. Far from seeing the publisher's dispositions in tactical terms only, this reflection is particularly relevant for the main argument of this book as we question the role of small-scale publishing houses, to remove them from the prejudices related to 'art for art's sake' and recontextualise them within the compelling dynamics of the Italian field of poetry publishing in the 1950s, when the relation between taste and sociality tended to be more univocal.[1]

---

1   The French model cannot, however, be applied to all periods, as Warde and Savage (2009) have exhaustively explained, and this confirms the need to analyse the specificity of historical as well as national dynamics.

Publishing ran in the family, and when Vanni Scheiwiller succeeded his father Giovanni, at only 19 years old, the Scheiwiller publishing house was already a symbol of prestige for closed literary circles. In the column 'Italia sott'occhio – America col cannocchiale' [Italy in view – America with a telescope], published in the weekly *Il Borghese* on 9 December 1965, the famous writer Giuseppe Prezzolini highlighted the typographic and textual elegance of Giovanni Scheiwiller's publications as a model that writers should aspire to in order to distinguish themselves from the commercialised book production of the time:

> esser pubblicato da Scheiwiller che non pagava o pagava poco, fu nel mondo un simbolo di nobiltà letteraria [...] In questi tempi di pubblicità e di collettame editoriale, di strombazzamento e di gonfiamento di tirature, di vendita di libri come se fossero ceste di pomidoro, il nome di Giovanni Scheiwiller è un esempio: insegna che l'"alienazione" non esiste che per chi l'accetta. (Kalczyńska, 2000: 186)
>
> [to be published by Scheiwiller. who paid poorly if at all, was a symbol of literary nobility [...] In these times of frenzied and haphazard advertising and publishing, of print-run proclaiming and inflating, of books that are sold as if they were tomatoes, Giovanni Scheiwiller's name is an example: he teaches that 'alienation' exists only for those who accept it.]

The young Scheiwiller not only followed but deepened his father's unconventional attitude by significantly widening the literary borders of the publishing house through the introduction into the catalogue of the most innovative examples of post-war Italian and foreign literature: 'accanto ai nomi di Joyce e Pound (nume tutelare) figurano oggi con ammirevole spregiudicatezza quelli di Céline, Evola, Pizzuto, Gadda' [next to such names as Joyce and Pound (tutelary deity) he now puts, with admirable irreverence, those of Céline, Evola, Pizzuto, Gadda] (Romano, 1986: 23). This more ambitious project, especially in relation to foreign poetry, not only configured Scheiwiller as a Bourdieusian 'new entrant' in the publishing field in the 1950s, but also granted him the possibility of moving more decidedly beyond the general limits of the modernist vogue of Italian Hermeticism and successfully projecting the Italian cultural scene into a trans-European realm.

From this nonconformist position, the small-scale publisher operated in accordance with his heretical habitus, which the greater agility of his business structure could sustain, thus giving life to a highly refined publishing project.

In the figure of Vanni Scheiwiller, the publisher coincided with the editorial committee. This permitted the small-scale publisher substantial freedom of choice, particularly when considered alongside the more limited sphere of action of Sereni at Mondadori and the Einaudi editors, who negotiated strategies on relatively democratic terms with the publisher Giulio Einaudi and the editorial board. Promoting innovative foreign poets, a prestigious paratextual format and elitist textual practices, along with strategic narratives to distinguish himself from other cultural operators, further strengthened Scheiwiller's positioning in the field of poetry publishing. Notwithstanding some contradictions in narrative and translation practices, Scheiwiller's publishing and editorial strategies challenge the uncritical view of the small publisher as a peripheral agent, sealing instead his image as a central agent of specialised publishing who did much to reconfigure Italian publishing and culture.

2.1.1 'All'insegna dell'eccentricità': the choice to publish Ezra Pound

The processes involved in the publication of Ezra Pound's poetry provide an insightful example of Vanni Scheiwiller's radicalisation of his father's dispositions, and show clearly how the very specific cultural and political anxieties of national history interacted with transnational intellectual dynamics, thus articulating the publisher's identity and his function in the publishing field. Scheiwiller used to define himself as 'il più eccentrico degli editori milanesi' [the most eccentric of Milanese publishers] (Novati, 2020: 23). The adjective 'eccentric', as derived from medieval Latin *eccentricu(um)*, signifies here how he felt himself to be outside the centre/canon. Giovanni Scheiwiller had already published Pound's *Profile* in 1931, followed five years later by *Confucius: Digest of the Analects*. Publishing Pound at the beginning of the 1950s was an even more daring and risky operation, 'eccentric' both in terms of the political and ideological conventions and the aesthetic models of the time.

Italy was, with difficulty, emerging from the fall of the Fascist dictatorship, and ambiguous attitudes could be questioned. Between 1941 and 1943, Pound threw accusations at the Anglo-American allies, while expressing solidarity with the Fascist regime via Italian radio. This action resulted in a charge of treason issued by the American government. Following a psychiatric report in 1945, the poet was declared mentally ill and was interned in the federal criminal hospital of St Elizabeth's in Washington, where he stayed until 1957. He thus represented for some an inconvenient figure, left at the margins of the world poets' community for his behaviour in support of fascism. For Scheiwiller, however, the publication of Pound's works might – consciously or not – become a potential fund of symbolic capital, a valid means of reinforcing the heretical position of the small-scale publisher: the connection with the American author could not only facilitate the construction of a radical project that, moving from a cosmopolitan afflatus, developed into a more articulate transnational strategy for Scheiwiller, but also make it possible for him to enter the political and aesthetic national debate by challenging its taboos.

In tirelessly defending Pound, Scheiwiller fought against the positions of other Italian intellectuals, especially left-wing figures such as Fortini, who refused to accept the political attitude of the American poet and wrote a slanderous article against Pound in the journal *L'Avanti* on 6 February 1954. This friction carried with it a potential loss of social capital, which would have been disastrous in such a restricted field as that of poetry publishing in Italy. Such a risk was nonetheless compensated for by the added value of critical thinking that the publication of Pound's work entailed. By stressing his own willingness to clearly distinguish political judgement from questions of literary taste, Scheiwiller was in fact weaving a narrative of critical autonomy and irreverence, an attitude visible in the hyperbolic terms he used to declare that he 'ringrazi[ava] Dio tutte le sere per non essere un editore obiettivo: pubblic[ava] solo quello che [gli] piac[eva], fac[eva] di tutto per pubblicare quello che [gli] piac[eva]' [thanked God every night for not being an objective publisher, nor fair or politically committed: I publish only what I like, I do everything to publish what I like].[2]

The same attitude was reinforced in a few letters exchanged with another poet in Scheiwiller's catalogue: Rafael Alberti, whose political ideas opposed those of Pound. Scheiwiller stressed his own anti-fascist beliefs, but also captured – arguably in a more cosmopolitan fashion – the requirement for the publisher to judge not the political but the poetic side of an author: 'Circa la mia mania per Destra Pound: sono di famiglia ed educazione antifascista MA lui è un grande poeta e un *hombre todo hombre* (detto alla Unamuno) che ha sempre pagato di persona' [about my mania for right-wing Pound: I come from an anti-fascist family BUT he is a great poet and a *hombre todo hombre* (as Unamuno would say) who has always paid the price personally].[3] If cosmopolitanism could be conceived as a philosophy that 'urges

---

2 In 'Lettera a una signora perbene', preface by Vanni Scheiwiller to Biagio Marin's *La poesia è un dono* (Milan: Scheiwiller, 1966), now in Ferretti, 2009: 110.
3 APICE, VS, to Rafael Alberti, 29 November 1961.

us all to be "citizens of the world", creating a worldwide community of humanity committed to common values' (Vertovec and Cohen, 2002: 10), in Scheiwiller's case this would seem, on the surface, to lean towards humanism rather than shared political values.

Not only was the decision to publish Pound politically eccentric, but it also stood out from a largely Hermetic preference for T.S. Eliot. This is a crucial point which, once again, shows how Scheiwiller's translation choices not only expanded the transnational reach of the Italian cultural field of the time, but were also voiced as a response to its dynamics *and* successfully changed them. Though both poets represented the new path undertaken by modernist poetry and were promoters of significant formal innovations on the international level, Eliot had always received much more attention from Italian scholars and translators. Prominent recognition had already come as early as 1946, with the publication of *The Sacred Wood*, edited by Luciano Anceschi.[4] In 1949 the English Studies scholar Mario Praz was translating Eliot's work and, in the same year, Guanda published Eliot's poems translated by Luigi Berti. For the first translations of Pound's works, on the contrary, we have to wait until 1953, when Guanda published the *Pisan Cantos*, translated into Italian by the literary critic Alfredo Rizzardi. 1953 was also the year when Vanni Scheiwiller wrote to the American poet, who had already been interned in an asylum, to request a manuscript for publication.

Scheiwiller was not the only one interested in Pound, as the case of the *Pisan Cantos* suggests, but the echo of the American poet's reception clearly broadened and became more coherent thanks to the proactive Milanese publisher. The publication of Pound's work by Guanda was in fact troubled. In 1949 Ugo Guandalini wrote to the literary agent Erich Linder to enquire about the foreign rights of the American poet, to whom he intended to dedicate a book similar to Eliot.[5] From this, it was already clear that Guanda's purpose differed significantly from that of Scheiwiller: the Parma-based publishing house operated according to a wider interest in modernism that dated back to the Second World War, and in this context Pound represented just one of

---

4   For a more exhaustive bibliography on the Italian reception of T.S. Eliot, see Laura Caretti, *T.S. Eliot in Italia. Saggio e bibliografia; 1923–1965* (Bari: Adriatica, 1968).

5   FAAM, Linder Archive, file Guanda, Ugo Guandalini to Erich Linder, Parma, 18 and 23 May 1949. Guanda's project, however, suffered various delays, due to Pound's dissatisfaction with the work of the first translator (Ellemire Zolla) and doubts relating to the second potential translator (Carlo Izzo) (ibid., Ugo Guandalini, Parma, 23 May 1950). The restrictions imposed by Pound exhausted the publisher (ibid., Ugo Guandalini, Parma, 10 September 1951).

the most prominent figures of the literary movement; the Milanese publisher, on the contrary, recognised in Ezra Pound a nonconformist author who, we suggest, could signal the distinction of Scheiwiller from other small-scale publishers.

As such, thanks to Scheiwiller, in 1955 the journal *Stagione* devoted a special issue to Pound in collaboration with well-known Italian poets, and the following year it was the turn of *Nuova Corrente*. Furthermore, a petition by the famous poets Sergio Solmi and Diego Valeri, supported by Vanni Scheiwiller, began circulating in order to ask for Pound's release. From then, the publication of Pound's work by Scheiwiller became systematic, with annual or biannual frequency: *Tre Cantos* (Three Cantos, 1954); *Iconografia italiana – con una piccola antologia poundiana* (Italian Iconography – with a Small Poundian Anthology, 1955); *A lume spento (1908–1958)* (With Tapers Quenched, 1958); *Canto 98* (1958); *Catai* (1959); *H.S. Mauberley* (1959); *Canto 99* (1960); *Antologia classica cinese* (Chinese Classical Anthology, 1964); *Canto 90* (1966); *Ezra Pound tradotto da Giuseppe Ungaretti* (Ezra Pound Translated by Giuseppe Ungaretti, 1969); *Me felice/felice notte* (Myself Happy, Happy Night, 1972); *Stesura e Frammenti dei Cantos CX–CXVIII* (Writing and Fragments from Cantos 110–118, 1973). In addition to the translations of his poetry, numerous essays were reproduced: *Introduzione ai Nô* [Introduction to Noh] and *Lavoro ed usura* [Work and Wear] (both in 1954); *Confucio: studio integrale et l'asse che non vacilla* (Confucius: Integral Study and the Axis which Does not Sway, 1955); *Brancusi* (1957); *Gaudier-Brzeska: con un manifesto vorticista* (Gaudier-Brzeska: with a Vorticism Manifesto, 1957); *Rimbaud* (1957); *Nuova economia editoriale* (New Publishing Economy, 1962); not to mention translations by Pound himself (*Moscardino* by Enrico Pea, 1955), as well as, finally, the publications in English (*Section Rock-drill 85-95 de Los cantares*, 1955; *Thrones 96-109 de los cantares*, 1959). The presence of the American poet in Scheiwiller's catalogue was conspicuous, casting an eccentric 'aura' over the entire book production of the small-scale publisher.

2.1.2 Beyond personal taste: a cultural project of distinction

The choice to publish Ezra Pound was a propeller for a more structured publishing project: through translation, Scheiwiller could acquire a bank of symbolic capital enabling him to become more central in the field of poetry publishing while connecting him (and indirectly national poetry and culture) to the transnational sphere and feeding directly into transnational movements. This is evident in Scheiwiller's own words: in a letter to Pound, he outlined not just a subjective taste, relatively uncompromised by market influences and typical of his own dispositions, but a more wide-ranging project with a precise will for distinction:

> Abbiamo tanto bisogno di lei per seguire una linea (non solo di gusto), per salvare il salvabile [...]
>
> [...] Se si lascia andare lei, andiamo a rotoli tutti. Cioè quelli che le vogliono bene e che seguendo e leggendo E.P. credono di salvare il salvabile. È lei che ci ha insegnato a 'distinguere l'alto dal basso'. [6]
>
> [We need you very much to follow a line (not only aesthetic), to save whatever can be saved...
>
> If you give up, we all fall down. We as those who love you think, by following and reading E.P., we'll save whatever can be saved. It is you who taught me to 'distinguish the top from the bottom'.]

Scheiwiller intended to 'save whatever can be saved', that is, to succeed in an ambitious cultural operation which would involve the publication of 'disruptive' poetry capable of distinguishing itself from the current mediocre production. This nonconformist earthquake needed, however, an epicentre that was symbolic of a new way for contemporary poetry, an epicentre that Pound perfectly embodied. Endowed with international credit, but not yet canonised, the American poet was the ideal promoter of that formal innovation that Italian contemporary poetry was seeking, without being aligned with dominant aesthetics or post-war ideologies. Poetically innovative and politically controversial, the publication of Pound's work would represent the essential hinge for a publishing project that considered 'marginalità come valore' [marginality to be a value] (Ferretti, 2009: 18):

> Siamo noi che abbiamo bisogno di lei. Quasi tutto il mio lavoro è impostato su di lei [...][7]
>
> [It is us that need you. Almost all of my work relies on you.]

---

6   APICE, VS, to Ezra Pound, 14 April 1960, ms, and 18 July 1960, ms.
7   APICE, VS, to Ezra Pound, 16 January 1960, ms.

Faremo tante cose insieme, caro E.P., e se lei <u>funziona, funzionerò</u> anch'io.[8]

[We will do many things together, dear E.P., if you function, I'll function, too.]

From this perspective, translation provided a strategic continuity to this project and effectively cast Scheiwiller into a transnational horizon that forged his intellectual positioning abroad as well as within national borders.

Along with the publication of Pound's translations, the catalogue of contemporary foreign poetry was enriched by innovative literary proposals which ambitiously connected to transnational experimentalism or cultural ferments, thus enhancing the prestige of the publishing house. To this end, Schewiller also pragmatically exploited the transnational social networks and connections of national poets, particularly the future Nobel prize winner Montale, who had translated and continued to be in touch with the Spanish Jorge Guillén, published in 1958 (Chiappini, 2002).[9] The catalogue displays authors who had or would come to exercise a significant influence in world literature, published in translation by Scheiwiller often for the first time: the Greek poet Constantine Cavafy (*Poesie scelte*, Selected Poems, 1956);[10] US poets e.e. cummings (*Poesie scelte*, 1958) and William Carlos Williams (*Il fiore è il nostro segno*, The Flower is our Sign, 1958); James Joyce (*Musica da camera*, Chamber Music, 1961);[11] the Portuguese poet Murilo Mendes (*Finestra del caos*, Chaos Window, 1961);[12] the Spanish Vicente Aleixandre (*Picasso*, 1962);[13] the German poet Gottfried Benn (*Apréslude*, 1963);[14] the French Paul Valéry (*Cimitero marino*, Maritime

---

8 Ibid., 12 February 1960, ms.
9 The first edition of Guillén's poetry dated back to 1955, and was published by the Istituto editoriale Cisalpino (Milan-Varese) with a print run of 570 copies only.
10 Published as a book for the first time in Italy only in 1955 by the Lecce-based publishing house La Nuova Ellade. A first essay on Cavafy's poems was edited by the translator Filippo Maria Pontani and published in 1940 in the journal *Epitheoresis* (vol. 4, issues 8–9, August–September).
11 *Chamber Music* appeared in *Corrente* (15 March 1940, issue 18).
12 In 1959 Luciana Stegagno Picchio translated some poems by Mendes, published alongside the original lines, in 'La poesia in Brasile: Murilo Mendes', *Rivista di letterature moderne e comparate*, 12:1.
13 The Spanish poet had been previously translated by the well-known translator and poet Oreste Macrí in *Quaderni ibero-americani*, 3:11 (December 1951), and in a book by Dario Puccini (edizioni Sciascia, 1961).
14 Benn's poems had already been translated in 1954 by the famous Traverso for the

Cemetery, 1963); anglophone works by Conrad Aiken (*Mutevoli pensieri*, Variable Thoughts, 1963), W.H. Auden (*Per il tempo presente*, For the Present Time, 1964), and Marianne Moore (*Omaggio a Marianne Moore*, Homage to Marianne Moore, 1964);[15] the Hungarian Gyula Illyés (*Due mani*, Two Hands, 1966); T.S. Eliot (*Poesie giovanili*, Juvenile Poems, 1967); and the Greek Giorgos Seferis (*Note per una 'settimana'*, Notes for a 'Week', 1968). The publisher was aware of the added value that these poets could bring to the series 'Pesci d'Oro', identifying six goldfish in Guillén, cummings, Pound, Joyce, as well as French poet Jean Cocteau, and Spanish poet Pedro Salinas.[16] Here the precious metal is not only a qualifying adjective, but a symbol of the prestige that these poets brought with them.

To these authors who might appear more canonical, Scheiwiller added the poets of the collection 'Oltremare', which collected translations of more peripheral poets. The decision was in line with the more flexible plans of the small-scale publisher which allowed him to respond quickly, in terms of translation practices, to the transnational political and cultural events of the 1960s. This put his publishing strategies at the intersection between a cosmopolitan afflatus and the pressures of Italy's opening up to transnational movements and relationships after the Second World War. Between 1962 and 1966, collective poetic productions from Korea or Amerindian peoples, such as the Mapuche, were published as part of this initiative. These were accompanied by more politically committed books, such as the *Omaggio a Praga* (Homage to Prague, dedicated to the Czech poets of the Prague Spring in 1968), as well as the series entitled 'Il male di Grecia' (The Pain of Greece).

When, in effect, the translator Filippo Maria Pontani called on the small Milanese publishing house to ask for prompt publication of the Greek poems of Yiannis Ritsos as a concrete help to Greek intellectuals under the regime of the Colonels, Vanni Scheiwiller demonstrated much zeal – and a clearly anti-fascist stance – in embracing the cause and creating an ad hoc series. The latter was produced with more diligence than the volumes offered by medium- and large-scale publishers, such as Mondadori and Einaudi, in aid of the Greek cause, for wider structural reasons, as we will discuss later:

---

publisher Vallecchi.
15   1962 is the year of the Guanda edition.
16   APICE, VS, to Jorge Guillén, 23 June 1960. See also Milani, 2012: 104; Guillén and Scheiwiller, 2012, 125.

non è questa un'ennesima collana, per cui avrò più collane che libri nel mio catalogo. Se ciascuno di noi non saprà reagire in modo responsabile (farlo anche per i miei amici rivoluzionari in fuoriserie) una brutta mattina ci ritroveremo in Italia con uno o più colonnelli, come in Grecia. Perciò la collana sulla Grecia libera: per difendere la libertà di ciascuno di noi, anche se non condividiamo le idee politiche del poeta e forse neanche la sua poetica. Ma è un uomo privato nella sua libertà e lo dobbiamo difendere a tutti i costi.[17]

[This is not just another series, risking creating more series than books in my catalogue. If each of you cannot react in a responsible way (and do it also for my revolutionary friends out of a specific series), one sad morning we will find in Italy one or more colonels, as in Greece. Hence the series on free Greece: to protect the freedom of each of us, even if we don't agree with the poet's political ideas or even perhaps with his poetics. But he is a private citizen in his freedom and we have to protect him at all costs.]

The poetic sparks were promptly caught by Scheiwiller in the name of a translation engagement which valued above all (as in the case of Pound) intellectual freedom, as opposed to a more popular literary market constrained by specific series and objectives.

The chronology of publications supports the idea of a new publishing path that benefited from translation – and particularly from the translation of Pound's works – and could give value to eccentric positions within the domestic field of Italian poetry. The publication of Pound was followed by that of Italian poets who had been forgotten in the early 1950s by critical literature, such as Sbarbaro and Rebora, in 1954 and 1955 respectively (Ferretti, 2009: 14). After publishing Guillén for the first time, in 1956, this was succeeded by the publication of the so-called poets of the fourth generation, who leaned towards an anti-lyrical poetry attentive to objects, such as Nelo Risi, Giovanni Giudici, and Margherita Guidacci. The series 'Poeti stranieri tradotti da poeti italiani', launched in 1958, was then accompanied by the publication of the poets of the *Linea lombarda*, in particular Sereni, while 1965 became the year of the *Novissimi*. More innovative national publishing choices do not stand alone in the rapid flux of the catalogue but sit alongside contemporary

---

17 APICE, VS, to Filippo Maria Pontani, 1969.

foreign authors, functioning as a transnational legitimisation of the heretical positioning of Vanni Scheiwiller within the field of poetry publishing.

2.1.3 'All'insegna del pesce d'oro': elitist books for the elite

Once a prestigious literary catalogue had been built through strategic transnational projects and networks, its distribution had to be in line with the publisher's distinctive dispositions, not to discredit the symbolic capital of newly acquired refinement. This brings to light the importance in our analysis of the book as a material object, in relation to and beyond the textual practice of translation: the book format, its paratexts, as well as the distribution system all contributed to creating a sophisticated product in translation for a discerning elite. These elements fostered an idea of 'distinction' which not only strengthened the prestige of Scheiwiller's editions, but also provided the Italian readership with an elite way of accessing contemporary foreign poetry that would differ from the practices of larger-scale publishing houses.

Although Montale had defined Scheiwiller's cultural products as 'microlibri introvabili, illeggibili, inutilizzabili' [micro-books that are untraceable, unreadable, unusable] (Minuscoli, 1976: 745), the publisher saw them as the accomplishment of a cultural venture, the merits of which could be recognised only by a restricted readership:

> Questa nuova collana di poesia straniera del '900 in lingua originale si apre all'insegna del motto circolare *c'est ici qu'on prend le bateau* con cui Giuseppe Ungaretti chiudeva l'*Allegria di Naufragi* [...] Seguiranno testi in inglese, francese, tedesco, russo, etc., se i pochi tifosi della poesia in Italia e fuori sapranno mantenere a galla queste fragili barchette di carta che sono i buoni libri di poesia. *Nous savons que nous serons compris d'un petit nombre mais cela nous suffit.*[18]

> [This new collection of twentieth-century poetry in the original language opens with the circular motto 'it is here that we set sail' with which Giuseppe Ungaretti closed his *The Joy of Shipwrecks* [...] English, French, German, Russian, etc. texts will follow, if the few poetry supporters in Italy and abroad can keep afloat these fragile paper boats that are the

---

18 Introductory note by Vanni Scheiwiller to *Luzbel desconcertado* by Jorge Guillén, 1956 (Cadioli and Kerbaker, 2009: 132).

good poetry books. 'We know that we will be understood only by a small number [of people] but this is enough for us.']

Aware that his project of publishing contemporary foreign poetry in the original language would narrow the already small audience for poetic collections, the stance of Vanni Scheiwiller would seem adamant: he would not transcend the borders of the elite to reach a wider audience.

The publisher proposed to this niche market an edition that was minimal, yet refined, even in material terms. The small book format was traditionally linked to Giovanni Scheiwiller, who in the 1930s and 1940s opted for this style. The reasons were both economic, including paper rationing, and ideological, in opposition to the bigger Fascist books (Ferretti, 2009: 11). His son's decision to maintain this format encompassed both aesthetic reasons and probably the desire to capitalise on this already distinctive feature, which could have a bearing on the structures of the book market. In fact, the costs of lithography, as a preferred method of publishing, weighed heavily on the small-scale publisher's budget: 'stampo [questo libro] in litografia – non tipograficamente. Ma verrà più caro di quanto pensassi (prezzo di copertina intorno alle 5000 lire)' [I will print [this book] in lithography, not with typography. It will cost more than I expected (cover price around 5,000 Italian lira)].[19] At the same time, the extreme care in the format was a distinctive trait apt to acquire more prestige. The books became a union of poetry and art thanks to the intervention of artists or the poets themselves in designing the covers. The collaboration with renowned graphic designer Bruno Munari and his adaptation of the 'goldfish' to the style of the Movimento Arte Concreta [Movement of Concrete Art] (Cadioli and Kerbaker, 2009: 243–44),[20] as well as that with Rafael Alberti, who would design a book cover with his 'finissima penna un po' cocteauiana' [with his very fine pen, a bit Cocteau-style],[21] are illustrative.

Scheiwiller pointed out two strengths of the small book format. On the one hand, the creation of small, 'agile' books, which Scheiwiller named

---

19 APICE, VS, to Rafael Alberti, 25 February 1964, ms.
20 On Bruno Munari, see Aldo Tanchis, *Bruno Munari: From Futurism to Post-Industrial Design*, trans. by H. Evans (London: Lund Humphries, 1987), and more recently *Bruno Munari: The Lightness of Art*, ed. by Pierpaolo Antonello, Matilde Nardelli, and Margherita Zanoletti (Oxford: Peter Lang, 2017); *Bruno Munari: Aria Terra*, ed. by Guido Bartorelli (Mantua: Corraini, 2017).
21 APICE, VS, Paolo Franci, 16 August 1967.

'taschinabili' [pocketable] (Scheiwiller, 1983: 127–31), could increase their ease of circulation, as we see occurring with pocket books. On the other hand, the marked distinction between the aspirations of mass-produced, generic pocket books and these elitist texts further highlighted the prestige of Scheiwiller's books. In this vein, the small-scale publisher indicates an acute awareness of the urgency of gaining the symbolic capital that can orient the market in the elite genre of poetry. In other words, the 'goldfish' are less innocent than the rhetoric built around them. This is how Scheiwiller replied to the writer Elio Filippo Accrocca's request to print his book *Reliquia umana* [Human Vestiges] in a bigger format to include other poems and make a 64-page book as *Portonaccio*: 'I formati grandi – specie per la poesia – non vanno assolutamente e io non voglio dipendere dall'autore. Di più si dà un tono, una linea alla collana di giovani' [the big format books – especially for poetry – don't sell and I don't want to depend on the author. Plus, you give a tone, a line to the youth series].[22]

The collaborators understood this system very well. The correspondence with the poet-translator Francesco Tentori Montalto makes clear how the refined and elastic project was seen as a form of minimal craftsmanship, and distinguished Scheiwiller from other small-scale publishers, including Guanda, which were more apt to welcome substantial projects: 'mi piacerebbe veramente fare ambedue le cose con lei (sa forse che sto preparando per Guanda una grossa antologia della poesia sudamericana). Potremmo fare un'antologietta veramente essenziale, col meglio della lirica spagnola del Novecento' [I'd really like to do both things with you (you may be aware that I am preparing for Guanda a big anthology of South American poetry). We can do a truly essential small anthology, with the best of Spanish twentieth-century poetry].[23] In essence, Scheiwiller proposed a dividing line between himself and other specialised publishers, whose typographical practices already demonstrated a tendency towards the objectives of medium-scale publishers, such as the 'big anthologies'.

---

22 APICE, VS, to Elio Filippo Accrocca, 7 December 1954, ms.
23 APICE, VS, Francesco Tentori Montalto, Rome, 7 November 1956 (or 55?).

2.1.4 Disdain for economic capital?

The project of distinction undertaken by Scheiwiller was based on a rhetoric of disdain for the operational ways typical of larger-scale publishers. This does not mean that Scheiwiller disdained profit *tout court* in its diverse forms, as earnings ultimately allowed the cultural project to survive. He was fully aware of the production costs in the publishing market, as evidenced in his attention to literary prizes, supporting his authors for literary as well as financial recognition (Ferretti, 2009: 30). Having obtained significant symbolic capital of prestige and refinedness through the careful selection of foreign authors and the care put into the typographical format, the latter had to remain distant – at least in the public narrative – from economic capital.

In a letter to Alberto Mondadori on the works by Ungaretti translated by Allen Mandelbaum, Schewiller confessed the necessity to strike a balance between production costs and sales, trying to appeal to the generosity of the bigger publisher. A twofold rhetoric was used to convince Mondadori: Scheiwiller sought to play down the potential for the circulation of a certain work, by underlining how the print run was limited to half of that of an average Mondadori print run, and how the actual readers would be very few. He also emphasised the elitism of the format which rejected the more popular objectives of the bigger industry; the copies were numbered, the price per page quite high, the prefaces written by prestigious intellectuals:

> Le 'riserve' non sono solo del traduttore, ma dipende anche da me se ho un po' più di soldi o meno. La tiratura è limitata a 1000 copie numerate, il prezzo di copertina sotto le mille lire possibilmente. La prefazione, se riesco l'impossibile, di Eliot o di Pound. Mi raccomando alla sua generosità, per non essere gravati da altre spese. Lo scopo mio e di Allen è solo quello di far conoscere a quattro gatti di lingua inglese un po' di buona poesia italiana contemporanea e, possibilmente, di rientrare nelle spese di stampa.[24]

> [Not only does the translator have reservations, but also I myself, depending on whether I have spare funds or not. The print run is limited to 1,000 copies, numbered, the cover price under 1,000 Italian lira, if possible. The preface, if I can do the impossible, by Eliot or Pound. I plead

---

24 APICE, VS, file correspondence to Mondadori, to Alberto Mondadori, 8 September 1956.

with your generosity, so that I won't be oppressed by other expenses. My purpose and that of Allen is only to introduce a handful of people who can read English to a bit of good Italian contemporary poetry and, if possible, to stay within the printing costs.]

The wish to avoid exceeding the production costs is reaffirmed in a letter to Poggioli. Frustrated by the meagre profits, Scheiwiller drew on his network of influential relationships to ask for help in publicising his work: 'mi aiuti un po' per la diffusione del Salinas [...] Questo non è andato troppo... E le cartoline, un disastro: forse il 2% ha ordinato' [please help me a little with the circulation of Salinas' book [...] This has not sold much... And the postcards, a disaster: perhaps 2% of them have ordered].[25] The social capital Scheiwiller had accumulated via his (often very prestigious) collaborations could be deployed towards achieving the publishing success of his publications.

Analysis of the distribution modalities highlights some ambiguity: the publisher's written requests appear at times naive, while his management of the process is marked by much greater efficiency than that of the larger publishing houses. Beyond the system of purchasing postcards outlined above, Scheiwiller took care of the distribution in person, travelling by train and taking his books to bookshops spread across Italy. In this sense, the format of the book also facilitated its portability and helped to forge the publisher's identity as a mobile intellectual. Such an effective mode of distribution contrasts directly with that of larger-scale publishers, apparently unable to manage their stocks wisely and leaving them unsold in their warehouses.[26] In his wandering, the Milanese publisher preferred the big cities ('non amo troppo la provincia, che non compra non legge e non paga') [I don't like the small towns, that don't buy, don't read, and don't pay],[27] thus showing his willingness to reach the core of the publishing market, where the more active and curious readers were, but also, in general, the agents of the cultural and intellectual fields in Italy.

The pragmatic demands of the publishers were nonetheless partly downplayed in the meta-discourse that Scheiwiller strategically interwove. He cleverly reaffirmed his dissociation from the financial dynamics typical of the leading publishing houses: 'Che fare? Mi prendono per un Feltrinelli, scordandosi che faccio tutto da me in casa e con un capitale di partenza,

25 APICE, VS, to Renato Poggioli, 24 January 1958.
26 APICE, VS, to Libero de Libero, 11 February 1956, ms.
27 APICE, VS, to Ezra Pound, Tirolo, 18 March 1959, ms.

anno 1952, di duecentomila lire...' [What to do? They think I am Feltrinelli, forgetting that I do it all by myself at home and with a starting capital, in 1952, of 200,000 Italian lira].²⁸ As defined by Pound, the print run system at Scheiwiller's was based on an absolute loss, as 250 copies were printed on normal paper, 200 of which were sent as complimentary copies to libraries and 50 to the author; 25–30 were printed on refined paper – Japon – and sold at a high price to recoup the costs, without gaining considerable economic profits.

The above tirade against the bigger publishing houses was accompanied by the artisanal characterisation of his activity that Scheiwiller persistently insisted upon. The publishing correspondence and his friends' and collaborators' stories are marked by the narrative of a 'Pesce d'oro piccolissimo in mezzo a tanti enormi Pescicani editoriali' [very small goldfish among many, enormous publishing sharks].²⁹ In this respect, the eulogy of Mary de Rachewiltz, Pound's daughter, is interesting in that it upholds the idea of a rigorous artisan publisher:

> Vanni preparava il menabò con righello e forbici, gomma e matita, che si portava appresso, come pure campioni di carta per il testo e la copertina che doveva intonarsi con l'umore del contenuto, la data di pubblicazione coincidere con quella di nascita – o altra ricorrenza. Il numero delle copie da 5 a 500. Mille era il massimo. Numerate a mano, e certi numeri sempre destinati alle stesse persone. Poi i pacchetti con carta marrone e spago fine. Correttura fino a tre bozze prima del visto si stampi, e sempre in due, l'autore a leggere ad alta voce e l'editore a seguire sulla pagina. (Cadioli and Kerbaker, 2009: 60)

[Vanni used to prepare the paste-up with ruler and scissors, rubber and pencil, which he had always with him, as well as paper samples for the texts and the cover, which had to match the tone of the content, the date of publication should match the date of birth – or another event. The number of copies spanning 5 to 500. 1,000 was the maximum. Hand-numbered, and certain numbers always allocated to the same people. Then the packaging with brown paper and thin twine. Proofread up to three times before the imprimatur, and always in pairs, the author reading aloud and the publisher/editor following on the page.]

28 APICE, VS, file Mary de Rachewiltz, VS to Alfredo Rizzardi, 5 November 1962, ms.
29 APICE, VS, to Filippo Pontani, 2 July 1962.

Vanni Scheiwiller projected, and indeed to all extents and purposes embodied, the image of a passionate, bookworm publisher,[30] who did not have a reading committee (Spina, 2000: 286), and whose minimalism was set against the short-term economic objectives of the larger publishers.

If we uncritically accept this narrative, we risk perpetuating a solidly rhetorical image, a danger that Ferretti (2009: 55) acknowledges in reference to the wave of portraits offered by critics and collaborators alike after the death of the Milanese publisher. Scheiwiller's aim would seem in fact to have been much more subtle, and if interpreting it simply as a market-driven strategy would be entirely wrong, we should consider its publishing effects. Starting from his aesthetic and to an extent cosmopolitan dispositions, he sought to define forms of cultural distinction that, contrary to the more popular publishers, must be conceived within a long-term perspective of capitalisation. In a letter to Sereni, Scheiwiller made explicit his policy: to focus on the discovery of just one high-calibre poet who would emerge with time, thus making up for the probable losses caused by many other risky publications:

> A.S., anni 23, spara a zero – spesso senza mirare. Ha sbagliato con il suo romanzo ma ha tentato. Pubblicherà da me le sue poesie e sbaglierà, sbaglieremo, in parte. Ma ha tentato o ci siamo, in parte, esposti. Se dei 5 o 6 *novissimi* uscirà un Porta o un Porta e mezzo o anche solo mezzo, mi basta. Come dalla cosiddetta 3ª generazione Luzi e te, ma dopo tanti tanti anni. Il resto è cronaca, dettagli, niente d'importante: ciò che vale, si sa, resta e viene fuori col tempo.[31]

> [A.S., 23 years old, puts his all into it, without aiming properly. He made a mistake with his novel, but he did try. He will publish his poems with me and he will make a mistake, we will make a mistake, partially. But he tried and we did, partially, expose ourselves. If from the 5 or 6 novissimi one Porta or one Porta and a half, or just half, emerge, I will be happy. As for the third generation Luzi and yourself, but after many many years. The rest is irrelevant, detail, nothing important: works of value, you know, stay and emerge with time.]

---

30   APICE, VS, to Jorge Guillén, 27 November 1956, ms.
31   APICE, VS, to Vittorio Sereni, 8 January 1965, ms, with reference to a polemic in the leading newspaper *Corriere della Sera* sparked by an article by Spatula.

His narrative reinforced an elaborate operation of elite exquisiteness that, by translating eccentric personalities and opting for a refined typography, was intended to distinguish Scheiwiller from the other publishers of the field. Textual practice fitted coherently in this project of distinction, prompting us to discuss critically, also vis-à-vis national dynamics, the publisher/editor's engagement with transnational features at a more formal level.

2.1.5 Distinction in translation: the need for 'a poetic style'

The small book format contained translations compatible with the notion of elite refinement that Scheiwiller sought to promote, in accordance with his personal taste. In general, the translations showed attention to Scheiwiller's ideal readership, that is, the fine poetry connoisseur coinciding with the closed circle of cultural operators – like Vanni Scheiwiller himself, we might say. Our analysis of textual and paratextual features evidences how the transnational elements of poetic innovation were not only retained in the practice of translation, but potentially further intensified – or to use Antoine Berman's terminology, even 'embellished' (1984). This suggests a specific modality of transnational dialogue, whereby the encounter with contemporary foreign poetry stretches the Italian language further than the Hermeticists' philological attention; it goes beyond the formal structure and organisation of the literary content to focus instead on the construction of the imagery and tone, and adds to the refined, hence distinctive, style sought by the publisher. It also signals the degree of freedom that the editor/publisher saw in their reading, interpretation, and recontextualisation of the source text's linguistic/rhetorical as well as stylistic features; the latter are conceived in the broader sense of voice and 'culturally-bound and universal ways of expressing meaning' (Boase-Beier, 2006: 2), which makes style indicative of the source author's mindset and world view.

A case in point is the translation of Gottfried Benn's *Apréslude*, which Scheiwiller published in 1963. Until then, Benn had enjoyed limited fame in Italy, where he had only been translated as part of the *Antologia della lirica tedesca contemporanea* [Anthology of Contemporary German Poetry] in 1925 and in literary journals in the 1940s, before finally seeing his works published as a collection, translated by Traverso in 1954, in the 'Cederna' series produced by Vallecchi (Scuderi, 2006: 14–15). Traverso's version had elicited a substantial number of reviews and enjoyed a positive reception, particularly within Hermetic circles (De Lucia, 2018: 240–43), for his close attention to retaining as much as possible the rhythm of the poems through assonances, where rhymes were not possible (Scuderi, 2006: 45–47). The portrait offered by Traverso was thus that of a classical Benn (Miglio, 2014: 82), beyond his Expressionist features.

A translator, poet, and editor, as well as a scholar in German Studies interested in nihilist philosophy (Agazzi, 2018: 57), Ferruccio Masini was now tasked with the translation of Benn and offered the opportunity to provide an alternative reading of his poetry. In the early 1960s Benn's poetry had been canonised in Italy through Fritz Martini's *Storia della letteratura tedesca* [History of German Literature], translated by Alighiero Chiusano and published in 1960, within an intrinsically ontological and nihilist perspective (Miglio, 2014: 79), in line with Masini's interests. At a transnational level, this ill matched his contemporary reception in Germany, which was more centred on the closer relationship between aesthetics and history (Miglio, 2014: 80). However, at national level it represented an opportunity for the translator, as well as the publisher, to move away from the previous Hermetic interpretation.

In the preface to *Aprèslude*, Masini seemed to release himself from any attempt at making the obscure German poet 'understandable'. With the impossibility of offering a more prosaic translation, Masini's declared objective was that of preserving as far as possible those philosophical peculiarities in tone that distinguished Benn's poetry, at the price of readers' understanding:

> Benn stesso diceva che la poesia è per sua essenza l'intraducibile [...] Se anche potrebbe giovare al 'senso comune' ritradurre Benn, cercando di agevolare la sua intelligibilità, non si eviterebbe, con questo, il pericolo di alterare e corrompere il 'senso poetico', forse troppo difficile, forse quasi inaccessibile, ma pur sempre l'unico ed esclusivo *ens realissimum* di un'opera d'arte. (Masini, 1963: 15–16; partly in Milani, 2013b: 100)

> [Benn said that poetry is in its essence untranslatable [...] Even though the 'common sense' would benefit from re-translating Benn, trying to ease his being intelligible, we cannot avoid, with this, the danger of altering and corrupting the 'poetic sense', perhaps too difficult, maybe almost inaccessible, but for sure the unique and exclusive *ens realissimum* of a work of art.]

In this sense, Masini shunned Traverso's prosodic and formal attention to maintain 'quei preziosi sostantivi a tutto tondo propri della scrittura benniana' [those all-round precious nouns typical of Benn's writing] through the use of a more free verse (Scuderi, 2006: 48), which privileges lexical oppositions and semantic dissonances (Miglio, 2014: 84).

The publisher's attitude partly tallied with that pronounced by Masini, as the editorial history of Pound's *Antologia classica cinese*, published in 1965, demonstrates. Tellingly, Scheiwiller did not see translation as a 'popularising' attempt to bring foreign poetry, and here specifically Pound's modernism, closer to a wider readership, but as an attempt to keep intact the stylistic value of that poetry, beyond a philological or formal approach only. Similarly to *Aprèslude*, when faced with Pound's lines, the translator – the journalist and son of famous novelist Matilde Serao, Carlo Scarfoglio – was dealing not only with obscure language, but also content that was quite distant from the literary imagery of Italian readers. Unlike Masini, though, Scarfoglio adopted a translation strategy aimed at clarity and intelligibility, so as to benefit an average reader, as the translator explained in a few letters addressed to the publisher:

> Sono intimamente contento di aver fatto questo lavoro, col quale, credo, ho reso un servizio alla cultura italiana, rendendo leggibili e apprezzabili anche al lettore meno provvisto queste bellissime e sincere manifestazioni di sentimenti antichi [...][32]
>
> [I am intimately happy in having done this job – I think that with this I have made a useful contribution to Italian culture, by making readable and appreciable even for the less equipped reader these very beautiful and sincere manifestations of ancient feelings.]

Moreover, in the draft of the preface to the book later entitled 'Apology of the Translator', Scarfoglio dealt with the generic character of the work and discussed his own translating methods in language that could also be understood by a readership with no knowledge of ancient Chinese culture.[33] The translator proposed the use of a 'linguaggio piano e chiaro, in luogo di quello spesso oscuro di Pound' [plain and clear language, instead of that used by Pound, often obscure],[34] confident that Italian readers would be grateful for this. Scarfoglio concluded by underlining how, notwithstanding his efforts to inscribe the content of the work within a shared Italian historico-cultural

32 APICE, VS, file Ezra Pound, Carlo Scarfoglio to VS, Rome, 29 May 1961.
33 APICE, VS, file Ezra Pound, Carlo Scarfoglio to VS, Rome, 15 January 1962.
34 Ibid.

horizon – for instance, by making the Chinese dynasties closer to Roman foundations, thus domesticating the poems – he had lavished every care to translate in a way that, going beyond word-for-word translation, matched the tone of the poems in their plurality.[35]

The translator's preface was accused of being too long and essentially lacking arguments interesting enough to stimulate Scheiwiller's ideal reader. The publisher's comment with regard to the translation highlighted instead the impersonality of the language used by the translator, as, although it allowed for a more transparent understanding, it did not produce any stylistic elevation: 'Sinceramente all'inizio non ero troppo entusiasta della traduzione. Mi sto a poco a poco ricredendo (io infatti volevo la Guidacci): è una traduzione un po' grigia, cioè non brillante, però <u>solida</u>' [honestly, at the beginning I wasn't too enthusiastic about the translation. Little by little I am changing my mind on this (in fact I wanted Guidacci as translator): it is a bit of a grey translation, that is, not brilliant, but solid].[36] In the passage from its publication in a journal in 1956 to Scheiwiller's edition in 1964,[37] Scarfoglio's attention to the stylistic qualities of the foreign text increased significantly: it is probably this awareness that prompted Scheiwiller's judgement of 'solidity'.

Analysing the Italian version of the poem 'La fanciulla che va sposa' [The young women getting married], we note that in the first translation, Scarfoglio eliminated many figures of speech. In 1956 the translator opted for a choice of synonyms that bestowed a much higher specificity, by translating, for instance, the anaphoric 'Oh omen tree / [...] Oh omen tree' as 'Auspicioso arbusto [auspicious bush] / [...] auguroso pesco [augural peach tree]'. For 'such a solid fruit' Scarfoglio had offered a word-for-word solution: 'così solido frutto', with the consequent loss of assonance. In the 'Pesce d'Oro' book of 1964, Scarfoglio kept the adjective 'auspicioso', but amplified the figure of speech and reinterpreted the assonance of the English mute sibilant, by converting it, in the Italian, into a voiceless labiodental fricative, an alveolar vibrant and a voiceless dental stop: 'così forte frutto' [such strong fruit].

Yet Scarfoglio was not always able to achieve his target. More often, in order to produce a fluent reading whose lexical content would not be too distant from the original, the translator had to sacrifice some of the complexity of Pound's rhetoric. In translating the poem 'L'amica del principe'

---

35   Ibid.
36   APICE, VS, to Ezra Pound, 9 December 1958. See also Milani, 2012: 108.
37   The translation had already appeared in March 1956, in the journal *Nuova Antologia*.

[The Prince's Friend], other than the rhyme, the majority of the assonances and alliteration of the English vanished in the Italian version. As a result, 'toss and turn' was translated with a colourless 'ondeggiare e sparire' [to weave and vanish], the onomatopoeic 'bang the gong' with the plain 'battete il gong' [beat the gong]. The translator added a chiasm in the opening ('Nasconditi, disse il Falco Pescatore / Il Falco Pescatore, nell'isola sull'Ho' [Hide, said the fish-hawk / The fish-hawk, on the island of Ho] instead of 'Hid! Hid! The fish-hawk saith / by isle in Ho the fish hawk-saith'), but the ancient connotation of the English verb and the assonance of monosyllables which gave the strophe a singsong rhythm were not maintained. It was in effect a 'grey' translation, as Scheiwiller defined it, but for structural reasons rather than because of the translator's inabilities. The publisher was perhaps misled by the poetic exquisiteness that Pound was capable of when playing with archaic English, but Italian cannot always be so flexible. Scarfoglio did try not to excessively force the text, and his caution led to the publisher's unenthusiastic, but ultimately pragmatic, approval.

Vanni Scheiwiller's general editorial line presupposed, on the contrary, a different vision of poetry translation. Its reference points coincided with the transfer of the poetic sense of the work of art, and first and foremost its rhetoric and stylistic complexity. The combined approach of a poet-translator was therefore preferred, for the higher poetic sensibility that they could bring to the translation. In suggesting intellectuals that Rafael Alberti should contact for future collaborations, Scheiwiller privileged stylistic abilities over linguistic and literary expertise, which partly clashed with the philological approach that some Hermetic translators had suggested thus far. Hence, he deemed it better to rely on poet and translator Vittorio Bodini than Hermetic critic and full professor of Spanish literature, Oreste Macrí:

> Spero tanto nel futuro di fare qualcosa con lei (grosso editore-industriale permettendo) [...] Il Prof. Macrí è una persona seria e molto preparata: peccato che le sue versioni siano spesso <u>poeticamente</u> discutibili [...] Bodini: eccellente traduttore e buon poeta in proprio.[38]

> [I very much hope in the future to do something with you (big publisher-industrialist permitting). Professor Macrí is a professional and very well-informed person: it is just a pity that his versions are debatable from

---

38   APICE, VS, to Rafael Alberti, 29 November 1961, ms.

a poetic viewpoint [...] Bodini: excellent translator and a good poet himself.]

Doubts also arose with regard to the project of publishing some poems by Jorge Guillén, renowned for his pure poetry in the line of modernist essential features, and the proposal of Macrí as translator. Scheiwiller opposed the collaboration with the scholar, notwithstanding the clear benefit that his academic prestige would donate to the publishing house. The reasons lay in the arguable stylistic abilities of the critic; he was unable, as Scheiwiller saw it, to offer a translation that would be decently poetic, thus risking undermining the quality of the source text:

> Per *Càntico*: [...] pubblicare appena possibile la 1° edizione integrale [...] nella traduzione di alcuni poeti italiani (chiederei agli amici Sereni, Orelli, Zanzotto, Guidacci, Ungaretti oltre a Montale), NON di un chiarissimo Professore, bravissimo e preciso (credo) filologicamente MA NEGATO ALLA POESIA. Cioè intendo 'alla resa poetica.[39]

> [On *Càntico*: publish as soon as possible the first integral edition [...] with the translation of some Italian poets (I would ask my friends Sereni, Orelli, Zanzotto, Guidacci, Ungaretti, in addition to Montale), NOT of a highly esteemed Professor, very good and precise (I think) from a philological viewpoint, but hopeless at poetry. I mean 'at poetic rendering'.]

For a small-scale publishing house specialising in poetry, the social capital that a collaboration with Macrí might have promised remained negligible if not supported by a textual refinement that cultural operators (critics, often poets themselves) could enjoy. Poet-translators were therefore preferable.

In line with Scheiwiller's nonconformist intellectual attitude and the value he placed on craftsmanship, the actual translation, the textual interaction between source and target text, was key in the capital-acquisition process and ultimately most significant in shaping the identity of the elite publisher. This is why Scheiwiller pushed for an agreement between the foreign poet's peculiarities and those of the Italian poet-translator, in the conviction that the synchrony of these perspectives would lead to a prestigious translation:

---

39 APICE, VS, to Jorge Guillén, Rome, 3 July 1960, ms. In Guillén and Scheiwiller, 2012: 49, 128–29.

Se vede Macrí, gli dica che Vanni non odia nessuno: ma dissente da lui, pur ammirando la sua filologia e preparazione. I poeti devono essere tradotti da altri poeti congeniali. Questo il mio dissenso da lui. Senza odio né antipatia. MA io ho la mia linea di gusto – sbagliata o no – e la seguo a tutti i costi.[40]

[If you see Macrí, please tell him that Vanni does not hate anybody: but he disagrees with him, although he admires his philology and preparation. Poets should be translated by other suitable poets. This is my disagreement. Without hatred or dislike. BUT I have my own line of taste – right or wrong – and I will follow it at all costs.]

Our analysis of the narrative of critical and independent judgement that marked Scheiwiller's publishing venture from the outset – his 'personal taste' – reveals again a more subtle project of distinction. Once more, the selection of poets that shared a similar poetic background, rather than collaboration with the eminent scholar, reflected the aim of enhancing the prestige of his publishing product.

This can be teased out more fully if we examine the editing process adopted by Scheiwiller in the case of Adelina Aletti's translation of ten epigrams by Jorge Guillén. Aletti's poems *Giorni d'acqua* [Days of Water] had been published in 1975 by Scheiwiller, while her translation, though well received by Guillén (Guillén and Scheiwiller, 2012: 226), ultimately remained unpublished, with the Spanish text featuring alone in the book. Such a choice reinforced the exclusiveness of the text, fully coherent with the elitist intentions and habitus of the small-scale publisher; at the same time, this almost anti-translation tactic suggests a resistance to transcultural communication, as in the earlier launch of his series of foreign poets in the target language. It is worth noting that Scheiwiller, as editor, constantly raised the register, resulting in exaggeratedly noble tones or added semantic features that are noticeably distant from the poetic text of the original. In an attempt to cultivate further refinement, Scheiwiller accented elements of Guillén's pure poetry, while the Spanish poet had preferred in his text a precise control of language, pondering the value of each single word.

Consider, first of all, the line 'donde el vestido yo se desvanece' [where the clothing 'I' vanishes], translated by Aletti as 'dove l'abito 'io' non ha più senso'

---

[40] APICE, VS, to Jorge Guillén, Montorio Veronese 24 September 1960, ms. In Guillén and Scheiwiller, 2012: 49.

[where the clothing 'I' has no longer meaning].[41] The editor/publisher sought to add a further meaning to that 'vestido', intended as 'costume', by resorting to the Latin word *persona* as 'mask of the self'. Similarly, for the phrase 'el mesurado octubre', translated literally by Aletti as 'ottobre moderato' [moderated October], the publisher proposed a much more elaborate solution, 'la dignità ottobrina' [October dignity], that was eventually rejected, the formula 'cadenzato ottobre' [rhythmic October] being the final option. As a result, a rhythmic over-meaning and a sort of propulsion of beauty were produced as opposed to the hint of simplicity that the Spanish text conveyed: 'delirio de hermosura / que al fin no altera el mesurado octubre' [delirium of beauty / that finally does not alter the measured October]. The metaphor of the shortness of life, 'la vida / tan corta, se deshace en polvareda' [life / so short, it falls apart in dust], proposed by Aletti through the mechanical action of crumbling, was furthermore turned into the more impalpable image of vanishing, whereas the 'polvareda' became higher in register, transformed from the humble 'polvere' [dust] to the more ineffable 'polverio' [cloud of dust]. A similar operation was carried out on 'hermosa catedral / se eleva, muy segura' [beautiful cathedral / rises, very confident]. The word-for-word rendering 'bella cattedrale, si eleva molto sicura' became 'splendida cattedrale, s'innalza con slancio' [splendid cathedral, rises with panache], through the substitution of the qualifying adjective with a superlative and the transformation of the adjective 'segura' into a noun. Introducing the assonance of the sibilant also made it possible to further stress the majesty of the building – an accent that was not present in the rhetorical design of the Spanish original. In sum, we can infer from Scheiwiller's modifications an elaborate textual practice intended to tailor contemporary foreign poetry for a restricted audience, and further signify the distinction of the Milanese publisher. This outlines an articulate relationship between an ambitious engagement with transnational movements, particularly the radical experimentation of modernism, wavering at times towards cosmopolitan afflatus, and a close connection with specialised readerships in the publishing process, culminating at times in an over-appreciation of stylistic features.

These findings call for a more critical understanding of the function of small publishers, which certainly needs to take into account the crucial importance of their aesthetic dispositions, but also needs to question their

---

41   APICE, VS, translation draft by Adelina Aletti, *10 epigrammi* by Jorge Guillén, first draft on 4 February 1976 and the second on 27–28 May. Handwritten corrections by Vanni Scheiwiller. Also partly in Milani, 2012: 109.

sociological 'marginality' and pay attention to the materiality of book production. Scheiwiller's catalogue was structured around the translation of similar authors and models, which eventually represented a source of conspicuous prestige for the small-scale publisher. To maintain this prestige, the selection of foreign poets was supported by an appropriate book format and by a refined textuality lent by the particular contribution of poet-translators. In this way, the small volumes of the 'Pesce d'Oro' were constructed and sustained in a distinctly refined space that the publisher amplified by developing narratives, both in the meta-publishing discourse and in the paratextual apparatus, that expressed his dislike of the heteronomous factors implicated in cultural production (and especially social and economic capital). In the relatively autonomous field of poetry publishing, this strategy – whether conscious or unconscious – increased the prestige of Scheiwiller and located him at the end of the 1950s in a much more central position that that of his medium- and large-scale competitors.

2.2 Mondadori's 'Lo Specchio' and translation: between canon and *antiprogrammaticità*

In the 1960s the new distribution of forces in the poetry publishing field questioned the traditionally autarkic direction of large-scale publishers. Along with the 'translation turn' of small-scale publishing houses that, like Scheiwiller, had been acquiring more centrality, the crisis of national poetry – the mainstay of the large-scale publishers' catalogues – meant they rapidly lost prestige. In 1956 Mondadori did not hold the central position in the field of poetry in which, only ten years earlier, it had seemed unshakable: it needed to reconsolidate. To do so, the Milanese publishing house decided to break the traditionally domestic boundaries of its specialised poetry series 'Lo Specchio' and to welcome into the catalogue contemporary foreign poets. At the beginning, the series featured only one translated title per year (out of eight titles published in 1957 and seven in 1958), but this figure grew steadily in the 1960s, reaching at least two per year, with four foreign collections published in 1968 – nearly 60% of the annual poetry production, as quantitative analysis in Appendix 2 outlines. The publication of foreign poetry proved, however, a less straightforward process than we might imagine for a large-scale publisher with economic means and an established poetry series already in place, thus attesting to the greater dynamism of small-scale publishing houses in the poetry field and to the complexity of negotiations among agents.

Within the proto-industrial model of Mondadori, which favoured short-term investments, 'Lo Specchio' had to proceed with much more caution than the small publishers and to rely on sufficiently secure banks of cultural capital. In line with this more traditional approach, Mondadori's selection of foreign poets initially indicated a more conservative attitude. Only later in the 1960s, thanks to the cultural dispositions of new editors-in-chief such as Vittorio Sereni and the development of a much more dynamic publishing field, would the poetry series embrace more systematically literary experimentation in translation and connect with transnational movements in more flexible ways. Contemporary foreign poetry thus not only became a means of affirming canonical power; it generated the innovation and formal prestige that allowed Mondadori and his editors to position themselves more firmly within the Italian cultural field. At both stages, the readership influenced, in a more or less explicit way, the publishing process as well as textual practice. Contrary to the elite narrative developed by Scheiwiller, Mondadori – as a large-scale publisher – targeted a broader lay public by tailoring translations in such a way as to provide Italian readers with a blend of foreign yet accessible features. This strategy enabled 'Lo Specchio' to regain a prominent position in the poetry publishing field in the 1960s.

2.2.1 The search for 'le massime voci della poesia straniera': 'Lo Specchio' in the late 1950s

At the end of the 1950s, at least five years later than Vanni Scheiwiller, Mondadori finally opened the list of 'Lo Specchio' to foreign poets. The initial search for established authors showed the enduring conservatism of the large-scale publishing house: 'established' for the Milanese publisher meant canonical and potentially more popular poets, in an attempt to strike a balance between international literary recognition and economic exigencies related to publishing sales. On 12 March 1959, when Alberto Mondadori presented the new direction of 'Lo Specchio' to Rafael Alberti, he stressed the desire to align canonical foreign poets with equally canonical Italian authors so as not to diminish the value of the latter. It was important that the choice was based, even before stylistic qualities, on the position held by the contemporary foreign poets in the transnational canon, though filtered through their Italian reception:

[nel]la collezione mondadoriana che forse Lei conosce [...] sono presentati tutti i più grandi poeti italiani, e, [in essa] abbiamo cominciato a pubblicare, con testo a fronte, le massime voci della poesia straniera, quali Ezra Pound, Juan Jiménez, T.S. Eliot, eccetera.[42]

[[in] the Mondadori series that perhaps you know [...] all the major Italian poets are published, and [within it] we have started publishing, in parallel text format, the best representatives of foreign poetry, such as Ezra Pound, Juan Jiménez, T.S. Eliot, etc.]

By 1959 T.S. Eliot had been the tutelary deity of Italian Hermeticism for decades; three years earlier the Spanish poet Jiménez, influenced by Symbolism and the idea of art for art's sake, was awarded the Nobel prize for literature and had already been published in Italy in 1946 by Guanda; at the end of the 1950s Pound had been widely published by small publishers.

In the search for cultural capital, Mondadori's editors in 1958 supported the publication of Gottfried Benn, probably relying on the greater fame that the German poet had enjoyed throughout the 1950s at national and transnational levels; the award in 1951 of the Georg Büchner prize, the most prestigious literary accolade in Germany, had sealed Benn's widely affirmed European status, while Traverso's translation in 1954 had canonised the German poet within a Hermetic framework. Although in the end Mondadori did not pursue the publication of Benn due to copyright issues, archival materials reveal the shifting attitude of Mondadori editors towards transnational poetic dynamics, and how this would have an impact on publishing strategies at national level. In April 1958 Elio Vittorini's notes sang the literary praises of Benn not only in Germany, but more interestingly in relation to the Italian poetic canon. Vittorini's metric of comparison is a clear example of how, when selecting foreign poets, contributions had been assessed thus far against national paradigms in a hierarchical, arguably 'international' way, with the result that they were virtually inscribed within the domestic literary system and incidentally taken out of the specificities of their source culture.

Such a literary short circuit is also figurative of the peculiar reception of foreign authors, based on, in this case, a translation – that of Traverso – which erased in part Benn's expressionism (Scuderi, 2006: 16–24). Benn was praised by Vittorini for continuing Rilke's decadent path and for his 'sviluppi

---

42 FAAM, AM, to Rafael Alberti, 12 March 1959; also in Mondadori, 1996: 624. Alberti would publish his *Poesie* with 'Lo Specchio' in 1964.

rinnovatori per cui si può dire che corrisponda a quello che è Ungaretti per l'Italia' [innovative developments that made him what Ungaretti is for Italy].[43] The German poet was compared to Ungaretti not only as one of the pioneers of formal innovation but also as one of the most established poets in Italy; indirectly, Benn was included in a Hermetic lineage that did not necessarily reflect his early career, when he moved around the expressionist lines of the *Die Brücke* movement. This judgement would not seem to acknowledge a wider transnational perspective that, moving from an Italo-centric perception, could productively connect Italy with contemporary foreign contributions.

Editor Lavinia Mazzucchetti,[44] a scholar and expert in German literature, had on the contrary bestowed an aura of transnational prestige on Benn and defined him as 'nome insomma che, non per confronto diretto, ma per risonanza, può essere accostato a un Ezra Pound americano' [a name that, not in direct comparison, but by resonance, can be put side by side with an American Ezra Pound].[45] Mazzucchetti's intuition appears to broaden the horizon, demonstrating her acute understanding of how poetic dynamics were changing transnationally in a more experimental direction. In other words, it shifted the focus, when discussing publishing strategies, from the national borders and their traditionally dominant Hermetic aesthetics, to transnational poetic movements currently influencing Europe. The name of Pound is interesting in this context as a clear indication of Mondadori's awareness of the new competitors in the field. Comparing Benn to Pound, instead of any other poet, acknowledges indirectly the relevance of Vanni Scheiwiller – who incidentally would publish Benn in 1963, offering an alternative perspective on the German poet beyond the Hermetic interpretation.

Pound's editorial history unveils in even more lucid terms Mondadori's initial caution towards contemporary foreign poetry. Mondadori had already considered publishing the American poet in the late 1940s, well before the more systematic interest shown by small-scale publishers, but the translation by Luigi Berti of Pound's work, purchased in 1948, was put aside by Alberto

---

[43] FAAM, *Segreteria Editoriale Estero – Giudizi di Lettura* [hereafter SEE – GDL], file Gottfried Benn, note by Elio Vittorini, 4 April 1958. See also Milani, 2013b: 103.

[44] More broadly on Lavinia Mazzucchetti, see *Lavinia Mazzucchetti: impegno civile e mediazione culturale nell'Europa del Novecento*, ed. by Anna Antonello and Michele Sisto (Rome: Istituto di Studi Germanici, 2017), and *Come il cavaliere sul Lago di Costanza: Lavinia Mazzucchetti e la cultura tedesca in Italia*, ed. by Anna Antonello (Milan: Fondazione Arnoldo e Alberto Mondadori, 2015).

[45] FAAM, SEE – GDL, file Gottfried Benn, reader's report by Lavinia Mazzucchetti, 21 March 1958.

Mondadori. The publisher cited the difficult economic conditions of post-war publishing in Italy as his reason.[46] 'Lo Specchio' nonetheless dominated the poetry publishing field in the second half of the 1940s, confuting in part Alberto Mondadori's declared motive. The rejection of Pound probably had more to do with the publisher's prudent attitude, since in the immediate aftermath of the Second World War Pound had a weaker position in the world literary system, and certainly in Italy.

Eleven years and a few translations by other publishers later, in 1959 Pound's name returned. The translation carried out by scholar Alfredo Rizzardi, however, aroused anger in the American poet, who was not satisfied with Rizzardi's translation skills.[47] In reviewing the translation, the translator and critic of US literature Fernanda Pivano also indicated some perplexities about the literary value of the selection and translation of this text.[48] Commercial success was nevertheless assured by the world fame that Pound appeared to have acquired for reasons beyond poetry and linked to political events.[49] This exposes the variation in the reception of Pound's work in Italy: the debate around Pound's trial that concluded in 1958 with the return of the poet to Italy, where he lived until his death in 1972, had obscured the complexity of his poetry, but conversely afforded him wider recognition in Italy. In 1960 Pound's *Selected Poems* were finally published in Rizzardi's translation, and confirmed Pivano's sales prediction: the first print run (2,131) sold out in 1961, when a second edition of 2,790 copies was published. A third edition followed in 1969 (1,505 copies, hardback) and a

---

46 FAAM, SEE – GDL, file Ezra Pound, Alberto Mondadori to Robert Knittel, 4 December 1948: 'In consideration of the difficult situation of the Italian book market, we though [sic] better to postpone our decision to better times. At that time, however, we bought a very good translation of said poesies [sic] made by a renowned translator Mr. Luigi Berti, and said translation is still with us.'

47 FAAM, SEE – GDL, file Ezra Pound, to Alberto Mondadori, Rapallo, 11 March 1959.

48 On the figure of Pivano as a translator, see Blossom S. Kirchenbaum, 'Fernanda Pivano: Italian Americanista, Reluctant Feminist', *VIA: Voices in Italian Americana*, 7:2 (1996), 83–100; Paolo Biamonte, *Fernanda Pivano. Biografia minima* (Naples: Tullio Pironti Editore, 2000); Elena Tapparo, *Fernanda Pivano e la letteratura americana* (Civitavecchia: Prospettiva, 2006); Andrea Romanzi, 'L'*Urlo* di Fernanda Pivano: The History of the Publication of Allen Ginsberg's 'Howl' in Italy', *The Italianist*, 41:3 (2022), 1–22.

49 FAAM, SEE – GDL, file Ezra Pound, reader's report by Fernanda Pivano, 27 May 1958.

fourth (2,027, paperback), in line with the usual print runs for such Italian poets as Saba and Ungaretti.[50]

Where external factors could not drive the publication, according to Mondadori editors, readers tended to seek some rhetorical and formal accessibility in poetry; texts that were neither obscure nor too popular. In 1953 this led the publishing house to reject Pound's fellow Imagist Conrad Aiken, whose refined style was deemed suitable for a restricted circle of readers only.[51] Aiken would finally be published in 1968, but only because he was included in the translator's notebook by Salvatore Quasimodo, *Da Aiken e Cummings*. The status of the Italian poet thus opened the doors of the publishing world to the foreign author, and not the other way around, with the implicit risk of favouring an established domestic tradition over more productive transnational connections. Mondadori thus ran the risk of repeatting the exact same mistake made only a few years earlier by creating a counterproductive stagnation of the catalogue: new publishing agents and much livelier competition in the field would avert, at least partially, this possibility.

2.2.2. Vittorio Sereni and the 'anti-programmatic' line in the 1960s

The bureaucratic dispositions of a large-scale publisher such as Mondadori were not always cast-iron; they also reflected external stimuli and the individual inclinations of editorial agents. The appointment of Vittorio Sereni as editor-in-chief in 1958 was significant in this respect, as it brought to Mondadori an 'anti-programmatic' attitude that, as far as poetry production was concerned, was projected substantially towards a transnational opening.[52] Probably thanks to the relative absence of commercial limitations dictated by an elite genre such as poetry and the social capital that the Italian poet brought with him in terms of literary relationships, Sereni enjoyed some freedom as editor-in-chief of 'Lo Specchio', despite the normally hierarchical organisation within Mondadori (Ferretti, 1999: 119). This enabled him to introduce innovations in line with his own poetic experience, albeit constantly trying to

---

50 Print runs consulted at FAAM.
51 FAAM, *SEE – GDL*, file Conrad Aiken, reader's report by Ruth Domino-Tassoni on *Ushant*, 22 June 1953.
52 See Ferretti, 1999: 122 and more generally, for an exhaustive overview of Vittorio Sereni's publishing activity, not only restricted to 'Lo Specchio', as in this chapter.

strike a balance with Arnoldo Mondadori's own vision and with the specific dynamics of the publishing field.

Mondadori's choice to appoint Sereni certainly had to do with his experience in a large company like Pirelli, but also with his social networks in the Italian literary field, beyond his personal friendship with Alberto Mondadori (Ferretti, 1999: 18–22). At the end of the 1950s, Sereni was an established poet of the so-called *Linea lombarda*, and a relevant figure in the poetic debates in Italy: he had already translated literary works (in particular, the work of William Carlos Williams in 1957), had run publishing series at Le Edizioni della Meridiana, and contributed to, and would continue to contribute to, literary journals such as *Questo e altro* (1962–64). Here, poetry (*questo* = this) and reality and society (*altro* = other) were conceived as related, but not in the radical way suggested by either Pasolini's *neosperimentalismo* [neo-experimentalism], or the soon-to-be-born Gruppo 63. Art critic and Gruppo 63 member Renato Barilli offers a rather stimulating analysis in this sense: Sereni would soon launch 'Il Tornasole' [Litmus] (1962–68), a literary series conceived with the aim of cautiously welcoming some stylistic innovations, 'purché queste si presentassero in abiti decorosi e compassati, senza abiurare in modi troppo vistosi rispetto alle linee della tradizione' [as long as these were presented in decent and staid clothes, without retracting too vigorously from tradition] (Barilli, 1995: 241). With this comment, Barilli neatly summed up Sereni's strategy of embracing a new poetic language but without the extremes of the *neoavanguardia*.

In ten years, from his appointment in 1958 to 1968, Sereni successfully published in 'Lo Specchio' several poets who moved within his own poetic area or could productively dialogue with it, such as Luciano Erba, Giovanni Giudici, Giovanni Raboni, and Andrea Zanzotto (Ferretti, 1999: 124). A glance at the data collected in Appendix 2 shows nonetheless that the number of Italian poets akin to Sereni's poetics was not as high or as radical as that of foreign poets. The reactions within national poetic circles, and the dynamics of the literary canon, restricted the room for manoeuvre for a conservative publisher; space in the catalogue also had to be reserved for the canonical poets who had been published in 'Lo Specchio' since the 1940s, such as Ungaretti, Quasimodo, Sinisgalli, Saba, Solmi, and Valeri. Sereni was fully conscious of these complexities (Ferretti, 1999: 62) and saw the selection of foreign poets as to a certain extent 'safer'. Indeed, its influence on the national field was not immediately perceived by the agents involved, and, having already gone through a process of publication and legitimation, it was seen as less questionable:

i nomi sono di per sé opinabili, oggi più che mai: di qui l'opportunità di uscire dal terreno italiano abbastanza spesso e il più significativamente possibile, e di non uscire dal presente immediato per dare ogni tanto qualche rapido ritratto di uno straniero o di un italiano di ieri o ierlaltro che risulti utile nell'ordine della loro ricerca.[53]

[the names [of contemporary Italian poets] are in themselves debatable, today more than ever: hence, the opportunity to go beyond the Italian terrain quite often and most significantly, and not to leave the contemporary age, to offer only every now and then some quick portrait of a foreign poet, or of an Italian poet of yesterday which could be helpful to show their poetic quest]

His flexible programme's emphasis on publishing foreign poetry made possible an efficient revitalisation of 'Lo Specchio', in line with the pressing interests of a changing literary field at the end of the 1950s; the 'canon' had to leave room for more receptivity towards new poetic tendencies, as per Sereni's habitus. In addition, the publication of foreign poetry represented for Sereni a means of self-legitimation within the poetry field. Sereni's imprint was especially recognisable for the attention paid to American poetry, particularly William Carlos Williams, a beloved reference point who Sereni would translate for a decade (1951–61), and the poets affiliated with the Black Mountain Group, such as the American Robert Creeley.

The influence of Sereni's dispositions on the selection of foreign poetry was, however, not absolute, and despite his transnational connections and interests, he could not override the publishing dynamics that informed Mondadori internally, nor, externally, the Italian publishing field. Mondadori editor Oreste del Buono (Mannucci, 2014: 27) suggested that Sereni's role could be accurately described as that of a 'direttore letterario' [literary editor-in-chief] rather than 'direttore editoriale' [publishing editor-in-chief], given the focus on literary choices as opposed to managing publishing expectations. Sereni himself maintained that he did not pay attention to print runs, since a book was appealing to him only if it had literary value; a perspective that has helped to shape Ferretti's slightly romanticised narrative of 'a poeta e di poeti funzionario' [a poet and poets' official]. We argue instead that, although Sereni's own dispositions certainly remained key to his practice, he also had

---

53 FAAM, *Direzione letteraria* [hereafter *DL*], file *Paragone*, Vittorio Sereni to Cesare Garboli, 19 March 1965.

to be tactical and adopt a more flexible approach vis-à-vis the publishing demands and Mondadori's delayed engagement with foreign poetry. The Mondadori series could not linger on the republication of foreign poets who had already been translated or were soon to be translated by other publishing houses – much as they appealed to the editor-in-chief. In a fiercely competitive context, they were increasingly forced to anticipate literary trends instead of relying on established authors.

The publishing history of American poet Marianne Moore aptly illustrates this situation. In 1962 scholar and translator Agostino Lombardo – who in 1957 in *Realismo e simbolismo* (Rome: Edizioni di Storia e Letteratura) suggested moving beyond the American myth of the 1930s to search for the most authentic voices of the US tradition between, literally, realism and symbolism (Bosco Tedeschini Lalli, 2008: 29) – pushed to have Cristina Campo translate Moore for Mondadori. 'Con molto rammarico' [with great regret],[54] Sereni had to reject the proposal, not only because Guanda would publish Moore's *L'insidiosa molestia della corazza* [*The Insidious Modesty of Armor*] that very year, but also because of the urgency for 'Lo Specchio' to 'guardare alle cose che sono in movimento più che alle cose che hanno una fisionomia già precisata' [stick to a publishing line more focused on developments in world poetry rather than on consolidated and established values].[55]

Mondadori's task was now to 'prevenire semmai gli altri rispetto alle nuove voci della poesia contemporanea' [to reach the new authors of contemporary poetry before others].[56] Continuing along the well-trodden path, according to Sereni, would only allow the publishing house to fill academic niches, a task more appropriate for a specialised small-scale publisher than for the publishing giant. 'Lo Specchio' ought to expand its catalogue to feature new tendencies (provided they coincided with more vibrant trends), in order to 'riguadagnare il tempo perduto e le varie occasioni perdute in passato' [make up for wasted time and the various wasted opportunities of the past]. This search for innovative foreign contributions was not only new for Mondadori, but risked clashing with the very nature of 'Lo Specchio', where only more established poetic forms had been published. Sereni had to use the means available in the multi-layered Milanese publishing structure wisely, and to 'far intervenire il proprio gusto personale rispetto alla poesia

---

54 FAAM, *SEE – GDL*, file Marianne Moore, Vittorio Sereni, 1 April 1962, ms.
55 FAAM, *SEE – GDL*, file Marianne Moore, Vittorio Sereni, 28 December 1961.
56 Ibid.

di oggi, ma limitatamente alla piuttosto complessa situazione editoriale' [use [his] own personal taste in relation to contemporary poetry, but only within the limits of the complex publishing situation].[57]

The editor-in-chief decided to utilise less canonical series as a temporary location for foreign poets *in fieri*, which enabled him to acquire their copyrights while avoiding the potential 'downgrading' of 'Lo Specchio' to an experimental collection. This is precisely what happened with Denise Levertov, as the editor explained lucidly in the same letter to Lombardo cited above. Sereni was keen to claim the poet for Mondadori's catalogue; her style, informed by English Romanticism and included in the 1947 anthology edited by Kenneth Rexroth, *New British Poets*, was gradually changing through her encounter, via poet Robert Creeley, with Sereni's beloved William Carlos Williams and the Black Mountain Group, who 'helped her to extricate herself from merely received diction and imagery, not rooted in authentic experience' (Hollenberg, 2013: 155). The editor-in-chief suggested acquiring the rights to Levertov for the more experimental 'branch' of Mondadori, 'Il Saggiatore', with a view to featuring her in 'Lo Specchio' at a later stage. This way, he could both anticipate his publishing competitors and maintain an 'appropriate' stylistic level in the poetry series.

The editorial decisions followed this route. In 1961 Lombardo appreciated the incisiveness of Levertov's poetry in expressing feelings in a concrete manner,[58] but glimpsed also some affectation,[59] which precluded publication as part of 'Lo Specchio'.[60] Three years later, in 1964, in the less bureaucratic environment presided over by Sereni, Lombardo finally proposed featuring Levertov in the series as an established poet, who had received recognition in the 1960 anthology edited by Donald Allen, *The New American Poetry, 1945–1960*, and who had engaged with literary traditions (notably Hasidism) and achieved a stylistic transition with *The Jacob's Ladder* (1961). The poetry collection was 'a significant development in Levertov's growth as a lyrical poet' (Hollenberg, 2013: 195) which would continue the direction undertaken by 'Lo Specchio' with the Black Mountain Group and US poetry trends, perfectly fitting with Mondodori's purposes:

---

57   Ibid.
58   FAAM, SEE – GDL, file Denise Levertov, reader's report by Agostino Lombardo on *The Jacob's Ladder* 1961, 13 November 1961.
59   Ibid.
60   Ibid.

> Se lo 'Specchio', come mi sembra di capire, non vuol limitarsi a pubblicare poeti per così dire classici ma intende presentare personalità mature sì, ma ancora in sviluppo, credo che la Levertov meriti pienamente di apparire in tale serie, e tanto più che la sua poesia è sommamente indicativa della direzione in cui (o un ritorno a William Carlos Williams) si muove buona parte della poesia americana contemporanea.[61]

> [If 'Lo Specchio', if I am not mistaken, does not want to limit itself to the publication of so-called classical poets, but intends to present personalities that are mature but with still more to give, I believe that Levertov fully deserves to appear in this series, especially since her poetry is extremely indicative of the direction that (or a return to William Carlos Williams) a good part of contemporary American poetry is moving towards.]

Sereni's editorial work therefore proceeded to establish a subtle but fruitful compromise between his own idea of poetry and the internal conditions of more conservative publishing. But in order to operate in a field where the force of small- and medium-scale publishing houses was central, power relationships had also to change: Mondadori was required to set aside artisanal models in the name of bureaucracy. Starting from the mid-1960s, in fact, the presence of Einaudi began to threaten copyright acquisitions of both foreign and Italian authors. Mondadori displayed a more severe attitude towards publishing concessions, including for instance the possibility of a Mondadori author, such as poet Camillo Pennati, having his poems, and not merely his translations, published by Einaudi.[62] In a note to the chief executive, Sereni acknowledged that this request by Pennati was an effect of the establishment of Einaudi's new 'Collezione di poesia',[63] revealing the changed dynamics of the field. A similar approach was taken with the Greek poet Constantine Cavafy, whom Sereni greatly admired. Einaudi was interested in publishing a *plaquette* of the Greek poems translated by Nelo Risi, and requested the rights to do so. Although in the past a similar proposal would not have posed an issue, Mondadori now categorically refused to relinquish its rights, since an Einaudi publication would damage Mondadori's sales.[64]

---

61 FAAM, SEE – GDL, file Denise Levertov, reader's report by Agostino Lombardo on *O Taste and See*, 5 November 1964.
62 FAAM, DL, file Camillo Pennati, Vittorio Sereni, 8 October 1964.
63 Ibid., 28 September 1964.
64 FAAM, DL, file Nelo Risi, Ufficio Contratti, 21 June 1965.

The competition was not limited to the exchange of publishing favours; it heavily impacted translation trends and the geographical spread in the selection of foreign poetry. Whereas in the 1960s 'Lo Specchio' evidenced a clear preference for anglophone poets, who represented nearly half of the overall contemporary foreign poets published in the series, further poetic traditions had now to be included to match the new transnational horizons of other publishing houses. In this regard, the issue of contemporary French poets is enlightening. At the end of the 1950s, contemporary French poetry was not normally published in 'Lo Specchio'. The rationale was quite simple: poetry readers in Italy were highly educated, and they were able to read French poems in the original language. An exception was nonetheless made in 1971 with the publication of Francis Ponge, translated by Piero Bigongiari, the same post-Hermetic translator whose poems, in the 1950s, had received a lukewarm reception. The justification for this publication choice appeared to lie with Ponge's stylistic talent in the use of poetic prose,[65] and his relationships with Surrealism, Dadaism, and the *NRF*.[66] However, looking at the wider trends in the field of poetry publishing, we contend that one of the main demands faced by Mondadori was that of matching the growing publishing competition. The reason for ending the 'embargo on French poetry', as Sereni defined it in a letter to French author André Frénaud, was Mondadori's reassessment of its position after Einaudi had enlarged the selection of French poetry in its catalogue:

> Pour ce qui concerne ta situation chez les éditeurs italiens, j'ai besoin d'abord de savoir si tu as ou non une option chez Rizzoli. Mais je dois te dire aussi que la situation a beaucoup changé depuis nos propos faits à Paris il y a dix ans. A ce temps là on avait exclu de présenter dans la Collection 'Specchio' les poètes français. Après on a commencé à y songer car les concurrants (Einaudi, Rizzoli) ont commencé à publier des poètes français. On ne pouvait pas laisser faire et alors c'est pour ça que l'on a accepté une suggestion d'Ungaretti pour Ponge, une suggestion de Bigongiari pour Bonnefois, et moi-même j'ai fini par proposer une traduction du dernier Char, comme j'avais déjà traduit les *Feuillets d'Hypnos*.[67]

---

65   FAAM, *SEE – GDL*, file Francis Ponge, Cin Calabi to Carmela Capocci-Gallimard, 6 May 1965.
66   Ibid., reader's report by Marco Forti on *Le grand recueil* 1961, 12 May 1965.
67   FAAM, *DL*, file André Frénaud, Vittorio Sereni, 26 October 1970.

[The situation has changed significantly since the proposals we decided upon in Paris ten years ago. At that time we excluded the possibility of publishing French poets in 'Lo Specchio'. We have now changed our mind since the competitors (Einaudi, Rizzoli) have started publishing French poets. We cannot allow that, and this is why we have approved a proposal by Ungaretti for Ponge, a translation by Bigongiari for Bonnefoy, and I have myself ended up suggesting a translation of the late Char, since I have already translated *Feuillets d'Hypnos*.]

Not only publishing dynamics but also transnational political movements made their way into the editorial strategies of 'Lo Specchio', signalling a much more tangled web of connections between Italian publishers and foreign cultural agents than could have been envisaged, especially for a conservative series such as 'Lo Specchio', only twenty years earlier. In the 1960s some politically committed foreign poets found their place in Mondadori's poetry series, such as Spanish poet Gabriel Celaya, not purely by virtue of their poetic value. What was the reason for this inclusion? Some translation choices related to key twentieth-century historical events, such as the Spanish Civil War or the Resistance movement, may be correlated with the intellectual trajectory of Sereni and his dialogue between poetry and 'other' ethical and societal upheavals (Ferretti, 1999: 124). If we instead take into account the ongoing transnational dialogue pervading the Italian publishing scene in the late 1960s, such an angle brings to the fore two stimulating images, helpful in reassessing both the perception of Italy as much more ingrained and central within the post-war transnational intellectual field than generally perceived, and that of Mondadori as more disposed to political tides than one might expect a conservative publisher to be.

Celaya was indeed published in 1967 as a militant representative of contemporary Spanish poetry, both for marketing reasons – on the wave of the general interest in Spanish exiles – and political reasons – as an 'act of political solidarity' against Franco's dictatorship;[68] the publication was suggested by the politically committed poet and intellectual José Augustin Goytisolo and the influential Catalan publisher and editor Josep Maria Castellet,[69] and was probably inscribed within the wider transnational anti-Francoist project of the 'Comitato italiano per la libertà del popolo spagnolo' [Italian Committee for the Freedom of the Spanish People], which saw the active presence among

---

68 FAAM, *SEE – GDL*, file Gabriel Celaya, note by Vittorio Sereni, 19 July 1962.
69 Ibid., note by Vittorio Sereni, 22 October 1962.

others of Alberto Mondadori, Giulio Einaudi, and Giangiacomo Feltrinelli (Fernández, 2020: 10):

> Celaya non è un gran poeta ma oggi rappresenta in poesia la nuova resistenza spagnola assai più degnamente di quanto non facciano i nuovi prosatori. Per mancanza di maestri più autorevoli (morti o dispersi fuori di Spagna) i giovani poeti vedono in lui l'esempio di una poesia affondata nelle radici popolari, chiaro strumento di lotta.[70]

> [Celaya is not a great poet but he represents today, in poetry, the new Spanish resistance much more worthily than the new novelists do. Due to the lack of more authoritative masters (dead or missing beyond Spain), the young poets see in him the example of a poetry based on popular roots, a clear weapon in the fight.]

The political peculiarity of Celaya's case was further emphasised by the choice of translator, who rather than being a refined poet, needed to be a figure who shared the same political position,[71] in a very similar fashion to the Einaudi series of the 1950s, 'Poeti stranieri tradotti da poeti italiani'.

Yet the book was not as successful as the editors had hoped, since more than half of the 2,000 print run remained unsold.[72] In order to be more effective, the opening to transnational political movements demanded to be undertaken more carefully and to be matched to the dispositions and interests of Mondadori's readership. Unsuccessful initiatives such as that with Celaya led to the rejection in the late 1960s of Greek poet and left-wing activist Yiannis Ritsos. Included in the corpus of neo-Greek poetry that more authoritative figures such as Cavafy and Seferis – published respectively in 1961 and 1968 – already sustained, Ritsos and his opposition to the Greek military junta, which saw him imprisoned in 1967, could find a place in the catalogue as a political act, in the same way Celaya did. The financial risk appeared too high, though. In addition, arguably the power relationships in terms of the transnational connections at stake were not wholly comparable, since no influential foreign intellectuals or publishers

---

70 FAAM, SEE – GDL, file Gabriel Celaya, reader's report by Vittorio Bodini on *Poesia*, 9 July 1962.
71 FAAM, SEE – GDL, file Gabriel Celaya, Vittorio Sereni to Dario Puccini, 15 May 1963.
72 Ibid., note by Marco Forti to Vittorio Sereni, 22 June 1970.

had championed the publication of Ritsos except scholar and translator Filippo Maria Pontani:[73]

> Editorialmente non direi che si bruci dal bisogno di tradurre in Italia un poeta rispettabilissimo ma forse di misura non assoluta, e per di più di una cultura poetica relativamente marginale come quella neogreca che esiste, in verità, perché sono esistiti Seferis e, soprattutto, il grande Kavafis. In questo senso una decisione per Ritsos dovrebbe essere negativa, anche se verrebbe scelto e tradotto da un traduttore inappuntabile come Pontani; ma potrebbero anche prevalere considerazioni di ordine politico e umano verso un coraggioso poeta militante, e allora il mio parere editoriale infine negativo, potrebbe, al lume di questo altro punto di vista, mutare di segno. Ma non so se, su questa base, la nostra casa editrice, già molto impegnata con i poeti stranieri, voglia affrontare un'operazione meritoria, ma di prevedibile perdita.[74]

> [From a publishing perspective, I wouldn't say that we cannot wait to translate in Italy this very respectable poet, though perhaps not of absolute value, and what's more from a relatively marginal poetic culture like the neo-Greek one, which actually exists only because of Seferis and, especially, the great Cavafy. In this sense, we should reject Ritsos, even if he were to be translated by so irreproachable a translator as Pontani; but political and human considerations might prevail in favour of a brave militant poet, and so my publishing rejection could, in the light of this other viewpoint, change. However, I am not sure if, on this basis, our publishing house, already much involved with foreign poets, would risk such an initiative, which is praiseworthy but likely unsuccessful.]

The publication seemed therefore more suited to a small-scale, more agile and militant publisher; this is why Sereni would suggest to Pontani the politically committed Editori Riuniti, close to the Italian Communist Party and better

---

73 This is certainly not to downplay the importance and role of Filippo Maria Pontani (full professor at the University of Padua since 1966 and winner of the translation prize 'Premio Monselice' in 1972) in the literary and scholarly field in Italy, but to outline the difference in terms of transnational power relationships from Celaya's case. On Pontani, see *Autografi letterari romanzi e neogreci: due giornate di studio in memoria di Filippo Maria Pontani – Padova, Accademia galileiana, 24–25 ottobre 2013*, ed. by Kostis Pavlou and Giorgio Pilidis (Padua: S.A.R.G.O.N, 2015).

74 FAAM, SEE – GDL, file Ritsos, Marco Forti to Vittorio Sereni, 26 September 1968.

placed to ensure an expeditious publication, as the promptness of Scheiwiller in publishing Ritsos himself had already demonstrated.

Mondadori editors were normally attentive to sales and, more generally, audience receptivity, certainly more so than Scheiwiller, but also in greater measure than Einaudi. To emulate the typical specialisation of small-scale publishing houses would be counterproductive and unfeasible in a proto-industrial set-up like that of Mondadori. Indeed, when in 1963 poet and political activist Joyce Lussu – whose translation rationale will be examined in more detail in Chapter 3 – proposed to Sereni the translation of Serbian poet Vasko Popa, complexities arose and led to a rejection. Lussu had met Popa in Belgrade (Trenti, 2009: 130), but the poet, a modernist author of refined formalism in constant dialogue with Surrealism and Balkan folkloric tradition, was still unknown in Italy.[75] At the beginning of the 1960s, Popa had obtained a brief mention in the journal *Europa letteraria* (issue 18, December 1962, p. 39), where it was noted that he had been awarded the Branko prize for poetry, having already been translated into French and German, and was awaiting an Italian translation.

Despite this literary accolade from one of the oldest cultural-scientific institutions in former Yugoslavia, Popa could not feature in 'Lo Specchio' as the poet was not yet established worldwide nor well received in the national canon, nor did he belong to any widespread literary or extra-literary transnational trends, as in the case of Celaya or the French poets. On this occasion, Sereni expressed Mondadori's more conservative position, unable to specialise in intriguing yet marginal foreign poets – in terms of strength of innovation but most particularly in terms of presence in the wider transnational canon – as the more agile small-scale publishers could do:

> La cosa sarebbe possibile solo in due casi: a) qualora si trattasse di una novità sconvolgente; b) qualora l'opera di Popa raggiungesse o per intima forza propria o per fatti di ordine esteriore un indiscutibile livello di notorietà internazionale [...] Il mio consiglio è di tentare per il momento altre strade: Guanda, Edizioni dell'Avanti, Editori Riuniti, ma soprattutto farei il possibile per interessare Guanda, o anche Lerici. Questi sono editori più adatti a seguire specificatamente il cammino di questo o quel poeta straniero contemporaneo, tenendolo nella cerchia di lettori

---

[75] The first Italian translation to be published as a single volume occurred only a decade ago (Prenz, 2008).

in qualche modo specializzato. Noi siamo piuttosto destinati a tirare le somme e a fare il punto.⁷⁶

[It would be possible only in two cases: a) if it were an unprecedented novelty; b) if Popa's work reached either on its own or through external factors an indisputable level of international fame [...] My suggestion would be to try for the time being other paths: Guanda, Edizioni dell'Avanti, Editori Riuniti, but I would do my best to interest Guanda or even Lerici. These are publishers more suitable to follow specifically this or that contemporary foreign poet, and keep him within the circle of a somewhat specialised readership. We are rather destined to settle accounts and review.]

More precisely, the issue that constantly resurfaced in the publishing correspondence was the lack of an elite readership for a supposedly more critical 'venture' of 'Lo Specchio'. This happened, for instance, with American poet Theodore Roethke, who received several awards in the USA and was translated by Mariolina Meliadò.⁷⁷ We will discuss the translation at length in the following section; suffice to note here that *Sequenza nordamericana* [*Northamerican Sequence*], published in 1966, was well received by critics, but only half of the copies printed were sold by 1967.⁷⁸ This did not allow the publishing house to proceed with the publication of Roethke's subsequent *Collected Poems*.

A similar situation occurred with Thom Gunn. Gunn was first published in Italy by Mondadori, but of the 1968 edition of *I miei tristi capitani* [*My Sad Captains*], with a 2,500 print run, 1,490 were still unsold in 1971.⁷⁹ Such a peculiar publishing issue sheds light on the role of bureaucratic complexities, which are neglected by a solely aesthetic analysis. The losses were indeed substantial, but if Gunn's new poems were rejected by Mondadori, the copyright arrangements would enable Mondadori's competitors – namely Rizzoli, since Einaudi had rejected Gunn in June 1967 following editor Giorgio Manganelli's negative judgement (Manganelli, 2016: 66) – to acquire

---

76   FAAM, DL, file Joyce Lussu, Vittorio Sereni, 24 April 1963. Partly in Milani, 2012: 106.
77   FAAM, SEE – GDL, file Theodore Roethke, Raffaele Crovi to Mariolina Meliadò, 11 March 1965.
78   Ibid., Marco Forti to Donatella Ciapessoni, 6 April 1967.
79   FAAM, SEE – GDL, file Thom Gunn, Marco Forti to Vittorio Sereni, 19 July 1971.

them; the risk was that they could intrude into the protected anglophone space that had been for so long the sole dominion of the Milanese publishing house.[80] The 1975 proposal for the publication of English poet Philip Larkin, firmly in line with Mondadori's interest in the New Movement,[81] was deemed by Marco Forti too risky from an economic perspective. Mondadori opted for a publishing expedient that would actually better suit its competitor Einaudi, which was interested in publishing Larkin.[82] Forti suggested leaving the publication of an entire book to Einaudi, and putting forward only a selection of poems for the more agile and experimental series 'Almanacco dello Specchio' [Specchio's Yearbook].[83]

No hesitation was shown, however, over the publication of *City Without Walls* (1969) by W.H. Auden, albeit his earlier book, *L'età dell'ansia* (*About a House*), published in 1966, had sold only 565 copies (out of 2,021) by February 1970.[84] Among the most representative contemporary anglophone poets, along with Pound, Auden brought with him vast cultural capital as a favourite for a Nobel prize,[85] and the profit he promised could not be left for other publishers to seize. Literary prizes were important to Mondadori, as a prize-winning author could rapidly increase the prestige of the publishing house as well as boosting sales.[86] Although poetry could be seen as an elite genre, a compromise with the expectations of a large publishing house's

---

80   Ibid.
81   FAAM, SEE – GDL, file Philip Larkin, reader's report by Agostino Lombardo on *High Windows* 1974, 9 September 1975.
82   Less than ten years earlier, in 1967, Manganelli was not, however, impressed by the English poet (Manganelli, 2016: 61). Larkin was nevertheless published in 1969, translated by Renato Oliva and Camillo Pennati. For an overview of the challenges of translating Larkin into Italian in terms of imagery and prosody, see Enrico Testa, 'Translating Larkin', in *Twentieth Century Poetic Translation: Literary Cultures in Italian and English*, ed. by Daniela Caselli and Daniela La Penna (London: Continuum, 2008), pp. 135–44.
83   FAAM, SEE – GDL, file Philip Larkin, note by Marco Forti to Vittorio Sereni, 24 November 1975.
84   FAAM, SEE – GDL, file W.H. Auden, Vittorio Sereni to Marco Forti, 11 March 1970.
85   Ibid., Marco Forti to Vittorio Sereni, 10 March 1970.
86   This was true of both poetry and novels. A case in point is Guatemalan novelist Miguel Angel Asturias, whose novel *Une certaine mulatresse* was sought after merely because he was a candidate for the Nobel prize. FAAM, SEE – GDL, file Miguel Angel Asturias, reader's report by Paolo Caruso on *Une certaine mulatresse* 1963, 15 October 1965.

readership had also to be struck. This was not limited to the selection of contemporary foreign poetry, but was also key to the textual practice.

2.2.3 Accessible translations: 'Lo Specchio' for 'il lettore medio di poesia'

The policy adopted in the practice of translation reflected the multiple demands that both foreign and domestic poets had to satisfy. Scrutiny of the publishing correspondence confirms an aesthetic impatience, anticipated in the late 1950s, with the increasingly stagnant Hermeticism: editors tended to favour poetic expressions which were anchored more in the realistic representation of the external world. Furthermore, Mondadori's ever-broadening popular readership, reflected in the proposal to publish contemporary Italian poetry in the pocket-sized series 'Oscar',[87] had an impact on the poets' reception and prompted a search for greater reading accessibility. Doubts were voiced with regard to poets who seemed otherwise firmly in line with Mondadori's anglophone trends. American poet Charles Olson, whose highbrow language, full of allusions and references to the past, went on to influence postmodernist writers, is a clear example: Forti was unsure about the publication for a number of reasons, including the cultural background, considered too distant from Italian readers, the difficulty of translating Olson's experimentally abstract style, and especially the inaccessibility of a poet who was much more allusive than his peers Robert Frost or William Carlos Williams.[88] Conversely, overtly direct language was not acceptable either. Contemporary French poet Jacques Prévert – interestingly, one of the sources of long-term income for the small-scale publisher Guanda – was, according to Sereni, too close to contemporary *chansonniers* and too 'facile' [easy].[89] Publication would make sense only if the publishing house prioritised the function of the Italian poet-translator over the foreign poet.[90]

Our analysis of the translations, carried out from the references suggested in the publishing correspondence, confirms a consistent editorial tendency

---

[87] Enrico Falqui proposed publishing an anthology of contemporary Italian poetry as a pocket-sized book to Alberto Mondadori and Sereni in 1965. The proposal, however, did not lead to any concrete publications, because of editorial complexities in the selection and division of poets and the fact that Falqui abandoned the project in 1968.
[88] FAAM, SEE – GDL, file Charles Olson, reader's report by Marco Forti on *The Maximus Poems*, 23 February 1966. See also Milani, 2012: 111.
[89] FAAM, SEE – GDL, file Jacques Prévert, Vittorio Sereni's reader's report, 6 April 1955.
[90] Ibid.

to approve target texts that were able to lexically adhere to, and eventually mildly enhance, rather bare source texts. Contrary to Scheiwiller, Mondadori editors had to be translators first, and, as required, poets second. This signals a different relationship with foreign poetry, one that in part recognises the relevance of transnational elements and their potential to interact with and disrupt outdated uses of the Italian language, but also one that does not forget the ultimate purpose of accessibility for their ideal readership. While reviewing a sample translation of Cecil Day Lewis's poems by Mario Cicognani – whose poems were rejected as stiffly Hermetic just a few years earlier – Agostino Lombardo raised in lucid terms the issue of finding a common policy to adopt in translation practice. The proposed publication of Day Lewis, one of the most representative authors of the Auden group in 1930s England with their sociopolitical engagement, is intriguing given the traditionally conservative attitude of Mondadori, especially if we bear in mind that the 1930s poets had not been translated in Fascist Italy. They had reached Italy only in the post-war period via Guanda's anthology *Poesia inglese contemporanea: da Thomas Hardy agli apocalittici* [Contemporary English Poetry: From Thomas Hardy to the Apocalyptics], edited by Carlo Izzo in 1950. The reasons for this delay were mainly related to their 'impoetico' [unpoetic] (Capoferro, 2004: 313) style, charged with lower registers and ideological stances, which did not find favour with the Hermetic translators but attracted the interest of Italian intellectuals in the aftermath of the Second World War. Day Lewis's crime fiction, published under the pseudonym of Nicholas Blake, had already been translated by Mondadori, but when it came to poetry translation, a more subtle editorial strategy was required.

In his reader's report in 1963, Lombardo was worried about finding univocal translation criteria to give coherence to the corpus of foreign poetry in the catalogue and to represent a precise approach that would distinguish Mondadori from its competitors. Lombardo was inclined towards translations that were able to offer 'una assoluta e letterale fedeltà al testo originale [...] con un uso della lingua italiana il più possibile lontano dallo "stile di traduzione"' [an absolute and literal faithfulness to the original text [...] using an Italian language as far as possible from a 'translating style'].[91] This was feasible, according to the scholar, if Mondadori chose translators who were extremely competent in the foreign and Italian language, and with the

---

91 FAAM, *SEAI*, file Mario Cicognani, reader's report by Agostino Lombardo on Cecil Day Lewis's poems translated by Mario Cicognani, 14 February 1963. The translation texts have not, however, been preserved.

necessary modesty to understand that 'che sta[nno] appunto traducendo e che non [possono] sovrapporsi al poeta tradotto' [they are *translating*, and they cannot displace the translated poet].[92]

The use of an outdated term such as 'faithfulness' marks an understanding of translation as an ancillary activity *at the service* of the source text, but paradoxically Lombardo also foregrounded a domesticating approach whereby these translations had to present a fluid rendering that could insert them within the system of domestic poetry production. In terms of the most appropriate approach to the sociopolitical interests of an author such as Day Lewis, Lombardo seemed to privilege *ante litteram* a dynamic equivalence, as defined one year later – but not available yet in Italian translation – by Eugene Nida (1964), over an adherence to the pure metrical form, which risked leading to an entirely new composition. The 'documentary' translation by Cicognani, which mirrored the metrics of the source text – as per functionalist theory (Nord, 1997) – had incongruously fallen into an 'instrumental' translation which created a new act of communication between the source and the target text:[93]

> la decisione di adottare sempre gli endecasillabi lo porta, gradualmente, a sopprimere parole anche importanti del testo, ad aggiungerne altre, ad aggiungere intere frasi, a proporre insomma nuovi modi di leggere queste poesie. Ora, tutto questo è, a mio avviso, inaccettabile, proprio perché, muovendo da un lodevole tentativo di riprodurre attraverso l'endecasillabo il movimento ritmico di Day Lewis (e non è detto che tale verso sia sempre il più adatto), il Cicognani passa a creare delle composizioni nuove, interessanti quanto si vuole, ma che tradiscono la lettera e lo spirito della poesia tradotta.[94]

[the choice of constantly using hendecasyllables led him, gradually, to cut out significant words, and add others, and whole sentences – in sum, to propose new ways of reading these poems. This is, in my opinion, unacceptable, precisely because, moving from a praiseworthy attempt

---

92 Ibid.
93 As evidence of the risk of contradictions in the redundant use of dichotomies in Translation Studies, 'instrumental' has been characterised by Lawrence Venuti in his provocative *Contra Instrumentalism: A Translation Polemic* (Lincoln, NE: University of Nebraska Press, 2019) as a mere reproduction of the source text, as opposed to the more fruitful hermeneutic approach which conceives of translation as an interpretative act.
94 FAAM, *SEAI*, file Mario Cicognani, reader's report by Agostino Lombardo on Cecil Day Lewis's poems translated by Mario Cicognani, 14 February 1963.

at reproducing, through the hendecasyllables, Day Lewis's rhythmic movement (and this metre is not necessarily always the most suitable), Cicognani ends up creating new compositions that may be appealing but that betray the words and the spirit of translated poetry.]

The strategy suggested by Lombardo marked a break with the translation practice that Hermeticism had so far supported. Hermetic translators, and Oreste Macrí in particular, had seen translation as an autonomous creative activity – though with a focus on philological analysis – at the intersection between translation and the translator's own poetic practice (Capoferro, 2004: 308). Lombardo would seem to recommend instead a more subordinate approach, in line with the 1960s Italian trends in poetry translation that will be discussed in Chapter 3.

More interestingly, Lombardo framed this requirement in terms of offering readers 'la presentazione in buon italiano di un poeta straniero' [the presentation of a foreign poet in good Italian].[95] More so than Lombardo's suggestions in relation to the proposed translation of Day Lewis, this sentence illustrates the two translating principles upheld by Mondadori, which seem to reach a compromise between two approaches that Venuti (1995) would provocatively present as a dichotomy. On one side, Mondadori editors privileged a domesticating tendency, by interpreting the target text as a poetry production in Italian, whose formal rules had to be respected in order to ensure readability for the publisher's ideal reader, the average Italian. On the other, this trend coexisted with a foreignising approach, as the translation had also to present to the Italian readership the stylistic peculiarities of foreign poetry.

Such a compromise was exactly the reason why Mondadori came to reject another translation by Cicognani, that of another figure affiliated with the Auden group, the Irish-born poet Louis MacNeice. According to Lombardo, in Cicognani's translation, the original poetic pattern had been destructured, and the constitutive elements were reduced or amplified to then be recomposed in a new literary context – the contemporary Italian poetry of *I Novissimi* and their multilingualism. To the editor, this seemed disconnected from the 1930s context of the politically committed Auden group, and the result was a cultural eradication of the foreign author to the sole benefit of the Italian poet and translator:

---

95   Ibid.

> A parte certi errori, e a parte le omissioni, le aggiunte, ecc – sempre inammissibili quando si traduce un poeta – il continuo inserimento di parole e frasi inglesi e specialmente francesi o addirittura latine è assolutamente ingiustificabile, anche se il Cicognani cita l'esperienza (del resto abbastanza provinciale e incolta) dei cosiddetti poeti 'nuovissimi' o 'novissimi' che siano [...] Traducendo così, si sradica completamente MacNeice dalla sua cultura, dalla sua esperienza, dal suo tempo; si crea una nuova poesia, o esercitazione poetica, che ha le sue giustificazioni in sede ben diversa.[96]

> [Apart from some mistakes, apart from some omissions, or additions, etc. – always unacceptable when one translates a poet – the continual insertion of English, and especially French or even Latin, words and sentences cannot be justified, even though Cicognani quotes the experience (however rather parochial and uncultured) of the so-called 'nuovissimi' or 'novissimi' [...] Translated this way, MacNeice is completely uprooted from his culture, experience, time: a new poem, or poetic exercise, is created and with an entirely different rationale.]

Lombardo's judgement is revelatory on two accounts. First, it unveils a rather simplistic interpretation of MacNeice's work as tied to left-wing protest, neglecting that the poet's attention towards linguistic artifice could 'actually invigorate and diversify everyday experience [and that he] sometimes indulged in artifice in the different sense of unproductive verbal contrivance' (Underhill, 1992: 223). Secondly, it outlines the different positions within the Italian poetry field, with Mondadori situated at the opposite end of the spectrum to Gruppo 63 and *I Novissimi*. MacNeice would subsequently be translated by Francesca Romana Paci only in 1974, with rich footnotes detailing geo-cultural information on Ireland and Great Britain, and in a more prosaic version than that offered in 1950 in *Poesia inglese contemporanea: da Thomas Hardy agli apocalittici* (see, for example, 'Sunday morning' – 'But listen, up the road, something gulps' // 'Ma *ascolta*, in cima alla strada, qualcosa *tiene di colpo il fiato*' (MacNeice, 1974: 56), whereas Guanda's anthology used a higher register with 'Ma *odi* [hark] in cima alla strada, un *singulto* [a more literary version of a gulp]' (Izzo, 1950: 385)).

---

96 FAAM, *SEAI*, file Mario Cicognani, reader's report by Agostino Lombardo on Louis MacNeice's poems translated by Mario Cicognani, 14 February 1963.

As Mondadori saw it, poetry translation could – at least in theory – help renovate the Italian language by offering readers new content and forms, but only if translations did not become a sterile space for private stylistic exercise, but a fertile area of comparison with foreign literature. The publishing history of Thom Gunn's *I miei tristi capitani*, translated in 1968 by anglophone literature scholar Camillo Pennati, depicts well the struggle to strike a balance between foreign lines and domestic conventions. Initially associated with 'The Movement', a literary movement of anti-Romantic, rational and controlled English poetry, Gunn moved to the USA in the mid-1950s and in the 1960s started to explore freer poetic forms and flouted social norms of the time with his homosexuality and use of drugs. His style was attentive to physical sensation, and his voice, perceived as 'humane, direct, candid, unselfconscious, personal, and, apparently, objective' (Weiner, 2009: 3), was still unpublished at the end of the 1960s in Italy. Yet in the first proposed draft, the translation appeared to have missed the stylistic peculiarities of the poet, and to have misinterpreted the purpose of translation in relation to potential innovation of the Italian language. The grammar and lexical mistakes would seem to obscure the meaning of the lines and made it even more difficult for the reader to understand Gunn's poems. Furthermore, the stylistic level of the translation was not uniform, moving between an excessively informal register ('sì che il mio sbaglio è peggio[re]' [sic] / 'yes my mistake is worse'),[97] and an overly refined one ('qui m'è più rezzo la brama' / 'here the yearning is more umbriferous for me').[98]

Although conscious of Gunn's use of classical style as well as his ironic use of vulgar terms, Arnoldo Mondadori himself suggested that Pennati edit his translation and employ more incisive language: the Italian language might be historically grounded in a fixed literary style but it should not sound too arcane.[99] The issue revolved around the lack of suppleness in Pennati's translation: the translator's style did not capture Gunn's ability to juggle with different tones. A poet himself, whose *L'ordine delle parole* [The Order of Words] had been published by Mondadori in 1964 and whose poems had been prefaced by Salvatore Quasimodo in 1960 (in their English-language version, *Landscapes*), Pennati was characterised, according to Fortini, by a certain 'difficoltà' [obscurity],[100]

---

97 FAAM, *SEAI*, file Camillo Pennati (translations Gunn), Arnoldo Mondadori, 16 March 1965.
98 Ibid.
99 Ibid.
100 FAAM, *SEAI*, file Camillo Pennati, reader's report by Franco Fortini on *Le radici* and *Dal profondo*, 22 September 1959.

which appeared not to be Hermetic but related to an obsolete use of rhetorical devices that invalidated a more concrete representation and ended up sounding 'barocche' [baroque].[101]

Fruttero and Lucentini's precise evaluation of the draft translation outlined the translator's mistaken typology, both in terms of grammar and style.[102] In particular, they noticed an unsuitable 'domesticating' tendency,[103] which brought Gunn's lines closer to the Italian cultural horizon, but with parochial results. For instance, to 'dance hall' the translator applied the regional folklore of an outdoor dancing platform, typical in Emilia Romagna, 'balera'; 'Charing Cross Road' became quite literally an obsolete 'via Charing Cross'; and 'Miss Brown and Miss Jones' were turned into 'signorina Franchi e signorina Rossi'. Some of these examples would be slightly modified in the final parallel text version (following Fruttero and Lucentini's suggestions); however, the examples of translation choices which aimed to elevate the tone of Gunn's poems were countless. Some of these deforming tendencies of 'ennoblement', as Berman would call them (1984), were also noticed by the reviewers: '"Trattengo ancora Eden" [I still hold Eden]. È come tradurre, credendo di rendere chissà quale sfumatura, go to hell come "va a inferno"' [It is like translating, thinking of rendering with who knows what nuance, 'go to hell' as 'vai a inferno'].

In addition to textual issues, the paratextual elements of Pennati's translation did not match Mondadori's principle of reader accessibility. The preface prepared for the book was deemed as too specialist, more suitable for an academic journal than for a poetry volume.[104] The contribution was stilted due to the use of weighty adjectives and vague literary references,[105] probably because Pennati envisaged that his audience would be an academic one. The final version featured instead a preface by Lombardo who situated Gunn's poetry in the wider context of contemporary English poetry in a more didactic

---

101   FAAM, *SEAI*, file Camillo Pennati (translations Gunn), note by Marco Forti to Vittorio Sereni, 27 June 1966.

102   Ibid., report by Fruttero. It is worth remembering that Carlo Fruttero and Franco Lucentini worked as editors and translators at Einaudi for decades, and were also editors-in-chief for Mondadori's science fiction series 'Urania' for more than two decades from 1961 to 1986.

103   It should be pointed out that Venuti uses the term *domesticating* to refer to the text as a whole and not to the single translation choices.

104   FAAM, *SEAI*, file Camillo Pennati (translations Gunn), note by Vittorio Sereni to Raffaele Crovi, 2 May 1963.

105   Ibid., preface by Camillo Pennati, London, 19 March 1963.

way. Lombardo's introduction brought together his reading of the 1956 *New Lines* anthology, Robert Conquest's editorial notes, and Giorgio Melchiori's 1956 essay 'Il Nuovo movimento e i giovani arrabbiati' [The New Movement and the Angry Young People] (*I Funamboli*), tracing a brief outline of the Movement, whose generally disillusioned, anti-symbolic and anti-ideological stance upheld Gunn as its most productive representative (Lombardo, 1968: 22). Pennati criticised the preface for its elementary character as unbefitting an informed reading,[106] but his more scholarly perspective did not seem to correspond to the popularising intentions of the Milanese publisher.

In light of these two objectives – proximity to the original poetic style and accessibility for the Italian reader – other translations had to be 'normalized' (Milani, 2012: 110). In 1965 Mary de Rachewiltz translated what she thought 'translatable' of Denise Levertov,[107] thus denouncing at the outset a supposedly opportunistic selection criterion. Forti appreciated the selection, while pointing out the translator's slight bias towards 'femminili' [feminine] poems against the more ethical and intimate production.[108] Here the editor seemed to neglect a fundamental element in Levertov's poetry that the translator had instead acutely perceived, thus partly diminishing the function of the English-born American poet in terms of social critique and cultural activity. Critical literature on Levertov has in recent decades reassessed her relationship with William Carlos Williams beyond their immediate stylistic similarities and their shared call for immediacy; specifically, it has shed light on how their symbolism was closely connected to an ideological commitment, and particularly the way that 'the feminine and the maternal become important figures for alternative authority, which is at times cast in idealized terms – through mythologizing, essentializing, generalizing – but is also insistently developed through the material contexts of cultural activity' (Kinnahan, 1994: 125). In his introduction to the book, critic Aldo Tagliaferri nonetheless put forward a more didactic psychoanalytic interpretation, identifying the 'feminine' in terms of Jung's archetype, noticeable in the lunar symbolism pervading Levertov's poems (Tagliaferri, 1968: 15).

Forti was more thorough when assessing the translation at the linguistic level, raising some doubts in relation to the general sense of extraneousness to

---

106 FAAM, SEAI, file Camillo Pennati (translations Gunn), to Vittorio Sereni, 10 November 1966, ms.
107 FAAM, SEE – GDL, file Mary de Rachewiltz, to Vittorio Sereni, Brunnenburg, 30 September 1965.
108 Ibid., note by Marco Forti to Vittorio Sereni, 24 January 1966.

the standard Italian language. Especially in terms of lexis, the editor noticed on occasion archaic solutions, more reminiscent of Pound's translations of Dante than of Levertov's style:

> La traduzione è indubbiamente interessante dal punto di vista poetico e può fare un ottimo effetto, purché venga un po' revisionata e normalizzata dal punto di vista dell'italiano [...] A volte esagera e certe parole 'anticate' sembrano uscite dal laboratorio dantesco di Pound [...] Dovrà insomma trattarsi di una revisione che non si sovrapponga in nessun modo alla qualità di fondo [...] che sono originali e ben azzeccate per il testo, ma ne corregga soprattutto alcune manchevolezze scolastiche di lingua italiana.[109]

> [The translation is undoubtedly interesting from a poetic viewpoint and can have a powerful effect, as long as it is slightly edited and normalised in terms of the Italian language [...] Sometimes [the translator] exaggerates and some 'antique' words seem to have come out of Pound's Dante laboratory [...] What is needed is some editing that does not alter [its] basic qualities in any way, which are original and well suited to the text, but that can correct some schoolbook lacunae in the Italian language.]

As the translation did not include footnotes, in order to further help the reader Forti advised tailoring a short preface that could situate Levertov's work within contemporary anglophone poetry and, more importantly, provide the 'average Italian reader' with all the necessary details and information in order to understand and appreciate it.[110] Tagliaferri's introduction satisfied these needs and the book would be launched in such literary journals as *Paragone* and *La Fiera letteraria*.

In the final version, however, the distance from Levertov's stylistic traits was still perceivable and we can observe two contradictory operations: Levertov's elliptical syntax was simplified; at the same time, a constant raising of lexical register produced extraneous effects. This is the case with the poem 'About marriage', a plea about the lack of obligations and ties in marriage. The most ambiguous and syntactically complex 'it's not / irrelevant / I would be / met / and meet you' has been synthesised in the use of verbs, in

---

109   FAAM, SEE – GDL, file Mary de Rachewiltz, note by Marco Forti to Vittorio Sereni, 24 January 1966.
110   FAAM, SEE – GDL, file Mary de Rachewiltz, Marco Forti, 22 May 1966.

contradiction to Levertov's typical ellipsis of the auxiliary, in 'non è / da poco / vorrei / ci / incontrassimo'. Conversely, the insertion of *dolcestilnovo* terms such as 'meriggio' [literary for 'noon'] or 'frescura' [chillness] clashed with the more ordinary 'Saturday afternoon' and 'cool air' (Levertov, 1968: 226–27), whereas 'a veil of quiet' was rendered by the adjective 'pellucida quiete', related more appropriately to anatomy or biology than the veiled quietness of a park. In similar terms, the translation of 'laced / here and there with feathery groves' ('With eyes at the back of our heads'; Levertov, 1968: 22) as 'qua e là trinato di pennuti arbusti' ('Con gli occhi sulla nuca', 23), where 'trinato' conveyed a further sense of triple division compared to the original, risks overexaggerating the perhaps more intimate idea of 'in-dreaming, actual sleeping dreaming, and also the process of imagining [...] a desirable place to go' that Levertov herself suggested for the poem (Brooker, 1998: 75–76).

Even when the symbolism appeared more informed by Aztec mythology, as in the poem 'Xochipilli', or was powerfully vivid, as in 'The Communion', the strategy of ennoblement undertaken by the translator did not enhance the power of the images; it made them more obscure, by relying more heavily on the use of adjectives than the noun-focused poetry that Levertov advocated. 'Thatch' became 'ramaglia' [dead branches] ('Xochipilli'; Levertov, 1968: 130–31), rather than simply 'paglia' [straw], whereas 'hump and perch' was translated with the rare adjectives in Italian 'appollaiate gibbose' [hunchbacked and perched] ('The Communion'; Levertov, 1968: 86–87). In the opening of the poem 'Song for Ishtar/Canto per Ishtar', where sacred images and profane language are daringly intertwined, the translator's archaic use of language makes for a stilted read, diminishing the alliterating rhythm of the original, laid over ordinary words: 'The moon is a sow / and grunts in my throat / Her great shining shines through me / so the mud of my hollow gleams / and breaks in silver bubbles' became 'La luna è una *troia* / mi mugola in gola / irradia e illumina per me / sicché il *brago* nella mia fossa luccica / e mignola d'argento' (Levertov, 1968: 174–75). Once again, there was a clear clash in the passage from 'troia', charged with a vulgar sense, rather than the fauna-based choice of 'scrofa', and the Dante-inspired 'brago' preferred to the more neutral and literal 'fango', which would have allowed the continuation of the animal metaphor in more immediate terms.

What Mondadori sought in a translator was something different, as clearly explained with the praise of translator Mariolina Meliadò's work:

Mi ha favorevolissimamente impressionato il lavoro di Mariolina Meliadò: per la padronanza, teorica e pratica, del mestiere di traduttrice, e per la capacità di arrivare, con un sistema di accerchiamento linguistico (ma qui è stilistica anche il più astratto rilievo) al centro di verità della poesia. Ecco una persona da agganciare stabilmente, anche per lavori critici. Prefazione e nota si integrano a vicenda e sono un'ottima presentazione del poeta.[111]

[Mariolina Meliadò's work has very favourably impressed me: for the both theoretical and practical translation competence, and for the ability to penetrate, with a system of linguistic encirclement (but here even the more abstract remark is stylistic) the centre of the poetic truth. She is a person who should be hired permanently, also for the critical works. Preface and notes are well integrated and are a very good presentation of the poet.]

In 1966 Meliadò translated Theodore Roethke's *Sequenza nordamericana e altre poesie*, which included a selection of poems from *Open House* (1941), *The Waking* (1953), for which he received the Pulitzer prize in 1954, and *The Far Field* (1964). The translation was introduced by a preface by Lombardo and by Meliadò's own note on the translation. This unusual practice was possibly due to two paradoxically coexistent reasons: one pertaining to gender and power dynamics, one to editorial approaches. Although a study of women translators and their role in translation and canon formation as in Woods (2011) is beyond the scope of this book, it is clear nonetheless that poetry publishing in the decades under consideration was a quite male-oriented domain, probably because of the prestige afforded to poetry in the then literary system. Key agents such as Fernanda Pivano were exceptions, whose cultural capital derived from their literary fame and wealth of literary networks. Meliadò's name was certainly not as popular, and she was probably in need of a male figure who could bestow legitimacy upon her – in this case scholar and editor Lombardo. The other reason most likely lay in the opposite, yet complementary, perspective provided by the two prefaces, which taken together offered readers an exhaustive overview; interestingly, women translators could provide a more informed approach, as we will see, though their function was arguably reduced to a 'note' rather than a 'preface'. Lombardo situated Roethke's poetry within a wider anglophone literary tradition, spanning Blake, Yeats, Eliot, Pound, and William Carlos Williams

---

111 FAAM, *SEAI*, file Agostino Lombardo, note to Vittorio Sereni by Maria Teresa Giannelli, 18 February 1965.

– identifying the influence also of John Donne, Walt Whitman, William Wordsworth, Emily Dickinson, and even Dante, which an intertextual analysis of the American poet outlined less than ten years later (La Belle, 1976). Meliadò privileged a sophisticated linguistic analysis which presented to the reader the main challenges of the translation.

Biographical information on Mariolina Meliadò is scarce, but we should note that her work is exemplary of the greater theoretical awareness that translators showed during the 1960s, the result of a new direction in linguistics, and of a new conception of the translation on the part of Italian agents. George Mounin's *Les problèmes théoriques de la traduction* [Theoretical Problems of Translation] had been published in Italian translation by Einaudi in 1965 and had been reviewed by Aldo Rossi in *Paragone* the same year, marking the beginning of a new 'scientific' approach to the activity of translation.[112] Beyond these structuralist approaches, Meliadò demonstrated a more philosophical awareness of translation, quoting at the start of her translation note Walter Benjamin's 'The Translator's Task', published by Einaudi in 1962. Drawing on Benjamin's discussion of 'literality', Meliadò explained that she wanted to reproduce Roethke's syntax that was modulated according to the emotional situation, which also informed the peculiar rhythm of the US poet (Roethke, 1966: 33).

If Roethke's crystal-clear language, though imbued with symbolism, tended overall to dominate, a key challenge for her was the use of childish language, which does not normally produce in Italian the same empathy that it inspires in English. In 1963 Meliadò published one of the first scholarly essays on Roethke to appear in Italy,[113] in which she discussed in detail the American poet's articulate use of childish images and nursery rhymes, which she did not simply connect to his biography but interpreted more acutely in relation to images of sex, death, and the sense of guilt of Puritan adulthood (Meliadò, 1963: 433–34). Meliadò sought to recreate this effect through a salient use of rhetorical devices such as onomatopoeia and assonance, inserted in a fluid metrics, based on a 'criterio accentuativo, o di cadenza'

---

112 Earlier works were Contini's essay 'Di un modo di tradurre' [Of a Way of Translating] (1946) and Benvenuti Terracini's 'Il problema della traduzione' [The Issue of Translating] (1957).
113 Roethke's poems, 'Elegy' and 'Words for the Wind', had already been translated in *Inventario* in January 1960, while in 1961 American scholar Lynne Lawner had published a brief essay (Lawner, 'Tre nuovi') on three American poets, which included Roethke alongside Wilbur and Lowell.

[accentuative criterion, or rhythmic cadence] (Roethke, 1966: 37) more than on the rigid number of syllables. The result was a translation graphically in line with the facing-page text which enabled the Italian reader to enjoy the compelling and immediate rhythm of Roethke's lines.

The footnotes were rich in cultural references to Roethke's literary reflections. In addition, Meliadò offered precise explanations of the covert irony, or of the reasons behind a particular metric structure, to signal to the reader when her translation choice was distant from the literal sense. In other words, Meliadò produced an almost self-sufficient version in terms of reading enjoyment; still, the more attentive reader was given the opportunity to fully grasp the serious work of the translator. In the poem 'I cry, love! Love!', the obscure – to an Italian reader – use of nouns in the stanza 'What's a thick, Two-by-two's a shape, / This toad could waltz on a drum; / I hear a most lovely huzza: / I'm king of the boops!' (Roethke, 1966: 152) were clearly explained in a footnote: 'toad' as a tender diminutive of Theodore, translated literally in Italian as 'rospo', and 'boops', an onomatopoeic sound invented by the poet to indicate be-bop jazz, inscribed within an Italian lexical context with an equally onomatopoeic 'da-dda-dda'. Similarly, in the poem 'The Far Field', European birds were found as correspondents to typical American ones (Roethke, 1966: 316, 39, 439n), and a footnote revealed the reference to foreign culture.

Meliadò's pedagogic approach corresponded perfectly with Mondadori's twofold objective of accessibility and accuracy, as did poet and translator Giovanni Giudici:

> Giudici ha reso molto bene quel tanto di cantilenante, di felicemente e amabilmente rimato, quell'atmosfera ora di nostalgica rammemorazione e ora di più cupa e nostalgica riflessione, che mi pare distinguere il mondo di Ransom. È riuscito a darne il tono 'sudista' con l'uso di qualche vocabolo desueto che (come Ransom) ora adopera sul serio, e ora ironicamente [...] Per il resto il libro va bene e mi pare rappresenti compiutamente l'autore nei suoi diversi mondi e aspetti.[114]

> [Giudici rendered very well that singsong, happy and sweet rhythm, that atmosphere of at times nostalgic remembrance and at times darker

---

114 FAAM, SEAI, file Giovanni Giudici, note by Marco Forti to Vittorio Sereni on *Poesie scelte* by John Crowe Ransom, Milan, 22 June 1966. See also Milani, 2012: 110. In Italian, also in Franco, 2018: 128. For a comprehensive analysis of Giudici's translation activity, including the translation of Ransom's poetry, see Franco, 2020.

nostalgic reflection, which seems to me distinctive of Ransom's world. He succeeded in conveying the South American tone by using some obsolete words that (as does Ransom) sometimes seriously, sometimes ironically [...] For the rest, the book is good and I think it fully represents the author in his diverse worlds and aspects.]

In a note to Sereni,[115] Forti praised Giudici for having appropriately painted US poet John Crowe Ransom as a representative of the New Criticism movement and as a ruralist opposed to Roosevelt's industrialist policies. This is particularly interesting as Mondadori wanted Ransom's translator to be a 'militant' poet. As such, we shall unpack Giudici's habitus beyond his well-known socialist ideas. In fact, this supposed 'militancy' would seem to be rendered via a stylistic – rather than political – consonance with the US poet in terms of close attention to prosody and rhyme, which ultimately became a pivotal element of Giudici's own writing (Franco, 2018: 121–24; 2020: 203–04).

Ransom's 'anti-romantic' and 'anti-positivist' ideologies had been discussed at length in one of the first essays on the US poet by scholar Remo Ceserani in 1960; Ceserani dismissed these to an extent as nostalgia rather than political philosophy, in favour of an analysis that emphasised Ransom's interest in language and its articulate techniques. In his introduction to the translation, Giudici partly undermined the strength of the US poet's wider poetics and, from a critical point of view, claimed him as a formalist, though less relevant than the Russian formalists. The translator's interpretation failed to acknowledge the cultural and political stance offered by Ransom's poems, and specifically how his 'intertwining poetic and cultural theories [...] participate in constructing new models of culture [...] and conceive of this cultural "whole" as itself a spatialized aesthetic object [...] grounded in the physical region and represent[ing] the fusion of art and economy' (Aronoff, 2013: 137–38). Through his reading, though, Giudici indirectly assumed a position within poetic discussions of Marxist approaches connecting art and social context, which conceived of literature as a self-referential artistic object and upheld that poetic value should not be limited to the acceptance or rejection of the intentions and contexts that shaped it (Ransom, 1971: 12).

Giudici's reflections demonstrate the 'complexity' of his theoretical positions (Neri, 2018: 80), from the moral and political perspective of his

---

115 FAAM, *SEAI*, file Giovanni Giudici, note by Marco Forti to Vittorio Sereni, 13 December 1966.

poems and essays to a formal attention to poetry as stylistic practice. The first draft of Ransom's translation was produced in 1965 (Franco, 2018: 123), but the book was only published in 1971. In 1968 Giudici completed his translation of Yury Tynyanov's 'The Problem of Verse Language', in which poetic language was conceived as an autonomous entity, with the concept of rhythm crucial for both phonetics and semantics (Neri, 2018: 75–81). On the contrary, just few years later in 1972, Giudici discussed the relationship between poetry and technology in the context of information and communication in an essay, 'La letteratura verso Hiroshima' [Literature towards Hiroshima], published in the journal *Rivista IB*; here, poetry was seen as a political act which needed to surprise and provoke the reader.

In terms of translation practice, Giudici's 'translation ideology' has been seen as a foreignising approach that, drawing on Tynyanov's distinction between poetic and everyday language, sees poetry as ontologically 'foreign' (Blakesley, 2014: 136–39). To a certain extent, our analysis upholds such a reading. Going back to Forti's note to Sereni, the editor identified in Ransom's poetry a striking rhythm that Giudici was able to reproduce through lexical expedients, as evident from the choice of the title, *Le donne e i cavalieri* [Women and Knights], deemed as 'ironicamente ariostesco' [ironically Ariostan].[116] According to Giudici, Ransom's value lay in his linguistic mastery, which bestowed a highly connotative charge upon the linear structure of his poems. This characteristic brought with it specific translation challenges for Giudici, who acknowledged that he had to 'sacrificare una traduzione letterale per la rima' [sacrifice a word-for-word translation for the rhyme],[117] given the key function of this rhetorical device in enhancing Ransom's use of irony and ambiguity.

The Italian poet and translator made a consistent effort to keep the alternating rhyme in the quatrains, sometimes adapted to a cross rhyme, as in the case of the opening poem 'Janet waking/Il risveglio di Giannina'. The poem touches upon universal themes such as the end of childhood through a salient use of rhymes ironically counterposing banality and seriousness of tone, Janet's deception and her supposed awakening (Wasserman, 1968: 149; also Franco, 2020: 215). Giudici suggested a sequence of rhymes slightly different from the ABBA rhyme scheme in the original, but the solution (ABAB) showed creativity and acumen, influenced also by Pascoli in the use of affectionate names (Franco, 2020: 215): 'One kiss she gave her mot<u>her</u> /

---

116 Ibid. In Italian, also in Franco, 2020: 208.
117 Ibid., to Vittorio Sereni, 17 January 1965. In Italian, also in Franco, 2020: 211.

only a small one gave she to her dad<u>dy</u> / Who would have kissed each curl of shining ba<u>by</u>; / no kiss at all for her broth<u>er</u>' became 'Un bacio diede alla mamma. *Piccolo* / appena un altro ne diede al papà, / che del suo bel tesoro avrebbe baciato ogni *ricciolo*. / E al fratello per niente nessun bacio' (Ransom, 1971: 86–87). More generally, in line with Giudici's own interests, the attention to prosody stands out when comparing the source text and the target text (Zucco, 1993). In 'Winter remembered', for instance, Giudici kept the same prosodic length in the stanzas, thanks to carefully considered syllabic insertions, as in 'And in the wood the furious winter blowing' / 'e nel bosco il *gran* [my italics] soffio del vento furioso' (Ransom, 1971: 20–21), thus proposing inventive solutions that used the Italian language in a creative and flexible way.

As further evidence, in the introduction to *Lady Lazarus e altre poesie* [Lady Lazarus and Other Poems] by Sylvia Plath, published in 1976 and winner of the Monselice prize for translation the following year, Giudici claimed to disagree with the idea that the translator had to make the foreign text his own. As a 'facitore di versi' [doer [rather than a creator] of verse] (Plath, 1976: 12), according to Giudici the poet-translator should instead use his craftsmanship to select the main qualities of the foreign poem – in the case of Plath, in terms of lexis – and maintain the extraneous effect. In 'The Applicant/L'aspirante', a sarcastic reflection on the societal expectations of a marital relationship, the translation of the line 'naked as paper to start' did not keep a prosodic continuity with the original, but relied upon the slightly extraneous syntactic construction: 'nuda per cominciare come una pagina bianca' [naked to start as a blank page] (Plath, 1976: 22–23). The function of the translation was, according to Giudici, that of 'essere al servizio' [being at the disposal] (Plath, 1976: 14) of the foreign text, and if this would seem to be true in terms of language, arguably Giudici failed to acknowledge here the thematic relevance of the feminist claims by attributing the voice of the poem to a feminine subject instead of the predominant male one (Franco, 2020: 227).

Giudici's translation skills and his elastic adaptation to foreign prosody could not, however, neglect certain publishing constraints, meaning that his tendency towards foreignising strategies had to coexist with a domestic approach. In relation to Ransom's translations, from the outset the project was influenced by the need to produce an accessible translation: all poems whose linguistic wordplays were 'inafferrabili, quasi riservate al *clerc* di lingua inglese' [incomprehensible, almost reserved for a clerk, native speaker of English] (Ransom, 1971: 13) had to be discarded from the collection. The original selection by Lombardo (Franco, 2018: 125), as an avid reader of Ransom's poetry since his *Realismo e simbolismo*, was rejected partly on the basis of its poetic content and particular references, likely to be too cultivated for the Mondadori readership:

> 'Lady Lost' è intraducibile perché basata tutta sul gioco verbale fra Lady Lost (il titolo e il tema della poesia) e Lady-Bird che nel testo inglese suggerisce una graziosa associazione, ma che in italiano non può tradursi con altra parola che 'coccinella'; 'What Ducks Require' sarebbe una buona poesia, anzi una bella poesia, ma è troppo condizionata da una rigorosa associazione tra ritmo e rima, che è la sua struttura essenziale e che in italiano scomparirebbe del tutto; 'Address to the Scholars of New England', infine, è troppo 'dotta', non riesce a interessarmi.[118]

> ['Lady Lost' is untranslatable since it is all based on wordplay between Lady Lost (the title and topic of the poem) and 'lady-bird', that in the English text has a graceful association but in Italian can only be translated by <u>coccinella</u>; 'What Ducks Require' would be a good poem, even a beautiful poem, but it is too conditioned by a rigorous association between rhythm and rhyme, which is its essential structure and that in Italian would completely disappear; finally, 'Address to the Scholars of New England' is too 'cultivated', I cannot get interested in it.]

Forti's judgement supported Giudici's selection, in the name once again of reader accessibility: 'io sarei favorevole all'eliminazione di "Uomo senza il senso di direzione" e di "Testa dipinta" che, fra le poesie più tarde, offrono non comuni difficoltà anche a un lettore abbastanza allenato' [I would be in favour of eliminating 'Uomo senza il senso di direzione' [Man without a sense of direction] and 'Testa dipinta' [Painted Head], that, among the later poems, offer unusual difficulties even for a reasonably well-trained reader].[119] These poems were nonetheless included in the final version, but it is true that they were the least successful. In particular, the assonance and consonance of 'Painted Head' was very difficult to render in Italian without completely changing the lexical meaning. Looking more closely at the last stanza ('The *b*ig *b*lue *b*irds sitting and *s*ea-*s*hell flats / and caves, and on the

---

118 FAAM, *SEAI*, file Giovanni Giudici, to Vittorio Sereni, 17 January 1965.
119 FAAM, *SEAI*, file Giovanni Giudici, note by Marco Forti to Sereni on *Poesie scelte* by John Crowe Ransom, 22 June 1966, ds.

iron acropolis / To spread the hyacinthine hair and rear / the olive garden for the nightingales') (Ransom, 1971: 128), we notice that the Italian translation kept only the concluding line's alliteration ('l'orto degli ulivi per gli usignoli'), while the rhythm is broken and the striking rhetorical weave created by Ransom has vanished ('ai grandi uccelli azzurri che covano e agli alvi / di conchiglie marine e sulla ferrea acropoli / per spandere le chiome di giacinto e nutrire / l'orto degli ulivi per gli usignoli' [Ransom, 1971: 129]). Our examination challenges Blakesley's analysis, which focuses on how Giudici's translations figured 'at least six different secondary linguistic aspects [...] the conservation of the same amount of verses in a poem; enjambements; raising of the register for poetic power; *added assonance and alliteration*; omission of words; and the foreignization of Italian syntax and the introduction of foreign vocabulary into Italian' (2014: 160, my italics), but ultimately gives credit to the challenges of each single translation.

A partly 'domesticating' tendency can be seen in the 11-page-long commentary penned by Ransom, the *Prelude*: the translator was indeed worried that the numerous references to highbrow literature could be felt as extraneous by the reader.[120] The text would in the end be translated, but Giudici's own preface warned the reader of its 'un po' curioso, un po' macchinoso' [rather curious, rather intricate] nature (Ransom, 1971: 14). Giudici's introduction is fascinating as it indicated what kind of readers the translator and the publishing house had in mind. Forti commended the paratext, for it was able to join a critical, in-depth analysis of the history and culture of the foreign text and a 'lettura corrente e adatta a ogni pubblico' [fluent read appropriate for any readership].[121] Presenting Ransom's work, Giudici underlined its metric and stylistic precision and the need for the translator to adopt a strategy that would 'puntare subito sul possibile' [focus immediately on what is possible] (Ransom, 1971: 16). The translator revealed how he had skimmed over the rhetorical devices in order to focus only on the most evident and most easily enjoyable elements, such as the ironic tone and the system of metaphors that created a thematic union, starting from the female characters and the theme of death. What is more stimulating for our analysis is the image Giudici gave the reader, as a metaphor for the ultimate sense of this publication. Why indeed translate such a rhetorical poet, so closely related to the specific context of rural America that the translator was

---

120 FAAM, *SEAI*, file Giovanni Giudici, to Vittorio Sereni, 17 January 1965.
121 FAAM, *SEAI*, file Giovanni Giudici, note by Marco Forti to Vittorio Sereni, 13 December 1966.

often forced to explain the poetic design so as to make it accessible for the reader? The reason lay precisely in the work's highly refined status, suitable for an average reader who was concerned with his cultural standing. *Le donne e i cavalieri* had a similar function to a 'vino d'annata' [vintage wine] or smoking a 'pipa di marca' [branded cigar] (Ransom, 1971: 17): a sign of distinction.

Through a mixture of domesticating and foreignising approaches, as Lombardo and the Mondadori editors had in mind, 'Lo Specchio' thus succeeded in presenting to 'the average poetry reader' a foreign perspective that fully met all expectations: cultivated but accessible; accurate but not pretentious. This textual practice would in theory be able to appeal to a different section of the poetry market and, at the same time, allow Mondadori to regain a more central presence in the poetry publishing field. The sales of Plath's *Lady Lazarus*, more so than those of Ransom's poems, seemed to confirm the success of the project: the 2,558 copies printed in January 1976 had sold out by December of the same year. This was followed by a second (1,564), and third (1,622) edition in March 1977, and finally a fourth (2,180) edition in 1980, figures which demonstrate not only a strong interest in the US poet (confirmed by the publication in English of her letters in 1975, thirteen years after her suicide), but also the significance of Giudici's translation prize in 1977, which gave sales a further boost.

If, in the 1950s, the small publishing houses had been able to shatter Mondadori's monopoly over poetry production, the 1960s saw the large-scale Milanese publishing house reposition itself in the field. Under Vittorio Sereni's editorship, 'Lo Specchio' used translation as a means to navigate a new path between canonical prestige and much-needed literary innovation, between national as well as transnational changing dynamics, in order to achieve the cultural capital necessary to re-emerge as a central player. Thanks to the production of poetry books which detached themselves more and more from Hermetic influences and engaged with contemporary poetry trends in new ways, Mondadori re-established an active relationship with poetry readers in Italy. Its success was also thanks to generally accurate but accessible translations which provided different forms of transnational dialogue at the junction between foreignisation and domestication. Situated precariously between the increasingly solid position of small publishers and the success of the large publishers' revival strategy, the medium-scale publishing houses, represented by Einaudi, had to carve out their own space in a field comprised of fluid forces.

2.3 Einaudi and paperback poetry

After the 'Poeti' initiative, conceived in the immediate aftermath of the Second World War, had been abandoned, and the 'Poeti stranieri tradotti da poeti italiani' series had ceased publication, at the beginning of the 1960s Einaudi surprisingly found itself with 'nessuna presenza nel campo della poesia' [no presence in the poetry publishing field].[122] Its absence was especially notable in the dynamic context of the time, when economic prosperity and market opportunities brought new life to the publishing industry and cultural debates regarding poetry in Italy resurfaced. In a poetry publishing field characterised by plural forces, the Turinese publisher attempted to position itself by placing itself at the confluence between the elite focus of the small-scale publishers and the more popular orientation of the larger-scale publishing houses. Like other medium-scale publishers, Einaudi ought to satisfy the demands of a varied middle market while upholding its status as an 'editore di cultura' more markedly devoted to cultural innovation. If the former allows publishers to survive, the latter represents a necessary source of legitimation. From this (partly oxymoronic) perspective, the publication of foreign rather than national poetry provided a flexible and productive solution. Foreign poetry had the potential to appeal to an audience beyond the poetry specialists, and act as an agent of cultural renewal at the transnational level. This was particularly evident in the increasingly internationalist outlook of political-cultural activism in the 1960s, in conjunction with the coming to the fore of university students as a significant cultural force for innovation in this decade in their quest to explore what cultures outside Italy offered. Einaudi was thus identifying a new, and potentially large and durable, readership, and positioning itself as an intellectual publisher in the poetry field.

In the mid-1960s, Einaudi therefore embarked once again on the path of poetry publishing, but with an innovative format. The brand-new poetry series, 'Collezione di poesia', was of a dichotomous nature from the early stages of conception, in line with the specific position of the medium-scale publisher described above. Einaudi editors aimed at designing a series that could derive a certain level of credit from the charismatic figure of an editor and/or a poet who would orient its tastes; at the same time, the poetry collections had to offer more variety in terms of foreign poetry selection, ensuring the publisher multiple sources of prestige. In other words, the question was not just *who* to

---

122 AE, minutes of the meeting held on 22 May 1963, Cesare Cases. Also in Munari, 2013: 738.

translate, but also crucially *how* to translate and publish specific authors. The solution that the Turinese publisher adopted was a 'iniziativa mista, di classici italiani e stranieri, di grandi moderni soprattutto stranieri, e (forse) qualche italiano, nuova scoperta o outsider' [mixed initiative, comprised of both Italian and foreign classics, of important modern poets, especially foreign ones, and (perhaps) some Italian ones, a new discovery or an outsider];[123] it interwove the cultural capital offered by already established figures (the 'classics') with the symbolic capital of literary innovation derived mainly from foreign poets.

As such, Einaudi's 'Collezione di poesia' could represent a threat both to Mondadori's cultural capital and Scheiwiller's prestige, and a chance for the Turinese publishing house to assert its own identity in the field. By taking advantage of authoritative editors, by crafting an agile yet refined format, and by introducing increasingly innovative foreign literary elements, the publishing house was finally able to carve out a solid position within the poetry publishing field. More interestingly, thanks to poetry translation and its transnational intellectual value, in the late 1960s Einaudi successfully re-functionalised the cultural identity of Italian intellectuals, a project it had been engaged in since the post-war 'Poeti' initiative. The following sections will detail some of the fundamental components of Einaudi's publishing project: the book format and the readership, as well as the selection of national and foreign collaborators.

2.3.1 Plaquettes *for a 'bazaar' collection: the strategy of the refined paperback*

Given Einaudi's objective of appealing to a wider audience, the format of the books needed careful consideration. Einaudi's paratexts reveal immediately the subtle dynamics of a field dominated by small and large-scale publishers: in order to establish its own place, the Turinese publishing house offered the graphical sophistication associated with the former, as well as specific paratextual elements (prefaces and notes, in particular) to appeal to a wider readership, though with a markedly politico-cultural attitude. In practical terms, Einaudi was required to choose between expensive lengthy volumes and books at a relatively cheap price, as the metaphor of the 'bazaar' used by the German Studies specialist Cesare Cases aptly synthesised: 'la nuova "Collezione di poesia" è la stessa cosa del Bazar o Rinascente di cui si parlò a Rhêmes o è la collana grossa diretta da

---

123 AE, file Lucia Sollazzo, Italo Calvino, 27 April 1964.

Solmi, Vittorini, Montale?' [is the new 'Collezione di poesia' the same thing as the Bazar or Rinascente store that we discussed in Rhêmes-Notre-Dame or is this the big collection edited by Solmi, Vittorini, Montale?].[124] As Mondadori's *opera omnia* had already been rejected by Giaime Pintor as early as 1943, Einaudi opted for the flexible model adopted by the small publishers.

The format chosen for the 'Collezione di poesia' was an object-book similar to Scheiwiller's micro-texts; typographically refined books which presented a small selection of poems – normally forty – by a single poet or multiple authors. The publishing house could rely on the collaboration with well-known graphic designers such as Bruno Munari and Max Huber, who were responsible for the covers of many Einaudi editions from 1962 to 1972. What was particularly distinctive about the 'Collezione di poesia' was its simple and elegant white covers, which usually featured an extract from the book printed in black. This paratextual choice reflected Giulio Einaudi's fascination with the books of the leading French publisher Gallimard, which he described as 'insuperabili nella loro semplicità grafica, nella loro capacità di invogliare la lettura' [unbeatable in their graphical simplicity, in their ability to encourage reading] (Einaudi, 1988: 108; Munari, 2016: 35). Einaudi perceived Gallimard as the publishing house 'affine' [most similar] to his own and strove to represent in Italy the same stature and intellectual commitment that Gallimard represented in France. The paratext was a strategic means of fashioning this sought-after transnational dialogue, as demonstrated by the direct 'transfer' of the titles of Gallimard series to the Turinese publishing house, such as the 'Collection blanche'/'Collezione bianca' (Munari, 2016: 50). Minimalist and refined, the covers of the 'Collezione di poesia' obtained a favourable welcome and rapidly became a synonym of prestige. A quick overview of the reviews illustrates the narrative that developed around the editions of the 'Collezione di poesia', seen as a 'un piccolo (soltanto di formato!) gioiello' [small (but only in terms of format) jewel!],[125] whose elegance and seemingly elite status attracted the reader. The symbolic capital that Einaudi acquired through these sophisticated books was notable and made the series a natural competitor to Scheiwiller – but with even wider transnational ambitions.

As with Scheiwiller's *plaquettes*, the advantages of such a book can also be identified more pragmatically on an economic level, in terms of carving out

---

124 AE, file Cesare Cases, to Guido Davico Bonino [hereafter GDB], Rome, 2 January 1963.
125 AE, *recensioni*, T.S. Eliot *La terra desolata*, 20 May 1965.

Editors, Habitus, and Translation

a niche in the market of copyright acquisition. Giulio Einaudi used this very argument in his attempt to convince Mario Luzi – a celebrated Mondadori author, whose works were also published in *plaquette* by Scheiwiller – to publish some of his unpublished poems in the 'Collezione di poesia' series. Featuring only a small number of poems, the Einaudi edition could function as a pre-launch, which would not compromise – but could theoretically increase – the appeal of a subsequent comprehensive Mondadori volume. At the same time, such a strategy would enable Einaudi to publish those poets 'a cui guardiamo con grande stima, [che sono] ormai legati ad altri editori' [that we much value, who are by now tied to other publishers]:[126]

> la collana, destinata com'è a raccogliere brevi scelte, quasi prologhi o preannunzi a future più ampie raccolte, consente, per la sua stessa natura, anche ad un autore legato ad altri, di concederci per intanto delle 'editio minor', senza per questo urtare la suscettibilità di un eventuale editore d'ufficio. Ho visto per esempio di recente il suo [...] nel magma pubblicato da Scheiwiller. Un volume di analoghe dimensioni che raccolga suoi versi per ora inediti, potrebbe benissimo comparire in questa sede senza pregiudicare una prossima 'editio maior'.[127]
>
> [The nature of series, which intends to present only small samples, almost prefaces or pre-announcements of wider collections of poems, means that even an author tied to other publishers could give us for the time being an *editio minor* without offending a potential official publisher. For instance, I have recently seen your [...] in the jumble published by Scheiwiller. A book of similar dimensions that would present your still unpublished lines could certainly appear in our collection without jeopardising a further *editio major*.]

Because the Einaudi *editio minor* was not ostensibly in direct competition with the products of Mondadori and the like, it was generally tolerated,[128] enabling Einaudi to open a gap in the large-scale publishers' potential monopoly of publishing rights. Additionally, the publications were also accepted by the

---

126 AE, file Mario Luzi, GE, 11 September 1964.
127 Ibid., GE, 11 September and 8 October 1964.
128 We should, however, note that this practice was in some cases opposed so as not to overshadow the primary edition – this was the case, for instance, with the publishing rights of Cavafy at Mondadori.

small publishers in the name of their potential for the 'exchange of similar favours', as in a pragmatic way Giulio Einaudi revealed to Sergio Solmi.[129]

Unlike the small-scale Milanese publisher, Einaudi sought to offer an object-book to a broader public than merely poetry specialists. Mindful of its post-war intention to foster an intellectual community through its publishing projects, the Turinese publishing house reworked the *plaquette* model into a prestigious paperback. This is confirmed by the announcements made by the publisher, eager to present the 'Collezione di poesia' to a wider audience, and by the data related to print runs. The latter showed average numbers of about 3,000 copies for each single-author book, which was three times more than Scheiwiller's average, and slightly higher than Mondadori's average of 2,500 copies. They also reached 5,000 copies in the case of wide-ranging anthologies that might interest a larger proportion of readers. In comparison to other collections, these were not excessively high numbers in terms of print runs (the print runs of the 'Supercoralli' series established in 1948 to publish literary masterpieces were at least four times greater); yet 3,000–5,000 copies can be considered quite significant for the notoriously restricted market of poetry publishing.

Finally, the price of 800 Italian lire was, if compared to the 2,000 Italian lire of 'Lo Specchio' books and 1,000 Italian lire of Scheiwiller's *plaquettes*, in line with Einaudi's aim to have a more popular appeal, as it was an accessible figure even for students with limited financial resources. When presenting the collection, Giulio Einaudi expressed this strategic combination of price and prestige:

> Tjutčev, Beckett e Brecht inaugurano la nuova 'Collezione di poesia' Einaudi [...] Con i suoi volumetti di formato tascabile e di prezzo economico, la collana vuole proporre al grande pubblico la vera poesia d'ogni tempo e paese, dai classici antichi ai più recenti esperimenti.[130]

> [Tyutchev, Beckett, and Brecht launched the new Einaudi Collezione di Poesia [...] With its fairly priced paperback books, the collection intends to offer to a wide audience the true poetry of every time and country, from the ancient classics to the most recent experiments.]

---

129 AE, file Sergio Solmi, GE, 13 November 1968.
130 AE, *recensioni*, file Brecht (*Libro di devozioni domestiche*).

The 'wide audience' targeted by Einaudi was made up of 'persone colte, studenti e giovani' [well-educated people, students and young people],[131] as internal correspondence reiterated. In a letter to Fortini, Guido Davico Bonino – who effectively oversaw the 'Collezione di poesia' – suggested republishing Paul Éluard's poems to give younger people the opportunity to read at a cheap price the French poet, who was seen as relevant politically.[132]

Affordable pricing was not the sole strategy adopted by Einaudi editors in order to reach university students. The paratexts, specifically clear and informative introductions, helped situate the foreign authors within a historical and literary horizon to such an extent that they could almost function as textbooks. In the case of German scholar Anselmo Turazza's preface to the collection of poems by the early twentieth-century German humorist Christian Morgenstern, what was needed was 'una voce d'enciclopedia, una conferenza di studenti della terza liceo' [an encyclopaedic entry, a lecture for pupils about to finish secondary school], accessible to students with little or no knowledge about Morgenstern.[133] From an editing perspective, some revisions had to be carried out to simplify difficult passages: this would ease the understanding of the textual analysis for the benefit of those people who did not belong to the 'happy few' (in English in the document), particularly younger readers or those less 'equipped' from a cultural viewpoint.[134]

The final version of the preface began with a lively portrait of Morgenstern, but the remaining three-quarters interestingly situated the poet within the German tradition, hinting at the potential rivalry with Stefan George – translated into Italian at length under the Hermetic influence – and sealing, through German essayist Eugen Gottlob Winkler's words, Morgenstern's poetic validity over George (Morgenstern, 1966: 6) and his proximity to Hölderlin and Rilke. The introduction concluded with a brief linguistic excursus on Morgenstern's work and the parodic effects produced by the names of the main characters in his poems. Drawing on academic sources, the paratext was therefore utilised to provide readers with informative analyses, but also to position Einaudi's publication against the traditional transnational approach of the literary canon. Overall, whereas Einaudi's typographical apparatus was oriented towards the acquisition of a bank of symbolic capital through its refinement, the parameters related to the audience and reception

131 AE, file Salvatore Quasimodo, GE, 18 June 1963.
132 AE, file Franco Fortini, GDB, 13 May 1965.
133 AE, file Anselmo Turazza, Mario Losano, 6 December 1965.
134 Ibid., Mario Losano, 19 December 1965.

adopted a more popularising perspective, though maintaining a distinctive style. The most practical way of obtaining a more dominant position in the poetry publishing field lay, however, in the selection of authors and, especially, of translators.

2.3.2 Translators as bearers of prestige

Translation is a form of legitimisation from which both authors and cultural mediators can benefit (Heilbron and Sapiro, 2002: 5). The value of a translated text does not rely solely on the languages involved in the translation process, but also on the related literatures and cultures in the world's literary field, as well as on the position of the translators as cultural agents in their specific national field. Acquiring literary prestige can thus be related as much to the established position of the translator as to the translated author. Precisely in the former modality, translation was the tactic that would enable Einaudi to emerge from the margins of the poetry publishing field (Milani, 2017: 301).

In terms of copyright acquisition, one strategy was, as we have seen, that of publishing only a small selection of poems by a prestigious author. But authors could also be included in Einaudi's catalogue as translators. Candidates for the role of translators were poets of an established reputation, essayists, and especially distinguished scholars, who also could append, as a guarantee, 'un sigillo accademico di garanzia' [an academic seal] (La Penna, 2003: 301) to the translations. The latter was particularly important for Einaudi, whose intended readership was largely composed of students, and enabled the 'Collezione di poesia' to secure a first, fundamental bank of symbolic capital. In a letter to the anglophone literature scholar and translator Giorgio Melchiori, Giulio Einaudi outlined openly this strategy: 'A noi dispiace un po' non dare il testo di Yeats, ma dispiace di più non pubblicare le versioni di Melchiori' [We would be sorry not to publish Yeats's text, but we would be even more sorry not to publish Melchiori's versions].[135] Although these were judged by Melchiori as 'piuttosto letterali che poetiche' [almost more literal than poetic],[136] from Einaudi's perspective the prestige derived from collaborating with Melchiori as a translator was more advantageous than the reputation derived from the publication of the foreign text alone.

The correspondence with Mario Praz, renowned scholar of English Studies, is another telling example. Thanks to his established academic

---

135 AE, file Giorgio Melchiori, GE, 11 November 1964. Also in Milani, 2017: 302.
136 Ibid., GE, 16 November 1964. Also in Milani, 2017: 302.

position both in Italy and the UK, Praz was a desirable translator for Einaudi, for 'qualche versione inedita che potrebbe innalzare il prestigio di questa serie' [some [of his] unpublished translations that could increase the prestige of this series] as well as for already published translations that had not yet been reprinted.[137] Faced with Praz's hesitation, Einaudi sought to assure the scholar that he would be placed alongside similarly esteemed figures, enumerating a distinguished 'Parnassus' of poet-translators and scholars, including Sergio Solmi translating Arthur Rimbaud, Valeri translating a notebook of contemporary French poets, and Melchiori translating Yeats.[138]

As with the 'Poeti stranieri tradotti' series, the main intent became that of focusing on the fitting encounter between the foreign poet and the translator, with the latter becoming the occasion for a highly refined production that would cement the future of the 'Collezione di poesia'. In this first stage, the value of the series resided primarily on the figure of the translator as an Italian cultural mediator, bearer, and at the same time recipient of prestige. This is clearly shown by the discussion arising in an editorial meeting when Calvino suggested shaping the collection around the foreign author; not privileging certain translators or translations questioned the very principle on which the 'Collezione di poesia' was based, provoking objections from Vittorini and Davico Bonino. Translations could not simply *support* the foreign text; rather, they should be a fundamental element of the publication:

> VITTORINI: Ma per presentare così dei grandi poeti c'è la NUE; per la collana di poesia ci vuole il grande traduttore. [But for the big poets there is the NUE [Nuova Universale Economica], for the poetry collection, we need a 'big name' translator [...]
>
> DAVICO: [...] C'è una distinzione di partenza. Nella collana di poesia la scelta parte dal traduttore. [There is a distinction from the start. In the poetry collection, the selection starts from the translator]
>
> EINAUDI: [...] Per la poesia aspettiamo il traduttore. Se troviamo un gigante contemporaneo lo mettiamo nei 'Supercoralli' [...] Lascerei la collana di poesia agli incontri fra traduttori e poeta.[139] [For the poetry

---

137 AE, file Mario Praz, GE, 14 September 1964.
138 Ibid., GE, 9 October 1964.
139 AE, minutes of the meeting held on 31 March 1965.

collection, we wait for the translator. If we find a contemporary literary 'giant', we will publish it in the Supercoralli collection [...] I would leave the poetry collection to the encounters between translators and poets.]

In the early days of the series, the translators were thus granted freedom in selecting the source texts, thanks to the reputation that they enjoyed in their specific professional field. Often, though, their freedom was mundanely reduced to pragmatic criteria of 'translatability', as happened with the famous poet and translator Maria Luisa Spaziani, who translated the French Symbolist and then *fantasiste* poet Paul-Jean Toulet in October 1964, just one month after the launch of the 'Collezione di poesia'. In her later notes on editing and translating, Spaziani advocated for the translator to offer 'un testo che sembri scritto in italiano, ma proprio da quell'autore, in quell'epoca storica e con quel bagaglio di pensieri, esperienza, uso della lingua, scelta di stile' [a text that would seem to be written in Italian, but from a certain author, in a certain historical time, and with a certain baggage of thoughts, experience, use of language, choice of style] (Spaziani, 2015: 133). In other words, she privileged a target text that was mindful of the historical peculiarities of the foreign language and style. In translating Toulet, Spaziani appeared nonetheless to have made an opportunistic selection, whereby she sifted only the poems which could be translatable.[140] The publisher was not hugely concerned; in fact, Einaudi's purpose was to publish a specific *translator* – Spaziani – and not a specific *author* – Toulet. The publishing house even suggested that Toulet could be replaced by another poet, such as the earlier Romantic poet Marceline Desbordes-Valmore – one of the reference points of Spaziani, who devoted university courses to the French poet (Scotto, 2015: 21) – if that would ensure a more prompt publication.[141]

Textual practice was in part negatively influenced by these first directions, with superficial attention given to the stylistic aspects of the translation, as in Rodolfo Wilcock's translations of Samuel Beckett's poems, published in 1964. A friend of Jorge Luis Borges, the Argentinian poet and translator Wilcock was already a published author in Italy (by Bompiani, Il Saggiatore, as well as Guanda, which published his Spanish poems in 1963); he was chosen by Davico Bonino, in agreement with Calvino, for his supposed suitability for Beckett's avant-garde poetry.[142] The fact that he translated, along with

---

140   AE, file Maria Luisa Spaziani, to GDB, Rome, 15 May 1965.
141   Ibid., GDB, 2 October 1964. See also Milani, 2017: 302.
142   AE, file Rodolfo Wilcock, GDB, 15 November 1963. Wilcock, however, had

Sanguineti, Alberto Rossi, and Alfredo Giuliani, Joyce's poems for Mondadori in 1961 surely supported this viewpoint, as much as his editorship of the Europe-leaning *Sur* (Puglisi, 2002: 2), in which he showed a more nonconformist attitude than the main editor Victoria Ocampo (Salvioni, 2002: 60).

When looking at Wilcock's translations, we find, however, that Beckett's poems remained cryptic, notwithstanding the rich series of encyclopaedic and philological notes, as well as a brief introductory note that 'aiut[i] il lettore a "capire" il più possibile queste poesie, per lo più incomprensibili' [would help readers to understand these largely incomprehensible poems as much as possible].[143] In general, the translation did not follow closely either the semantics or syntax of the source text, and appeared to have underestimated the linguistic challenges it posed, a point raised by critics at the time. Margherita Guidacci – incidentally, praised by Scheiwiller as a translator endowed with refined poetic taste – identified some inaccuracies in Wilcock's translations that rendered certain elements of Beckett's poems unnecessarily obscure.

If we compare Wilcock's and Guidacci's translations, the very short poem 'Da Tagte Es' was not 'una delle sue più decise incursioni nell'incomunicabilità' [one of [Beckett's] most decisive intrusions in the domain of incommunicability] (Beckett, 1964: 7), as Wilcock maintained, but 'tutt'altro che incomprensibile' [anything but incomprehensible],[144] as Guidacci put it. The lexical choices do not suit the funereal context described by Beckett ('sheet' was intended as 'shroud' and not 'sheet of paper'), nor do the syntactical mistakes (relative pronouns related to the second person singular, or ellipsis of the auxiliary 'to have' in the final line);[145] in addition, the poem – part of a series of poems following the Provençal troubadours' model and set at dawn, as the time when the poets could see their lovers again – alludes to an added bodily image of 'falling or fallen moisture' (Kosters, 2018: 139), that Wilcock's translation ignores:

Redeem the surrogate goodbyes / the sheet astream in your hand / who have no more for the land / and the glass unmisted above your eyes. (Beckett, 1964: 58)

---

objections, particularly in relation to the lack of time to produce an accomplished version. See ibid., to GDB, Rome, 14 May 1964, ms.
143 AE, file Rodolfo Wilcock, GDB, 25 May 1964.
144 AE, *recensioni*, Beckett – *Poesie in inglese*, Margherita Guidacci in *La Fiera letteraria*, 25 October 1964.
145 Ibid.

> Redimi gli addii surrogati: il foglio fluente nella tua mano / che altro non hanno per la terra: / e il vetro terso sopra i tuoi occhi [Redeem the surrogate goodbyes: the sheet of paper astream in your hand / which have no more for the land / and the glass unmisted above your eyes]. (Beckett, 1964: 59)

> Redimi i surrogati dell'addio / col sudario fluente tra le mani / tu che non hai più nulla per la terra / ed hai il vetro snebbiato sopra gli occhi [Redeem the surrogates of the goodbyes / the sheet astream in your hand / you who who have nothing left for the land / and you have the unmisted glass over your eyes].[146]

Recently, Franco Buffoni has shown more enthusiasm for Wilcock's translation skills and particularly his use of prosody and metrics, able to make Italian even more fluid than English. An example Buffoni cites is the poem 'Alba', where the line 'that you shall establish here before morning' is rendered literally through the Italian hendecasyllable 'che stabilirai qui prima dell'alba', with an ictus of 6, 7 and 10, or 5, 6, 7 and 10, depending on the speed of pronunciation (Buffoni, 2012: 121). Yet Buffoni also recognises some of Wilcock's shortcomings, precisely at the level of lexis. The choice to translate a line from the poem 'Serena I', 'ah father father that *art* in heaven', with 'ah padre padre che sei *in cielo*' [ah father father that you are in heaven] missed for instance the archaism of 'art' that a more traditional 'che sei nei cieli' would have captured (Buffoni, 2012: 123). More interestingly, Mario Praz – who, we have just seen, had been reassured about the calibre of the translators featured in the series – was concerned that sloppy grammatical mistakes (such as the translation of 'many a funnel' with the singular form, which Wilcock himself noticed at a later stage)[147] would damage the reputation of all Einaudi's translators.[148] Too much freedom for translators could threaten rather than boost Einaudi's social capital.

---

146   Ibid.
147   AE, file Rodolfo Wilcock, to GDB, 20 June 1965, ms. See also Milani, 2017: 303.
148   AE, file Mario Praz, to GE, 16 September 1964. Melchiori's review was actually more positive and deemed the translations 'excellent'; AE, file Giorgio Melchiori, to GE, 15 September 1964.

2.3.3 The selection of foreign poets: distinction and marginality

Praz's concerns help to articulate a delicate aspect of the planning: the precise demands of Einaudi's most suitable target audience. Reliance on what can be seen as the translator's 'author function' (Foucault, 1977; 1981) is understandable at the launch stage, when the publisher needs to quickly accrue prestige in an indirect way and attract the readership's attention. In the long term, though, it could become counterproductive. The Turinese publishing house had to quickly modify its tactics and choose more rigorously not only its translators, but also its poets. Foreign authors were now perceived not only as bearers of established cultural capital, but as possessing a noteworthy documentary and cultural force, as they were inserted into the wider literary and cultural debate of their time. As such, they could represent a significant publishing novelty (Milani, 2017: 303).

The reasons for this change of strategy had to due with the modified position of Einaudi in relation to national and transnational relationships at a political level, in particular with the Italian Communist Party. The Hungarian Revolution of 1956 had unsettled the ideological positions of the post-war period and had caused many Einaudi editors, most notably Calvino, to renounce their membership of the Party. The beginning of the 1960s had also broadened the perspective towards political and cultural movements well beyond Italy and Europe, thus sparking a transnational interest in literatures traditionally perceived as peripheral. The new strategy was also related to the publishers against whom Einaudi had to renegotiate its own politically committed position by seeking out alternative transnational relationships. In the publishing field of the 1960s, Einaudi was expected to grant a distinct symbolic identity to its poetry series and detach itself from Mondadori's 'Oscar' series, since 'il pubblico che cerca [...] sul catalogo Mondadori, Rizzoli, ecc, cerca semplicemente una lettura; chi legge da noi cerca un filone che non è puramente quello della scrittura' [the audience that looks for a book [...] in Mondadori or Rizzoli catalogues, simply seeks an easy read; those who read an Einaudi book seek a line that is not purely that of readability].[149] At the same time, it was necessary to dissociate themselves from the publishing initiatives of the newcomer Feltrinelli, in order to reach a 'new' public that was not only younger but also intellectually lively:

---

149 AE, minutes of the meeting on 17 January 1979, Roberto Cerati.

Mentre Feltrinelli intende le collane economiche come una possibilità di rifondere tal quali i libri di maggior prezzo dopo un breve o lungo periodo dalla pubblicazione e di metterli a disposizione di un pubblico più largo, ma non diversamente qualificato, Fortini e Panzieri, parlarono al congresso sostenendo il punto di vista opposto e cioè la necessità di individuare un pubblico nuovo e di impostare tutte le collane economiche nello sforzo di produrre dei libri nuovi per un pubblico nuovo.[150]

[While Feltrinelli conceives of its paperback editions as a possibility for selling again, in the exact same form, more expensive books, a short or long time after their initial publication, and making them available for a wider, but not diversely qualified, audience; at the congress Fortini and Panzieri supported the opposite view, that is, the need to identify a new readership and set out all the paperback collections with the aim of producing new books for new readers.]

In other words, Einaudi had to produce books for a new student readership, which did not simply mean manufacturing 'paperback' editions, since as reiterated in the following years by Einaudi editors, 'il lettore che compra il libro Mondadori si assume meno responsabilità rispetto a un libro Einaudi' [the reader buying a Mondadori book takes fewer responsibilities than an Einaudi book];[151] they needed to imbue them with a clear intellectual mark, and arguably a political responsibility: 'libro da GE, [anziché un libro] da GGF: di quelle cose svelte, da discutere e far discutere, che piacciono a Nanni Balestrini' [a GE book, [instead of] a GGF book: these books completed in a rush, in order to debate and raise debates, that Nanni Balestrini likes].[152]

The first foreign authors featured in the series were Brecht, Beckett,[153] and the nineteenth-century Russian poet Tyutchev. As outlined by the Slavicist Vittorio Strada, Tyutchev was cultivated as a poet, influenced by German poetry and philosophy, but more didactic in his political affiliation.[154] His

---

150 AE, minutes of the meeting on 13 June 1962, Franco Fortini. Also in Munari, 2013: 630.
151 AE, minutes of the meeting on 17 January 1979, Franco Fortini.
152 AE, file Edoardo Sanguineti, GDB, 4 October 1968. Also in Milani, 2017: 303.
153 Both authors were more widely known as playwrights, with Beckett's main plays having been translated by Carlo Fruttero just a few years earlier, in 1961. After a first negative review by Tommaso Landolfi in 1953, Beckett was welcomed into the series by Giorgio Manganelli (Angelucci, 2018: 21–40).
154 AE, file Tommaso Landolfi, reader's report on Tyutchev by Vittorio Strada.

poetry was nonetheless topical in the context of an interest of Europe–Russia relations, since he was most representative of pan-Slavism.[155] Tyutchev had already been published in *Il fiore del verso russo* (1947), translated by Poggioli, who as a 'transatlantic' comparatist and Slavicist had been based at Harvard University since the end of the war, and whose rejection of both right- and left-wing ideologies had provoked controversy with the PCI (Alcini, 2016). The latter deemed Tyutchev's more decadent poetry, unfavoured by the Soviet Union, to be anti-communist and did not appreciate the fact that the poet was presented in opposition to communist critics (Munari, 2016: 191). In the introduction to the 1964 edition, penned by Slavicist Angelo Maria Ripellino, Tyutchev was, however, portrayed as a poet closely related to society and its events, and as a much more restless persona than the image of an intellectual who had retreated into a superficial aristocratic world that was promoted by his contemporaries (Tjutčev, 1964: 5–6).

The preference accorded to the Russian author was also interesting in relation to the editorial habitus of Einaudi. The cultural mediators with the Soviet Union were, in addition to Poggioli, Pietro Zveteremich and Franco Venturi (Munari, 2016: 171–205). Zveteremich favoured a more orthodox Marxist-Leninist line and Soviet realism, and, in the immediate post-war period, represented an intermediary with Soviet institutions because of his linguistic skills; he nevertheless moved to Feltrinelli in 1955. Venturi was a publishing agent in Moscow who worked extensively to strengthen the relationships between Italian and Soviet historians. Despite their differences, these three figures perceived Russian literature as part of European literature and as in dialogue with Western production. The translation of Tyutchev was tasked to Tommaso Landolfi: close to Poggioli and Florentine Hermetics during the 1930s, he had embraced a more formalist approach to nineteenth-century Russian poetry, seeing it beyond the labels of Soviet realism and *impegno* (Pala, 2009: 100). The choice reveals Einaudi's aim to position itself in a broader transnational dialogue between Europe and the Soviet Union, and to shift – albeit with some domestic controversies, given the former proximity to Hermeticism of some of the agents involved – the ideological boundaries created in the post-war period.

On a further level, the decision to publish Tyutchev was for Einaudi a way to break into a poetry publishing field dominated by more heterodox agents. Soviet literature elicited the curiosity of more politically oriented

---

155 Ibid.

intellectuals and readers and prompted a fierce copyright competition. Yet such a 'struggle' risked diminishing the very value of the cultural product, which was not subjected to the most rigorous of publishing strategies and was often translated by non-experts. Einaudi intended to oppose the wider tendency that Ripellino – who had succeeded Zveteremich – described in rather apocalyptic tones:

> Da tutte le parti come sparvieri editori di tutte le dimensioni si buttano freneticamente sui poeti sovietici, tirandoli a sé come bretelle. È una vera orgia di corteggiamenti. Ora vogliono tutti pubblicare Voznesenskij, come se non bastassero le liriche che ho scoperto e tradotto io. C'è stato ieri a Roma Feltrinelli con tutto il suo stato maggiore, per firmare, in un impeto di epigonismo nauseante, un contratto con Voznesenskij, per una raccolta di poesie, che dovrebbe tradurre la solita ineffabile Olsufieva, con l'assistenza di Mario Socrate [...] La corsa ai sovietici si sta mutando in delirio. Appena noi apriamo uno spiraglio (e non c'è dubbio che siamo sempre noi ad aprirlo), torme di cavallette irrompono, per rimasticare la stessa *zvacka* [chewing gum]. Che si può fare per difendersi? Passa il gusto di tradurre, se qualsiasi farmacista o impiegato di associazioni semiculturali può, nel nostro campo, arramacciare versioni e parafrasi interlineari, senza il minimo fiuto poetico. Così ora appariranno dieci Voz a cui dei vari zveteremucci. E tutto sarà amalgamato in un'unica poltiglia amorfa e indistinta. Forse esagero, ma certo ci dovrebbe essere un modo di proteggersi da queste arpie che ci sporcano le mense.[156]

> [Everywhere, like sparrowhawks, publishers of any scale jump frenetically on Soviet poets, and clasp them to their chest as tightly as braces. It is a true orgy of courting. Now everyone wants to publish Voznesensky, as if the poems that I discovered and translated weren't enough. Yesterday Feltrinelli was in Rome with all of its chiefs of staff, in order to sign, under an impetus of nauseating imitation, a contract with Voznesensky for a collection of poems, that the usual ineffable Olsufieva, assisted by Mario Socrate, would translate [...] This race to publish Soviet authors is becoming delirium. As soon as we open a door (and there is no doubt that it is always us who open it), crowds of grasshoppers burst in, to chew over the exact same *zvacka*. What can we do to defend ourselves? We are losing

---

156   AE, file Angelo Maria Ripellino, to GE, 20 March 1962. Also in Ripellino, 2018: 63.

the will to translate if any pharmacist or employee of semi-cultural associations can, in our field, put together versions or interlinear paraphrases, within the minimum poetic taste [...] Perhaps I am exaggerating, but certainly there should be a way to protect ourselves from these harpies that soil our soup.]

In his remarks, Ripellino outlined a number of issues, not only in terms of the professionalism of translators in Italy and the indirect loss of prestige for Slavicist scholars, but more interestingly in terms of cultural relationships at national and transnational levels. Einaudi was perceived, in the eyes of the scholar and editor, to be more reputable than those cultural institutions primarily responsible for the distribution of Russian literature, which were normally connected to political interests.

This marked a willingness to draw a clear line against the practices undertaken by Feltrinelli, but also signalled Einaudi's distance from the channels of transnational dialogue between Italy and the Soviet Union. Voznesensky, one of the most representative poets of the Khrushchev thaw, was closely connected to Boris Pasternak, whose *Doctor Zhivago* had been published for the first time worldwide in 1957 by Feltrinelli. In a short memoir, Feltrinelli recalled his first encounter with Voznesensky, who had met him in Paris, where the poet had been enjoying a positive reception from the French press, and offered him an advantageous contract (Feltrinelli, 1999: 240–43). However, a sloppy translation produced by transnational intellectual networks combining a translator from Russian and an Italian poet or scholar would be detrimental to the reception of these Russian poets, with publishing, and crucially political, consequences for both Italian intellectuals and publishers, and potentially even Soviet–Italian relations. Fishing out an unpublished and culturally significant author such as Tyutchev represented a means of defence against Feltrinelli, and an indirect strategy to regain a position in the transnational space. The print runs confirmed the partial success of the initiative: by 31 December 1966, about 80% (3,590 out of 4,510) of the copies had been sold; in December 1972 a second edition of 7,044 copies would be published and 6,422 of them (around 90%) would be sold.[157]

In similar terms, the translation of French poetry would prove an innovative strategy that allowed Einaudi to explore an almost untouched

---

157   AE, sales figures, administrative charts provided to the author by Roberto Cerati, former president of Giulio Einaudi editore.

sector. As mentioned already, French poetry was normally published in the original language, with translations undertaken rarely and only by specialised publishers. Einaudi could bypass any competitors and address requests for unpublished productions directly to the French authors with whom Giulio Einaudi already entertained a dialogue, such as Surrealist poet André Frénaud.[158] The latter had strong links with Italian intellectuals, particularly Einaudi editors (Bricco, 1999; Grata, 2013): he had been 'scouted' in Italy by Vittorini and translated in *Il Politecnico* in July–August 1946 with a short introduction by Fortini. Frénaud was then published by Il Saggiatore (1962) and translated by fifteen Italian poets and published by Scheiwiller (1964). In 1969 the French poet was awarded the Etna-Taormina prize for foreign poetry precisely because of the Einaudi edition. This movement beyond the Alps also generated a change of perspective in the policies of large-scale publishers, as the troubles Mondadori experienced with the publication of French poetry demonstrated.

In more general terms, faced with the heterodox (Feltrinelli) as well as orthodox (Mondadori) forces of an increasingly composite publishing field in the 1960s, the symbolic capital necessary to affirm Einaudi's own centrality could derive from the dialogue with unexplored or even marginal areas of foreign literature, which now indicated innovation and noteworthy cultural topicality. With their assumption of a dynamic transnational perspective and the development of an increasing interest in foreign literatures and cultures, the peripheries produced greater innovation. We cannot deny that this interest in cultures beyond Europe underlined a changed conception of the relationship between cultures, for instance from a postcolonial perspective, where translation assumed a crucial role in questioning (or maintaining) existing power relationships (as shown first by Bassnett and Trivedi, 1999; Tymoczko, 1999). The relationship between Italy and 1960s anti-colonial movements was particularly problematic: whereas many Italian left-wing intellectuals endorsed the cause and expressed solidarity, in a line of continuity with anti-fascist and Resistance movements, a denial of the legacy of Fascist colonialism and the general lack of engagement with this aspect of Italian history and the country's responsibilities allowed racist elements to resurge in post-war Italian culture.

In the case of such publishers as Mondadori with Caribbean novels, the agents were more interested in 'the exotic, picturesque contents of Caribbean

---

158   AE, file André Frénaud, GE, 30 March 1965.

literature than in its historical, ideological, and political significance, but also sometimes actively opposed the circulation of texts containing anticolonial or pro-Black identity claims' (Pennacchietti, 2018: 412). In our reading of the archival correspondence of the publishers under investigation, this racist element did not emerge in foreign poetry production as it did decisively in foreign novel production, although uncritical or myopic views on minorities – including gender – were present. This is not to dismiss the underlying presence of racism in Italian publishing, an aspect of Italian publishing that bears further investigation beyond the sociological analysis of this book. Our point here is that in being 'ex-centric', peripheral literatures became a potential bank of significant symbolic capital (Boschetti, 2010: 14) that Italian publishers in the 1960s could indirectly exploit in more or less critical ways.

Einaudi's strategy did move towards 'allargare il discorso della collana anche alle zone più periferiche e trascurate' [opening the discourse of the series also to the most peripheral and neglected areas].[159] It was part of a wider project in the Turinese publishing house, as Calvino had already discussed with Ripellino in 1963:

> scoprire e lanciare autori ancora non noti da noi sarebbe la vera cosa da fare. Perché quando se ne accorgono in Francia o nel mondo anglosassone, e il nome dell'autore comincia a diventare editorialmente appetibile, magari è troppo tardi.[160]

> [to fish out and launch authors who are as yet unknown is what we should really do. Since as soon as they are discovered in France or in the Anglo-Saxon world, and the name of the author starts becoming palatable, it may be too late.]

As such, in 1972 a poet outside the category of 'canonical' such as Carles Riba could be praised as 'uno dei maggiori poeti della Catalonia' [one of the most representative poets of Catalonia].[161] Not even ten years earlier, the same Catalan poet had been rejected because he was largely unknown in Italy: 'non abbiamo nulla contro l'idea di tradurre testi come Vicente Huidobro e Carles Riba (che del resto candidamente ignoriamo), ma preferiremmo, se possibile,

---

159   AE, minutes of 3 March 1965, GDB.
160   AE, file Angelo Maria Ripellino, Italo Calvino, 20 November 1963.
161   AE, minutes of 13 December 1972, GDB.

presentare prima figure più "canonizzate"' [we don't have anything against translating such texts as Vicente Huidobro and Carles Riba (who besides is largely unknown), but we prefer, if possible, to present first more 'canonical' figures].¹⁶² Riba had in fact been translated only once into Italian, in a selection of a dozen poems translated by Giuseppe Sansone and published by the small publisher De Luca in Rome in 1962. Intriguingly, in his introduction to the foreign poems, which were without footnotes and notably preceded by, rather than following, the Italian versions, Sansone had presented Riba's poetry as 'pure' in terms of form and 'passionate', but only from an aesthetic, not political, perspective (Sansone, 1962: 3). In his introduction to the Einaudi edition of the translation of *Elegies de Bierville*, Sansone stressed instead the political weight of Riba's work, which was labelled as a moment of inner investigation and fundamental questioninig triggered by the urgency of political events rather than a simply hedonistic work (Riba, 1977: vii–viii). Sales figures, perhaps boosted by political events related to student protests and the demand for Catalan autonomy in the early 1970s, confirmed the effectiveness of the new strategy, since 2,725 of the 3,035 copies published in 1977 were sold, with the remaining ones offered as free copies.

Among the most 'peripheral' proposals, attention was also given as early as 1966 to Portuguese literature, currently untranslated and therefore potentially profitable.¹⁶³ Einaudi editors wanted to offer a composite portrait of Alexandre O'Neill, an anti-fascist poet whom translator and political activist Joyce Lussu had met in Lisbon and considered 'representative of Portugal's renewal' (O'Neill, 1966: 11). Although O'Neill's fame resided in surrealist poetry, his use of experimental and visual forms was intended as a strategy of political denunciation of Salazar's dictatorship (Ledesma, 2018). O'Neill was, however, not only a valuable option for his political stances, but for his formal innovations, which would distinguish him from obsolete elegiac codes. Such a philological focus partly clashed with Lussu's more intuitive translation strategy (Trenti, 2009: 124), a point that will be explored more fully in Chapter 3. The dialogue between Davico Bonino and Lussu shows that, in the selection of poems, the translator was encouraged to favour those featuring O'Neill's most distinctive stylistic qualities, stressing his ironic vein or including his portraits of local accents:

---

162 AE, file Vittorio Bodini, GDB, 29 December 1964.
163 AE, file Joyce Lussu, GDB, 16 October 1964.

metterei comunque l'accento su un certo colorismo lusitano, affettuoso e ironico insieme, quello, per intenderci, di autoritratto, Portogallo, i ciechi, gente da beffe e danno, i vecchi di Lisbona, piuttosto che sull'aspetto populista-didascalico di 'La piuma capricciosa' (che mi sembra l'aspetto più datato e facile di questo poeta).[164]

[I would put, however, the accent on a certain Lusitanian colour, emotional and ironic the same time; that, to be clear, of self-portraits, Portugal, blind men, people making jokes or doing harm, the old people in Lisbon, rather than the popular-didactic character of 'La piuma capricciosa' (that seems to me the more outdated and simple of this poet)].

Ho qui la sua scelta che approverei al 90%, escludendo soltanto due o tre poesie [...] che mi pare insinuino un'ombra di patetico e di elegiaco in quella che mi sembra la vena più schietta di O'Neill, che è di natura ironico-grottesca, molto ben rappresentata da tutto il resto della sua scelta.[165]

[I have here your selection, 90% of which I would approve, and exclude only two or three poems [...] that seem to me to insinuate a shadow of pathos and the elegiac in what seems the more honest vein of O'Neill, which is of an ironic-grotesque nature, very well represented by the rest of your choices.]

The public seemed again to enjoy this choice: between sales (2,632) and free copies, the print run of 3,006 soon sold out. In offering not only cultural references that could be inscribed within contemporary debates but also literary innovation, the strategy of more peripheral poets resolved those doubts related to an overly canonical approach. It is now necessary to deepen our inquiry, to examine the extent to which these choices were also connected to multifaceted sociological dynamics pertaining not just to the publishing and political, but most interestingly to the Italian literary and intellectual fields.

---

164   AE, file Joyce Lussu, GDB, 22 December 1964.
165   Ibid., GDB, 6 April 1965.

2.3.4 The neoavanguardia *and public intellectuals*

To appeal to a 'lettore Einaudi tipo' [ideal Einaudi reader],[166] a reader with literary *and* cultural interests,[167] editors and translators had to draw on works that were able to raise both historico-cultural and documentary attention. This eventually triggered some attention to politics, as in the case of Scottish poet Hugh MacDiarmid. In British literary history, MacDiarmid is seen as a key figure for his linguistic experimentation with the Scots language; his more politically committed works, though, inspired by his joining the Communist Party in the mid-1930s, gradually shifted to English and did not find a place either in Scottish or English literary canons (Lyall, 2011: 68–70). In his initial reading in 1967, Giorgio Manganelli – whose role as Einaudi editor will be discussed in more depth later – was interested in the formal experiments between the directives of modernism and the Scottish popular tradition[168] in MacDiarmid, largely unknown in Italy. Only two of MacDiarmid's poems had in fact been translated in Izzo's *Poesia inglese contemporanea da Thomas Hardy agli apocalittici*; there, the editor had given a more political appraisal insofar as the Scottish poet was deemed to practise 'il più ortodosso Comunismo' [the most orthodox communism] (Izzo, 1950: 235). These political affiliations were, apart from MacDiarmid's aesthetic and formal experimentalism of the highest calibre, intriguing for Manganelli: 'È scrittore letteratissimo e passionatissimo, nazionalista scozzese e leninista, un casino di gran classe che a mio avviso non dovremo lasciarci sfuggire, prima che Tanassi Big Brother occupi la appena polverosa poltrona della Cultura popolare' [He is a very literary and very passionate writer, Scottish nationalist and Leninist, a refined chaos that we shouldn't leave to others, before Big Brother Tanassi occupies the dusty chair of popular culture]. The reference to socialist politician Mario Tanassi indicates a publishing choice that could spark political debate: MacDiarmid's mixed political positioning between nationalism and communism, which made his canonisation in Britain problematic, could conversely have made his publication in Italy more palatable for Einaudi.

The conception of nationalism foregrounded by MacDiarmid was shaped around his own subjectivity and articulated through the representation of a fragmented and contested geography of marginal Scottish areas (Sassi, 2011:

---

166 AE, file Francesco Leonetti, Italo Calvino, 15 July 1960.
167 Ibid.
168 AE, file Giorgio Manganelli, to Paolo Fossati, probably before 30 June 1967; also in Billiani, 2007b: 149; Manganelli, 2016: 84.

118–21). Still, Manganelli's reading seemed to overlook the political potential of MacDiarmid's transcultural discourse and revolutionary connection of the local to the global; the editor perceived it as an excessively local expression, linked to the historical-political events of Scotland, which might have been difficult for Einaudi readers to access: 'molto pettegolo e senilmente vanitoso: ma il peggio è che fa un gran discorrere di faccende scozzesi, che mi sembrano di interesse più che tribale' [gossipy and vain in a senile way: but the worst is that he talks a lot about Scottish affairs, which seem to me more of tribal interest].[169] This was arguably the reason why the publication did not go ahead; despite the missed opportunity in terms of postcolonial discourse, Manganelli's comments alert us to a shift in the mechanisms of poetry selection, with greater attention given to foreign poets loaded with more decisively political features.

Discussions around the publication of contemporary Greek poets are, in this sense, revealing. Translator Margherita Dalmati proposed the publication of poems by Cavafy, 'l'unica voce della Grecia moderna che può arrivare oltre i confini linguistici ed è già arrivata; e non arriverà mai in questo Paese, [poiché] il poeta di oggi non può più "cantare", deve "parlare"' [the only voice in modern Greece that can reach beyond linguistic borders and has already reached out; but it will never reach this country [as] today's poets cannot 'sing' any more, they should 'talk'];[170] Dalmati's remarks signal already a new understanding of poetry as not simply limited to individual expression, but more widely connected to the elaboration of political discourses. But poetry that put documentary before lyricism could not find a place at Einaudi, mainly because when the proposal arrived in 1960, the 'Collezione di poesia' was yet to be launched. Mondadori's 'Lo Specchio' could profit from this opportunity.

In 1968 the translator Filippo Pontani proposed to Einaudi another Greek poet in exile, Yiannis Ritsos. According to Pontani, who we have seen championing Ritsos's cause with several Italian publishers, the authority that Einaudi enjoyed in the political debate would grant greater visibility to such an urgent publishing venture, in the name of a timely assumption of civic responsibility against the right-wing dictatorship in Greece:

> Credo che l'editore Einaudi sia il più adatto a lanciare il poeta in Italia, rendendo omaggio alla sua dignità artistica, alla sua incrollabile fede

---

169 AE, file Giorgio Manganelli, to Paolo Fossati, Rome, 16 August 1967.
170 AE, file Margherita Dalmati, to GE, 1 January 1960.

politica e alla sua attuale sofferenza [...] Occorrerebbe un impegno dell'editore a far presto. Ci terrei molto a pubblicare ora questo libro: è l'unico modo che ho di assumere una posizione morale e politica contro il fascismo greco, e sono certo che l'editore condividerà questo orientamento.[171]

[I believe that the publisher Einaudi will be the most suitable to launch this poet in Italy, and will pay tribute to his artistic dignity, to his unshakeable political faith, and his current suffering [...] This is a case where prompt action is required. I would very much like to publish this book now: it is the only way that I can take a moral and political stance against Greek fascism, and I am sure the publisher will share this.]

For practical reasons related to publishing planning, Ritsos would only find a place in the very busy catalogue of the 'Collezione di poesia' in the 1970s; despite its political orientation, a medium-scale publishing house, as much as a large-scale publisher, could not give the Greek case the same dedication that a small publisher like Scheiwiller could.

Structural limits did not distract Einaudi from accomplishing other documentary objectives, as with the publication of Jiří Orten's poems in diary format. The Jewish poet, murdered under the German occupation, bore witness to minority literatures under the Nazi dictatorship.[172] The timing of the publication, around the 1968 Prague Spring, indicates immediately an intention to connect with the wave of renewed transnational interest in Czech culture. The reading offered by other Italian literary agents unveils, however, a further layer of interpretation, tied up in the dynamics of the Italian literary field. Let us consider a review, published in *Il Resto del Carlino* on 10 March 1970, by Beniamino Dal Fabbro, an eclectic intellectual with a nonconformist attitude who tended to engage in polemics against trends that he perceived as hegemonic (Cantini, 2011: 35). Dal Fabbro attacked the status attributed to foreign poetry, seen as more 'prestigious' than Italian poetry, based on the stereotypical fascination with foreign literature often observed in cultural elites (Bollati, 1983). Behind this appeal to foreign poetry, the critic saw the intents of the *neoavanguardia*: the publication of Orten's poetry under the title *La cosa chiamata poesia* [The Thing Called Poetry] disclosed, according to Dal Fabbro, a Crepuscular echo as an attempt to overcome Hermeticism and

---

[171] AE, file Filippo Maria Pontani, to Carlo Carena, Padua, 7 October 1968, ms.
[172] AE, file Giovanni Giudici, to Italo Calvino, Milan, 26 May 1967.

make space for the *neoavanguardisti*. Tellingly, as late as 1969, Einaudi had published the anthology *Poesia italiana del Novecento* [Twentieth-Century Italian Poetry], edited by one of the most representative authors of Gruppo 63, Edoardo Sanguineti, who put forward the idea of retracing the origins of twentieth-century Italian poetry in Crepusculars and Futurists:

> Si fosse presentato negli uffici Einaudi un poeta italiano d'oggi, bene o male vivente, con una sua raccolta di poesie diaristiche, intercalate da brevi prose, relative agli anni tra il 1938 e il 1941 [...] sarebbe stato estromesso a precipizio e forse inseguito dai gorilla di redazione per il Viale Umberto Biancamano. Céco, ebreo e morto, Jiri Orten, *nom de plume* per Ohrenstein, aveva invece tutti i caratteri per rendere accettabile e pubblicabile il suo manoscritto, oltre all'indubbia qualificazione di poeta. Non è mancata [...] l'imposizione di un titolo fazioso e inesatto, sebbene dedotto da un contesto dell'Orten: *La cosa chiamata poesia*. Come a richiamare, in modo anche troppo esplicito, Gozzano e quei crepuscolari di cui oggi ci si serve, con massicci appoggi antologici, per mandare all'aria Ermetici e post-Ermetici e per aprire il varco ai chimismi strutturalistici dei neo-sperimentali, edosintattici e neo-transimentali.[173]

> [If one of today's Italian poets, more or less alive, came to the Einaudi headquarters with a poetic diary, interspersed with short prose pieces, referring to the years 1938–1941 [...] he would be expelled immediately and perhaps chased by the editors' bodyguards along Viale Umberto Biancamano. Czech, Jew and dead, Jiří Orten, pseudonym of Ohrenstein, instead meets all the criteria to have his manuscript published, more than the indubitable qualification of poet. They also imposed [...] an inexact and partisan title, although deduced by some contextual info from Orten: *La cosa chiamata poesia*. As a way to recall, in an overly explicit way, Gozzano and those Crepuscular poets that we use today, with substantial anthological supports, to throw to the wind Hermeticists and post-Hermeticists and to open the window to structuralist, edo-syntactic and neo-transmental chemisms.]

Sanguineti was not an anomalous reference: in a synergistic exchange between culture, literature, and publishing, many of the Einaudi editors

---

173 Dal Fabbro, 1976.

– perhaps most notably Guido Davico Bonino – turned their attention towards the *neoavanguardia* during the 1960s. It is precisely the relegitimation of this movement, whose time appeared to be over at the end of the 1960s, that represents a stimulating line of interpretation in our analysis of Einaudi's translating strategies. In placing foreign production and Italian poets in the same frame, the latter indirectly benefited from the authority of the former. Scrutiny of the 'Collezione di poesia' catalogue alongside the collaborators' correspondence illustrates Einaudi's intention to create several anthologies in the fashion of the *neoavanguardia*, which in its turn referred back to the French intellectuals of *Tel Quel*. Davico Bonino said as much in a letter to Gruppo 63 poet Antonio Porta:

> La tua proposta di giovani poeti ispano-americani mi interessa molto: si tratterebbe, se interpreto rettamente, di un'antologia che fa *pendant*, non solo esteriormente, a *I Novissimi* e a *Tel Quel*. Il mio sogno è infatti di allineare, uno all'anno, dei panorami giustamente faziosi della ricerca poetica dei giovani, paese per paese.[174]

> [Your proposal of young Latino-American poets really interests me: what you have in mind, if I have understood correctly, [is] an anthology which would be in line, and not only from an external viewpoint, with *I Novissimi* and *Tel Quel*. My dream is indeed to align/present, annually, some rightly partisan overviews of the younger poets' poetic investigations, country by country.]

In that anthological 'allineamento' [line-up], within a decade Einaudi published not only *I Novissimi* and the *Tel Quel* poets, but also German, South American, US, Spanish, and British poets, as well as those of Central America; all not only bearers of literary innovation, but representatives of a transnational interest in European and especially extra-European countries and their cultural dynamics. The minutes of the editorial board of 20 May 1969 confirm Davico Bonino's attempt to publish a poetry anthology, edited by Porta, devoted to the 'neo-avanguardia ispano-americana' [Hispanic American neo-avant-garde]. Although the project did not come to fruition, as the following year Porta would edit *Poeti ispano-americani*, published by Feltrinelli, the title suggested by Davico Bonino lays out a crystal-clear

---

174 AE, file Antonio Porta, GDB, 22 April 1969. Partly in Milani, 2017: 305.

intention of highlighting the proximity of the *neoavanguardia* to the Hispanic movement. Seen from a wider perspective, these systematic publications reveal an ambitious cultural operation, which resides in a transnational network of diverse cultural and literary features, with *I Novissimi* being inserted in a pivotal position. Through the assimilation of the avant-gardes of other countries, the *neoavanguardia* was *de facto* included in the transnational debate. The comparison with foreign literatures endowed the Italian poets and intellectuals with enough legitimacy to overcome national literary borders and obtain transnational significance (Milani, 2017: 305–06).

Under the aegis of the *neoavanguardia*, the 'Poeti' initiative of the 1940s was effectively resumed, albeit in different ideological and publishing terms. First of all, the static category of *impegno* formulated in the immediate aftermath of the Second World War could no longer be applied to the sociocultural context that had characterised Italy since 1956 and was shaped further by the events of 1968.[175] Despite its many heterogeneous components, Gruppo 63 was firmly united against politically committed objectives and reaffirmed that the formal dimension should be approached as a space of conflict and innovation (Barilli and Guglielmi, 1976: 17). Poets therefore had to formulate an alternative conception of the relationship between reality and literature which could assume the shape of a cultural debate on a transnational scale. Secondly, the publishing conditions at Einaudi had radically changed. If, in the first place, the weak status of national poetry and the impossibility of finding a synergy between politically committed foreign and Italian poets had ensured the failure of previous initiatives, the more powerful position of Einaudi at the end of the 1960s could legitimise this series, and especially the publication of less canonical authors, as the bearer of cultural innovation. The creation of 'public intellectuals', able to overcome the restrictive borders of the literary field, was now more solidly grounded.

At the end of the 1960s – almost three decades after the expression of its objective to create a 'fronte della cultura' – the Einaudi publishing house seemed finally able to confer upon poets and translators, through contemporary foreign poetry, the status of public intellectuals, with the additional intention of relegitimising the experience of Gruppo 63 and assuming a decisive position within the literary field. The relationship between Einaudi

---

175 Burns (2001: esp. 13–58, for the 1950s–1970s) argues against a static and purely ideological interpretation of the category of 'impegno', suggesting instead a more ductile and 'fragmented' phenomenon, which individual writers negotiate in relation to their audience, publishers, and the wider society.

and the *neoavanguardia*, often neglected in favour of the more obvious synergy between Gruppo 63 and Feltrinelli or between Calvino and Einaudi, is instead key to establishing in more precise terms the interaction between the new publishing direction and the principles of the *neoavanguardia* in textual practice.

2.3.5 Habitus and the neoavanguardia: a distinctive style

The editing process relies on the interaction between the dispositions of the agents involved therein: editors, translators, publishers, and readers. In the translation process, however, negotiations are not limited to the human agents' habitus: the translated text enters this network and undergoes alterations due to the collaboration among the agents themselves (Buzelin, 2007). In the microcosm of Einaudi, notwithstanding the allegedly 'democratic' procedures, the specific habitus of each editor influenced and was influenced to a certain extent by the translation products. Textual practice thus followed a very different direction than the one envisaged at the launch of the 'Collezione di poesia': influenced by current literary dynamics also at the national level, it now engaged much more closely with foreign styles and formal innovation. In other words, textual practice appeared decidedly mindful of the need to relate to the complex 'literariness' of the source text, which 'has much to do with the style of a text, with its marked and distinct use of features such as voice, metaphor, ambiguity, repetition and defamiliarization' (Wright, 2016: 5).

In a similar fashion to O'Neill's publication, the more markedly political content had now to coexist with the editors' interest in the *neoavanguardia* principles of linguistic experimentation. Both the French specialist Guido Neri, a translator and scholar close to the *neoavanguardia*, and the English Studies expert Manganelli, poet, novelist, and theoretician of the *neoavanguardia*,[176] undertook more formal research when selecting the foreign text and devoted specific attention to the stylistic components in their editing of the translated texts. In line with the general dispositions of the editorial staff, the greater refinement in the choice and revision of translations corresponded to the third source of symbolic capital necessary in the redefinition of publishing roles in the poetry field. The books of the 'Collezione di poesia' acquired a bank of literary innovation that consolidated Einaudi's position in

---

176 On the figure, at times controversial, of Manganelli within Gruppo 63, see Barilli, 1995: 246–52.

the poetry publishing field, without neglecting the commitment to accessibility for its student readership.

A clear sign of this change of direction was the doubts raised regarding the selective criterion adopted by Maria Luisa Spaziani, who 'tende a dare di Cocteau le cose più leziose, più classiche e meno stuzzicanti, e in più cerca le più facili da tradurre' [tends to represent the more affected, the more classical and less stimulating things by Cocteau, and what's more, looks for the easiest ones to translate].[177] Just a few years earlier, the work of Spaziani had not been contested but promoted and included among the first publications of the series, as it was necessary for an initial, more cautious, strategy of accumulation of symbolic capital. Now, the poetic selection was governed by the degree of formal complexity that the foreign text could offer, in line with a greater interest in the cultivated poetry favoured by Gruppo 63.

In this context, the French surrealist avant-garde assumed a key position on account of its iconoclasm and linguistic experimentation, which questioned current literary tradition and had informed French culture more broadly, to the point that 'negli ultimi 20 anni è diventato definitivamente chiaro a tutti (alla fine anche in Italia) che tutto ciò che c'è di vivo in Francia – come poesia, romanzo, teatro, saggistica – ha avuto rapporti in un modo o nell'altro col surrealismo' [in the last twenty years it has definitely become clear to everybody (and finally even in Italy) that everything topical in France – such as poetry, novel, theatre, essay – has in some way or another a relationship with Surrealism].[178] Neri proposed that the 'Collezione di poesia' move in the same direction of overcoming an obsolete system of literary values by shifting the Italian post-war interest in Surrealism (centred mainly on Paul Éluard for his social commitment) towards avant-garde language through the publication of other key French surrealist poets. These were chosen in particular to suit the interests and trends of the *neoavanguardia* poets, and included Blaise Cendrars, published in 1958 by Scheiwiller and in 1965 by the Nuova Accademia; the still unpublished Max Jacob; Henri Michaux for his combination of existential anguish and linguistic experimentation; as well as Pierre Reverdy, translated by Antonio Porta and published in 1972.[179]

Yet not all French surrealists found a place in Einaudi's catalogue. Neri refused the surrealist poems of British-born poet Joyce Mansour, a truly transnational figure who grew up in Egypt and wrote in French, noting 'non

---

177   AE, minutes of 11 June 1969, Guido Neri. See also Milani, 2017: 304.
178   AE, file Guido Neri, to GDB, 1965.
179   AE, file Guido Neri, to GDB, 1965.

c'è la novità di ricerca formale che giustifichi la pubblicazione' [there isn't that innovation in terms of formal research that could justify the publication].[180] The minutes did not include any further comments by Neri; we can nonetheless surmise that the stark symbolist imagery in Mansour's erotic poetry,[181] close to André Bréton, would not be perceived as a step forward in the French Symbolists' stylistic quest; a 'rather daunting poem and probably the least read' (Andrews, 2004: 71) work by Raymond Queneau, *Petite cosmogonie portative* [Small Portable Cosmogony] (1950), would be published instead, because of his ties to the Einaudi editors.

In spite of its length of some 1,300 alexandrines, Queneau's poem fully suited the new direction undertaken by 'la linea migliore della "nuova avanguardia"' [the best line of the 'new avant-garde'], with its linguistic experimentation, indebted to James Joyce's use of rhetorical devices, and the mixture of scientific and refined registers in 'lo scientismo (sempre semiserio) di Queneau' [the (always half-serious) scientism of Queneau]. The results of such a ludic linguistic exercise touching upon recent scientific discoveries would produce not only a cultivated, but also 'divertent[e] (cioè non solo raffinat[a], ma spiritos[a])' [fun (that is, not only refined, but funny)] reading,[182] a kind of 'hermeneutic vertigo' (Andrews, 2004: 80). This intriguingly seems to imply a demand for a more specialised cultural background than the Einaudi student readership was likely to possess. Besides the affinities with Gruppo 63, the poem aligned more closely with Calvino's *Cosmicomiche* [Cosmicomics] (1965) and his interest in science and cosmogony; Calvino had Queneau's novel *Les fleurs bleus* [The Blue Flowers] translated in 1967, thus showing a wider interest on the part of Einaudi in the French author. The Italian translation, *Piccola cosmologia portatile* by Sergio Solmi, was published in 1982, together with an afterword by Calvino.

Manganelli's proposals were similarly informed by extensive linguistic research, often focused on revamping more experimental authors. Since 1949 Manganelli had provided *La Fiera Letteraria* with monthly reviews of British or American authors (Papetti, 2000: 188) and, over the course of his career, he translated several contemporary anglophone poets, including South African born David Wright, and poets connected to the Movement in England, including Thom Gunn, Philip Larkin, as well as less renowned figures such as Donald Davie, John Wain, and Kingsley Amis (Leotta, 2007:

---

180   AE, minutes of 2 February 1966, Guido Neri.
181   This would remain unpublished in Italy until the 2000s.
182   AE, file Guido Neri, reader's reports, n.d.

202–03). Driven by these interests, Manganelli strove to shift the focus of the reception of anglophone poets in Einaudi from more canonical, or previously ideological lines, by paying attention predominantly to stylistic experimentation rather than simply political content *per se*.

His recommendations also tactically connected to other publishers' strategies by proposing alternative poetic choices within the same literary movements. Accordingly, Manganelli supported the publication of Elisabeth Bishop for the formal elegance of her poetic production. An established US poet, who had been nominated Poet Laureate in the USA in 1949 and was awarded the Pulitzer prize for poetry in 1956, the choice to publish Bishop would not represent a literary discovery; it would closely mimic, though, Mondadori's research in the domain of US poetry and its interest in Marianne Moore. Einaudi was in fact interested in publishing Moore in the 'Supercoralli' series in November 1969, although the translation by Aurora Ciliberti appeared too 'slow' and 'languid' for Moore's rapid use of monosyllables (Manganelli, 2016: 272). Bishop thus represented a good option: 'Elisabeth Bishop: direi di sì, è poetessa di singolare, metallica, eleganza, non proprio una Marianne Moore, ma certo sottile, ed invecchiata con tanta grazia, senza sgarbo [...] Non sarebbe una scoperta, ma una finezza sì' [Elisabeth Bishop: I would say yes, she is poet of a peculiar, metallic elegance, not really a Marianne Moore, but certainly subtle, and aged with such grace, without rudeness [...] It will not be a new discovery, but an excellent one, yes].[183]

Moving to contemporary British poetry, in his essays Manganelli had lamented the lack of imaginative language or ingenious rhetoric, and – Larkin excepted – a non-ideological but academic finesse (Manganelli, 1960: 38–40). This immediately strikes a parallel with the Italian *neoavanguardia*. Manganelli's first suggestions included war poets related to both the First and Second World War who were not well known in Italy, such as Keith Douglas and Edward Thomas, as well as W.S. Graham, affiliated with the neo-Romantic poets including Dylan Thomas (Manganelli, 2016: 63). None of these poets were in the end published, but the suggestions acknowledged an interest in war poetry beyond its documentary value. In this respect,

---

183   AE, file Giorgio Manganelli, to Paolo Fossati, Rome, 22 September 1968. Also in Manganelli, 2016: 73–74. Manganelli would, however, remove a prose story from Bishop's *Questions of Travel* collection, on account of its being 'femminesco' [womanish] (ibid.), a derogatory comment that recalls Forti's comments on the translation of Denise Levertov, and that signals a myopic view of US feminist poetry.

Manganelli praised the complex stylistic techniques used by W.H. Auden, suggesting that, rather than the political themes normally discussed by the Anglo-American poet, these were the main reason he should be considered for publication. The editor preferred the multifaceted mixture of registers, 'colloquiale, lirica, drammatica, sarcastica, sermoneggiante' [colloquial, lyrical, dramatic, sarcastic, sermonising], in Auden's *Poems* to the corrosive content of the play *The Dance of Death*, 'con tanto Marx adoperato in modo estrosamente cabarettistico' [with a lot of Marx used in an ingeniously cabaret-style way], despite the greater pertinence of the latter.[184]

Textual practice was inevitably influenced by these new directions, seeking to strike a balance between formal experimentalism and accessibility. Looking at readers' reports on foreign works that would later be refused publication can, in this sense, contribute to an alternative history of publishing (Ferretti, 2012: xii). In revising some of the translation proposals, the Einaudi editor constantly called for highly skilled translators equipped with a stylistic sensitivity. This was not the refined poetic taste privileged by Vanni Scheiwiller, which in some cases was not in accordance with the foreign lines; Manganelli would seem to be talking about an ability to adapt the Italian version to the stylistic needs of the source text through a precise formal coherence. We shall look briefly at a couple of examples in which Manganelli discusses the syntactic fluidity and lexical references, in search of solid linguistic-rhetorical devices. The translations of Robert Browning by one of Melchiori's pupils, Nereo Condini, revealed shaky stylistic abilities, but suggested that competent editing might be able to shift the drafts towards a more effective rendering:

> traduce discretamente, con qualche irregolarità. I suoi difetti sono, alternativamente, un cattivo gusto poetico (*yellow hair* tradotto capelli di croco) e una durezza non risolta, per cui il suo italiano talora tradisce il sottostante inglese [...] Tuttavia ha un <u>certo senso dello stile</u>, e forse, controllato, potrebbe fare un decoroso lavoro.[185]

> [he translates in a decent way, with some irregularities. His limits are, alternatively, bad poetic taste (*yellow hair* translated as saffron hair) and an unresolved hardness, hence his Italian still betrays the underlying

---

184 AE, file Giorgio Manganelli, to GDB, Rome, 29 September 1970. Also in Manganelli, 2016: 89.
185 AE, file Giorgio Manganelli, to GDB, Rome, 27 January 1966. My underlining.

English [...] However, he has a certain sense of the style, and perhaps, with some guidance, could do an appropriate job.]

The translation of Thomas Hardy by Franci Zignani, a pupil of Carlo Izzo and specialist in Hardy (Manganelli, 2016: 247), was rejected on account of linguistic inaccuracies ascribed to the shortcomings of the translator, who did not capture the refined style of the foreign poem; she systematically translated unusual terms with everyday ones: '*postern* diventa porta, *warped* è curvato, *quittance* è (ohimé) trapasso e il *dawnfall hawk* diventa un ornitologicamente improbabile falco della rugiada' [*postern* becomes 'door', *warped* is 'bent', *quittance* is (dear me) 'passing away' and *dawnfall hawk* becomes an improbable, from an ornithological perspective, hawk of the dew].[186] A note on the translation of Marianne Moore makes the stylistic direction proposed by Manganelli even clearer. Here the style is required to move in a rhythmic way, in an attempt to give life to a marked prosody. The normally more wordy Italian should speed up to follow the monosyllabic cadence of the English language: 'la traduzione esaminata è linguisticamente competente, ma stilisticamente un po' lenta. Forse è una specifica difficoltà della Moore, che ricava molti dei suoi effetti dalla sveltezza monosillabica della sua lingua; l'italiano è di troppo più languido' [the examined translation is linguistically competent, but stylistically a bit slow. Perhaps this is the specific difficulty in translating Moore, who accomplished her results through the monosyllabic swiftness of her language: the Italian here is much more languid].[187]

Going through Manganelli's reader reports, style was seen as ultimately a literary endeavour on the part of the translator. The Einaudi editor's outlook was thus a far cry from Mondadori's intent to remain as close as possible to the source text but simultaneously assist comprehension. In Agostino Lombardo's reader's report on the translations of Cecil Day Lewis, for example, it was precisely translator Mario Cicognani's poetic ambitions and particularly the adherence to the precepts of the *neoavanguardia* that were questioned. Manganelli's judgement was more positive: 'è una buona, talora assai buona, traduzione, anche se ho segnato qua e là qualche inesattezza, o qualche aggiunta di fantasia' [it is a good, even very good in places, translation, even if I have underlined here and there some uncertainties, or even creative

---

186 AE, file Giorgio Manganelli, to GDB, Rome, 27 January 1966.
187 AE, file Giorgio Manganelli, to GDB, Rome, 25 January 1970. Also in Manganelli, 2016: 79–80.

additions];[188] the issue pertained instead to the foreign author, who appeared to be the most traditional of the Auden group and too outdated for the new directions of the 'Collezione di poesia'.[189]

It was because of such a conception of style that Manganelli accepted – although with reservations – the translation of Katherine Mansfield's *Poemetti* [Short Poems] by Gilberto Altichieri. Guanda had already published a version in 1942, but Altichieri's revisions moved systematically away from the source text. Altichieri substituted the syntactically rhymed strophes and the childish vocabulary of the New Zealand poet with more polished syntax and a vocabulary that substantially elevated the register. As an example, we shall dwell on the fragmented syntax and the insertion of a subordinate clause in contrast to the more fluid use of coordinated sentences by Mansfield in the poem 'Little brother's secret': 'But one night it rained / and I woke up and I heard him crying: / Then he told me' // 'Ma una notte, destata da uno scroscio (But one night, awakened by pounding) / D'acqua, mi raggiunse il suo pianto (of water, his cry reached me) / e sciolse il faticoso nodo (and unleashed the laborious knot)' (Mansfield, 1970: 26–27). Manganelli did not approve of this emphasis; nonetheless, he deemed the translator's operation refined from a stylistic viewpoint, given the internal coherence of Altichieri's translation choices:

> L'Altichieri è un fine letterato, e la sua traduzione è stilisticamente interessante, sebbene io non la trovi a me congeniale [...] gonfia un po' la poesia dura, e acerba, della Mansfield: ma è cosa più che decorosa [...] Le traduzioni in bozza mi sembrano più brusche, più svelte. Insomma, un lavoro interessante ma forse da non pubblicare senza darci un'occhiata. Parere che vuol essere positivo.[190]

> [Altichieri is a fine literary man, and his translation is stylistically interesting, although I don't find it suitable for me [...] he slightly exaggerates the hard, and raw, poems by Mansfield: but this is more than decent [...] The draft translations seem to me more abrupt, swifter. Anyway, an interesting job that perhaps cannot be published without a second look. A judgement that wants to be positive.]

---

188 AE, file Giorgio Manganelli, to Paolo Fossati, Rome, 19 October 1968.
189 AE, minutes of 22 October 1968, GDB.
190 AE, file Giorgio Manganelli, to Paolo Fossati, 22 September 1968. Also in Manganelli, 2016: 73.

Editors, Habitus, and Translation 151

The wider, more structural disposition towards formal experimentation notwithstanding, the specific habitus of each editor had to enter into negotiation with the intentions of a medium-scale publisher interested in keeping a sufficient degree of accessibility for a student readership, both at a literary and prosodic level. The translation of the sixteenth-century poet Jean de Sponde – an author who Manganelli had already rejected as 'poeta difficile, ermetizzante, intellettualistico' [difficult, Hermetic-prone, intellectualistic][191] – was criticised by Neri for the rhythmic solution adopted by the translator, which hampered a more agile version of the Baroque poet. The option of a closed metrics triggered some rigidity in lexical solutions, with consequences both on the level of intelligibility and stylistic rendering: 'altre soluzioni sono oscure e contestabili; certe costruzioni sono inaccettabili nell'italiano moderno [...] frequenti costruzioni contorte (ad esempio quelle del tipo "un punto per di più che lo nasconde di una nuvola in volo"' [other solutions are obscure and questionable; certain constructions are not acceptable in modern Italian [...] frequent contorted constructions (for instance, of the likes of 'un punto per di più che lo nasconde di una nuvola in volo'... a point that what is more would hide it from a flying cloud].[192]

The objective, for the French Studies expert, was instead to adhere closely to the stylistic peculiarities of the source text, including paying attention to the lexical weave which in translation should seem neither obscure nor mundane to modern readers: 'Mi riferisco ai vari "brama", "fralezza", "e che?", "cui" usato come accusativo ecc., e al ricorso delle dieresi di comodo per guadagnare una sillaba e far tornare il verso a tutti i costi' [I am referring to the various 'brama' (yearning), 'Fralezza', 'e che (and that)', 'cui (whose)' used as accusative, etc., and the use of convenient diaeresis in order to earn a syllable or make the verse right in any possible way]. Trite solutions, or selections 'legger[e] e di maniera' [light and mannered],[193] should therefore be avoided as they would invalidate the formal refinement.[194]

Such a viewpoint was not shared only by language-specific experts, but more importantly by editor-in-chief Davico Bonino. In a negative review of the unpublished translation of Emily Dickinson's poems by Lucia Sollazzo – a poet in her own right and cousin of the highly influential and recognised critic

---

191   AE, file Giorgio Manganelli, to GDB, Rome, 7 March 1965.
192   AE, file Guido Neri, remarks on Eurialo De Michelis's translations of de Sponde, n.d.
193   Ibid.
194   AE, file Guido Neri, to GDB, Rome, 22 September 1965, on Faccioli's translations of Apollinaire.

and writer Anna Banti – Davico Bonino highlighted once again the need to avoid an excessive adherence to the rhetorical structure of the original, but also to limit any lingering over superfluous lexical preciousness. Davico Bonino's very specific comments stressed the requirement for a translation to constantly bear in mind the readers' expectations. The ultimate purpose was to facilitate as much as possible the enjoyment of the foreign text without making it more difficult for the reader:

> Nella poesia 303, 'attention' viene reso, per ragioni di assonanza, con un incomprensibile (nel contesto) 'attesa' [...] Anche il linguaggio è prezioso più del necessario: accade così che un umile 'apron' (grembiule) diventi 'zendado' [...] troppo spesso si ha l'impressione di eccessiva tensione, quasi di sforzo. La poesia della Dickinson può raggiungere un pubblico relativamente largo anche in Italia, come dimostrano le traduzioni che già esistono. Non mi pare che la via da lei scelta possa favorire l'incontro: direi – se posso essere franco – che anzi la complica, sovrastrutturando all'eccesso una parola poetica che va resa invece per 'diminuendo'.[195]

> [In poem 303, 'attention' is rendered, for reasons of assonance, by 'attesa' (wait) which cannot be understood (in the context) [...] The language itself is more precious than is necessary: a humble 'apron' (*grembiule*) becomes 'sendal' (*zendado*) [...] too often one has the impression of an excessive tension, almost an effort. Dickinson's poetry can reach a relatively wide audience even in Italy, as the existent translations demonstrate. I don't think that your strategy favours the encounter: I would say – if I can be honest with you – that it actually complicates it, excessively imposing a poetic word that should be rendered instead by diminishing it.]

Experimental exploration was important, but the audience should be at the core of both translators' and editors' views, and the essential criterion of judgement.

Each contemporary foreign poetry publication in the 'Collezione di poesia' shows the constant urgency for Einaudi to strike a balance between two opposing demands – autonomous and heteronomous – from paratextual choices to the selection of both authors and translators to textual practice. On the one hand, the intention to reach a student readership led Einaudi to favour

---

195 AE, file Lucia Sollazzo, GDB, 30 January 1974.

affordable paperbacks with didactic prefaces and intelligible texts by drawing on renowned scholarly or literary figures who could attract this younger audience. On the other, cultural ambitions inserted those same books within a more refined framework, placing the emphasis on innovative poetic content, and promoting engaged formal research thanks to the interaction with the *neoavanguardia*. In these terms, after several failed attempts, through a savvy interaction of national and transnational agents and features, Einaudi finally asserted its position in the poetry publishing field and, at the same time, brought to fruition that more widely militant cultural operation that it had pursued for so long.

To conclude, if the publication of contemporary foreign poetry became at the beginning of the 1950s and more widely in the 1960s a publishing venture for small-, large-, and medium-scale publishers alike, the specific modalities and strategies undertaken by each varied according to the publishing and editorial habitus. These necessarily interacted with the national, and transnational, dynamics of the field, suggesting a more articulate picture of the publication of foreign poetry in Italy, and of Italian culture at large – from Scheiwiller's ambitious project, hinged as it was on Pound's 'distinctive' experimentalism, through Mondadori's more cautious opening to transnational ferments particularly via anglophone poetry, to Einaudi's transnational relegitimation of *neoavanguardia* intellectuals.

Reading between the lines, elements pertaining to the history of translation practices in Italy have emerged – as have practices of interaction with transnational authors and movements. The selection of foreign authors was not univocal, but moved from investigations of the nonconformist (Scheiwiller) or culturally innovative (Einaudi), to the necessary compromise between innovation and tradition (Mondadori). Likewise, each publisher sought after different typologies of translators and textual practice, in line with their respective intents and ideal readership: Scheiwiller's project of distinction led him to seek out refined poet-translators; Mondadori looked for translator-poets who could generate philologically accurate but accessible foreign poems; and Einaudi, which initially desired self-consecrated translators endowed with great linguistic freedom, and subsequently 'experimental' translators, able to embrace more rigorous but still accessible formal investigation. Our sociological analysis of the readers' reports on contemporary foreign poetry has not only called into question the supposed 'naivety' of small-scale publishers, but also cast light on partly neglected or less explored cultural and literary paths in medium to large-scale publishers, as in the case of the function of the *neoavanguardia* in Einaudi, or the political take of some of Mondadori's publications (such as Celaya). These are key elements that contribute to (re)writing the history of each publisher. We now move to the level of micro-analysis and examine the extent to which the above dynamics are visible in a specific typology of publishing product: anthologies of contemporary foreign poetry.

CHAPTER THREE

Contemporary Foreign Poetry Anthologies for New Cultural and Publishing Horizons

The publication of foreign poetry anthologies between the 1930s and the mid-1950s, a practice initiated by the Hermetic tradition, was not unimportant, featuring key works for the aesthetic reception of European languages such as *Lirici spagnoli* [Spanish Poets] by Carlo Bo (Milan: Edizioni di Corrente, 1941), *Poesia inglese contemporanea: da Thomas Hardy agli apocalittici* edited by Carlo Izzo (Parma: Guanda, 1950), or *Poesia spagnola del Novecento* [Twentieth-Century Spanish Poetry] edited by Oreste Macrí (Parma: Guanda, 1952).[1] From the late 1950s, the presence of anthologies of contemporary foreign poetry became nevertheless much more systematic in the catalogues of Italian publishing houses, and significantly expanded beyond the usual Eurocentric boundaries. Guanda was particularly active; its publications included *Poesia ispano-americana del '900* [Twentieth-Century Hispano-American Poetry] (1957) and *Poesia americana del '900* [Twentieth-Century American Poetry] (1963).[2] Feltrinelli was also present in the market with roughly six titles,

---

1   In addition to the translation notebooks by Ungaretti (Rome: Edizioni di Novissima, 1936), Montale (Milan: Edizioni della Meridiana, 1948), and Traverso (Rome: Edizioni di prospettive, 1942), it is worth acknowledging at least *Poesia americana contemporanea e poesia negra* (1949, new edition 1953), edited by Izzo and published by Guanda. The Parma-based publisher also offered *Nuova poesia francese* [New French Poetry] by Bo (1952), and *Poesia russa del Novecento* [Twentieth-Century Russian Poetry] by Ripellino (1954).
2   Guanda's publications also included *Nuova poesia negra* [New Black Poetry] (1962), *Poeti delle Antille* [Poets of the Antilles] (1963), *Poesia americana del '900* [Twentieth-Century American Poetry] (1963), *Poeti algerini* [Algerian Poetry] (1966), *Poesia inglese del '900* [Twentieth-Century English Poetry] (1967), *Poeti romeni del*

including *Poesia russa del Novecento* [Twentieth-Century Russian Poetry] (1960).³

This trend became dramatically more marked from the 1960s onwards. Our quantitative analysis of the catalogues of Italian publishers confirms that in the 1960s and 1970s, the space allocated to foreign poetry anthologies was proportionally much more visible than earlier (Appendix 2). All three publishers under investigation engaged at some level with the publication of anthologies, which normally attracted a wider readership than other poetry titles. Scheiwiller's publications included *Poeti stranieri del '900 tradotti da poeti italiani* [Twentieth-Century Foreign Poets Translated by Italian Poets] (1956), *Poeti slavi* [Slavic Poets] (1956), *Lirici greci contemporanei* [Contemporary Greek Poets] (1965), *Poeti olandesi* [Contemporary Dutch Poets] (1966), *Poeti ciprioti contemporanei* [Contemporary Cypriot Poets] (1967), and *Poeti croati moderni* [Modern Croatian Poets] (1975). Mondadori published few titles: *Lirici tedeschi* [German Poets] (1959), *Lirici francesi* [French Poets] (1960), *Tradurre poesia* [Translating Poetry] by Joyce Lussu (1967), and *Poesia sovietica degli anni '60* [1960s Soviet Poetry] (1971). In Einaudi's catalogue, poetry anthologies featured more substantially with such titles as *Quaderno francese del secolo* [French Notebook of the Century] (Valeri, 1965), *Poeti di* Tel Quel [Tel Quel Poets] (1968), *Giovani poeti tedeschi* [Younger German Poets] (1969), *Quaderno di traduzioni* [Translations' Notebook] (Solmi, 1969), *Giovani poeti sudamericani* [Younger South American Poets] (1972), *Giovani poeti americani* [Younger American Poets] (1973), *Giovani poeti spagnoli* [Younger Spanish Poets] (1976), *Giovani poeti inglesi* [Younger English Poets] (1976), *Poeti simbolisti francesi* [French Symbolist Poets] (1976), and *Giovani poeti dell'America centrale, del Messico e delle Antille* [Younger Poets of Central America, Mexico and the Antilles] (1977).

What were the reasons behind this notable increase of anthologies in the market? And how do these poetry products change in comparison with those

---

dopoguerra [Post-War Romanian Poetry] (1967), and *Nicaragua ora zero: antologia della poesia nicaraguense rivoluzionaria* [Nicaragua Zero Hour: Anthology of Revolutionary Nicaraguan Poetry] (1969).

3   Other titles are *Poeti americani da E. Robinson a W.S. Mervin* [American Poets from E. Robinson to W.S. Mervin] (1958), *Spagna poesia oggi. La poesia spagnola dopo la guerra civile* [Spanish Poetry Today. Spanish Poetry after the Civil War] (1962), *Poesia degli ultimi americani* [The Latest American Poetry] (1964), *Poeti ispano-americani contemporanei* [Contemporary Hispano-American Poets] (1970), and *Poesia operaia tedesca del '900* [Twentieth-Century German Working-Class Poetry] (1974).

inspired by the Hermetic tradition? By looking into how the relationships and mechanics of the literary field, as well as the habitus of publishers and editors, influenced the specific cultural product of the anthology, in this chapter we will discuss whether and to what extent the latter developed in relation to the negotiations over capitals in the field. We will test the role that translators were originally conceptualised to perform as bearers of prestige and ask whether this would become less significant, and whether especially medium- and large-scale publishers would instead privilege a more strategic selection of contemporary foreign poetry. The hypothesis is that in the passage of time between the 1950s and the 1970s, poetry translation ceased to be the domain of poetic ambitions for the translator, to become instead a means for the publisher to engage in cultural and political projects at the transnational level. As a result, textual practice increasingly tended to act as a simple support for the foreign text rather than an opportunity for creative writing. Such an approach effectively debunks the idea of poetry translation as only an aesthetic-driven activity, an argument that this book has sustained throughout, and brings back a more nuanced perspective on the supposedly progressive function of small- and medium-scale publishers in engaging in a transnational dialogue with other poetic and cultural movements.

3.1 Lines of inquiry and an attempt to classify anthologies

From an etymological viewpoint, an 'anthology' is a repertoire of the best expressions; it envisages a selective action which produces evaluative categories and judgements of value on the part of the editors, seen to a certain extent as second authors who select and recontextualise relevant materials (Seruya et al., 2013: 7). As such, anthologies are key for analysing the very criteria of selection, along with 'the underlying taste of individual agents of the community they belong to, of publishing and book-market mechanisms, of fluctuations in cultural importance' (Seruya et al., 2013: 5). In what they exclude as much as what they feature, translation anthologies embody the editor's subjective perception of poetic value, depending on the freedom allowed by their publishers; the greater the freedom, the more editors can have a pivotal role in steering the reception of foreign poetry at large, and in building the literary canon at a national as well as transnational level. Instead of 'canon', Capoferro prefers to talk about 'repertori formali e ideologici' [formal and ideological repositories], since the notion of canon is 'conservativa, sincronica, normativa: non rende conto della dialettica tra tradizione e innovazione su cui si fondano le dinamiche della cultura' [conservative, synchronic, normative; it does not acknowledge the dialectic between tradition and innovation that cultural dynamics are based upon] (2004: 303). Capoferro's argument is logical. However, in the context of this book the concept of canon, according to the limits just mentioned, can be applied to the intended normative function of some translation anthologies, insofar as they suggest poetic hierarchies, geographies, and models not only for foreign poetry, but notably also for contemporary Italian literature.

Translation anthologies can offer readers a collection of poems from one foreign author, but they can also be 'bilateral' or 'multilateral (world literature)', including a single or several source languages and cultures (Seruya et al., 2013: 6). Crucially, the multiple functions they indicate enable us to shed light on the interaction between transnational publishing dynamics and literary and cultural phenomena to a greater extent than translations that present single poets only. Their very concept implies a desire to reach a wider audience, including literary critics and specialists, students, and readers who will use the anthology as a valid instrument of cultural and literary instruction. Even within the elite domain of foreign poetry, these anthologies have therefore broader commercial implications than other cultural products, which allows us to articulate more fully the interweaving of cultural and publishing factors. Their larger transnational scope also helps us to analyse in detail cross-cultural perceptions and interactions. In their intrinsic capacity to group together in one place authors belonging to culturally and geographically heterogeneous domains, these anthologies represent a sort of adjuvant in developing a transnational dialogue among cultures; they can function in *relatively* more neutral terms as a repository or an educational instrument, informing their readers about 'other' cultures and connecting their shared traits, or as a more partial and tendentious means of introducing foreign elements that could modify the current literary domain in the target culture, with potential political repercussions. Investigating the selection criteria and the behind-the-scenes procedures related to the production of bilateral and multilateral anthologies thus provides a composite view of the editors'/publishers' literary and ideological perspectives and a better sense of how the dialogue between Italy and transnational cultural phenomena was shaped.

A taxonomy of anthologies has been suggested by other scholars (Seruya et al., 2013: 5–6), but for the purposes of our inquiry into the Italian book market we need to find more specific criteria in terms of both content and structure. This can more productively outline not only the particular models, but more importantly their development: this evolution affects the very concept of the anthology and the role played by foreign literature in the publishing and cultural sector. Based on the featured content, we can identify three main types of anthologies in the Italian publishing field from the 1950s to the 1970s. The first type, already common in the decades prior to the 1950s, is the so-called 'quaderno di traduzioni' (translation notebook), where the selection of poetic materials is based not on the capital carried by foreign poetry, but on that of the translator as the mediator *par excellence*. In the 1960s, however, the translation notebooks would see their presence diminished in the catalogues of the publishing houses examined here. Gradually, publishers moved towards other cultural products. First, they broadened their literary horizons and shifted towards a more diverse range of foreign cultures with sporadic anthologies that shift, at least theoretically, to a 'world' dimension, nonetheless maintaining firmly the role of the editor. These are the 'antologie mondiali' [world anthologies]. In the Italian field of cultural studies, the term 'mondiale' has been widely used as a synonym for Goethe's *Weltliteratur* (Bond, 2014: 416), and this partly tallies with its uncritical use on the part of 1960s Italian editors. However, if world history usually transcends the national as a category of analysis (Clavin, 2005: 435), this is not the case for the Italian 'antologie mondiali', which are instead firmly rooted in national literature. In the context of such a taxonomy, the term also relates in part to a 'global' perspective related to the phenomenon of increased connection (before 1980s globalisation) in the European cultural space and beyond, still articulated around the role of the nation (Sapiro, 2009b: 5–25). Secondly, anthologies presenting poets belonging to the same foreign country or, somewhat uncritically, to the same geo-linguistic area started to grow in popularity. The 'antologie di Paese' [anthology of a country] – borrowing Davico Bonino's words from an earlier chapter – would become the most popular publishing option, indicating a new interest in the politico-cultural topicality of foreign poetry, but also a myopic perception of such concepts as language, culture, and nationhood.

3.2 Evolution of the anthological models: the sunset of the translation notebooks

Still at the beginning to the 1960s, translation notebooks represented a means of consecration (Heilbron and Sapiro, 2002: 3) for the publishing houses. The value of the publication lay in the literary quality of the translated text more than the cultural meaning derived from the selection of foreign poetry (Billiani, 2007b: 152). The cultural operation behind the translation notebook was intended to increase both the prestige of the translator, by consecrating their talents in dialogue with authoritative foreign poets, and of the publisher. This implied at times a less critical engagement with transnational literary movements for the scope of the target text. Throughout the 1960s, however, the diminishing prestige of this format reflected the decline of the Hermetic tradition, which relied on the anthology format, and the rise of a more meaningful dialogue with transnational phenomena in cultural terms.

The translation notebook format was not only exploited by the small-scale publishers, whose structure led them more naturally to embrace this cultural product, but also by the larger-scale publishing houses such as Mondadori and Einaudi as a rapid way of accumulating cultural capital in periods of stagnation. One example is offered by Diego Valeri's translations published at the end of the 1950s, when Mondadori was trying to regain some centrality in the field by welcoming translations into its catalogue while also capitalising on the canonical status of some of its long-term contributors. The publishing process relied essentially on the literary figure embodied by Valeri, as demonstrated by the paratextual materials. Vittorio Sereni called for a 'notarella sul tradurre' [brief note on translating], that 'accentua – e giustifica – il criterio personale della scelta e del "modo" della traduzione' [would highlight – and justify – the personal criterion of the choice and the 'mode' of translation].[4] Sereni intended to enhance the subjectivity of the creative act, which was deeply connected to the intellectual prestige of the Veneto-based poet, already featured in 'Lo Specchio',[5] a full professor of history of Italian literature at the University of Padua and tireless contributor to literary journals such as *L'Approdo*.

Valeri's note – an excerpt from one of his university lectures (Albanese and Nasi, 2015: 177) – bolstered his status as a poet-translator through two precise rhetorical strategies. On the one hand, he emphasised his ability as a translator, remarking upon the linguistic difficulties that emerged from translating both French poets – due to the consonance with the Italian

---

4   FAAM, *SEAI*, file Diego Valeri, Vittorio Sereni, 29 December 1958.
5   Before 1959 (the year of publication of *Lirici tedeschi* [German Poets], his first translation notebook), Valeri published four titles in less than ten years: *Terzo tempo* [Third Time] (1950), *Poesie vecchie e nuove* [New and Old Poems] (1952), *Fantasie veneziane* [Venetian Fantasies] (1953), and *Il flauto a due canne* [Double-reeded Flute] (1958).

language, which would deceive the translator (Valeri, 1960: 316) – and German poets. He made the readers acutely aware of the:

> più arduo, certamente, compito del traduttore italiano, che ha da piegare ai suoi fini, e senza che lo sforzo si avverta, una lingua elaborata e definitivamente fissata nella sua morfologia e nelle sue articolazioni sintattiche da sette secoli d'ininterrotto travaglio letterario. (Valeri, 1959: 210)

> [more demanding, certainly, task of the Italian translator, who, without making his efforts known, has to bend to his needs an articulate language, definitely fixed on its morphology and its syntax from seven centuries of uninterrupted literary labour]

On the other hand, Valeri focused on the need for the translator not to be simply a philological expert, but to possess that 'sensitivity' which would ensure that one was unequivocally recognised as a poet. In short, to overcome that untranslatability of poetry famously suggested by Benedetto Croce, Valeri promoted translation as a poetry exercise in the target language. The role of foreign authors was in the end made relative and subject to the purposes of the poet-translator, as shown in the continued Hermetic influence in his selection of German (mostly Romantic or decadent, spanning Goethe, Hölderlin, von Hoffmansthal, Rilke, and Hermann Hesse) and French Parnassians (from sixteenth-century classicism to nineteenth-century Symbolism, including Louise Labé, Pierre de Ronsard, Joachim du Bellay, Charles Baudelaire, Paul Verlaine, Arthur Rimbaud, and Stephan Mallarmé, among others). Such a 'classical' take was firmly in line with Valeri's own poetic practice, which 'resisted the exorbitant formal tendencies of his contemporaries' (Peterson, 2010b: 114), and 'represent[ed] the continuation of the lineage of Baudelaire in Italy' – a poet praised by Valeri for his combination of innovative content and rigorous form (Peterson, 2010b: 127). Valeri stated that his choice avoided any historical literary hierarchy – something, we might argue, that was difficult to avoid, at least indirectly – thus reiterating the centrality of his own translating activity as poetic endeavour: 'quest[e] raccolt[e] [...] non ambiscono a dare, in traduzione italiana, il *meglio* della lirica tedesca e di quella francese. Esse vogliono essere soltanto due *antologie delle mie traduzioni poetiche*' [These collections [...] do not strive to give, in Italian translation, the *best* of both German and French poetry. They want simply to be two *anthologies of my poetic translations*] (Valeri, 1959: 212).

With similar objectives in mind, in the mid-1960s Einaudi discussed publishing translation notebooks as a potential means of increasing the prestige of the brand-new 'Collezione di poesia'. To draw on the cultural capital of the translators, Giulio Einaudi proposed to Attilio Bertolucci the publication of 'un quaderno di A.B. traduttore' [a notebook by A.B. translator],[6] a project that never came to fruition, while in its catalogue we find *Quaderno francese del secolo* [French Notebook of the Century] (1965), again by Valeri, probably for the exact same reasons mentioned earlier.

Yet in a matter of years cultural and pragmatic reasons accelerated the decline of the translation notebooks. Throughout the 1960s there was an increasing willingness, on the part of both editors and publishers, to offer their readers literary choices that could spark political debate, in line with the cultural needs of new audiences, as we have seen particularly in relation to Einaudi. Translation notebooks were seen in part as a parochial reflux of the Hermetic tradition and therefore rejected. In addition, the anthological model of the *quaderno* tended to lose value with the passing of time, meaning it became less profitable. This was most probably due to its strict link with the figure of the translator, usually more ephemeral than highly recognised international poets who seemed to overcome with ease the limited boundaries of the specialist audience. Publishers preferred to focus on more cohesive books which over time could gather established cultural capital, and ultimately economic profit.

From that perspective, despite the normally conservative habitus typical of large-scale publishing, since the beginning of the 1960s Mondadori had started to voice doubts regarding the function of the translation notebooks, which necessarily implied compromising the role of the poet-translator. In this respect, it is worth analysing the events related to Piero Bigongiari's translation notebook, *Il vento d'ottobre: da Alcmane a Dylan Thomas* [October Wind: From Alcmane to Dylan Thomas] (1961). Arnoldo Mondadori initially demonstrated a substantial interest in the book: on 23 January 1959 he stated that the book could complement the relaunch of 'Lo Specchio', in a similar fashion, in principle, to Valeri's translations.[7] Sereni made clear the publishing significance of this translation notebook in terms of the Mondadori reader's expectations: the translation notebook would assume the guise of a small booklet, allowing the readers to step into the poet-translator's shoes and

---

6 AE, file Attilio Bertolucci, GE, 14 September 1964.
7 FAAM, *SEAI*, file Piero Bigongiari, Arnoldo Mondadori, 23 January 1959.

assemble their favourite poems.⁸ In other words, the translation notebook served the purpose of creating a bond between readers and translators that would nurture the readers' ambitions and virtually elevate their status, arguably as a source of distinction.

The publishing project, however, was greeted with resistance by the editorial board. Echoing the case of Bigongiari's poems, according to Fortini, the issue revolved around the limits of offering to readers a cultural perspective strictly linked to the now stagnant Florentine Hermeticism, of which Bigongiari was felt to be among the less convincing representatives. In his evaluation, Fortini expressed concerns around an inadequately discerning editorial selection, which reflected a cautious resort to the foreign element through already widely known authors; the only feature that came out in favour of the translation notebook was the potential it could display as a work of synthesis recording the relationship between Hermeticism and foreign poetry:

> il libro rappresenta benissimo un gusto ben preciso, quello 'fiorentino' ed 'ermetico', nella sua doppia fase, quella precedente e quella seguente la guerra. Per quella precedente valgono i nomi di Scève, Ronsard, Mallarmé, Éluard; per quella successiva, gli endecasillabi che traducono Gregorio di Nazianze e i testi di D. Thomas [...] Fatte dunque tutte le riserve [...] bisogna dire che una antologia di questo tipo è, come in uno 'Specchio' retrovisivo, esemplare e, a suo modo, utile.⁹
>
> [The book represents very well a precise 'Florentine' and 'Hermetic' taste, in its double phase, before and after the war. For the one preceding the war, we could list such names as Scève, Ronsard, Mallarmé, Éluard; for the one following the war, the hendecasyllabic translation of Gregory of Nazianzus and the poems by Dylan Thomas [...] With all these reservations [...] we have to say that an anthology like this is, as a review, exemplary and, in its way, useful.]

In addition to the list of poets just mentioned, the book also included Pierre Reverdy, Francis Ponge, and René Char, all inspired by 1930s French Surrealism; Jorge Guillén, representative of the '27 generation in Spain; Rafael

---

8   Ibid., note by Vittorio Sereni to Alberto Mondadori, 1 June 1959.
9   FAAM, *SEAI*, file Piero Bigongiari, reader's report by Franco Fortini on *Vento d'ottobre*, 3 June 1959.

Alberti; the modernist Hart Crane; and intriguingly a Hermetic four-word poem 'Mattina' [Morning] by Giuseppe Ungaretti, translated into French, as well as a poem written in French by Bigongiari himself. Bigongiari's Hermetic taste not only influenced the selection of poems, but also the linguistic features of the translation. According to Fortini's reading, Bigongiari's version was emulative of Ungaretti's Hermetic conciseness exemplified precisely in that 'M'illumino d'immenso' [lit. immensity illumines me],[10] while the footnotes added a lyric and less lucid tone,[11] almost a paratextual exercise of that 'embellishment' technique.

It is interesting to note how, among all the translated poets, Fortini preferred Bigongiari's attempts at translating Dylan Thomas, since the British author's style seemed to purify the Florentine poet's Hermetic voice of the obsolete pattern work of 'cadenze pre-belliche' [pre-war cadences].[12] Capoferro has outlined numerous shortcomings in Bigongiari's translations, including a misleading elevation of register and an inability to maintain an alliterative rhythm. Viewing these inadequacies in their intertextual dimension makes evident a certain informality of style in Bigongiari's translations as opposed to his poems (Capoferro, 2004: 313), thus partly corroborating Fortini's evaluation. Significantly, Fortini's remark on the linguistic function of rejuvenating outmoded styles is not only telling of his perspective against Croce's idea of poetry's untranslatability, but also of his idea of translation as active engagement with foreign languages in terms of cultural, and here linguistic, renewal (Albanese and Nasi, 2015: 148). Following Fortini's mixed reading, Sereni's doubts about the risks of this publication filtered through in a letter to Bigongiari on 2 February 1960. Here, the editor-in-chief at Mondadori gave rather feeble excuses – saturated publishing programmes and excessive publication costs – while the actual deterrent was probably uncertainty over whether the work would sell well. The publication of *Il vento d'ottobre* had therefore to wait until the following year, in 1961; the project envisaged a print run of about 2,990, in line with the average numbers for 'Lo Specchio' titles, and a hardback edition at 2,000 Italian lire.

A further indication that both cultural and publishing orientations had started to envisage a new model of the translation notebook – more attentive to the cultural weight of foreign poetry, but where the translator still maintained a pivotal role – was the anthology edited in 1967 by Joyce

10 Ibid.
11 Ibid.
12 Ibid.

Lussu. This publication is of particular interest for the main argument of this book, insofar as it signals the desire on the part of some Italian intellectuals for translation to allow them to cross cultures based on shared narratives of political commitment. Beyond the scope of our study, it also alerts us to one of the first publishing ventures in which women translators were also the sole editors of their books thanks to the cultural capital acquired in their professional fields.

The proposed title was emblematic of the central role embodied by the translator's perspective: *Tradurre poesia* contained not only the cultural but also the most significant political encounters that the translator had engaged in throughout her intellectual activity as a militant anti-fascist. Lying outside academic or (post-)Hermetic networks, Lussu had a radical conception of translation as 'a participative, collaborative and conversational praxis' (Taronna, 2017: 153). Lussu used to reach out to peripheral and dissident poets in languages she could not speak through an intermediary language, engaging with them in oral conversations or asking them to self-translate their works; this not only escaped any stale idea of philological accuracy but put forward a radical act of *trans*cultural rewriting. In broader terms, she conceived translation as both a public act, insofar as translations can tell a story, and a collaborative endeavour, in which she, as a cultural mediator, was able to give voice to minor poets (Capancioni, 2011: 178), or enable in theory, in Gayatri Spivak's terms (1988), the subaltern to speak. In allowing the authors to 'intervene' also in the paratexts (notes/prefaces) as part of their interlocutory relationship, Lussu could raise awareness of political inequalities without exoticising them (Taronna, 2017: 158–62). It would, however, be disingenuous to fail to perceive that Lussu's attempt implicitly, though perhaps unconsciously, created a hierarchy between the availability of her means in terms of bestowing visibility and the lack thereof of the source authors; nonetheless her project was particularly innovative vis-à-vis the common perception of poetry translation as a mainly individual, aesthetic exercise for the purposes of the target poet's recognition.

We can also notice an interesting shift in approach, in line with the Italian anti-colonial internationalism that 'saw decolonization movements of the 1960s and 1970s as an ideal continuation, in the postwar period, of anti-fascist struggle', but failed to critically engage with Italy's own colonial past (Srivastava, 2018: 13). Lussu's book suggested a new conception of space based on a subjective, and markedly politico-literary, perspective on borders, which traced an innovative geography that avoided such concepts as nationhood and language, and found its meaning in a poetry translation that was a manifestation of a cosmopolitan 'umanesimo' [humanism] in terms of shared values and solidarity. Borrowing her words from the cover page, poetry translation was:

> non è arido esercizio accademico e filologico sulle complicazioni grammaticali e sintattiche di una lingua [ma] sforzo per comprenderla, è quasi riviverla. Basta solo (ma è indispensabile) avere col poeta il denominatore comune della posizione dell'uomo nei confronti della vita
>
> [not a sterile academic and philological exercise in the grammatical and syntactic hurdles of a language [but] an effort to understand it, to almost relive it. It is enough (but this is essential) to share with the poet the common denominator of a human outlook on life]

According to the editor and translator, her own personal narrative of anti-fascist commitment represented, in practice, a potential platform for this transcultural dialogue. She started from real experiences, which were part of her own militant narrative, and in the poem selection she, according to Forti's reader's report, privileged foreign authors who could conjugate poetic activity and political commitment, able to 'realizzare la propria autentica vocazione creativa e poetica all'interno di movimenti di liberazione di pari passo con la loro azione politica' [fulfil their own authentic creative and poetic vocation within the movements of freedom, hand in hand with their political action].[13] The geographical space was particularly composite, spanning from Denmark to Angola, so that the authors presented did not seem to have any linguistic or geographical affinities but instead shared values such as 'l'amore per il mondo, l'impegno nella lotta per modificarlo, la carica e l'impegno rivoluzionario in senso storico e politico' [love for the world, political commitment in the struggle to modify it, revolutionary drive in a historical and political sense] (Lussu, 1967: 5). This proposed line of continuity between her own perspective and that of the source authors appears, once again, unaware of the different power relationships they enjoyed, both as compared with Lussu and among each other (also, interestingly, no female authors were included in the book).

Beyond these shortcomings, publishing concerns also emerged. From a strictly thematic viewpoint, Sereni aimed to offer readers an evocative overview without political implications, hence his suggestion that Lussu would

---

13 FAAM, SEAI, file Joyce Lussu, Marco Forti's reader's report on *Incontri con i poeti*, 13 October 1965.

need to 'rendere meno perentorie le conclusioni del confronto tra la politica turca e quella dei partiti italiani' [make the conclusions with regard to Turkish politics as well as Italian political parties less dogmatic].[14] Mondadori could not play the dissident and polemical role that smaller publishers advocated; it was not 'le edizioni *Avanti!* né Porticati né Guanda!' [Avanti! Editions, nor Porticati or Guanda!][15] The issue lay, furthermore, in making such heterogeneous material appealing to Mondadori's 'lettore medio' [average reader],[16] that is, a reader who is generally quite knowledgeable, with a covert political interest, intrigued by innovative literary movements but, at the same time, in need of paratextual references to explain less common cultural territories. Lussu did furnish the book with biographies, separated from the poems but still part of the text, as evidence of the fact that individual history participated in the poetic production. Yet Forti advised supplying bio-bibliographies of all the poets presented, in order to guide the reader.[17] Notes were also required because Lussu tended to adopt a foreignising or 'indigenising' approach in marking and exposing readers to foreign political terms (Taronna, 2017: 157), and left foreign words in the text to enrich the target audience's vocabulary and knowledge of specific political contexts. Drawing on Spivak, it was a conscious political act to allow the subaltern to speak the language that the colonisers had forbidden (Lombardo, 2008: 40), but, we argue, with the limitations outlined earlier.

Mondadori's wariness regarding the content and paratextual apparatus of this eccentric publishing project was offset by the opportunity it presented to exploit the appeal of new poetic elements and attract a wider audience. Following Lussu's heterodox habitus and enthusiastic approach, such a special translation notebook could revitalise Mondadori's conservative reputation. At the same time, the book adhered to a less revolutionary, more didactic trend that could project it beyond the restricted circle of experts, with easy-to-follow divisions according to geopolitical areas and translations that responded well to the demands of the aforementioned 'lettore medio'.[18] As a result, Forti advised a change of title to *Incontri coi poeti del terzo mondo* [Encounters

---

14 FAAM, *SEAI*, file Joyce Lussu, Vittorio Sereni, 21 April 1966.
15 Ibid., note by Vittorio Sereni to Marco Forti's reader's report, 18 May 1966.
16 Ibid., Marco Forti to Vittorio Sereni, 16 September 1966.
17 FAAM, *SEAI*, file Joyce Lussu, Marco Forti's reader's report on *Incontri con i poeti*, 13 October 1965.
18 Ibid.

with Third World Poets] as being more appealing to the readership,[19] perhaps reminiscent of the Third Worldist interests shown by Italian intellectuals in those decades, but also with colonialist connotations. Lussu rejected that title, but the final product did include the additional details requested by the editors.[20] The texts chosen by Lussu, often anonymous political chants, could not be inserted in 'Lo Specchio' as they would undermine its prestige and clash with the generally more canonical offer.[21] They ultimately found a more appropriate home in the general series.

In the end, what was the function of this anthology? Sereni's answer to Lussu's query as to whether the chosen foreign poets should be previously unpublished in Italy, or whether they could have already been published in journals (but not books),[22] indicates that the anthology was intended to tap into the wider cultural operation that connected Italy with transnational movements historically. The selection criterion was not just that of seeking unpublished authors – literary discoveries that, we might argue, better suited small publishers – but that of 'l'informazione' [providing information], in the same way as, Sereni explained in the letter, publishing an innovative poem by an already established author would constitute a relevant addition to an ongoing literary and historical dialogue.[23]

The translation notebooks privileged wider historical overviews, often determined by canonical perceptions, of foreign cultures, and utilised them tactically to increase the prestige of the poet-translator within the national literary field. Notwithstanding the still fundamental role of the translator in articulating the relationships with the target culture, with Lussu's anthology the demands for a dialogue with foreign cultures moved progressively towards a – relatively – more critical engagement with key poetic facts or products that could advance the audience's understanding of cultural phenomena or movements at the transnational level. Similarly, the anthological formats which found space in the publishing catalogues in the early 1960s, starting from the 'world' anthologies, signalled the slow decline of the Hermetic idea of the translation notebook and the gradual passage towards an alternative, although not yet fulfilled, presentation of foreign poetry.

19 Ibid.
20 Ibid., Marco Forti to Vittorio Sereni, 16 September 1966.
21 Ibid., Marco Forti to Vittorio Sereni, 24 October 1966. See also Del Zoppo, 2022: 138.
22 FAAM, *SEAI*, file Joyce Lussu, to Vittorio Sereni, 8 July 1963.
23 Ibid., Vittorio Sereni, 16 July 1963.

3.3 Beyond Hermeticism? The role of the 'antologie mondiali'

At the end of the 1950s a new type of poetry anthology emerged which gathered together a range of diverse linguistic, cultural, and geographical areas. In a more pointed way than we observed in *Tradurre poesia*, in these 'antologie mondiali' the geographical space was broadened but national borders remained solid: in the list of contents, poets were rigidly located within national segments ('British poets', 'Spanish poets', etc.); the theoretical framework developed by the editors served to draw out the commonalities of the different sections and avoid excessive sectarianism. Though the titles suggested a publication with historical value (*Poesia straniera del Novecento, Poeti stranieri del Novecento*), specific poetic and cultural realities were not the main factors that shaped the anthology. Rather, the anthology was a geo-poetic map, allowing the editors to reaffirm their own perspectives, whether aesthetic or ideological, and to carve out their position in a transnational space of affiliated poetics. The role of the editor's symbolic capital came back to the fore in these anthologies, in a similar way as it did in translation notebooks. The difference this time was that the editors' prestige entered into negotiation with the historical and informative nature of the 'antologia mondiale', negotiations which also depended on the trajectory of each specific publishing house within the wider cultural and literary field in Italy and beyond at the beginning of the 1960s. We can thus see the 'antologia mondiale' as a transition point between the obsolete model of the translation notebook, where the editor had a pivotal function, and the 'antologie di Paese', which would prevail from the mid-1960s, and in which translation practice became increasingly distant from the editor's own poetic exercise.

The possibility of having editor and publisher coincide was, if certainly less frequent, not impossible in the artisan-like structure of Italian publishing, as in the case of *Poeti stranieri del Novecento tradotti da poeti italiani* (1956), both edited and published by Vanni Scheiwiller. While the featured content places this cultural product in the category of the 'antologie mondiali', its format and purpose were far from being simply a textbook. As with other publications, Scheiwiller privileged the encounter between poet-translator and foreign poet, where the translation was mainly a stylistic exercise for the poet-translator. The anthology lost its evaluative function for foreign literature to express instead the dispositions of the editor/publisher, and in practical terms was largely indistinguishable from the translation notebook.

As we can read in a publisher's note at the end of the book, Scheiwiller put together translations which primarily satisfied his own stylistic sensitivity rather than the literary hierarchies developed by the critics, who he sarcastically dubbed 'specialists'. This less philological trend reaffirmed Scheiwiller's refined translation practice, which interestingly, in its own way, intended to move away from Hermeticism:

> questa raccolta di POETI STRANIERI del '900 tradotti da poeti italiani ha carattere di *strenna* – non è un panorama critico – e segue la linea del gusto dei poeti (intendi *poeti traduttori* e pochi *traduttori poeti*, di mio gusto). Quindi si spiega l'esclusione di qualche poeta 'maggiore' e l'inclusione di altri meno noti o meno 'importanti' (per gli 'specialisti'). (Scheiwiller, 1956: 130)

> [this collection of twentieth-century FOREIGN POETS has a character of *strenna* – this is not a critical overview – and follows the line of taste of those poets (I mean poet-translators and a handful of translator-poets that I like). Hence, the exclusion of some 'big' poets and the inclusion of some less well-known or less 'relevant' (according to the 'specialists')]

In the preface to the anthology – a reprint of an appendix to the anthology *Poeti antichi e moderni tradotti da Lirici Nuovi* [Ancient and Modern Poets Translated by New Poets] (1945) – Sergio Solmi reiterated this point by advocating that he went beyond a dichotomy between 'literary' translator and 'personal' translator. The former was seen as a diligent driver of the poetic text in another language, who maintained content and form as much as possible, although that honest practice gave shape to a 'una scolorita suggestione dell'originale, incorporata in un esemplare letterario che rappresenterà tuttavia, fatalmente, il punto di vista – linguistico, estetico, storico – da cui opera il traduttore. Poesia in iscatola' [colourless reflection of the original, embodied in a literary element that will nonetheless represent, fatally, the linguistic, aesthetic, historical perspective from which the translator operates. Poetry-in-a-box] (Scheiwiller, 1956: 5). 'Personal' translators – which would seem to strike a chord with Folkart's later highly individualistic approach (2007) – were accused, instead, of suffocating the particularities of foreign poetry in their interpretations.

A third modality beyond these ineffective strategies of, respectively, bland foreignisation and overwhelming domestication, had therefore to be pursued: one that could balance a relevant proximity to the source text with the experienced translator's personal engagement with its foreignness. This entailed not simply an ability on the part of the translator to 'imitate' the tone and style of the source text (Albanese and Nasi, 2015: 144), but arguably the insertion of that translation within the poet's domain, his 'respiro profondo' [deep breath] (Scheiwiller, 1956: 5). Drawing on Sela-Sheffy (2014: 50) and her use of the notion of 'identity negotiation' in creating personal identities as complementary to Bourdieu's habitus, we note how Solmi identified here several 'specific role-images' and 'occupational ethoses' in order 'to make sense of [his] job and claim occupational dignity'; more interestingly, these 'role-images' prompt the employment of certain norms in translators' performances. Following Solmi's reasoning, translators spurned strictly informative approaches and saw the foreign text as a means to develop their own stylistic horizons. Although Scheiwiller rejected Macrí-style philological translators – and with him, Hermetic approaches more broadly – his 'antologie mondiali' moved again in the lineage of the Hermetic-inspired translation notebooks, whose survival seemed to be prolonged in the small-scale publishing houses which still relied on the *plaquette* as a refined encounter between poet and translator.

The idealistic, and to some extent radical, perspective adopted by Scheiwiller could not be assumed by larger-scale publishers with their bureaucratic constraints. This did not mean that editors could not impose their own perspective, as this depended on the power relationships within the publishing structure. As a result, a return to the translation notebook was still possible, as with *Poesia straniera del Novecento* [Twentieth-Century Foreign Poetry], published in 1958 by Garzanti and edited by Attilio Bertolucci. As a poet, translator, and intellectual attentive to foreign literature and fascinated in particular with late nineteenth-century poets (Lagazzi, 1981), Bertolucci was esteemed by the often fickle Livio Garzanti, who gave the Emilia-based poet free rein (Ferretti, 2004: 405). In the end, the anthology reflected more the elite interests of Bertolucci than the popular intentions of a large publisher such as Garzanti.

The extended geo-linguistic focus of *Poesia straniera del Novecento* broadened the national poetic boundaries well beyond the more well-trodden European paths by including Danish, Czech, Russian, Hungarian, and Greek poets. This was not driven by the desire to offer a wider audience a more extensive perspective on contemporary foreign poetry, but addressed a specialist audience of linguistic experts in these particular literatures (Bertolucci, 1958: xi). In line with the ornate style coursing through the editor's veins, the selection of poems aimed to provide readers with access to predominantly unpublished poetic voices, saving the latter from the oblivion to which they would otherwise be condemned, as Bertolucci maintained in his introduction (1958: xii). Specifically, within the various geographical sections into which the anthology was divided, French poetry was assigned a primary role, both from a qualitative and quantitative viewpoint, and was the first and largest section. The choice of poets was nonetheless less canonical and included peripheral voices such as the Christian-inspired Pierre Emmanuel, and René Guy Cadou, who was much influenced by Pierre Reverdy's surrealist poetry but was certainly less well-known.

If we look closer, though, such a different geo-poetic map also mirrored Bertolucci's attempt to legitimise his position within the Italian literary field. Connected to such names as Charles Baudelaire and William Wordsworth, Bertolucci's 'pastoral poetics [was] anything but naive or rustic' (Peterson, 2010a: 95), and his mixed-genre prose even demonstrated postmodernist traces (Jewell, 1992): the poet would seem to be reaffirming his prestigious place to his readers. In the paratextual discourse, particularly in the bio-bibliographical profiles presented at the end of the book, typical of a larger-scale publishing production, Bertolucci moved towards a re-evaluation of his literary work. First, he elaborated an indirect simile in placing the poems of French poet Toulet, who critics compared to Bertolucci himself, alongside Apollinaire's *Alcools* (Bertolucci, 1958: 797), defined as 'il più caro e il più nuovo poeta del primo Novecento' [the dearest and most innovative poet of the early twentieth century] (Bertolucci, 1958: 799). Later still, with regard to the *fantasistes* school that Toulet belonged to, Bertolucci rejected the critique of parochialism that had been levelled at these poets, suggesting once again a mediated reconsideration of his own style in terms of attention to local traditions and of the genuine relationship with nature that he shared with them (Bertolucci, 1958: 801).

Still in the context of re-evaluating minor poets, Bertolucci's anthology proceeded to reconsider some consolidated values of both English, Irish, and US poetry, according to a 'rediscovery' that had deep roots in the nineteenth century. As such, the anthology included Bertolucci's most beloved poets, such as Thomas Hardy for his celebratory localism of Dorsetshire, or W.B. Yeats, who was reassigned a prestigious role as 'il più puro, oltre che il più grande, poeta della letteratura inglese del Novecento' [the purest, as well as the greatest, poet of twentieth-century English literature]. There were, however, doubts concerning Auden, Eliot, and Pound, whose radical formal experimentalism was put into question. In particular, despite his admiration for Auden's wordplay, Bertolucci criticised the Anglo-American poet for his lack of spontaneity (Bertolucci, 1958: 819), a necessary criterion that poets had to satisfy in order to be included in the anthology. Similarly, Bertolucci highlighted Eliot's cold, intellectual vein, which greatly influenced world poetry, but according to the Italian poet only 'in senso tecnico' [from a technical viewpoint] (Bertolucci, 1958: 817). Finally, on the same page, it was Pound who received an even more dubious judgement:

> alcune cose ci convincono appieno, molte altre meno; il furore, più che impeto, verbale che nasconde? Quando potremo leggere, compiuti, i *Cantos* [...] saremo in grado di dire se oltre che un grande formatore di poeti, Pound stesso è un grande poeta.
>
> [some things seem to us fully convincing, others much less; what does the verbal fury, more than passion, hide? When we can read, fully finished, the *Cantos* [...] we will be able to say whether, beyond being a great mentor for poets, Pound himself is a great poet.]

The distance from Pound's experimentalism and the attention paid to the delicate tones of the *fantasistes* was fundamentally typical of Bertolucci's poetic practice; yet Bertolucci's critique aligned his stance with the poetic generation of the 1910s and contrasted sharply with both the Hermetic inclination towards Eliot and the unreserved inclusion of Pound as a tutelary deity demonstrated by Scheiwiller.

In the translation practice, *Poesia straniera del Novecento* expressed a different intent to the stylistic exercises of the translation notebooks, as per the objectives of the large-scale publisher Garzanti. Bertolucci notified the reader that the translation was a 'grigio surrogato' [grey substitute] (Bertolucci, 1958: x), apt to offer a rendering that most closely reflected the source text. The translation method that he proposed was that of 'piccole infedeltà ai fini di una fedeltà vera' [small infidelities for the purpose of a truer fidelity] (Bertolucci, 1958: x). It is almost an *excusatio non petita*: the editor seemed to be aware of the skilled linguistic abilities of his audience and to want to justify the distance they might experience from the original version. Borrowing his own words, Bertolucci was conscious that a growing proportion of Italians (especially poetry readers, who generally represent an elite sector of mass culture) could access the source texts and clearly identify the differences from the target texts. Those readers tended to use translations as a support, and providing them with parallel texts enabled them to discover (or read again) the foreign poem in the original language:

> E poiché l'italiano medio va sempre più imparando le lingue straniere [...] ci potrà pure essere più d'uno che sarà grato a questo volume di avergli

fatto per la prima volta posare gli occhi su versi come 'Ce toit tranquille où marchent les colombes' oppure 'That is no country for old men. The young...' oppure 'A la cinco de la tarde' oppure 'O Brunnen-Mund, du gebender, du Mund'. (Bertolucci, 1958: x)

[And since it has become more and more commonplace for the average Italian to learn foreign languages [...] there may be more than one reader who will be grateful to this book for encouraging them to look at such lines as 'This quiet roof where doves walk' or 'That is no country for old men. The young...' or 'At five in the afternoon' or 'O fountain mouth, you giver, you mouth' for the first time.]

Still linked to traditional practices, however, the anthology kept the traces of the reception of foreign poetry within Italian culture (Capoferro, 2004: 317), insofar as it privileged versions which were, by then, obsolete. In addition to contributions by one of the most representative critics of the 1930s, Emilio Cecchi, there were several translations by Traverso, as well as Montale and Ungaretti. The result was that an anthology of the late 1950s still clung to the translation zeal and talent of a past season. Notwithstanding the intentions of a different textual practice, the move away from the translation notebook happened only at a theoretical level. Indeed, the anthology still drew on a sector of collaborators who were rooted in interwar Hermeticism and maintained many features of the translation notebooks, primarily in relation to the role played by the editor. The passage towards new anthological models was therefore extremely slow not only for small-scale, but also for large-scale publishers.

Some partial elements of renewal can be identified in the publications of medium-scale publishing houses such as Einaudi. An intriguing combination of the legacy of the translation notebooks and the new format of the 'antologie di Paese' was *Poeti del Novecento italiani e stranieri* [Twentieth-Century Foreign and Italian Poets], published in 1960 as part of Einaudi's 'Supercoralli' series, and edited by Elena Croce. Rather than being an Einaudi cultural product, we could more appropriately define this book as the work of the editor, in possession of significant cultural capital derived from her influence in the Italian cultural field, as a prominent figure of the intelligentsia, active essayist, and founder of literary journals. In crafting *Poeti del Novecento italiani e stranieri*, there were nonetheless instances where Croce's habitus needed to negotiate with Einaudi, particularly in relation to the translation modalities. The latter progressed more systematically towards a mere reading support, moving away from the model of the translation notebook (Milani, 2013a: 8–11).

Daughter of Benedetto and wife of Raimondo Craveri, with whom she ran the journal *Lo Spettatore italiano*, Elena [Craveri] Croce coordinated the salon of the Craveris as a lively forum of debate for both Italian and foreign intellectuals (*Elena Croce*, 1999: 85). She was also active in politics, with the proposal of a historic compromise between Catholics and communists (*Elena Croce*, 1999: 30). In addition, she was among the founders of the journal *Botteghe Oscure*, and an advisor to the journal on account of her capital in social networks (Sullam, 2016: 171). Interestingly, her obstinacy in the role as journal editor-in-chief led her to refer to the products as *her* journals, because 'anche se vi è stata una serie di direttori, fu la mia ottusa tenacia a farle' [even if there had been a series of editors-in-chief, it was my stubborn perseverance that made them] (*Elena Croce*, 1999: 31), indicating how marked her presence would be as an editor and the force of her intellectual stance.

Poeti stranieri del Novecento italiani e stranieri enacted a process of (re)legitimation of her main theoretical and cultural assets through the strategic use of paratexts, as Capoferro underlines:

> fungendo da riduzioni portatili del canone, le antologie possono reificare un progetto culturale, dargli peso e sostanza; grazie alla loro agilità possono garantirgli una diffusione più rapida, persino prolungarne la vita: non è un caso che *Poeti del Novecento italiani e stranieri* sia uno degli ultimi sussulti del crocianesimo agonizzante. (Capoferro, 2004: 321)

> [by functioning as portable reductions of the canon, anthologies can reify a cultural project, give it weight and substance; thanks to their agility, they can ensure it has a more rapid diffusion, even extend its life: it is not by chance that *Poeti del Novecento italiani e stranieri* was one of the last thrusts of the agonising crocianesimo]

In the introduction, Croce asserted that she was moving away from conventional value schemes by adopting Crocean-historicist terms and by approaching the selection of poets from an aesthetic instead of an 'ethical-political' perspective (Croce, 1960: vi). She wanted to trace a 'history' of contemporary poetry, in which the evaluative categories coincided with the search for a 'linguaggio creativo, nuovo ed originale e al tempo stesso classico e perenne' [creative language, new, original and at the same time classic and eternal] (Croce, 1960: vi). The editor thus shunned a purely informative function, privileging instead an aesthetic approach.

Roles and positions within world literature were (re-)interpreted from this new viewpoint, and both cultural and symbolic capitals were redistributed. This reveals, once again, how Italian intellectuals sought to engage with transnational movements and relate them to the developments of the contemporary literary field, either by questioning or celebrating the latter; yet the evaluation here tended to anchor transnational features within domestic aesthetic coordinates. The post-war documentary value of French poetry and the prestigious role it had enjoyed with the literary avant-gardes was now felt as obsolete (Croce, 1960: x). On the contrary, Spanish poetry found a much more central position as the 'misura più alta della moderna poesia europea' [best example of modern European poetry] (Croce, 1960: xii), thanks to the authors that inspired the poetic period in Spain in the early twentieth century: Machado, Lorca, Jiménez, Guillén, and, more recently, Alberti. According to Croce, they all successfully moved the poetic axis towards a classical tradition. We see already the editor embracing the canonised line of Spanish poets who had been widely translated in Italy before and after the Second World War, but with a distinct aesthetic label ('classical') which elevated them above historical events – particularly their political activism in the Spanish Civil War which neorealism had consistently drawn upon.

Associated with the contemporary Spanish tradition, British poetry was re-evaluated starting from the Irish poet Yeats, as had Bertolucci; the two evaluations are not superimposable, though, as here the rediscovery is perceived in terms of retaining traditional and popular roots (Croce, 1960: xiv). The concept of 'popular poetry', in relation to art poetry, had a long formulation in Benedetto Croce's thought, and it is worth noting here its potential intuitive function in expressing universal feelings (Bronzini, 1986: 28). In similar terms, Russian poetry found a place in the anthology, but was relegated to a much more peripheral position than Spanish production on account of a supposed lack of an articulate poetic history. German poetry was excluded from the most distinctive ideological movements, such as expressionism, while the overview of US poetry was very brief, due in part to the intellectual attitude that Croce saw in it and did not seem to appreciate. In the preface, the editor devoted in the end only a handful of words to T.S. Eliot, normally privileged by Hermeticism. Croce's intentions were therefore notably different from *Poesia inglese del '900* (1950), edited by Izzo and published by Guanda, in which Eliot's work was a focal point and opened the anthology. This different spatial collocation was also symbolic of the great influence of the US poet on the Hermetic movement that was still prominent in 1950s Italy (Capoferro, 2004: 314). Pound received similar treatment, given his increasing prominence in contemporary cultural debates as an inspirational figure of innovative formal models. Similarly to Bertolucci's anthology, *Poeti italiani e stranieri del Novecento* opposed historical and contemporary formalist movements.

However, the essentially Crocean approach adopted by the editor clashed with the general mindset that Einaudi had promoted since the development of the 'cultural front' in the aftermath of the Second World War,[24] a stance that was made concrete with the publication of Antonio Gramsci's *Quaderni del carcere* [Prison Notebooks] between 1947 and 1951. With this publication, the influence of Gramsci's thought – and particularly the conception of the 'organic' role of the intellectual – became more systematic among Italian thinkers, although mediated by Croce (Gundle, 1995), as intellectuals seemed to hold the opinion that 'the only way to move beyond Croce [appeared to be] through a thorough immersion in Croceanism' (Leavitt, 2017: 396). Emblematic of the process of cultural renewal sought after Fascism, Gramsci, who sustained an in-depth critique of the concept of history as well as art as pure intuition theorised by Croce, was proposed as a model to shape innovative forms of political commitment in cultural production, including publishing practices. Hence, the primary function that Einaudi attributed to publishing the anthology was that of informing readers about foreign literary trends and generating a transnational dialogue that could critically question the current terms of the Italian literary and cultural debate and subvert obsolete acquisitions. Such an intent is exemplified by Calvino's remarks, who through the anthology hoped to 'dare un panorama che serva anche di informazione, oltre che di revisione critica' [give an overview that could serve for information, as well as critical revision]:[25] in other words, a comprehensive selection of contemporary world literature, in which the selective criterion broke from tradition to offer new cultural models. The evaluation of poetry thus became a document of cultural and historical reflection. Nonetheless, it is likely that Einaudi's weak position in the poetry publishing field at the beginning of the 1960s forced the publishing house to rely on Elena Croce's reputation, which explains the final product's aesthetic orientation.

The silence of those who were absent produced an intense echo. In the reviews published in key – and not always ideologically oriented – literary

---

24 See also Billiani, 2007b: 140–41.
25 AE, file Elena Craveri Croce, Italo Calvino, 10 January 1958.

journals, particularly Traverso's assessment in *L'Approdo letterario*, and Luigi Baldacci's scathing comments in *Paragone* (1961),[26] doubts were expressed regarding the lack of a section on South America, Portugal, or Hungary, areas of unrest in the late 1950s and therefore of much cultural interest. Croce explained in her overview that she had deliberately avoided these areas as they merited more than a hasty glance. According to the editor, the results that had already appeared in other anthologies, which she perceived as sterile and superficial, did not do justice to these literatures and cultures:

> È senz'altro un peccato escludere i greci (come gli ungheresi, etc) e gli americolatini: dei quali non si potrebbe mettere il solo Borges [...] Piuttosto varrebbe davvero la pena [...] di fare sia della poesia che della saggistica dell'America latina dei panorami che non siano quelli desolanti sinora apparsi.[27]

> [It is certainly a pity to exclude the Greek poets (as well as the Hungarian, etc.) and the South Americans of whom we feature only Borges [...] What would be of great value [...] is an overview of South American literature and essays that goes beyond the dreary publications we have seen to date.]

In the exact same way, a structural limit is evident in Croce's transnational approach in that she generally privileged cultural capitals derived from already established literatures, in contrast to *Poesia straniera del Novecento*. Once again, this rationale did not conform to Einaudi's vision of the function of the anthology, in which foreign authors active in the lively, global literary debate were a necessary feature so as to consecrate their status and shape the cultural expectations of Italian readers. Calvino lamented, in particular, the lack of such relevant poets as Borges, as the anthology would represent a good platform for the promotion of the Argentinian author,[28] who was in the end included, as well as Cavafy, who not only represented substantial cultural capital that would increase the value of the anthology, but was also already popular in Europe through translations into other languages. Excluding them meant risking falling behind the pace of current cultural debate.[29]

---

26 AE, recensioni, *Poeti del Novecento italiani e stranieri*.
27 AE, file Elena Craveri Croce, to Italo Calvino, 26 September 1960.
28 AE, file Elena Craveri Croce, to Italo Calvino, 23 September 1960.
29 Ibid.

In crafting the anthology, Elena Croce would seem to have moderated her perspective and negotiated with the dispositions of the Turinese publishing house. Though in her introduction, she claimed to have applied a 'criterio oggettivamente estetico' [objectively aesthetic criterion] (Croce, 1960: vii) which avoided ideological influences, the editor appeared on occasion to compromise with Einaudi's more politically oriented approach and selected a number of poets as politically charged carriers who could orientate the field dynamics. On 30 November 1960 Croce informed Fruttero that she would include Erich Kästner in the anthology. Kästner was a German poet of generally anti-conservative views, and she acknowledged that his presence would balance out the contributions of excellent poets whose values were too distant from the anti-fascist Einaudi habitus. The evaluation of critic Gilberto Finzi appears in hindsight an accurate one: 'un fatto non di puro gusto, criterio a cui la Croce si è appellata, ma piuttosto legato a un preciso clima sociale-politico-culturale dominante' [not a product dictated by pure taste only, the criterion that Croce claims, but linked instead to a precise predominant socio-politico-cultural climate].[30]

The compromise between the different habitus of agents involved in the publishing process was also explicit in the actual texts of the anthological product, in which diverse needs had to strike a balance. At times, the result was much more innovative than the 'crocianesimo agonizzante' [agonising Croceanism] that Capoferro (2004: 321) mocked. At the beginning of the 1960s, the cultural environment was rapidly changing, and readers' expectations were projected towards more popular horizons: it was essential to provide 'una interpretazione chiarificatrice del testo' [a clarifying interpretation of the text] for these readers' benefit.[31] Croce's intention was that the crystal-clear presentation of the textual elements would make foreign poetry more accessible to this new readership. Her project challenged the anthologies that preceded it and rejected Bertolucci's obscurity: against what was perceived as a sort of bourgeois 'exquisite salon tokens' – elegant but lacking clarity[32] – she would privilege 'biografie molto molto secche, dati ragionati e basta' [very, very dry biographies, annotated data, that's all].[33]

---

30   AE, *recensioni*, *Poeti del Novecento italiani e stranieri*, n.d.
31   AE, file Elena Craveri Croce, to Luciano Foà, 12 November 1958.
32   AE, file Elena Craveri Croce, to Italo Calvino, 8 November 1958.
33   Ibid.

Translations had therefore to conform to her principles, and Croce affirmed that she was willing to annoy the translator-poets for the sake of clarity.[34]

In textual practice, the function of the anthology entered the wider debate on the role of translation as cultural practice and its potential to question and forge cultural models. Croce proposed a firmly anti-Hermetic conception of poetry translation. This was not only reflected in the choice of poets, who were in part the exact opposite of those predominant at the peak of Hermeticism, but was articulated in the choices of cultural agents, questioning how the practice of translation had inserted these poets into the Italian literary tradition. In the editor's view, the selected translators should not belong to poetic circles but be 'traduttori "accademici" [...] Quindi nutriti di alta dignità letteraria (nonché capaci di tradurre ritmicamente)' ['academic' translators [...] thus nourished with great literary dignity (as well as able to translate with rhythm)].[35] Croce suggested, for instance, Giorgio Melchiori as an English Studies expert, and the assistant of the renowned French Studies professor, De Nardis, for the French-language texts.[36] As such, the anthology would benefit from the specifically academic prestige of the translators and would not fall into the stylistic obscurity of more radical literates.[37] The academic seal would please Einaudi following the early developments of the 'Collezione di poesia'.

Elena Croce put herself forward as a translator for most of the poems, and offered a word-for-word rendering that then had to be copy-edited by a much more 'poetic' hand.[38] She rejected the possibility of a 'pura traduzione interlineare' [pure interlinear translation],[39] as it appeared too difficult; she chose instead an approach informed by formal equivalence, 'letterale seguendo il verso' [with literal rendering, following the line],[40] to be applied to the ex novo translations. Existent versions, such as Traverso's, could be used but – conversely to the ethics of Bertolucci's *Poesia straniera del Novecento* – not assumed as a model.[41] If we compare, for instance, Traverso's version of Yeats's poem 'Sailing to Byzantium', included in Bertolucci's anthology, with Giorgio Melchiori's translation, published in Croce's anthology, the two

34 Ibid.
35 AE, file Elena Craveri Croce, to Luciano Foà, 12 November 1958.
36 Ibid., to Italo Calvino, 8 November 1958.
37 Ibid., to Italo Calvino, 26 October 1958.
38 Ibid.
39 Ibid.
40 Ibid.
41 Ibid.

target texts appear considerably different. Traverso clearly indicates a poetic intention in his attempt to deconstruct the syntagma ('nor is there <u>singing school</u> but studying' / '*e altra non c'è scuola di <u>canto</u>*'), and in adding a poetic rhyme, 'monuments of **its** own magnificence' / '*che studiare i trofei del **proprio** [of his own] vanto*' (Bertolucci, 1958: 272–73). Melchiori's version ('*ne v'è altra scuola di canto se non lo studio / dei monumenti della sua magnificenza*' (Croce, 1960: 26–27) demonstrates instead a more literal adherence to the foreign text, resulting in a more accessible version, both from a syntactical and lexical viewpoint, and more suitably conveying the poet's desire for the unity of physical and metaphysical.

Croce's drive towards clarity of expression bespoke a pragmatism even in terms of marketing. In a letter to Calvino in 1958, Croce advised replacing a translator for the Russian texts with her sister, who was experienced in publishing matters from her role as editor and translator, and who also had an understanding of marketing. In other words, an editor who kept a close eye on readers' expectations. The 5,000 copies sold in the first two years rewarded this more populist strategy, which not only satisfied the need to present material in an intelligible way to readers who were unfamiliar with elite interpretations, but also that of countering the contemporary perception of poetry translation as obsolete, which could harm the potential transnational dialogue with other cultures:

> Grazie ancora per l'Antologia, che mi ha dato tante soddisfazioni di leso provincialismo, e che Calvino dice si sarebbe addirittura anche venduta [...] rivendico quindi i meriti dell'antitecnicismo.[42]
>
> [Thanks again for the anthology which gave me great satisfaction in offending parochial attitudes, and that Calvino says has even been selling [...] I thus claim the credit for this anti-technicism.]

The dialogue between Einaudi and Croce nonetheless indicates how issues related to the translation approach were multifaceted. One significant editing challenge was how to create the necessary harmony between the different translations, partly already published, which were featured in the anthology. The publishing house called for a general uniformity of tone, privileging a certain poetic elaboration since 'le versioni già esistenti

---

42 AE, file Elena Craveri Croce, to GE, 10 January 1962.

(che, come Lei giustamente osserva, è inutile rifare) sono quasi sempre poeticamente "elaborate", in grado "di stare in piedi da sole"' [the already published versions (that, as you [Elena Croce] rightly observe, it is useless to do again) are almost always poetically 'articulate', able to 'stand on their own feet'].[43] This inevitably engendered a selection of textual materials based on the sole criteria of poetic rendering and their ability to imbue the target text with a dignified literary value.[44] An agreement between the intrinsic value of foreign poetry and the insertion of the translated text in the complex literary system of poetry in the Italian language had to be reached.

These theoretical intentions were, however, difficult to put into practice and, in initial drafts, there was some discrepancy between the translations.[45] As Calvino outlined, there were 'quelle che opportunamente seguono un criterio di limpida fedeltà interlineare' [those which appropriately follow a criterion of lucid interlinear faithfulness], and among these he included Croce's own translations, and those which 'vogliono arrivare a una struttura ritmica autonoma' [want to achieve an autonomous rhythmic structure].[46] In addition to the inconsistencies between translations, Calvino also detected shortcomings in relation to that linguistic rigour that Croce put at the top of her priorities. The Einaudi editor lamented that the translation of Ransom's 'The Equilibrist' by Izzo, for instance, failed to take into account a number of idiomatic expressions: *stranger, tread light* became 'o straniero, calpesta la luce' [tread *the* light] instead of 'o straniero, cammina leggero'.[47] In the same poem, the rhetorical effect was misleadingly emphasised by the embellishment produced by the synecdoche 'al di sopra dello scheletro' [above the skeleton] for the line *infatuate of the flesh upon the bones*, denoting an excess of zeal that does not suit the prosaic context of this American poem. Izzo's version appeared to contradict his claim to be an 'ethical' (Morini, 2007: 22–26) translator who had to be humble before the source text, in terms of respecting its integrity and implicitly avoiding unnecessarily personalised or elite practices. Giudici's later translation sounded indeed closer to formal equivalence, maintaining the physicality of the bodily image: 'sia lieve il tuo passo / o viandante' [can your tread be light], and 'attaccata la carne alle ossa' [flesh attached to the bones] (Ransom, 1971: 121).

43   AE, file Elena Craveri Croce, Luciano Foà, 7 November 1958.
44   Ibid.
45   AE, file Elena Craveri Croce, Italo Calvino, 10 April 1959.
46   Ibid.
47   AE, file Elena Craveri Croce, Italo Calvino, 20 May 1959.

More generally, it was the lexical elements that created trouble; the editors lingered on this point and asked for revisions quite often, signalling once again the search for a translation that functioned primarily as a reading support. In e.e. cummings's poem 'Portrait', Izzo twisted the literal English text (*break onetwothreefourfive pidgeons justlikethat*) by turning the pigeons into 'vigliacconi' [cowards], who Buffalo Bill was able to [literally] 'stritolare unoduetrequattrocinque [...] come se niente fosse'.[48] The grotesque hyperbole risked undermining the dynamism of this image, in which Buffalo Bill, armed and at a gallop, smiled at death. In Maria Luisa Spaziani's translations of Toulet's poem, the translator's licence produced an over-correction of the source text, overstating the maritime environment that some lexical items, such as *plage* [beach] or *océan* [ocean], echoed. As a result, the French line *douce aux ramiers, douce aux amants* became 'dolce ai rematori e agli amanti' [sweet to rowers and lovers], when the meaning of the first term was actually simply 'colombi' [doves], as Calvino noticed.[49]

In the final version, lexical accuracy would be re-established, with Spaziani choosing 'tortore' [turtle doves] for *ramiers*, and Izzo modifying his version of 'o straniero, sia lieve il tuo passo'. Yet Izzo for one did not seem to take into account some of Calvino's other revisions, and the published text ultimately offered the same interpretation displayed by the draft translation, as evidence of the constant difficulty in finding some degree of uniformity in the negotiated solutions. Overall, though the editor remained firm in her Crocean-historicist, anti-Hermetic perspective, in a similar way to that observed in the other 'antologie mondiali', the key difference of *Poeti del Novecento italiani e stranieri* was that it upheld a more coherent approach to translation. It moved away from the patterns of translation notebooks and identified an alternative relationship both with translators, who were not necessarily poets, and with the wider literary field as a result of the new cultural needs of the 1960s and the shift away from Hermeticism. This ideally opened up some potential in terms of a more productive engagement with transnational ferments, which tended to remain nevertheless rooted in individual habitus and national dynamics.

---

48 AE, file Elena Craveri Croce, Italo Calvino, 20 May 1959.
49 Ibid.

3.4 New cultural and publishing orientations: the 'antologie di Paese'

The 'antologie mondiali' remained sporadic publications at the end of the 1950s. While the success of translation notebooks continued to diminish, one typology that enjoyed increasing prominence during the 1960s was anthologies devoted to a specific geo-linguistic area. Comparing the diverse habitus of the publishing houses and the peculiarities of the 'antologie di Paese' that each produced reveals multiple strategies and offers us a composite insight into this new cultural product: the continuation of the translation notebook for the small-scale publishers; the outright rejection of the new model by the large-scale publishing houses; and the innovative formulation of the medium-scale publishers, for whom the cultural themes of the anthology acquired increasing relevance when compared to the mere reputation of the editor. In favouring a concrete inclusion within the contemporary transnational dialogue, the production of 'antologie di Paese' endorsed the rise of the medium-scale publishing houses, and, simultaneously, further advanced the desired refunctionalisation of the cultural identity of Italian editors at the transnational level.

For small publishers such as Vanni Schieiwiller, the 'antologie di Paese' continued to simulate the typical features of the translation notebooks, and primarily the predominant role of the translator. The first example of such an anthology dates back to 1956: *Poeti slavi*, edited by Renato Poggioli, presented an unpublished collection of Bulgarian and Bohemian poems in 1,000 numbered copies. In the year of the Hungarian revolution in 1956, the publication undoubtedly had the potential to draw attention to wider political issues, if the bond between poet-translator and foreign poet was not the sole focus of the poetry collection. In his preface to the *plaquette*, Poggioli explicitly described the translations from the Slavonic languages as a linguistic exercise profoundly related to his own abilities, through which he could reach more meaningful results than with other literatures. Translation practice became first and foremost a stylistic exercise for the Slavic Studies specialist, and the selection of foreign poets was based largely on this purpose:

> Composti idealmente in margine alle mie prove iniziali d'interprete della lirica russa, tali esercizi s'apparentano meglio, non solo per affinità di lingua, a quello che resta il mio lavoro centrale di traduttore, piuttosto che alle fatiche, per così dire, estravaganti, con cui di quando in quando ho tentato di rendere in versi ed accenti italiani poesia d'altri mondi da quello slavo. (Poggioli, 1956: 7)

> [Ideally elaborated in the margin of my initial attempts as an interpreter of Russian poetry, these exercises are better linked, not only for their language, to what remains my core work as a translator, than to the extravagant, to put it this way, efforts that I made in order to translate into Italian lines and accents foreign poetry that was not Slavic.]

Three years later, in the introduction to *Poeti olandesi*, Giacomo Prampolini unapologetically explained that the choice of poems was based purely on his preferences; as a consequence 'parecchi poeti pur degni di nota sono rimasti fuori; qualcuno degli inclusi avrebbe meritato più spazio; infine, hanno sempre influito sulla scelta le preferenze del gusto personale' [several well-known poets have been excluded; some of those who have been included would have deserved more space; finally, the choice has always been influenced by the preferences of my own personal taste] (Prampolini, 1959: 9). In the introduction to *Poeti bretoni moderni* (1966), Prampolini again highlighted his somewhat haphazard criteria, insofar as he 'qualche volta ho dovuto rinunciare a una lirica molto bella, ma di difficile resa, e ripiegare su un'altra che meglio si prestava a essere tradotta' [had to give up on a very beautiful poem which was very difficult to render in Italian, and fall back on another one that lent itself to translation]. The translations were not even seen as ancillary texts and the source text was not published on parallel pages.

The small-scale publisher Guanda also proposed several 'antologie di Paese'; in most cases they were reprints, or updated editions, of the anthologies of poet-translators, who were often also academics, who gravitated to the Hermetic sphere, such as Carlo Bo and Francesco Tentori Montalto. We should remark here that Guanda's anthology of the *Poesia ispano-americana del '900* (1957) may also be considered part of the 'translation notebook' category based on a number of elements: the attempt to closely follow the metre system of the original, according to a truly 'mimetic' technique – if we borrow Translation Studies terminology (Jones, 2011b) – the total absence of footnotes, and, significantly, the signature of 'Francesco Tentori' in the introduction. The intellectual normally signed using both of his surnames when he operated as a translator, and simply as 'Tentori' when he acted as a poet (Dolfi, 2004: 17n): signing in this way reaffirmed the typical intentions of a poet-translator still operating in a largely Hermetic horizon.

This continuity between the 'antologie di Paese' of the small-scale publishers and translation notebooks was probably due to the intrinsic nature of the publishing model of the *plaquette*, which ennobled the exercise of style instead of ideologically tendentious or informative perspectives. The more heteronomous aspect of the anthological format – its potential as an instrument of cultural renewal or as a textbook – was also further removed from the purposes of distinction that characterised the small publishers. As a result, although the specialist publishers explored the new model, they did not fully embrace its particularities. For structural reasons their attitude to the potential renovation of cultural formats and patterns was more conservative than we might expect: the usual anti-conformism gave way to a tried-and-tested formula, a confirmed source of symbolic capital. This is an extremely relevant element in the less idealised and more objective re-evaluation of poetry publishing that this book has proposed from the very beginning.

Entirely different reasons deterred the large-scale publishers from adopting the new anthological format. Garzanti limited its anthological offer: in 1974 it published the monumental translation in two volumes of *Poesia spagnola del Novecento* edited by Macrí, still within a clear Hermetic taste. In Mondadori's case, the 'antologia di Paese' model received negligible attention in the catalogue of the poetry series. The reasons can mainly be found in the intrinsic structure of 'Lo Specchio', which usually published a generally exhaustive selection by a single author, instead of a product inevitably more limited in its dimension and completeness, as were anthologies representing whole countries or continents. Mondadori's editorial board was not completely uninterested in the 'antologie di Paese', recognising their significance as part of the general publishing trend of systematically broadening the publication of foreign poetry. In particular, Sereni suggested a translation notebook of new and emerging Polish poetry for the 'Medusa' collection, edited by Vittorini,[50] following the Polish October in the second half of 1956. The literature in question was considered extremely 'viv[a]' [lively], and produced 'intens[e]' [intense] voices at a literary level, but the publishing house could not afford to publish one single expression.[51] It would be more agile, from a publishing perspective, to publish the best-known voices and eventually extrapolate a book from these.[52] The proposal was rejected as probably too risky when compared to the more traditional Mondadori publications. Additionally, the sales figures for Tadeusz Różewicz – the only Polish poet who was already included in the catalogue of 'Lo Specchio' – had been disappointing.[53]

---

50 FAAM, *SEE*, file Tadeusz Różewicz, Vittorio Sereni to the Direzione letteraria, 27 August 1961.
51 Ibid.
52 Ibid.
53 Ibid.

The impossibility of engaging with the new anthological format because of financial demands relegated Mondadori to a more peripheral position, to the benefit of the medium-scale publishers. Only at the beginning of the 1970s would there be an exception with the publication of *Poesia sovietica degli anni Sessanta* (1971), edited by Cesare G. De Michelis, which featured translations by, among others, Giudici. As the back cover confirms, the publication had a 'sociological' intent, according to the wider spread of poetry from the Soviet Union in a Khrushchev-style protest. Paratexts were in line with Mondadori's practice; they presented detailed bio-bibliographical notes and a substantial apparatus of endnotes, with cultural references, geographical indications, and even critical yet mostly linguistic interpretations of the translations (especially with regard to wordplay and double meanings). Despite the limited number of titles, we can note a further development from Joyce Lussu's anthology, towards a translation released from poetic-empathic intentions. Reservations regarding the effective quality of foreign texts led the 'antologia di Paese' to find a sounder home in the more commercial collections, such as the monthly paperback 'Oscar' series, where the economic gamble was more likely to be repaid.[54]

At the Turinese publishing house Einaudi, the 'antologie di Paese' were not only included in series with wide circulation, but at the end of the 1960s found a specific place in the 'Collezione di poesia'. Drawing on its more consolidated position in the publishing field, Einaudi crafted an innovative anthological typology that finally brought to completion – although certainly not in exactly the same terms, and with some limitations as we shall see – the politico-cultural project that had been somewhat held back by Elena Croce's powerful influence over the 'antologie mondiali'. By reworking the models already pursued by both small- and large-scale publishers, Einaudi developed its 'younger poets' anthologies': a key cultural product able to fully promote the renewal of the contemporary literary and cultural environment.

Einaudi was not the only medium-scale outfit that moved towards this new trend, as the publication of foreign anthologies by its direct competitor, Feltrinelli, demonstrates. However, it was precisely in intensifying the more 'heretical' line that normally characterised the Milanese publishing house that Einaudi formulated its own anthologies. If we look closely at the Feltrinelli anthologies, starting from *Poeti americani: da E.A. Robinson a W.S. Merwin* [American Poets from E. Robinson to W.S. Mervin] edited by Roberto Sanesi

---

54 FAAM, SEE, file Günter Kunert, note by Marco Forti to Vittorio Sereni, 22 May 1967.

(1958), they essentially provided a historical perspective on past examples of foreign poetry. Through a systematic paratextual apparatus, Feltrinelli offered a synthesis of the most significant poets of the previous fifty years and potential reading interpretations even for future poetry movements, as outlined by the back cover:

> primo *ubi consistam* dal quale si potrà partire per altre letture: le introduzioni biografico-critiche e le minuziose note bibliografiche dedicate ad ogni autore hanno un respiro molto ampio, che troverà la sua miglior misura quando il volume avrà adempiuto in ogni lettore alla sua prima funzione di riordinamento o di scoperta e si verrà via via trasformando in una guida stimolata e sicura a *tutta* la poesia americana, di oggi e di domani.
>
> [first reference point from which the audience can move towards other readings: the bio-critical introduction and the detailed bibliographical notes devoted to each author have a wider scope; this will be achieved when the book fully satisfies its function of reordering and discovery for all readers, and becomes an ever more stimulating and established guide to the *whole* of American poetry, current and future.]

Einaudi moved instead towards a critical documentary overview, in search of the most topical political and cultural trends, which shifted decidedly towards a more dynamic engagement with transnational appeals. Such a perspective of literary investigation heralded the incontrovertible death of the poet-translator – the genre to which Sanesi belonged – while more generic cultural mediators, coming from outside the usual poetic or academic circuits, were legitimised.

In a more clear-cut way than both the translation notebooks and Feltrinelli's historical repertoires, the Einaudi 'antologia di Paese' exhibited from the outset an explicitly partisan perspective. As the art historian and editor Paolo Fossati reiterated, 'Einaudi non ha mai pubblicato antologie che non fossero "tagliate" che non rispondessero a certe, magari opinabilissime opzioni interrogative' [Einaudi has never published anthologies which did not have a specific angle, that did not respond to certain, perhaps very debatable questions],[55] thus corroborating the idea of a critical engagement with literary,

---

55 AE, file Francesco Tentori Montalto, Paolo Fossati, 10 July 1968.

as well as cultural, issues. In a letter to translator Ariodante Marianni, who proposed a translation of Emily Dickinson alongside an anthology of US poets, Davico Bonino expressed in unambiguous terms the intentions of the Turinese publishing house. The letter dated back to 1 October 1964, when the 'Collezione di poesia' was in its infancy: the editor suggested exploring alternative approaches to US poetry, distinct from Mondadori's path – which at that stage included the translation of Dickinson – since to request Dickinson's copyrights at that time would be seen as 'politically incautious' and would excessively unsettle the publishing equilibrium. On the contrary, Einaudi's anthological product had to promote an innovative critical approach by broadening the audience beyond poetry experts by means of an astute selection of contemporary foreign poetry which would develop the approach established by the literary journals and expand towards the most topical trends in US poetry. The poets of the Beat generation were identified as particularly pertinent to this aim:

> Mi pare meglio far subito gli americani. Qui però bisognerebbe restringere la scelta: la linea Williams è per definizione per gli addetti ai lavori, non giustifica un'antologia. Io farei un Poeti della *beat generation*, con cattiveria magari e mordente: e partirei da *Questo e altro*, mettendoci oltre a Ginsberg, Corso, Ferlinghetti, O'Hara e magari altri: in tutto una quarantina di poesie.

> [I think it would be better to do immediately the American poets [the proposed names were Williams, Levertov, Olson, Ferlinghetti, O'Hara, who were the poets that the translator had published in *Questo e altro* 4 (1963)]. But here we should restrict the choice: the Williams' line is by definition for poetry specialists, it doesn't justify an anthology. I would do one on the 'Poeti della *beat generation*', perhaps with a malicious edge: and I would start from *Questo e altro*, and I would put in addition to Ginsberg: Corso, Ferlinghetti, O'Hara, and maybe others: overall about forty poems.]

Similarly, the Dadaist anthology proposed by Luigi Forte in 1971 had to draw on a partisan selection and a subjective interpretative line, insofar as Fossati advised Forte that the overall intent was not just documentary.[56]

---

56 AE, file Luigi Forte, Paolo Fossati, 17 May 1971.

Einaudi's anthologies intended to assume a relevant critical function, as their main selection criterion was 'una giustificazione interna, di preciso carattere critico, [ch]e non si fondi soltanto su criteri cronologici generali (poeti del '900, poeti del primo e secondo dopoguerra)' [an internal justification, of a precise critical character, that did not merely draw on general chronological criteria (twentieth-century poets, post-WWI or WWII poets)].[57] The anthologies that started to fill the catalogue of the 'Collezione di poesia' at the end of the 1960s also aimed to capture the liveliest poets of specific geo-linguistic areas, those poets who had not yet achieved canonical status. Instead of privileging already 'classic' figures, the anthology sought to offer an informative perspective on the most current trends developing overseas, particularly through the work of the younger poets. This archived once and for all the historicist intentions of Elena Croce's anthology.

Under those terms, in 1969 Paolo Fossati illustrated to Nereo Condini, who had translated the Black Mountain poet Charles Olson for Guanda in 1947, the need to adopt a critical approach that could raise debate or even spark controversy ('ci si aspetterebbe un pizzico di, non dico manifesto, ma pepe' [we should expect a pinch of, I don't say too evident, pepper]).[58] Without this, the translator's work would appear 'troppo ampio, e troppo minimo, per essere, ai fini nostri, caratterizzante' [too wide, and too much of a summary, to be, for our purposes, distinctive].[59] Condini's proposal embraced 1960s US poetry, including such authors as Randal Jarrell, who was born in 1910, while the general chronological limits of the 'younger poets' anthologies' aimed to focus on the most contemporary poets from the 1930s onwards. These dates were seen as key for stimulating an effective 'intervention' in the cultural environment of the late 1960s through this publication. When discussing the anthology of US poets, Davico Bonino made clear the extent to which the 'biographical' detail was not ancillary, but fully responded to the demand for innovative poetic values. The literary fame of the foreign poet assumed therefore a much less significant role in the selection: the reputation was seen as an extrinsic value, since an anthology should, above all, discover new names.[60]

At a higher level, the cutting-edge formulation of the 'antologie di Paese' sounded the death knell for the Hermetic model of the translation notebook.

---

57   Ibid., Paolo Fossati, 12 October 1964.
58   AE, file Nereo Condini, Paolo Fossati, 21 January 1969.
59   Ibid.
60   AE, file Gianni Menarini, GDB, 16 July 1970. See also Milani, 2013a: 11–12.

This is exemplified by the rejection of Tentori Montalto's proposal to bring together in a translation notebook some of the Spanish and Hispanic South American poets he had translated over his career.[61] The selection criterion would not influence any historico-cultural line, other than at the level of individual taste, and the finished product would be 'insomma alla Valeri un esemplare quaderno spagnolo "del secolo" e più precisamente del mezzo secolo' [in Valeri-style, an exemplary Spanish notebook 'of the twentieth century', and more precisely of the first fifty years of this century].[62] Such an initiative would pose, first of all, publishing issues, since the strength of the translator's cultural capital was not enough to make significant economic profits. Davico Bonino revealed that Valeri's translation notebook had not been as successful as expected, given that the author was well-known,[63] and it had forced the publishing house to limit its translation notebooks to the work of Sergio Solmi. Yet the issue was much broader than a sales one and was also related to the contemporary cultural climate; in 1968 Tentori still wanted to promote a Hermetic perspective on the relationship between Italian and foreign poetry, which no longer made sense for the Turinese publisher in the new Italian publishing and cultural environment. Einaudi strongly felt the need to critically insert foreign poems into the national poetic horizon as part of a more productive transnational dialogue that could re-evaluate the historical-cultural meaning of both national and foreign poetry.

More specifically, Fossati's idea was to narrow down the selection to the most accomplished movement or poet,[64] particularly active in the last two decades.[65] Within that horizon, more unconventional profiles found a home, such as Cuba and Nicaragua. Cuban poetry had already featured in the *Poeti delle Antille* anthology (1963), edited by scholar Giuseppe Bellini and published by Guanda. However, in line with the typical dispositions of a specialised poetry publisher, the book had followed 'criteri personali' [subjective selection criteria], with a view to shedding light on 'le figure di maggiore risonanza' [the most relevant figures], and was explicitly addressed to a 'pubblico colto' [well-educated public] (Bellini, 1963: x):

61 AE, file Francesco Tentori Montalto, to GDB, 27 October 1968.
62 Ibid.
63 AE, file Francesco Tentori Montalto, GDB, 18 November 1968. See also Billiani, 2007b: 152.
64 AE, file Francesco Tentori Montalto, Paolo Fossati, 22 January 1968.
65 Ibid., Paolo Fossati, 24 May 1968.

a clearly ornate cultural product. Such a framework tended to obscure a more informative intent, evidenced both in the breadth of the introduction, which was essentially a historical overview, and in the glossaries that functioned as reading support.[66]

Einaudi, though, sought transnational poetic innovations starting from both internal and external cultural debates. As Fossati advised Tentori Montalto, the younger poets played a pivotal role in documenting the function of cultural renewal that poetry was assuming; their function was necessarily developing, precisely at the level of 'continuità supernazionale [sia] della specialità nazionale delle culture poetiche' [super-national continuity [and] of the national specificity of poetic cultures]:

> Direi che mancano i giovani [...] credo che la presenza di queste ultime leve si giustifichi ampiamente almeno per due ordini di motivi: il primo è che qualcosa si va muovendo, a ciò che giornali e gazzette ci dicono, profondamente nella vita sudamericana e con le frizioni generazionali implicite [...] Il secondo motivo è direi tale da coinvolgere il discorso stesso dell'antologia: che noi vediamo non come fissazione di un olimpo di valori, ma come rilevamento nel tempo di uno sviluppo, dallo ieri all'oggi, e quindi anche come sintomatica di impulsi innovatori, anche se non precisati ancora con la convinzione e il distacco assoluti della poesia con la P maiuscola.[67]

[I should say that we lack young poets [...] I believe that the presence of these latest figures is widely justified for at least two reasons: the first is that something is changing profoundly, according to what newspapers and chronicles tell us, in South American life and with the implicit generation struggles [...] The second reason is, I would say, that it involves the concept of the anthology itself: that we see this not as a fixation within a Parnassus of values, but as a review over time of a development, from yesterday to today, and thus also as symptomatic of innovative stimuli, even if these are not yet fixed with the full conviction and detachment of poetry with capital P.]

---

66   The same was true of other anthologies published by Guanda, such as *Lirica ungherese del '900*, edited in 1962 by the founder of Hungarian Studies at the University of Turin, Paolo Santarcangeli, and *Poesia greca del '900*, translated in 1957 by the Hellenicist Mario Vitti.
67   AE, file Francesco Tentori Montalto, Paolo Fossati, 21 June 1968.

The above vision clashed entirely with the intentions of the editor, who was not interested in documenting these ferments.[68] Tentori Montalto firmly believed that the anthology should instead assume an 'assolut[o]' [absolute] character,[69] proposing simply an overview of established foreign poets.

The dispute with the Hispanic Studies specialist revealed a precise generational transition in the Italian literary domain. The Hermeticists avoided experimentation, and their contemporary poetry anthologies were the result of a careful process of editing (Capoferro, 2004: 311): Macrí, who exalted that 'estremo rigore ermetico dell'antologia ispanoamericana di Tentori' [extreme hermetic rigour of Tentori's Hispanic America anthology] (Macrí, 2002: 45; Capoferro, 2004: 311), affirmed that he had excluded 'tutti gli ultraisti e popolareggianti pseudo-realistici cosiddetti impegnati' [all the so-called *impegnati* Ultraist and pseudo-realist popularising poets] (Macrí, 2002: 45). Tentori Montalto was indeed a steadfast representative of that Hermetic trend which appeared increasingly irrelevant given the 1968 movement's desire to reinterpret the relationship between literature and reality. For Einaudi, contemporary political reflections ought to be distinct from any relics of Hermeticism.

The urge for a more critical gaze on contemporary reality was linked to the discussion that had been first stimulated by the *neoavanguardia* and its attempt to relegitimise the category of *impegno* formulated in the aftermath of the Second World War. From this perspective, the anthology of German Dadaists edited by Luigi Forte mentioned earlier in this chapter was characterised by an attention to the political dynamics behind literary movements. Particularly interesting for the main argument we are advancing was the editor's intention to emphasise the link between the European avant-garde and the *neoavanguardia*, the 'parentela tra avanguardia storica e neo-avanguardia' [parenthood between the historical avant-garde and the *neoavanguardia*], thus placing the latter as a primary interlocutor in this transnational cultural dialogue.[70] With the intent of creating several anthologies of contemporary foreign poetry in the fashion of the *neoavanguardia*,[71] the 'antologie di Paese' became the cultural product *par excellence* to shape a network of transnational

---

68 AE, file Francesco Tentori Montalto, Francesco Tentori Montalto, n.p., 28 June 1968. See also Milani, 2017: 304.
69 Ibid.
70 AE, file Luigi Forte, project for a Dadaist anthology of German language, n.d., but presumably 1970.
71 See in particular the letter sent by GDB to Antonio Porta, quoted in 2.3.4.

exchanges that could intercede in the (re)legitimation of the literary and cultural models of Italian poetry.

In responding to the issues of the (post-)*neoavanguardia*, the sociological and documentary interest in emerging contemporary foreign poetry had to strike a balance with some form of cultural capital, as revealed by the processes of negotiation behind the anthology of South American poets (1972) edited by Umberto Bonetti, RAI collaborator in Uruguay, poet, and expert in South American literature. In Bonetti's vision, the anthology would be able to compete with other publications covering the South America area thanks to the search for innovative poetry, biographical data, and unpublished material. In the Italian literary environment, an interest in publishing South American poets who were not already canonical was lacking, and Einaudi would have filled this gap with its attention to the new representatives of this group. The anthology edited by Antonio Porta for Feltrinelli already mentioned devoted little space to authors born after 1930; as Bonetti explains in the correspondence, out of the 76 poets featured in the Feltrinelli anthology, only eight were young authors.[72] Bonetti intended also to position his anthology against other earlier products, including *Spagna: poesia oggi. La poesia spagnola dopo la guerra civile* [Spanish Poetry Today: Spanish Poetry after the Civil War]. The latter had been published by Feltrinelli in 1962 and drew on an earlier edition by Josep Maria Castellet, while Einaudi preferred to source contributions that had only been featured in journals with very limited circulation or new unpublished material.[73]

In the beginning, Bonetti's enthusiasm for this project pushed him towards privileging a framework that avoided a geographical division into countries and supported instead '"linee" di contenuto, essendo probabilmente la linea principale quella della poesia di contenuto sociale (o ribelle che dir si voglia)' [thematic lines, since the main line of this poetry is that of social content (or rebellion, as we'd say)].[74] The young age of all the selected poets would also represent an element of cohesion, and would confer homogeneity on the collection in terms of the social and political problems shared by these countries.[75] Poetry here became an expedient for an appraisal of transnational issues. Among these, other than the Cold War and the nuclear threat that European poets also experienced, there was a shared revolutionary

---

72 AE, file Umberto Bonetti, to GDB, 21 November 1969.
73 Ibid., to GDB, 9 January 1970.
74 AE, file Umberto Bonetti, to GDB, 21 November 1969.
75 Ibid.

climate against the influence of the USA; this generated a strong political consciousness particularly in the poets of the ironic and corrosive movement of anti-poetry, whose most famous proponent was the Chilean Nicaor Parra, and the conversational poetry of the Nicaraguan Cardenal. That said, such a publication risked erasing cultural differences between the several cultures, creating an artificial, and problematic, 'umbrella' of a wider South American 'Paese'.

Beyond Bonetti's intentions, Davico Bonino reaffirmed the need to critically justify choices, not only from an historico-sociological perspective, but also in terms of literary and stylistic value.[76] In another letter to Bonetti, Davico Bonico cited an interesting reflection by Calvino which manifested the desire for Einaudi to reformulate its political-cultural interest in more innovative terms than in the past, in order to distinguish the project of the younger poets' anthologies from the publishing trends already developed within the Italian field. Intriguingly, in line with the *neoavanguardia* intentions, the Einaudi editors commissioned anthologies of politically committed poets along the lines of a stereotypical post-war *impegno*, as 'non vogliamo più sentir parlare di letteratura e impegno civile dopo il ventennio di grossolani equivoci che questo ha trascinato con sé in Italia' [we don't want to hear any more talk of civilian literature and political commitment after two decades of rough misunderstanding that this had dragged with it in Italy].[77] The editor underlined, in particular, the danger of accounting for the less structured poetics, which took their pretext from historical figures who could be easily trivialised, as in the case of Marxist revolutionary Che Guevara; Einaudi required substantial literary innovation instead, 'poesie di alta tenuta, e soprattutto "diverse", non prevedibili' [high-quality poems, and especially 'different', unpredictable].[78] Faced with the impossibility of finding a stylistic uniformity among the various movements, Bonetti would focus mainly on the current of conversational poetry, striking a balance between cultural and literary needs, and received the approval of Davico Bonino for the selection of poets who were 'appassionati ma non candidi, impegnati ma non retorici' [passionate but not naive, politically committed but not rhetorical].[79]

The question of the literary value of the anthologies of contemporary younger poets was controversial, given the unrecognised status of the

76 AE, file Umberto Bonetti, GDB, 26 November 1969.
77 AE, file Umberto Bonetti, GDB, 8 June 1970.
78 Ibid., GDB, 24 November 1970.
79 AE, file Umberto Bonetti, GDB, 25 September 1970.

authors. Einaudi did not aim to seek political dissent *tout court*, as the latter should strike a balance with the poetic offering. When Crescenzio Sangiglio suggested collecting the poems of younger Greek poets, the editor Pontani raised doubts about both the quality of the translations, whose results did not seem satisfying, and the figure and orientations of the translator, as the excessive bias could damage the effectiveness of the anthological selection.[80] The same happened with the proposal for a collection of US poems on Vietnam, which Davico Bonino rejected as he opposed the use of sterile and propagandistic polemic for its own sake: 'io sostengo che ogni scrittore che usa le parole SS, nazismo, guerra, ecc., debba essere energicamente multato' [I believe that every writer who uses the words SS, Nazism, war, etc. should be vigorously fined].[81] It was also a pragmatic issue, given that the substantial increase of publications in the sector of politically committed poetry risked saturating the market. Guanda had already published books such as *Poesie e canti popolari arabi* [Popular Arab Poems and Chants] (1956) and *Poesie e canti popolari di pace cinesi* [Chinese Popular Poems and Chants of Peace] (1960), edited by Ester Panetta and Franco Cannarozzo respectively.

With regard to textual practice, the 'popular' line already undertaken by Elena Croce's anthology was going from strength to strength, in opposition to the typical patterns of the translation notebooks. On the one hand, it was not only poet-translators or academic translators who edited the anthologies, but more often cultural agents such as journalists or literary experts in a broad sense – Bonetti being a fitting example. On the other, in counter-trend to the elite conception of the poetic genre, publishers were urged to move away from the more specialist circles in order to reach younger readers, such as university students, who were interested in the cultural and political turmoil occurring at an international level. Einaudi had thus to undertake specific editing strategies, starting with the prefaces, which now offered not only a literary review but an informative perspective, and the paratextual supports.

In *Giovani poeti americani*, published in 1973, Gianni Menarini – at the time, a journalist for the newspaper *Il Resto del Carlino* and only later a published poet and writer, who had translated *Vietnam Poeti americani* [Vietnam, American Poets] in 1972 for Guanda[82] – adopted a 'tono giornal-

---

80 AE, file Carlo Carena, to Filippo Pontani, 5 March 1970.
81 AE, file Luca Fontana, GDB, 11 December 1967.
82 Interestingly, according to the translator (private correspondence, 21 June 2021), he had to legally force Guanda to publish the book, as the publishing house was less

istico informativo' [informative journalistic tone],[83] underlining the topical character of the selection of poets, among whom the 2020 Nobel prize winner Louise Glück stood out. Menarini not only traced an excursus of the most relevant canonical examples and poetic techniques, but also raised wide-ranging sociological questions, such as the differences in status (awards, university lectureships in creative writing) and circulation (public readings, insertion within the publishing institutions) of poetry in the USA and Italy. The translator's choice was endorsed by Davico Bonino, both in terms of writing style and for economic reasons: 'la scelta di un linguaggio criticamente più rigoroso non avrebbe giovato all'impresa, anzi, l'avrebbe inutilmente appesantita, mentre quello che dobbiamo ottenere, è rendere il libro invogliante' [the choice of a more critically rigorous language would have not benefited the initiative; it would have made it too demanding, while what we need to do is to make the book appealing].[84] From that perspective, Menarini had to revise the conclusion, devoted to dense biographies of US poets, as a way to increase their readability.[85] The aim of reaching an appropriately wide audience, thanks to the book's intelligibility, was also evident in the paratext, which emulated a literary history textbook, so that, as stressed by Davico Bonino with regard to *Giovani poeti sudamericani*, the bio-bibliographical notes of each poet were expanded to list full details of publication at end of the anthology.[86]

In line with this publishing strategy, the translation was intended simply to support the foreign poem, without becoming an exercise in creative writing for the translator. In accordance with the orientation of the publishing house, Menarini's version of the US poems maintained the narrative style of John Giorno, well-known for his journalistic representation of notorious deaths, which the translator replicated with a verb/subject inversion: 'Mrs. Kennedy / told the commission' // '*disse la signora Kennedy / alla commissione*' (Menarini, 1973: 64–65; see also Milani, 2017: 306). To support the reader in accessing the source text, the translator chose to leave lines in the source language in the poem 'Crickets' by Aram Saroyan, according to a 'zero translation' practice (Crisafulli, 2002: 38). Instead of producing a version with diminished

---

interested in the political take of this initiative given that the USA was withdrawing from Vietnam.
83 AE, file Gianni Menarini, GDB, 8 March 1972. Also in Milani, 2017: 306.
84 AE, file Gianni Menarini, GDB, 8 March 1972. Also in Milani, 2017: 306.
85 Ibid.
86 AE, file Umberto Bonetti, GDB, 25 September 1970. See also Milani, 2017: 306.

rhetorical weight, Menarini preferred to offer a precise interpretation of this onomatopoeic poem in a footnote:

> la *s* del plurale si moltiplica invadendo progressivamente l'intera parola e il suo spazio sonoro, fino a indicare una parentesi di silenzio nel frinire degl'insetti; la parola viene poi riassorbita dal graduale riaffermarsi – sempre da destra a sinistra – delle lettere originarie e del suono dei grilli. (Menarini, 1973: 205)

> [the 's' of the plural is multiplied, thus progressively invading the entire word and the sound space, until it points to a break of silence in the insects' chirping; the word is then reabsorbed again gradually with the returning – always from right to left – of the original letters and the crickets' sound]

For *Giovani poeti dell'America Centrale, del Messico e delle Antille* (1977), edited by Bonetti, Davico Bonino specified that translations should be as close as possible to the prosaic original text ('poeti che parlano basso, domestico, quotidiano' [poets who have a low, domestic, everyday voice]), and avoid a superfluous lyricism that would counteract the ultimate sense of the publishing project and risk reinforcing an obsolete practice. Bonetti fully understood the sense of Davico Bonino's words and responded to his demands by adopting a foreignising approach in terms of maintaining 'le "bruttezze", le ripetizioni, le oscurità del testo' ['the less harmonious things, the repetitions, the obscurities of the text] and providing readers with several explicatory footnotes. There is a pronounced contrast between this approach and that of the poet-translators, a reflection of Einaudi's new target audience: a student cohort more interested in the thematic or formal discourse interwoven by the foreign poet than in the translator's poetic abilities.

The 'anthologies of younger poets' represented an innovative project at a literary and cultural level, aiming to connect a wider domestic readership with the liveliest transnational poetic elements. They also provoked controversy at a transnational publishing level and at a national literary one. Analysing the debates that they stimulated affords us not only a more nuanced understanding of the publishing processes, but also a sharper focus on the underlying cultural dynamics that influenced the evolution of the anthological products themselves. Dialogue with European and extra-European poets inserted Einaudi into the wider publishing field in a global sense positioned in this way its involvement with transnational power relationships at stake conditioned its editorial strategies.

This is exemplified by the events related to the *Giovani poeti spagnoli* anthology (1976), translated into Italian by Rosa Rossi. Unlike the anthologies discussed earlier, this anthology drew on work featured in *Nueve novísimos poetas españoles* [New, Very New Spanish Poets] (1971), edited by the influential theorist of Spanish realism Josep Maria Castellet and published by Carlos Barral, co-founder with Giulio Einaudi of the Formentor International Prize. In accordance with the objectives of the younger poets' anthologies, Rossi called for the elimination from Castellet's anthology of a whole section devoted to the senior poets and a focus on three younger poets instead.[87] The selected poets would propose 'una critica condotta attraverso una diversa esperienza totale – nei confronti del realismo, *engagement*, ecc. degli scrittori più anziani' [a critique conducted through a different holistic experience – if compared to the realism, political commitment, etc., of the older poets], which fully corresponded with Einaudi's *neoavanguardia* perspective.

In a letter dated 29 February 1972, however, Davico Bonino expressed two concerns regarding the project. The first was structural: with such a small number of poets, the publishing house could not apply the collective category of 'anthology' to the collection. The second was of a more diplomatic character, and this is significant in relation to the hidden network of influence behind the publishing production. Rossi's editing was perfectly in line with the Einaudi project of the younger poets' anthologies; nonetheless, it had to be modified in the name of the delicate balance to be struck with Spanish editors and publishers, particularly Castellet, who 'è un amico oltre che di Barral, anche di questa casa editrice' [is a friend not only of Barral's, but also of this publishing house], and whose preface could not be excluded. Transnational networks did provide Einaudi with publishing opportunities, but these had to be carefully negotiated and balanced against the risk of losing the very element of political and cultural innovation that had prompted the need to go beyond national borders in the first place.

Constant negotiations within the national literary field also led to the production of anthologies that did not wholly conform to the guidelines explicated earlier in this chapter. The *Giovani poeti tedeschi* anthology (1969) unveils a compromise with the perspective of the editor Roberto Fertonani, German Studies specialist and Mondadori collaborator, whose vision

---

87 AE, file Rosa Rossi, to GDB, Rome, 16 February 1972.

contrasted with the *neoavanguardia* impulses that characterised Einaudi's orientation with regard to poetry. Fertonani envisaged an anthology that would lean towards a politically committed stylistic practice which was very different from the intentions of the *neoavanguardia*. That was in line with his overall translation approach, which in contrast to Croce's idea of translation as a new creation, conceived the activity of translation as a close and integral linguistic interpretation of the source text (Albanese and Nasi, 2015: 182).

Fertonani's editorial work demonstrated two typical elements of the younger poets' anthologies: the foregrounding of biographical data and an unabashedly subjective selection process. The Germanist adopted the criteria of Peter Hamm's anthology, published in Germany in the second half of the 1950s, which focused exclusively on poets who had been born after 1930. Furthermore, the bias of the selection ('non si tratta di un panorama equilibrato e imparziale delle correnti e delle personalità poetiche di maggior rilievo attive oggi in Germania' [this is not a balanced and impartial overview of the most relevant poetic movements and figures currently active in Germany]) (Fertonani, 1969: 5) aimed at gathering the most explicit representatives of the contemporary political discontent regarding both the US influence on West Germany and the communist influence on the GDR. Accordingly, Cesare Cases further restricted the selection, 'inserendovi solo i testi più polemici e aggressivi o comunque più affini a un discorso di carattere sociologico' [by including only the most polemical, aggressive texts, or those that could be related to a sociologically driven discourse] (Fertonani, 1969: 6; see also Milani, 2013b: 105–06).

In his review of politically committed German literature, however, Fertonani's intention went beyond that of providing readers with pure literary information. As the preface makes evident, the Germanist wanted to influence the contemporary status of Italian culture by making comparisons that advocated a return to Croce's positions in the neo-avant-garde formal quest, as well as praising the more articulate and effective attitude of German poetry vis-à-vis contemporary society (Fertonani, 1969: 6). From this perspective, in line with Enzensberger's declaration that poetry should be judged on the basis of its utility and documentary value, contemporary German poetry assumed the features of a politically committed genre which looked back to the style of Bertolt Brecht. Examining the repertoire of rhetorical devices and syntactical construction of the anthologised German poets, Fertonani outlined in his introduction how the themes of political discontent had changed, while the poetic structure remained linked to a desire to estrange the reader and to

more prosaic writing, in contrast with both the subjective lyricism and the radical, formal experimentalism endorsed by Gruppo 63:

> da Brecht hanno imparato anche la forma del discorso colloquiale, dell'epigramma conchiuso in brevi parole o il procedimento stilistico della *pointe*, del finale ad effetto che sorprende e strania il lettore [...] In generale lo stile che i giovani prediligono è volutamente prosastico nella *tournure* della frase, nella frequenza dell'espressione idiomatica, nell'uso malizioso del proverbio e del luogo comune. (Fertonani, 1969: 10)

> [from Brecht they have learned even the form of colloquial discourse, of the epigram expressed in short words or the stylistic procedure of the *pointe*, of the captivating conclusion that surprises and estranges the reader [...] In general, the style that the younger poets privilege is intentionally prosaic in the structure of the sentence, in the frequency of the idiomatic expression, in the mischievous use of the proverb and commonplace.]

It was not only the ambiguous cultural capitals derived from the (trans)national relationships that complicated the publishing project, but also elements linked directly to the poetic selection and textuality. In seeking to strike a balance between form and content, the question of whether or not to 'discriminare il risultato estetico sotto l'indiscutibile carica sociologica dei testi' [set aside the aesthetic result in favour of the undisputable sociological weight of these texts] (Fertonani, 1969: 11) remained open. German Studies specialist Giorgio Manacorda identified the poetry's lack of formal innovation as a shortcoming of the selection:

> Questa tendenza della giovane poesia tedesca è sociologicamente e politicamente interessante, ma corre il rischio di essere poeticamente sterile. Il discorso poetico di questi giovani tedeschi non sembra capace di una indicazione creativa e di rinnovamento per la poesia degli Anni '70, poiché prescinde dai problemi specifici della poesia, per fare del verso un mero strumento della lotta politica.[88]

> [This trend of the German contemporary poets is interesting from both a sociological and political viewpoint, but runs the risk of being sterile

---

88 AE, *recensioni*, 'La Polonia i polacchi e la Germania in due pezzi', *La Stampa*, 3 August 1969.

from a poetic one. The poetic discourse of these young Germans does not seem able to give a creative orientation, an orientation of renewal for 1970s poetry, since it overlooks the specific issues of poetry in order to make the lines mere instruments of political struggle.]

In particular, Manacorda criticised the complete subordination of style to content, which led the German poets to utilise direct rhetorical devices such as the diatribe, in lieu of more complex ironic language. Some critics saw this as a reprise of a Brecht-informed anti-lyricism, which did not seem to have assimilated former experimentalisms, rendering the poems stylistically obsolete and ineffective. In an internal editorial note, Claudio Magris had already outlined the issue of a poetic rendering which unsuccessfully sought to conjugate realism, social criticism, and formal experimentalism, but as a document of the latest German cultural orientations, he saw in it a 'notevole significato' [noteworthy significance].[89] Despite the controversial textual elements, the anthology seemed to satisfy the needs of a student audience willing to question the linguistic demystification proposed by Gruppo 63 in order to explore the terms of a different representation of reality. At the beginning of March 1971, the first print run of *Giovani poeti tedeschi* sold out,[90] demonstrating the novel value of this anthology in Italy.

To sum up, our targeted examination of the different anthological typologies featured in the catalogues of the small-, medium-, and large-scale publishers has exposed at a microscopic level of analysis how, in a new context of transnational historical and literary movements, the modalities of appropriating foreign poetry changed. The passage from Hermeticism to the *neoavanguardia* shifted the understanding of the very concept of 'anthology'. With the decline of Hermetic-inspired 'quaderni di traduzione', and the move to 'antologie mondiali' first and 'antologie di Paese' later, more attention was paid to the literary and/or cultural themes proposed by the foreign poets, and not the translators. This not only questions in part naive representations of small-scale publishers, but also the emergence of new types of cultural agents. We have traced the variable fortunes of the translator as a cultural mediator, spanning the central role of the poet-translators in the translation notebooks, thanks to their symbolic capital; the predominantly informative perspective

---

89 AE, file Claudio Magris, n.d. See also Milani, 2013b: 107.
90 AE, file Roberto Fertonani. However, the exact number of the print run was not recorded.

of the academic translators of the 'antologie mondiali'; and finally the non-specialist translators of the anthologies of younger poets, who had to satisfy more significant political-cultural needs. At the same time, by testing the extent to which the meta-editorial discourse was credible by setting it against the textual dimension, we have examined unpublished poetry translations which are normally neglected in canonical exchanges between Italian and foreign poets, and brought to the fore lesser-known translators and editors who instead largely contributed to the building of Italian culture in the decades considered. These figures deserve further analysis in their own right, which would enrich the history and historiography of poetry translation into Italian. The evolution of the anthologies of contemporary foreign poetry has thus offered an insight into changing historical contexts in which new cultural and literary models developed and specialist interests broadened, thereby anticipating some elements of the phenomenon of globalisation whose power as a cultural force would be increasingly felt from the 1980s onwards.

CHAPTER FOUR

Towards Globalisation, by Way of a Conclusion

This last, shorter chapter looks at the poetry publishing field established after 1969. The overview of the production of Scheiwiller, Mondadori, and Einaudi from the late 1960s to the mid-1970s reveals a paradoxical situation if compared to the publishing dynamics of the 1950s, when small-scale publishing had acquired a central position thanks to translation: the leading publishers regained strength through the publication of foreign poetry, and the small publishers, conversely, tried to maintain their position by drawing on contemporary Italian poetry. These new dynamics of publishing production anticipated the tensions that globalisation would exacerbate from the 1980s onwards: translation became not only common practice for larger publishers but also activated strategies to enhance cultural diversity for the smaller ones (Sapiro, 2010: 419).

The 1968 protests shook societal roles, political dynamics, and cultural traditions at the transnational level. They also coincided with an economic crisis affecting the publishing sector, which prompted a movement towards an industrial distribution system; it would lead in the 1980s to 'publishing without publishers' (Schiffrin, 1999), with a predominance of market rules over editors' literary and cultural aims. Within the Italian publishing houses, the 1968 movement modified the role of Italian intellectuals, who were no longer conceived solely as 'letterati editori', and deepened the effects of the process of industrialisation that had begun in the 1960s. In 1969 the first ever union strike in an Italian publishing house (at Il Saggiatore, Ferretti, 2004: 225) signalled a loss of prestige of this intellectual work (Piccone Stella, 1972: 243–58), now seen in terms of labour. The 1970s opened with the symbolic end of the 'editore protagonista' embodied by Arnoldo Mondadori and the entry of new professionals more closely bound to the industrial sector and its economic imperatives (Ferretti, 2004: 256–62).

If the increased polarisation of the market risked strangling the small-scale publishing houses, it did not univocally benefit the large publishers, particularly in the first half of the 1970s. The tendency to create cartels was counterbalanced initially by the fierce resistance of the medium-scale publishing houses, particularly those with a strong political orientation, in their attempt to maintain a presence in the field. Giangiacomo Feltrinelli's death in 1972 intensified the Milanese publishing house's political commitment with a move towards the publication of non-fiction in lieu of the literary series run by the *neoavanguardia* (Ferretti, 2004: 284–87). In 1974 Einaudi and more than fifty other publishers abandoned the Italian Publishing Association (AIE, Associazione Italiana Editori) now linked to the General Confederation of Italian Industry (Confindustria). Einaudi would, though, rejoin the AIE in 1975 (Ragone, 1999: 217–19). In 1977 Vanni Scheiwiller founded the 'Libri Scheiwiller' through a partnership with the banking system (Gibellini, 2007: 38) that, although inventive (Kerbaker, 2020), inevitably marked the end of the relative autonomy that Scheiwiller had enjoyed for decades. In this context, translation analysis unveils contradictory power relationships. Paradoxically, the larger-scale publishers' consistent broadening of the national poetic borders beyond Italy and Europe meant that they were unable to feature national poets in their catalogues. Contemporary Italian poetry thus turned into a source of distinction and a site of resistance for small publishers.

4.1 Publishing paradoxes in the 1970s

In the early 1970s the so-called 'return to poetry' (Luperini, 1981: 745) outlined a renewed interest in poetry as a genre, which at first strengthened the specialised function of the small publishing houses. However, with the progressive loss of the field's 'autonomy', small publishers were increasingly less able to release themselves from wider distribution channels; this caused an overlap of intents which partly distorted the boundaries between small-, medium-, and large-scale publishing. Each publisher had to weigh both the domestic and foreign offer of their poetry series, prompting a move towards more diversified formulae, addressing a new, dynamic audience mostly comprised of students.

The structure of larger publishing houses changed substantially in directions unexpected only a decade earlier. With Arnoldo Mondadori's death in 1971, his son Giorgio and his assistant Sergio Polillo became CEOs;

and with that, Sereni's editorial line, followed throughout the 1960s, lost power. Sereni's most experimental series – 'il Tornasole' – ceased publication, his creative freedom in 'Lo Specchio' was curtailed (Ferretti, 2004: 250–56), and from 1976 he worked for Mondadori only as a freelance editor (Ferretti, 1999: 159–63). The central role that Mondadori had occupied since the 1940s in the publication of canonical Italian poetry was also put into question; the major contemporary Italian poets were not as prolific as earlier – most of them were now in their seventies – or had moved to other publishers who could offer better remuneration:[1]

> la perdita di Zanzotto col suo relativo passaggio 'indolore' (cioè per scadenze di contratti) a Rizzoli è certa e, dopo l'acquisizione di Luzi da parte del nostro concorrente, ciò sancirebbe la fine di ogni nostra preminenza nel campo della poesia. Questo almeno proiettando un poco le cose nel futuro. Prego infatti ricordare in proposito che Saba, Quasimodo e Ungaretti sono morti e che Montale ha 75 anni.[2]

> [the loss of Zanzotto with his 'painless' passage (due to the end of his contract) to Rizzoli is now confirmed, and our competitor's acquisition of Luzi seems to seal the end of any pre-eminence on our part in the field of poetry. This at least if we think slightly ahead. I would like to recall that Saba, Quasimodo, and Ungaretti are dead, and Montale is 75 years old.]

'Lo Specchio' no longer acted as a source of long-term economic capital which brought awards and critical reception to Mondadori;[3] in addition, Mondadori's traditional role as the publisher of canonical poetry prevented it from creating spaces of innovation, to the advantage of its competitors. This was evident not only in domestic production, but especially in contemporary foreign poetry, whose low sales figures called for caution. As Sereni astutely identified, foreign contributions, with the more prestigious literary awards attached, were nonetheless the ones to bring substantial cultural capital to Mondadori in those years:

---

1   FAAM, *DL*, file publishing projects 1970, Vittorio Sereni to Sergio Polillo, 5 January 1970.
2   FAAM, *SEAI*, file Andrea Zanzotto, Marco Forti to Vittorio Sereni, 11 January 1971.
3   Ibid., Marco Forti to Vittorio Sereni, 17 June 1969.

se ne pubblicano sette o otto all'anno, equamente suddivisi tra italiani e stranieri. Non succede mai o quasi mai che un autore al suo primo libro venga qui inserito [...] Mi si dice regolarmente che sono troppi e si raccomanda la prudenza [...] Degli stranieri in genere si dice che vendono poco. Domanda: dobbiamo rinunciare agli stranieri? Però quando Seferis vinse il Nobel ci fece comodo averlo pubblicato.[4]

[we publish seven or eight books per year, equally split between Italian and foreign ones. New authors are practically never featured here [...] I am always told that there are too many and caution is recommended [...] Foreign authors, generally, aren't selling well, they say. Question: should we renounce them? However, when Seferis won the Nobel prize it was very convenient for us to have published him.]

The more conservative foundations of 'Lo Specchio' were also shaken by a freshly invigorated field and the emergence of a new audience, which Einaudi had already identified and addressed with its 'Collezione di poesia'.[5] Mondadori's poetry series was therefore in need of a further 'revitalisation', according to new internal and external dynamics: internally, because the launch of the bestselling pocket book series 'Oscar di Poesia' meant that 'Lo Specchio' had to become more innovative to avoid selling similar products to the same readership;[6] externally, because readers' expectations had changed and they now required more 'agile' books, both in terms of publishing package and literary content. The absolute value of consecration that the Mondadori *opera omnia* embodied lost credit and had to be substituted with more flexible books, with 'una veste grafica e un formato assolutamente diversi, più agile, più vivace' [an absolutely different graphic layout and format, more agile, more lively].[7]

Medium-scale publishers were not in a better position. With the 1969 crisis, Einaudi's financial struggles impacted its literary production: the sector released fewer and fewer new titles, privileging instead reprints in the

---

[4] FAAM, DL, file publishing policies, programmatic report by Vittorio Sereni, 15 January 1969.
[5] FAAM, SEAI, file Andrea Zanzotto, Vittorio Sereni to Marco Forti, 21 July 1969.
[6] FAAM, DL, file publishing projects 1971, memo by Vittorio Sereni to Sergio Polillo, 1971.
[7] FAAM, DL, file publishing policies, programmatic report by Vittorio Sereni, 15 January 1969.

'Coralli' and 'Supercoralli' series (Ferretti, 2004: 270–76). In the same way that the example of Gallimard's series had motivated Giulio Einaudi in the 1950s, at the end of the 1970s the 'Collezione di poesia' started looking at other foreign counterparts – though now based more on established cultural capital – as a response to Mondadori's transnational ambitions signalled by its investment on foreign projects. In particular, Fortini indicated the need to shake up the format of the *plaquettes*, and to opt for those fuller-bodied books that Einaudi editors had rejected in the 1940s. At the same time, Einaudi had to move away from conservative choices that would distance the student audience:

> Applicare il criterio di 3 in 1 o 4 in 1 (già dei 'Penguin', dei tedeschi e di Guanda) a un paio di volumetti della 'Collezione di poesia' che, invece di farla morire, bisogna rendere meno molle. Uno o due volumetti annui, sulle 200 pagine, stesso formato ma con nonnulla che renda identificabili, senza troppe spiegazioni ma con brevi introduzioni, possono presentare da tre a otto piccoli canzonieri nuovi ogni anno (con estratti, per narcisismi insaziati), mantenendo e legando a sé tutto un popolo nascente che diffama Einaudi come casa vegliarda e nemica del progresso.[8]

> [We should apply the 3 in 1 or 4 in 1 model (that Penguin, German publishers, and Guanda already use) to a couple of books in the 'Collezione di poesia' – instead of letting it die, we should reinforce it. One or two books per year, about 200 pages, same format but with a small detail that makes them identifiable, without too many explications but with short introductions, can offer from three to eight new poetry collections every year [...] thus keeping and winning the favour of the growing voices defaming Einaudi as old-fashioned and an enemy of progress.]

Fortini's comments triggered a debate within the editorial board between old and new entrants in relation to the pressure to publish Italian poets in an engaging way. Some wanted newer publishing formats in line with the more agile literary journals, such as Mondadori's 'Almanacco dello Specchio' launched in 1972, to reflect the dialogic and interactive transnational tendencies of the student movements and the Beat generation. Fortini, supported by Einaudi's longest-serving editors Calvino and Cases, suggested

---

8   AE, file Franco Fortini, to GE, 18 January 1978.

that employing a similar format would create a 'fastidiosissimo e pericoloso allevamento di pulci liriche' [very annoying and dangerous livestock of lyrical lice],⁹ difficult to manage in terms of social relationships and networks. This scepticism, coupled with the growing number of foreign poets in the 'Collezione di poesia', had prevented the series from accommodating contemporary Italian poetry throughout the 1970s: the more tendentious debates that accompanied the publication of these poets, a crucial source of symbolic capital in terms of innovation, found a more suitable home in the catalogues of small publishers:

> le difficoltà sono enormi: si pubblica un italiano ogni 80 stranieri d'ogni tempo e paese ed ogni volta a prezzo di lotte intestine a non finire¹⁰
>
> [the difficulties are huge: we publish one Italian for every 80 foreign poets from all periods and countries, and each time with endless internal arguments]
>
> Suggerimenti? Rivolgersi a Giovanni Raboni, che sta brillantemente dirigendo la nuova Guanda.¹¹
>
> [Suggestions? Ask Giovanni Raboni who is successsfully running the new Guanda.]

These words prompt further discussion. The publishing catalogues show a substantial change in the twenty-five years analysed (1951–77): in an attempt to fill the void of literary prestige that contemporary Italian poetry lacked, the medium- to large-scale publishing houses had published a significant number of contemporary foreign poetry titles. Their catalogues were now saturated, and they found themselves unable to welcome Italian poets. It might not be a coincidence that, at the beginning of the 1980s, both Fortini and Sereni published their own translation notebooks with Einaudi, as a way, if not to resurrect the model, then to find space and seal their careers as translators thus far. Translation had in fact entirely shifted the equilibrium of the poetry publishing field: while the small-scale publishers had been the first to embrace translation in order to renew national poetry, by the 1970s the

---

9   Ibid.
10 AE, file Nereo Condini, GDB, 28 January 1973.
11 AE, file Rosa Rossi, GDB, 20 December 1976.

publication of contemporary foreign poetry had become the prerogative of the larger publishers. In this new scenario, publishing contemporary Italian poetry represented an exception to the rule. Once again, it was the small-scale publishers who, seeking to redefine their own identity and centrality in the field, ultimately set the new trend by deciding to turn (back) to Italian poetry. Sereni had already outlined these changed dynamics in clear terms in 1973:

> È un affare serio. Garzanti pubblica uno o due libri di poesia all'anno. Einaudi fa ogni tanto un 'Supercorallo' di poesia, per il resto ha quella collezioncina bianca – molto simpatica – raramente destinata a poeti italiani [...] Che cosa rimane? Il solito Scheiwiller e poi Guanda, che non ho ancora capito se abbia chiuso o sia stato assorbito.[12]

> [It is a serious affair. Garzanti publishes one or two poetry books per year. Einaudi publishes every now and then a 'Supercorallo' of poetry, and for the rest it has that small white series – very nice – rarely devoted to Italian poets [...] What is left? The ever-present Scheiwiller and then Guanda, which I haven't quite understood whether it has closed down or been bought by other publishers.]

With Ugo Guandalini's death in 1971, Guanda had been in fact purchased by Garzanti. The move to Milan enhanced the literary identity – and more specifically the poetic identity – of the previously Parma-based publishing house: in 1974 it released the 'Quaderni della Fenice' ('the Phoenix Notebooks', an offshoot of the 'La Fenice' historical series), edited by poet Giovanni Raboni, which in contrast to its predecessor, privileged contemporary Italian poets (Milo De Angelis and Patrizia Valduga, among others).

The small publishers, though, no longer held the relatively autonomous position they had enjoyed in previous decades. If Guanda's dynamism implied a new vitality for the small-case publishing houses after the 1960s, when the larger publishers had regained some centrality, its operation under the aegis of Garzanti was also emblematic of new power relationships between Italian publishers. The larger publishers made use of formats ostensibly better-suited to small publishers, and this not from an illusory dismissal of marketing needs, but to satisfy the changed demands of a more specialised audience (Ferretti, 2004: 288–302). This phenomenon is not only relevant from a

---

12   FAAM, *DL*, file Francesco Tentori Montalto, Vittorio Sereni, 13 April 1973.

quantitative viewpoint, with 538 new publishing houses launched between 1970 and 1979 compared to the 211 created in the 1960s (Ferretti, 2004: 288),[13] but also in terms of field dynamics. With the increased literacy as well as the increased politicisation of the 1970s, the small publishers were able to carve out sites of resistance by focusing on literary experimentation and qualitative research, but risked being absorbed by the larger publishers when it came to distribution.

Their invisibility was due either to a continued reliance on artisanal distribution modes or to a loss of identity in the circuits of mass distribution. The problem envisaged by Vanni Scheiwiller as early as the 1950s had now become concrete. Scheiwiller was indeed forced to collaborate with other publishers, working as a consultant for Rusconi (Ferretti, 2009: 40), and to ask for help from banks and investors, as in the case of the 'Libri Scheiwiller', in order to overcome financial difficulties created by the 1977 economic crisis and made more acute by the increasing interference of new media (Santoro, 2008: 416–18). The illusion of a relatively autonomous poetry publishing field vanished as we approach the 1980s, and the binary opposition between smaller and larger publishers became less rigid. While the medium- to large-scale publishing houses reformulated their offer by drawing on the greater dynamism of the smaller publishers, the latter were absorbed into the larger structures.

4.2 Globalisation: future research directions and concluding remarks

Even in this new scenario, translation still finds a significant place in cultural production: although globalisation started to affect more closely the world publishing market at the end of the 1980s, in Italy it was somewhat anticipated by the field dynamics of the 1970s. When we talk of globalisation, it is important to avoid stereotypical representations of a phenomenon encouraging homogeneous trends only, by bearing in mind the Bourdieusian dualism of small- and large-scale circulation (Sapiro, 2010). In the former, coinciding with more elite genres such as poetry, a stronger linguistic diversity would emerge, while in the latter, anglophone and market-driven fiction

---

13 Book sales did not, however, increase progressively: the market fluctuated between the hard times of the 1972 crisis, the 1973–76 recovery, and a new decline after 1977 (Santoro, 2008: 414).

production seems to predominate. The pressing question for us is whether these reflections apply to the Italian case as well.

At the end of the 1970s the map of contemporary foreign poetry published in Italy was larger than just twenty-five years earlier. We have seen how the passage for both medium- and larger-scale publishers to the 'antologie mondiali' in the 1960s, and the 'younger anthologies' in the 1970s, suggested a further broadening of the national poetic borders towards a documentary interest in foreign cultural innovation. Within that context, more peripheral voices, such as South American poets, found a place with respect to a usually Eurocentric tradition. Einaudi's 'riunioni del mercoledì' [Wednesday meetings] reflected this change of perspective: critic and writer Malcolm Skey recommended opening the 'Collezione di poesia' to literatures from outside the consolidated European tradition, to include Chinese, Arabic, and Icelandic poets.[14] On 23 January 1980 Sergio Perosa proposed the name of the Australian poet Judith Wright for an anthology of anglophone countries,[15] while publishing African literature appeared compulsory for an offer that wanted to be truly 'global'.[16] Moving towards the 1980s, the linguistic spectrum became more varied and would seem to confirm that translation acted as a means of affirming cultural diversity in the most elite sectors such as poetry.

To confirm such trends, we need to test these enlarged borders against the historical framework of the time and against how foreign poetry interacted with the agents' positioning, articulated in the specific literary and publishing fields. As this book has demonstrated throughout, we cannot limit our analysis of the role played by translation to either a scrutiny of catalogues or an aesthetic analysis of a few translations from the sole perspective of translators. Any meaningful investigation of the publishing strategies of translation involves a rigorous study of the intricacies of the relationship between Italian publishing houses and contemporary foreign poetry, at a national and transnational level.

Thus far, *Publishing Contemporary Poetry* has shed light on these intricacies from the 1950s to the 1970s, when a significant, but under-investigated, 'turn to translation' took place. Traditional analyses tend to focus on single poets or to idealise the role of small publishers as disengaged in relation to marketing needs. We have instead problematised the study of poetry publishing by

14 AE, minutes of the meeting on 17 May 1978, Malcolm Skey.
15 AE, minutes of the meeting on 23 January 1980, Sergio Perosa.
16 AE, file Sergio Perosa, Carlo Carena, 18 May 1978.

interpreting translation as a fundamentally social practice in the negotiation between national and transnational agents and dynamics. The final result is an articulate perspective on poetry translation as a source of development of both cultural and publishing models in the post-war publishing field in Italy. This liberates poetry translation from being seen, reductively, as an elite practice, and gives it a significant cultural value, allowing it to cast light on wider dynamics in terms of publishing history and the history of culture. The publication of contemporary foreign poetry modified the field of poetry publishing, granting it a level of fluidity: once the small publishers had gained a relevant position, this prompted larger-scale publishers to embrace more innovative projects. Translation influenced the strategies of each publisher also in terms of domestic production: canonical poetry gradually lost its prestige and national poetics were questioned. Finally, translation helped publishers and editors to establish a more productive role for public intellectuals, by promoting anthologies of historical and sociological interest and by creating a platform for dialogue, through translations, for younger audiences in Italy and transnational cultural movements.

Although we could not examine a larger number of publishers, the lines of inquiry established here will be useful for further studies investigating globalisation and publishing dynamics in the 1980s. The 1950s and 1960s represented a period of relative autonomy for the poetry publishing field in Italy – also due to the 'separatezza delle due culture' [separation between the two cultures] (Ferretti, 1994) – rendering Bourdieu's theoretical framework particularly apt for the aims of our research. The question of whether, with the progressive loss of autonomy, these analytical tools need to be fine-tuned to avoid an unproductive dichotomous vision, remains open. The new modalities of the publishing industry from the 1980s onwards are more intimately linked to digital communication technologies and relate to new models of professional agents. Future research will have the advantage of drawing on digital publishing catalogues and the potential opening of further publishing archives for materials related to the period from the 1980s to the 1990s. The prevalence of IT communication within editorial boards should also make the scrutiny of correspondence more complete, and convenient, in terms of time and resources. Researchers will also need to equip themselves with knowledge of international copyright and distribution laws, which in the more artisan-based publishing sector of the post-war Italian period allowed less stringent practices. The function of literary agents as gatekeepers will also need to be further emphasised as the close links between the Italian literary and publishing field evidenced more direct contacts between publishers and editors. More granularity of approach in terms of gender and inclusivity perspectives, as well as wider linguistic diversity through collaboration with specialists in specific foreign literatures and cultures, could be afforded now that the broad parameters have been outlined by our current inquiry.

Above all, to unveil the increasingly multifaceted process of translation, researchers will need to adopt an interdisciplinary methodology that allows the sociology of cultural production, cultural history, and literary criticism to interact for any effective analysis of the entangled history of publishing, culture, and translation. Therein, translation cannot be ancillary but has a key function as an element that primarily characterises cultural production in Italy. An analysis of Italian culture that does not take into account a transnational dimension will only provide myopic views. Besides, contrary to conceiving translation as a field on its own – which can have legitimacy when analysing translation as a profession (Sela-Sheffy, 2006) – our study has shown that translation is *not* an isolated activity, but should be inserted within the analytical horizon of the specific history of publishing, to critically rethink the function of foreign literature in the production of national culture. It is indeed within the *specific* context – cultural and historical – in which translation is inserted that researchers can eventually overcome the sterile dichotomies between hybridity and homologisation that discourses on globalisation often suggest, and enhance our understanding of how transnational practices did and will shape domestic cultures.

APPENDIX ONE

Numbers of contemporary poetry titles published in Italy, 1939–77

The charts below show the number of titles of contemporary Italian poetry, and contemporary foreign poetry in translation, published by the most relevant publishing houses in Italy from 1939 to 1977. They include the first editions – as indicative of the introduction rather than the reception of contemporary foreign poetry in the market, and thus demonstrative of the publishing strategies – listed in the catalogues of the main publishing houses specialising in poetry – the Parma-based small publisher Guanda, Vanni Scheiwiller, Mondadori and Einaudi, as well as the Milan-based Feltrinelli (1954–) and Lerici (1956–) – when cross-referenced with the national library catalogue OPAC SBN.

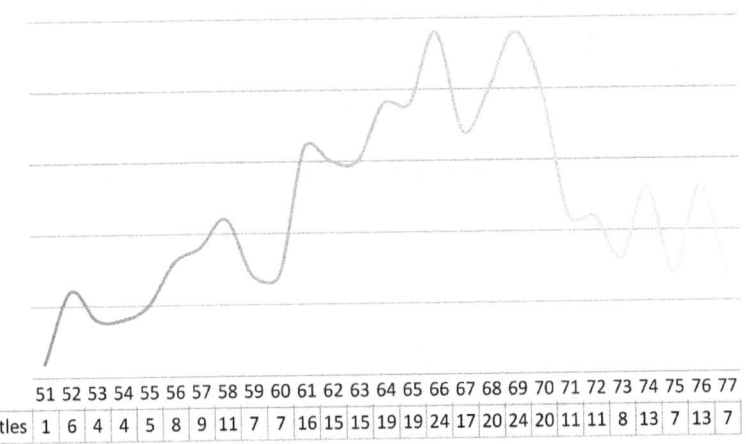

	51	52	53	54	55	56	57	58	59	60	61	62	63	64	65	66	67	68	69	70	71	72	73	74	75	76	77
Titles	1	6	4	4	5	8	9	11	7	7	16	15	15	19	19	24	17	20	24	20	11	11	8	13	7	13	7

Titles of contemporary foreign poetry (1951–77)

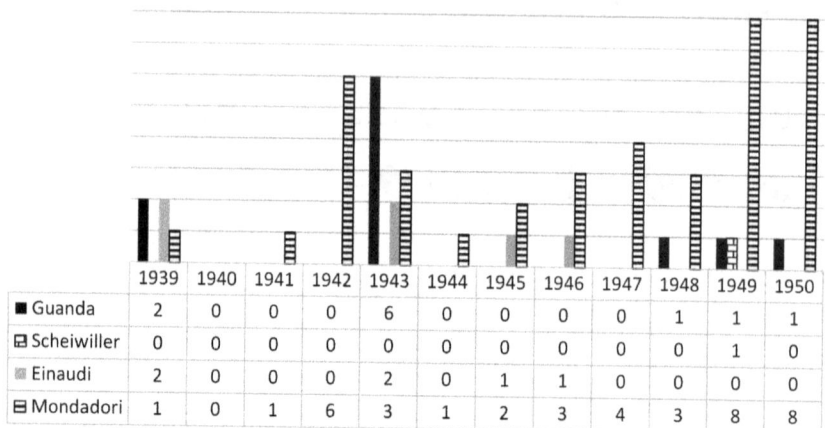

Titles of contemporary Italian poetry (1939–50)

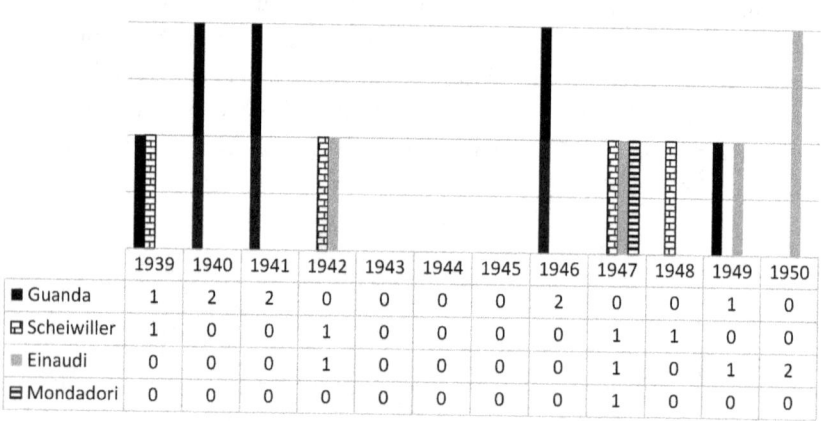

Titles of contemporary foreign poetry (1939–50)

Appendix One

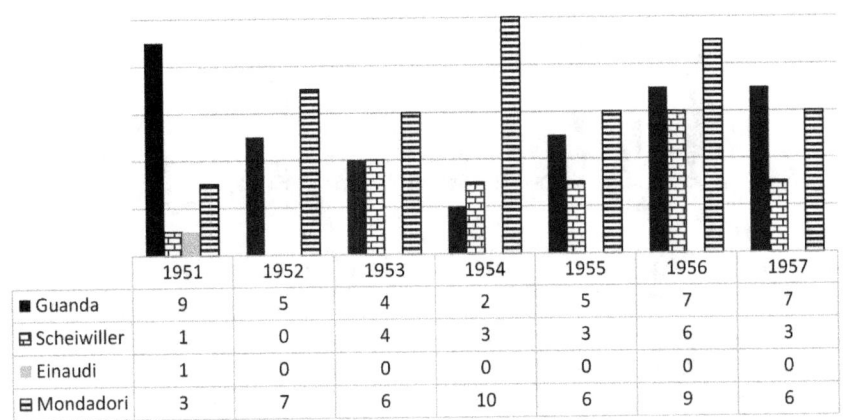

Titles of contemporary Italian poetry (1951–57)

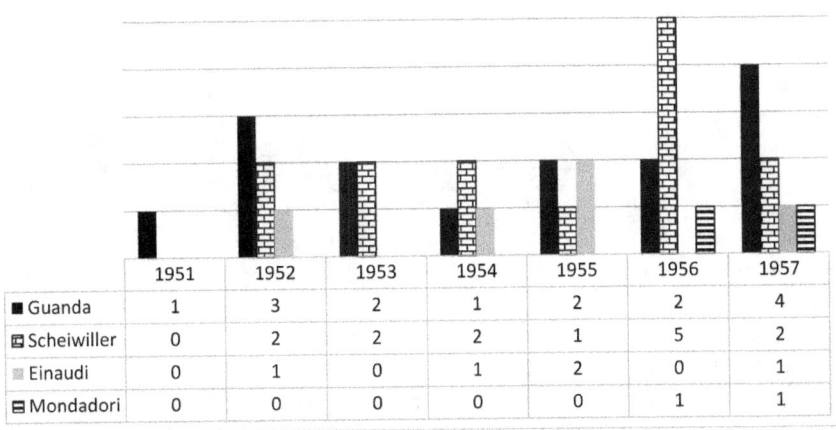

Titles of contemporary foreign poetry (1951–57)

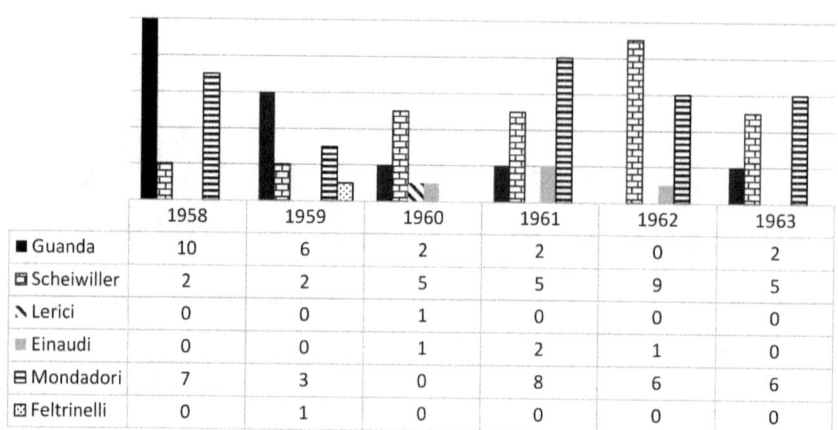

	1958	1959	1960	1961	1962	1963
■ Guanda	10	6	2	2	0	2
⊞ Scheiwiller	2	2	5	5	9	5
⃥ Lerici	0	0	1	0	0	0
▬ Einaudi	0	0	1	2	1	0
⊟ Mondadori	7	3	0	8	6	6
▦ Feltrinelli	0	1	0	0	0	0

Titles of contemporary Italian poetry (1958–63)

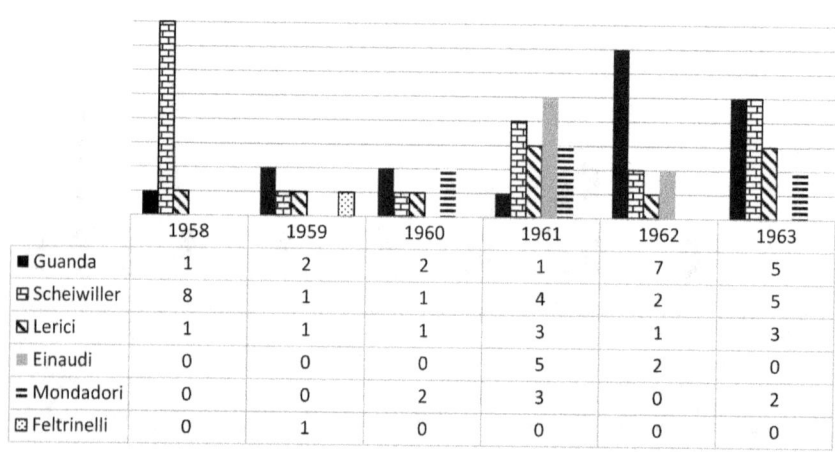

	1958	1959	1960	1961	1962	1963
■ Guanda	1	2	2	1	7	5
⊞ Scheiwiller	8	1	1	4	2	5
◨ Lerici	1	1	1	3	1	3
▬ Einaudi	0	0	0	5	2	0
= Mondadori	0	0	2	3	0	2
▦ Feltrinelli	0	1	0	0	0	0

Titles of contemporary foreign poetry (1958–63)

Appendix One

	1964	1965	1966	1967	1968
■ Guanda	2	1	0	1	1
▦ Scheiwiller	8	9	8	9	4
▩ Lerici	0	0	0	0	0
▓ Einaudi	1	6	2	3	5
☰ Mondadori	3	0	0	4	4
▨ Feltrinelli	1	2	3	1	5

Titles of contemporary Italian poetry (1964–68)

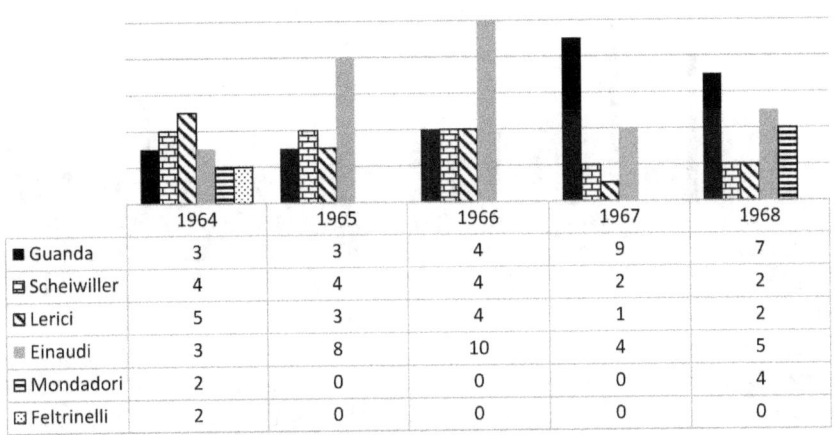

	1964	1965	1966	1967	1968
■ Guanda	3	3	4	9	7
▦ Scheiwiller	4	4	4	2	2
▧ Lerici	5	3	4	1	2
▓ Einaudi	3	8	10	4	5
☰ Mondadori	2	0	0	0	4
▨ Feltrinelli	2	0	0	0	0

Titles of contemporary foreign poetry (1964–68)

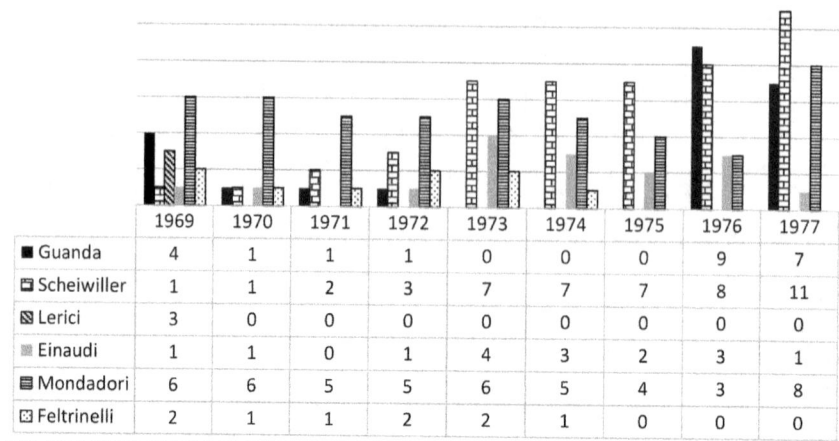

Titles of contemporary Italian poetry (1969–77)

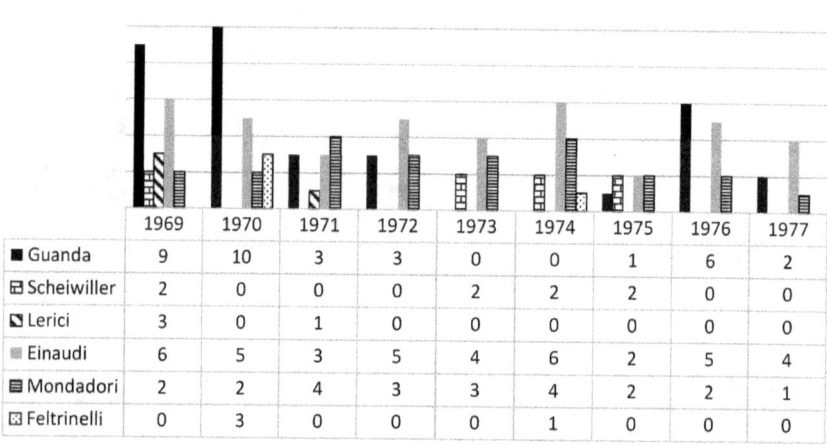

Titles of contemporary foreign poetry (1969–77)

Appendix One 223

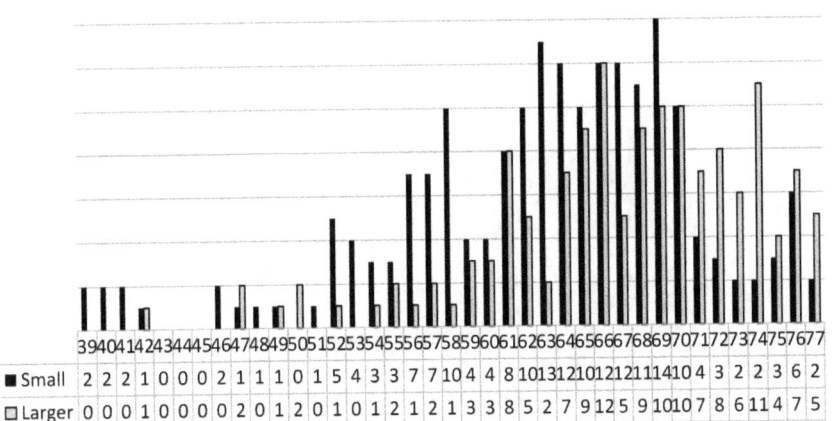

Titles of contemporary foreign poetry (1939–77)

APPENDIX TWO

Catalogue of contemporary Italian and foreign poetry titles published by Einaudi, Mondadori, and Scheiwiller, 1939–77

Below are listed the titles of contemporary Italian and foreign poetry (the latter highlighted in bold) published by the three publishers investigated: Einaudi, Mondadori, and Scheiwiller. Where available, print runs have been included. For Mondadori, these have been derived from FAAM and relate to the first editions only; for Einaudi, there are no specific data on first editions, and the print runs – made available to me by the former president of the Einaudi publishing house, Roberto Cerati – include all editions until 2010. The print runs below have been calculated on an average based on the number of editions; they are all plausible given the average print run of 3,000 copies (higher in the case of famous authors/translators).

Series 'Poeti' – Editore Einaudi (1939–60)

	Author	Title	Translator	Year
1	Montale, Eugenio	*Le Occasioni*		1939
2	Montale, Eugenio	*Ossi di seppia*		1939
3	**Rilke, Rainer Maria**	*Poesie*	Pintor, Giaime	1942
4	Jahier, Piero	*Con me e con gli alpini*		1943
5	Pavese, Cesare	*Lavorare stanca*		1943
6	Saba, Umberto	*Il Canzoniere*		1945
7	Fortini, Franco	*Foglio di via*		1946
8	**Éluard, Paul**	*Poesia ininterrotta*	Fortini, Franco	1947

	Author	Title	Translator	Year
9	Pavese, Cesare	Verrà la morte e avrà [...]		1951
10	Neruda, Pablo	Poesie	Quasimodo, S.	1952
11	Firpo, Edoardo	O grillo cantadò		1960

Series 'Collezione di poesia' – Einaudi (1964–77)

	Author	Title	Translator	Year	Print runs (editions)
1	Tyutchev, F.	Poesie	Landolfi, Tommaso	1964	3,022 (2)
2	Beckett, Samuel	Poesie in inglese	Wilcock, Rodolfo	1964	3,053 (7)
3	Brecht, Bertolt	Libro di devozioni [...]	Fertonani, Roberto	1964	3,682 (6)
4	Villa, Carlo	Siamo essere antichi		1964	3,991 (1)
5	Roversi, Roberto	Dopo Campoformio		1965	6,051 (1)
6	Bagritsky, Eduard	L'ultima notte	Strada, Vittorio	1965	4,045 (1)
7	Richelmy, Agostino	L'arrotino appassionato		1965	4,018 (1)
8	Luzi, Mario	Dal fondo delle campagne		1965	3,570 (9)
9	Eliot, T.S	La terra desolata	Praz, Mario	1965	3,996 (25)
10	Yeats, W. B	Quaranta poesie	Melchiori, Giorgio	1965	4,302 (19)
11	Valeri, Diego	Quaderno francese		1965	4,009 (1)
12	Neruda, Pablo	Poesie	Quasimodo, S.	1965	7,543 (31)
13		I Novissimi		1965	2,952 (5)
14	Blok, Alexandr	I dodici	Poggioli, Renato	1965	3,183 (4)
15	Holan, Vladimir	Una notte con Amleto	Ripellino, A.M.	1966	3,997 (1)
16	Toulet, Jean Paul	Poesie	Spaziani, M.L.	1966	4,023 (1)
17	Valéry, Paul	Il cimitero marino	Tutino, Mario	1966	3,248 (7)
18	Alberti, Rafael	Degli angeli	Bodini, Vittorio	1966	6,725 (2)
19	Morgenstern, C.	Canti grotteschi	Turazza, Anselmo	1966	4,026 (1)
21	Achmatova, Anna	Poema senza eroe	Riccio, Carlo	1966	3,399 (13)
22	Benn, Gottfried	Aprèslude	Masini, Ferruccio	1966	2,589 (4)
23	Prados, Emilio	Memoria dell'oblio	Tentori, Francesco	1966	3,057 (1)
24	Oppezzo, Piera	L'uomo qui presente		1966	3,053 (1)
25	O' Neill, Aleixandre	Portogallo mio rimorso	Lussu, Joyce	1966	3,066 (1)
26	Sachs, Nelly	Al di la della polvere	Porena, Ida	1966	6,010 (1)
27	Fortini, Franco	Foglio di via		1967	2,470 (4)

Appendix Two

	Author	Title	Translator	Year	Print runs (editions)
28	Frénaud, André	*Il silenzio di Genova*	Caproni, Giorgio	1967	4,009 (1)
29	Vallini, Carlo	*Un giorno*		1967	3,014 (1)
30	Simonotti Manacorda	*I banchi di terranova*		1967	3,006 (1)
31	Mayakovsky, V.	*Lenin*	Ripellino, A.M.	1967	9,753 (2)
32	Wilcock, Rodolfo	*Le parole morte*		1968	3,031 (1)
33	Yesenin, S.	*Pugacëv*	De Luca, Igino	1968	3,280 (4)
34		*Poeti di Tel quel*	Giuliani, Alfredo	1968	3,013 (2)
35	Caproni, Giorgio	*Il terzo libro e altre cose*		1968	4,056 (1)
36	Cavafy, C.	*Cinquantacinque poesie*	Dalmati, Margherita	1968	4,158 (12)
37	Char, René	*Fogli di Ipsos*	Sereni, Vittorio	1968	5,116 (1)
38	Corazzini, Sergio	*Poesie edite e inedite*		1968	2,188 (7)
39	Ceronetti, Guido	*Poesie. Frammenti [...]*		1968	3,018 (1)
40		*Giovani poeti tedeschi*	Fertonani, Roberto	1969	4,726 (3)
41	Berryman, John	*Omaggio a Mistress [...]*	Perosa, Sergio	1969	2,528 (2)
42	Ripellino, A.M.	*Notizie dal diluvio*		1969	3,006 (1)
43	Orten, Jiří	*La cosa chiamata poesia*	Giudici, Giovanni	1969	3,024 (1)
44	Larkin, Philip	*Le nozze di Pentecoste*	Pennati, Camillo	1969	3,016 (1)
45		*Quaderno di traduzioni*	Solmi, Sergio	1969	4,000 (1)
46	Bonnefoy, Yves	*Movimento e immobilità*	Grange Fiori, Diana	1969	4,137 (1)
47	Heym, Georg	*Umbrae Vitae*	Chiarini, Paolo	1970	3,027 (2)
48	Kunert, Günter	*Ricordo di un pianeta*	Forte, Luigi	1970	3,041 (1)
49	Aleixandre, Vicente	*La distruzione o amore*	Tentori, Francesco	1970	6,159 (2)
50	Goll, Ivan	*Erba di sogno*	Secci, Lia	1970	4,000 (1)
51	Mansfield, Katherine	*Poemetti*	Altichieri, Gilberto	1970	3,375 (3)
52	Quarantotti Gambini	*Al sole e al vento*		1970	3,000 (1)
53	Renart, Jean	*L'immagine riflessa*	Limentani, Alberto	1970	3,016 (1)
54	Valéry, Paul	*La giovane Parca*	Tutino, Mario	1971	3,459 (6)
55	Halas, František	*Imagena*	Ripellino, A.M.	1971	3,029 (1)
56	Benn, Gottfried	*Morgue*	Masini, Ferruccio	1971	3,612 (3)
57	Reverdy, Pierre	*Il libro di talento*	Porta, Antonio	1971	3,036 (1)
58	Moreno Villa, Jose	*Giacinta la rossa*	Bodini, Vittorio	1972	3,050 (1)
60		*Giovani p. sudamericani*	Bonetti, Umberto	1972	3,841 (3)
61	Jouve, Pierre Jean	*Paradiso perduto*	Risi, Nelo	1972	4,055 (2)

	Author	Title	Translator	Year	Print runs (editions)
62	Nouveau, Germaine	*I baci e altre poesie*	Frezza, Lucia	1972	2,521 (1)
63	Cabral De Melo Neto	*Morte e vita severina*	Ferioli, Daniela	1973	2,537 (1)
64	Giuliani, Alfredo	*Chi l'avrebbe detto*		1973	3,048 (1)
65		*Giovani poeti americani*	Menarini, Gianni	1973	3,525 (3)
66	Sollazzo, Lucia	*Unico Nord*		1973	2,539 (1)
67	Pennati, Camillo	*Erosagonie*		1973	2,542 (1)
68	De Andrade, Mario	*Io sono trecento*	Segre Giorgi, Giuliana	1973	3,034 (1)
69	Boll, Heinrich	*La mia musa*	Chiusano, Alighiero	1974	2,706 (3)
70	Strindberg, August	*Notti di sonnambulo [...]*	Oreglia, Giacomo	1974	2,392 (3)
71	Muir, Edwin	*Un piede nel'Eden*	Pellizer, Marina	1974	3,032 (1)
72	Parra, Nicaor	*Antipoesie*	Bonetti, Umberto	1974	3,032 (1)
73	Firpo, Edoardo	*O' grillo cantadò*		1974	3,565 (2)
74	Romano, Lalla	*Giovane è il tempo*		1974	6,039 (1)
75	Layton, Irving	*Il freddo verde elemento*	Lorenzini, Amleto	1974	3,012 (1)
76	Cavalli, Patrizia	*Le mie poesie non [...]*		1974	4,020 (1)
77	Loi, Franco	*Strolegh*		1975	3,054 (1)
78	Borges, Jorge Luis	*Carme Presunto*	Cianciolo, Umberto	1975	3,207 (6)
79	Martinson, Henri	*Le erbe della Thule*	Oreglia, Giacomo	1975	3,036 (1)
80	Sereni, Vittorio	*Gli strumenti umani*		1975	5,174 (2)
81		*Giovani poeti spagnoli*	Rossi, Rosa	1976	2,560 (2)
82		*Giovani poeti inglesi*	Oliva, Renato	1976	2,542 (2)
83	Mendes, Murilo	*Mondo enigma*	Cattaneo, Carlo	1976	2,517 (1)
84	Esenin, S.	*Anna Snegina*	De Luca, Iginio	1976	3,063 (2)
85	Ripellino, A.M.	*Lo splendido violino verde*		1976	2,044 (1)
86	Balestrini, Nanni	*Poesie pratiche*		1976	3,043 (1)
87	Éluard, Paul	*Poesia ininterrotta*		1976	6,038 (3)
88	Leonetti, Francesco	*Percorso logico*		1976	2,534 (1)
89		*Poeti simbolisti*	Viazzi, Glauco	1976	2,057 (3)
90	Biermann, Wolf	*Per i miei compagni*	Forte, Luigi	1976	7,156 (1)
91	Riba, Carles	*Elegie di Bierville*	Sansone, Giuseppe	1977	3,035 (1)
92	Jeffers, Robinson	*Cawdor*	Minuzzo Bacchiega	1977	2,055 (1)
93		*Quaderno di traduzioni II*	Solmi, Sergio	1977	2,058 (1)
94		*Giovani p. America C.*	Bonetti, Umberto	1977	4,109 (2)

Appendix Two

Series 'Lo Specchio' – Mondadori (1947–77)

	Author	Title	Translator	Year
1	Sinisgalli, Leonardo	I nuovi Campi Elisi		1947
2	Ungaretti, Giuseppe	Il dolore		1947
3	Montale, Eugenio	Ossi di seppia		1948
4	Sbarbaro, Camillo	Trucioli		1948
5	Ungaretti, Giuseppe	Da Gongora e da Mallarmé		1948
6	Montale, Eugenio	Le occasioni		1949
7	Antonino, Attilio	Sequenze d'autunno		1950
8	Cecchi, Emilio	L'osteria del cattivo tempo		1950
9	Chiesa, Francesco	L'artefice malcontento		1950
10	Gatto, Alfonso	Nuove poesie		1950
11	Saba, Umberto	Trieste e una donna		1950
12	Solmi, Segio	Poesie		1950
13	Valeri, Diego	Terzo tempo		1950
14	Bassani, Giorgio	Un'altra libertà		1951
15	Quasimodo, Salvatore	Dall'Odissea		1951
16	Zanzotto, Andrea	Dietro il paesaggio		1951
17	Borgese, Giuseppe A.	Le poesie		1952
18	Borlenghi, Aldo	Poesie		1952
19	Pavolini, Corrado	Natura morta		1952
20	Saba, Umberto	Cose leggere e vaganti		1952
21	Turoldo, David Maria	Udii una voce		1952
22	Valeri, Diego	Poesie vecchie e nuove		1952
23	Carrieri, Raffaele	Il Trovatore		1953
24	Ivancich, Adriana	Ho guardato il cielo e la terra		1953
25	Valeri, Diego	Fantasie veneziane		1953
26	Visconti, Marco	Poesie		1953
27	Zaleo, Lina	Il fiore dell'agrifoglio		1953
28	Arcangeli, Gaetano	Solo se ombra (1941–53)		1954
29	Gatto, Alfonso	La forza degli occhi		1954
30	Govoni, Corrado	Manoscritto nella bottiglia		1954
31	Manfredi, Antonio	Poesie		1954
32	Scotellaro, Rocco	È fatto giorno		1954

	Author	Title	Translator	Year	
33	Spaziani, Maria Luisa	Le acque del Sabato		1954	
34	Ungaretti, Giuseppe	Un grido e paesaggi		1954	
35	Ungaretti, Giuseppe	La terra promessa		1954	
36	Bona, Gian Piero	I giorni delusi		1955	
37	Flora, Francesco	Canti spirituali		1955	
38	Jona, Emilio	Tempo di vivere		1955	
39	Saba, Umberto	Preludio e fughe		1955	
40	Satta, Sebastiano	Canti		1955	
41	Turoldo, David Maria	Gli occhi miei lo vedranno		1955	
42	Piccolo, Lucio	Canti barocchi [...]		1956	
43	Quasimodo, Salvatore	Il falso e vero verde		1956	
44	Risi, Nelo	Polso teso		1956	
45	Sinisgalli, Leonardo	La vigna vecchia		1956	
46	Terra, Stefano	Quaderno dei 30 anni		1956	
47	Titta Rosa, Giovanni	Poesie d'una vita		1956	
48	Villaroel, Giuseppe	Quasi vento d'aprile		1956	
49	Arpino, Giovanni	Il prezzo dell'oro		1957	
50	D'Annunzio, Gabriele	Le martyre de [...]		1957	
51	**Drouet, Minou**	**Albero, amico**	Piceni, Enrico	1957	
52	Montale, Eugenio	La bufera		1957	
53	Ortolani, Sergio	Poesie		1957	
54	Quasimodo, Salvatore	Fiore delle Georgiche		1957	
55	Serafini, Giovanni	Barchette di carta		1957	
56	Zanzotto, Andrea	Vocativo		1957	
57	Bigongiari, Piero	Le mura di Pistoia		1958	
58	Carrieri, Raffaele	Canzoniere amoroso		1958	
59	Cattafi, Bartolo	Le mosche del meriggio, poesie		1958	
60	Cetrangolo, Enzio	I miti del Tirreno		1958	
61	Quasimodo, Salvatore	La terra impareggiabile		1958	
62	Rinaldi, Antonio	Poesie		1958	
63	Valeri, Diego	Il flauto a due canne		1958	Print runs
64	Leonetti, Francesco	La cantica		1959	1,019
65	Saba, Umberto	Cuor morituro [...]		1959	2,009

Appendix Two 231

	Author	Title	Translator	Year	
66	Valeri, Diego	Lirici tedeschi		1959	2,021
67	Erba, Luciano	Il male minore		1960	1,003
68	Noventa, Giacomo	Versi e poesie		1960	1,995
69	Piccolo, Lucio	Gioco a nascondere...		1960	2,014
70	Pound, Ezra	Le poesie scelte	Rizzardi, Antonio	1960	2,131
71	Quasimodo, Salvatore	Tutte le poesie		1960	
72	Valeri, Diego	Lirici francesi		1960	2,200
73	Betocchi, Carlo	L'estate di S. Martino		1961	1,978
74	Bigongiari, Piero	Il vento di ottobre [...]		1961	2,990
75	Di Pilla, Francesco	Tempo d'esilio		1961	
76	Gatto, Alfonso	Poesie		1961	1,989
77	Joyce, James	Poesie	Giuliani, Alfredo	1961	3,040
78	Cavafy, C.	Poesie	Pontani, F.M.	1961	2,704
79	Risi, Nelo	Pensieri elementari		1961	1,851
80	Saba, Umberto	Parole. Ultime cose		1961	2,021
81	Saba, Umberto	Il piccolo Berto		1961	1,995
82	Saba, Umberto	Preludio e fughe		1961	2,800
83	Ungaretti, Giuseppe	Il deserto e dopo		1961	3,546
84	Ungaretti, Giuseppe	Il taccuino del vecchio		1961	1,007
85	Bodini, Vittorio	La luna dei Borboni		1962	2,048
86	Gatto, Alfonso	Osteria flegrea		1962	2,006
87	Orelli, Giorgio	L'ora del tempo		1962	2,014
88	Sinisgalli	L'età della luna		1962	2,707
89	Valeri, Diego	Poesie		1962	2,021
90	Artoni, Gian Carlo	Lo stesso dolore		1963	2,050
91	Bellintani, Umberto	E tu che m'ascolti		1963	1,936
92	Carrieri, Raffaele	La giornata è finita		1963	1,966
93	Fortini, Franco	Una volta per sempre		1963	1,993
94	Hikmet, Nazim	Poesie d'amore	Lussu, Joyce	1963	2,006
95	Bigongiari, Piero	Torre di Arnolfo		1964	1,448
96	Cattafi, Bartolo	L'osso, l'anima		1964	1,465
97	Pennati, Camillo	L'ordine delle parole		1964	1,979
98	Różewicz, Tadeusz	Colloquio con il principe	Carlo Verdiani	1964	1,496

	Author	Title	Translator	Year	
99	Blake, William	*Visioni*	Ungaretti, Giuseppe	1965	
100	Borlenghi, Aldo	*Nuove poesie*		1965	1,977
101	Dal Fabbro, Beniamino	*La cravatta bianca*		1965	2,014
102	Giudici, Giovanni	*La vita in versi*		1965	1,952
103	Risi, Nelo	*Dentro la sostanza*		1965	1,998
104	**Robinson, Arlington**	*Uomini e ombre*	Giuliani, Alfredo	1965	3,042
105	Sereni, Vittorio	*Diario d'Algeria*		1965	3,005
106	Arghezi, Tudor	*Poesie*	Quasimodo, Salvatore	1966	1,624
107	**Auden, Wystan H.**	*L'età dell'ansia*	Rinaldi Antonio	1966	2,021
108	Gatto, Alfonso	*La storia delle vittime*		1966	3,050
109	Grande, Adriano	*La tomba verde [...]*		1966	2,050
110	Quasimodo	*Dare e avere*		1966	4,100
111	Raboni, Giovanni	*Le case della Vetra*		1966	1,937
112	**Roethke, Theodore**	*Sequenza nordamericana*	Meliadò, Mariolina	1966	2,120
113	Sinisgalli	*Poesie di ieri*		1966	2,015
114	Spaziani, Maria Luisa	*Utilità della memoria*		1966	2,049
115	Betocchi, Carlo	*Un passo, un altro...*		1967	3,130
116	Carrieri, Raffaele	*Io che sono cicala*		1967	2,061
117	**Celaya, Gabriel**	*Poesie*	Di Pinto, Mario	1967	2,003
118	Majorino, Giancarlo	*Lotte secondarie*		1967	1,541
119	Vigolo, Giorgio	*La luce ricorda*		1967	2,044
120	Bigongiari, Piero	*Stato di cose*		1968	1,565
121	**Gunn, Thom**	*I miei tristi capitani*	Pennati, Camillo	1968	1,914
122	**Levertov, Denise**	*La scala di Giacobbe...*	de Rachewiltz, M.	1968	2,120
123	Palazzeschi, Aldo	*Cuor mio*		1968	2,587
124		*Da Aiken e Cummings*	Quasimodo, S.	1968	1,953
125	**Seferis, Giorgos**	*Poesie*	Pontani, Filippo M.	1968	2,100
126	Solmi, Sergio	*Dal balcone*		1968	2,077
127	Zanzotto, Andrea	*La beltà*		1968	1,991
128	**Alberti, Rafael**	*Il poeta nella strada*	Bodini, Vittorio	1969	2,016
129	Bandini, Fernando	*Memoria del futuro*		1969	
130	**Bobrowski, Johannes**	*Poesie*	Fertonani, Roberto	1969	
131	Fortini, Franco	*Poesia e errore*		1969	

Appendix Two 233

	Author	Title	Translator	Year	
132	Gatto, Alfonso	*Rime di viaggio...*		1969	
133	Giudici, Giovanni	*Autobiologia*		1969	
134	Moretti, Marino	*L'ultima estate*		1969	
135	Carrieri, Raffaele	*Stellacuore*		1970	
136	Della Corte, Carlo	*Versi incivili*		1970	
137	**Huchel, Peter**	***Strade Strade***	Fortini, Franco	**1970**	
138	Risi, Nelo	*Di certe cose*		1970	2,107
139	Sinisgalli	*Il passero e il lebbroso*		1970	2,164
140	Spaziani, Maria Luisa	*L'occhio del ciclone*		1970	
141	**Tate, Allen**	*Ode ai caduti...*	Rizzardi, Alfredo	**1970**	
142	Valeri, Diego	*Verità di uno*		1970	1,676
143	Arcangeli, Gaetano	*Le poesie*		1971	1,551
144	**Creeley, Robert**	***Per amore***	Cacciaguerra, Perla	**1971**	
145	De Libero, Libero	*Di brace in brace*		1971	2,147
146	De Michelis, Cesare G.	*Poesia sovietica anni '60*	Giudici, Giovanni	1971	
147	Majorino, Giancarlo	*Equilibrio in pezzi*		1971	
148	**Montale, Eugenio**	***Satura***		**1971**	10,048
149	Moretti, Marino	*Tre anni e un giorno*		1971	
150	**Ponge, Francis**	*Vita del testo*	Bigongiari, Piero	**1971**	
151	**Ransom, John Crowe**	***Le donne e i cavalieri***	Giudici, Giovanni	**1971**	
152	**Alberti, Rafael**	***Roma, pericolo ...***	Bodini, Vittorio	**1972**	
153	Bigongiari, Piero	*Antimateria*		1972	
154	Bodini, Vittorio	*Poesie*		1972	
155	Cattafi, Bartolo	*L'aria secca del fuoco*		1972	
156	De Libero, Libero	*Scempio e lusinga*		1972	
157	Giudici, Giovanni	*O Beatrice*		1972	
158	**Olson, Charles**	***Maximus: poesie***	Sabbadini, Silvano	**1972**	
159	Palazzeschi, Aldo	*Via delle cento stelle*		1972	
160	**Ritsos, Yiannis**	***Prima dell'uomo***	Pontani, F.M.	**1972**	
161	Crovi, Raffaele	*Elogio del disertore*		1973	
162	Fortini, Franco	*Questo muro*		1973	1,560
163	Gatto, Alfonso	*Poesie d'amore*		1973	4,071
164	**Hughes, Ted**	***Pensiero-Volpe***	Pennati/Lombardo	**1973**	

	Author	Title	Translator	Year	
165	Moretti, Marino	Le poverazze		1973	
166	Pound, Ezra	Cantos scelti	de Rachewiltz, M.	1973	
167	Zanzotto, Andrea	Pasque		1973	
168	Bassani, Giorgio	Epitaffio		1974	
169	Betocchi, Carlo	Prime e ultimissime		1974	
170	Carrieri, Raffaele	Le ombre dispettose		1974	3,600
171	Char, René	Ritorno sopramonte	Sereni, Vittorio	1974	
172	Yevtushenko	Le betulle nane	Buttafava, Giovanni	1974	3,500
173	Cavafy, C.	Poesie nascoste	Pontani, Filippo M.	1974	
174	MacNeice, Louis	Poesie	Paci, Francesca R.	1974	
175	Moretti, Marino	Diario senza le date		1974	
176	Cattafi, Bartolo	La discesa al trono		1975	
177	Raboni, Giovanni	Cadenza d'inganno		1975	
178	Sinisgalli	Mosche in bottiglia		1975	
179	Snodgrass, W. D.	L'ago del cuore...	Binni, Francesco	1975	
180	Valeri, Diego	Calle del vento		1975	2,500
181	Celan, Paul	Poesie	Kahn, Moshe et al.	1976	
182	Cucchi, Maurizio	Il disperso		1976	
183	De Libero, Libero	Circostanze		1976	
184	Plath, Sylvia	Lady Lazarus	Giudici, Giovanni	1976	2,558
185	Risi, Nelo	Amica mia nemica		1976	
186	Cattafi, Bartolo	Marzo e le sue Idi		1977	

Scheiwiller (1951–77)

	Author	Title	Translator	Year
1		Poetesse del Novecento	Scheiwiller, Giovanni	1951
2		Proverbi cinesi	Prampolini, G.	1952
3		Hakai. Poesie giapponesi	Moretti, Franco	1952
4		250 proverbi negri	Prampolini, G.	1953
5	Bartolini, Luigi	Addio ai sogni		1953
6	Chiesa, Francesco	Alla chiesa fuggitiva		1953
7		50 pantun indonesiani	Prampolini, G.	1953

Appendix Two

	Author	Title	Translator	Year
8	De Libero, Libero	Ascolta la Ciociaria		1953
9	Bartolini, Luigi	Poesie per Anita e Luciana		1953
10		Omaggio a Rimbaud	Bacchelli, R. et al.	1954
11	Poeti italiani	Poesie alla madre	Scheiwiller, Vanni	1954
12	Spaziani, Maria Luisa	Primavera a Parigi		1954
13	Pound, Ezra	Tre Cantos	de Rachewiltz, M.	1954
14	Carli, Valeria	Il solco sottile		1954
15	Cappelli, Luigi	Cartoline di Roma		1955
16	Rebora, Clemente	Curriculum Vitae		1955
17		Lirici tedeschi	Valeri, Diego	1955
18	Merini, Alda	Paura di Dio		1955
19		Canti del Dalai Lama	Prampolini, G.	1956
20	Rebora, Clemente	Canti dell'infermità		1956
21	Parronchi, Alessandro	Coraggio di vivere		1956
22		In viaggio con Supervieille	Risi, Nelo	1956
23	Valeri, Diego	Metamorfosi dell'angelo		1956
24	Cristina, Campo	Passo d'addio		1956
25	Cavafy, C.	Poesie scelte	Pontani, F.M.	1956
26		Poeti slavi	Poggioli, Renato	1956
27	Sbarbaro, Camillo	Rimanenze		1956
28	Penna, Sandro	Una strana gioia di vivere		1956
29		Strofe del Vietnam	Prampolini, G.	1956
30	D'Arrigo, Stefano	Codice siciliano		1957
31	Risi, Nelo	Il contromemoriale		1957
32	Guidacci, Margherita	Giorno dei santi		1957
33		Poeti fiamminghi	Prampolini, G.	1957
34		Poesie degli Indios Piaroa	Costanzo, Giorgio	1957
35	Pound, Ezra	A lume spento	Scheiwiller, Vanni	1958
36	Pound, Ezra	Cantos 98	de Rachewiltz, M.	1958
37	Risi, Nelo	Civilissimo		1958
38	cummings, e.e.	Poesie	Quasimodo, S.	1958
39	Stefani, Armando	Fine del sentimento		1958
40	Williams, W.C.	Il fiore è il nostro segno	Campo, Cristina	1958

	Author	Title	Translator	Year
41	MacLeish, Archibald	*Four poems*	Guidacci, M.	1958
42	Auden, W.H.	*Good-bye to Mezzogiorno*	Izzo, Carlo	1958
43	Guillén, Jorge	*Poesie*	Montale, Eugenio	1958
44	Eliot, T.S.	*Poesie*	Montale, Eugenio	1958
45	Pound, Ezra	*Catai*	de Rachewiltz, M.	1959
46	Fabiani, Enzo	*L'anima in fiamme*		1959
47	Erba, Luciano	*Il prete di Ratanà*		1959
48	Pound, Ezra	*Cantos 99*	de Rachewiltz, M.	1960
49	Draghi, Piero	*Licenza di caccia*		1960
50	Bona, Gian Piero	*Il liuto pellegrino*		1960
51	Orelli, Giorgio	*Nel cerchio familiare*		1960
52	Pasolini, Pier Paolo	*Sonetto primaverile 1953*		1960
53	Bàrberi Squarotti, G.	*La voce roca*		1960
54	cummings, e.e.	*30 poesie*	de Rachewiltz, M.	1961
55	Simonotti-Manacorda	*I baffi di Blériot*		1961
56	Mendes, Murilo	*Finestra del caos*	Ungaretti, G.	1961
57	Guillén, Jorge	*La fuente*	Luzi, Mario	1961
58	Joyce, James	*Musica da camera*	Camerino, Aldo	1961
59	Caggiati, Marco	*L'invenzione della dolcezza*		1961
60	Laghlin, James	*Pulsatilla*	de Rachewiltz, M.	1961
61	Cattafi, Bartolo	*Qualcosa di preciso*		1961
62	Balestrini, Nanni	*Il sasso appeso*		1961
63	Valéry, Paul	*Il cimitero marino*	Tutino, Alessandro	1962
64	Cocchietto, Mario	*Dieci poesie*		1962
65	Bona, Gian Piero	*Eros anteros*		1962
66	Gherarducci, Vera	*Le giornate bianche*		1962
67	Messina, Francesco	*Ilaria e altre poesie*		1962
68	Sanguineti, Edoardo	*K. e altre cose*		1962
69		*Proverbi coreani*	Prampolini, G.	1962
70	Risi, Nelo	*Minime massime*		1962
71	Valeri, Diego	*I nuovi giorni*		1962
72	Jahier, Piero	*Qualche poesia*		1962
73	Merini, Alda	*Tu sei Pietro*		1962

Appendix Two

	Author	Title	Translator	Year
74		Antologia della lirica albanese	Koliqi, Ernesto	1963
75	Benn, Gottfried	Aprèslude	Masini, Ferruccio	1963
76	Giudici, Giovanni	L'educazione cattolica		1963
77	Raboni, Giovanni	L'insalubrità dell'aria		1963
78	Aiken, Conrad	Mutevoli pensieri	Quasimodo, S.	1963
79		Proverbi curdi	Prampolini, G.	1963
80	Luzi, Mario	Nel magma		1963
81	Guidi, Virgilio	Poesie brevi e d'amore		1963
82		Quaderno di traduzioni	Solmi, Sergio	1963
83	Valeri, Diego	La sera		1963
84	Orelli, Giorgio	6 poesie		1964
85	Pavese, Cesare	Poesie inedite		1964
86	Pound, Ezra	Confucio	Scarfoglio, Carlo	1964
87	Frénaud, André	Poesie	Bertolucci, A., et al.	1964
88	Porta, Antonio	Aprire		1964
89	Venchieredo, Paolo	Dodici poesie		1964
90	Selvatico Estense, D.	Un giorno all'improvviso		1964
91	Cardarelli, Vincenzo	Invettiva e altre poesie		1964
92	Pagliarani, Elio	Lezione di fisica		1964
93	Banus, Maria	Nuovi spazi	Vrinceanus, Dagos	1964
94		Omaggio a M. Moore	de Rachewiltz, M.	1964
95	Giuliani, Alfredo	Pelle d'asino		1964
96	Balestrini, Nanni	Altri procedimenti		1965
97	Fasani, Remo	Un altro segno		1965
98		Canti dei negri d'America	Griffini, G.	1965
99	de Rachewiltz, Mary	Il diapason		1965
100	Rebora, Clemente	Ecco del ciel più grande		1965
101		Lirici greci contemporanei	Dalmati, Margherita	1965
102	Hesse, Hermann	Poesie	Pocar, Ervino	1965
103		Poeti croati moderni	Trograncic, F.	1965
104	Garufi, Bianca	La fune		1965
105	Dazzi, Manlio	Peso della memoria		1965
106	Barile, Angelo	Poesie		1965

	Author	Title	Translator	Year
107	Valeri, Diego	*Poesie piccole*		1965
108	Rebora, Roberto	*Il verbo essere*		1965
109		*Poeti olandesi*	Prampolini, G.	1966
110	Sereni, Vittorio	*Frontiera*		1966
111	Camber, Giulio	*Anima di frontiera*		1966
112	Parronchi, Alessandro	*L'apparenza non inganna*		1966
113		**Canti degli Araucani**	Alberti, Aitana	1966
114	Ungaretti, Giuseppe	*Il Carso non è più un inferno*		1966
115	Testori, Giovanni	*Crocifissione*		1966
116	de Rachewiltz, Mary	*Di riflesso*		1966
117	Spatola, Adriano	*L'ebreo negro*		1966
118	Guerrini, Rosanna	*Invettive*		1966
119	**Illyés, Gyula**	*Két Kéz*	Risi, Nelo	1966
120		*Kabir*	Pound and Singh	1966
121	Pratolini, Vasco	*La città ha i miei trent'anni*		1967
122	Boccardi, Sandro	*Durezze e ligature*		1967
123	Carrieri, Raffaele	*La formica Maria*		1967
124	Antonicelli, Franco	*Improvvisi*		1967
125	Fasani, Remo	*La lezione del "Fiore"*		1967
126	Eliot, T.S.	*Poesie giovanili*	Sanesi, Roberto	1967
127		**Poeti ciprioti contemporanei**	Dalmati, Margherita	1967
128	Bodini, Vittorio	*Metamor*		1967
129	Draghi, Gianfranco	*Paracelso*		1967
130	Piccolo, Lucio	*Plumelia*		1967
131	Draghi, Piero	*Un attimo di attenzione*		1967
132	**Seferis, Giorgos**	*Note per una settimana*	Pontani, F.M.	1968
133	Goffi, Lento	*Dalla marca d'Oriente*		1968
134	Bertin, Mary	*Nebbia a Milano*		1968
135		**Omaggio a Praga**	Giudici, Giovanni	1968
136	Carpinteri e Faraguna	*Serbidiola*		1968
137	Marin, Biagio	*Tra sera e notte*		1968
138	**Ritsos, Yiannis**	*Poesie*	Pontani, F.M.	1969

Appendix Two

	Author	Title	Translator	Year
139		*Proverbi giapponesi*	Ricca, Giuseppe	1969
140	Cima, Annalisa	*Terzo modo*		1969
141	Fortini, Letizia	*Pena la vita*		1970
142	Gritti, Enzo	*Pienezza di vita cantata*		1971
143	Montonati, Ambrogio	*Trapezio*		1971
144	Borlenghi, Aldo	*28 Poesie*		1972
145	Bona, Gian Piero	*Alchimie della vita*		1972
146	Tanturri, Riccardo	*Alla fine della vita*		1972
147	Spezzotti, G. B.	*12 Poesie*		1973
148	Ramat, Silvio	*Corpo e cosmo*		1973
149	Fontanelli, Giorgio	*Georgicon*		1973
150	Provenzali, Delfina	*Il giorno fermo*		1973
151	Bortoluzzi, Emilio	*In viaggio*		1973
152	Principe, Quirino	*Il libro dei cinque sentieri*		1973
153	Negri, Renzo	*Parole nello spazio*		1973
154	**Michaux, Henri**	*Ombre per l'eternità*	Grange Fiori, Diana	1973
155	de Rachewiltz, Mary	*Processo in verso*		1973
156	**Pound, Ezra**	*Stesure Cantos 110-7*	de Rachewiltz, M.	1973
157	Calzavara, Ernesto	*Come se: infralogie*		1974
158	Goffi, Lento	*Evasivamente flou*		1974
159	Cima, Annalisa	*Immobilità*		1974
160	**Guillevic, Eugène**	*Inverno*	Provenzali, Delfina	1974
161	Guerrini, Adriano	*Jon il groelandese*		1974
162	**Mendes, Murilo**	*Mendes di domenica*	Cima, Annalisa	1974
163	Fortini, Letizia	*Il punto acerbo*		1974
164	Melotti, Fausto	*Il triste minotauro*		1974
165	Kacyzne, Alter	*Le perle malate*	Pizzetti, Ippolito	1974
166	Pola, Marco	*Cento poesie scelte*		1975
167	**Esteban, Claude**	*Dare un nome*	Provenzali, Delfina	1975
168	Zanotto, Sandro	*Il funzionario testimonia*		1975
169	Aletti, Adelina	*Giorni d'acqua*		1975
170	Novaro, Mario	*Murmuri ed echi*		1975
171	**Du Bouchet, André**	*Nella calura vacante*	Provenzali, Delfina	1975

	Author	Title	Translator	Year
172	Levi, Primo	*L'osteria di Brema*		1975
173	Bottiroli, Giovanni	*Parodia*		1975
174	Ricciardi, Luigi	*Specchi di nero*		1975
175	Turoldo, D.M.	*Fine dell'uomo?*		1976
176	Virgillito, Rina Sara	*I fiori del cardo*		1976
177	Laurenzi, Carlo	*L'illusione della solennità*		1976
178	Balestra, Tito	*Poesie di Liestal*		1976
179	Guerrini, Adriano	*Poesie politiche*		1976
180	Giubelli, Giovanna	*Se: diario*		1976
181	Angelini, Claudio	*Viaggio di nozze*		1976
182	Bernari, Carlo	*26 cose in versi*		1976
183	Santarcangeli, Paolo	*Resa dei conti*		1977
184	Pugliatti, Salvatore	*Canti di primitivi*		1977
185	Calzavara, Ernesto	*Cembalo scrivano*		1977
186	Quadrelli, Rodolfo	*Commedia*		1977
187	Silvera, Miro	*Liber singularis*		1977
188	Marrucci, Luciano	*Luci del Sagittario*		1977
189	Rebora, Roberto	*Non altro*		1977
190	Blandini, Arcangelo	*Poesie*		1977
191	Familiari, Rocco	*Ritratto di spalle*		1977
192	Forni, Pier Massimo	*Stemmi*		1977
193	Trombadori, Antonello	*I segni eugubini*		1977

Works Cited

Primary sources

Beckett, Samuel, *Poesie in inglese*, trans. by Rodolfo Wilcock (Turin: Einaudi, 1964).
Bellini, Giuseppe, ed., *Poeti delle Antille* (Parma: Guanda, 1963).
Bertolucci, Attilio, ed., *Poesia straniera del Novecento* (Milan: Garzanti, 1958).
Croce, Elena, ed., *Poeti stranieri del Novecento italiani e stranieri* (Turin: Einaudi, 1960).
Fertonani, Roberto, ed., *Giovani poeti tedeschi* (Turin: Einaudi, 1969).
Gunn, Thom, *I miei tristi capitani*, trans. by Camillo Pennati (Milan: Mondadori, 1968).
Izzo, Carlo, ed. *Poesia inglese contemporanea: da Thomas Hardy agli apocalittici* (Parma: Guanda, 1950).
Levertov, Denise, *La scala di Giacobbe e altre poesie*, trans. by Mary de Rachewiltz (Milan: Mondadori, 1968).
Lussu, Joyce, *Tradurre poesia* (Milan: Mondadori, 1967).
MacNeice, Louis, *Poesie*, trans. by Francesca Romana Paci (Milan: Mondadori, 1974).
Mansfield, Katherine, *Poemetti*, trans. by Gilberto Altichieri (Turin: Einaudi, 1970).
Menarini, Gianni, ed., *Giovani poeti americani* (Turin: Einaudi, 1973).
Morgenstern, Christian, *Canti grotteschi*, trans. by Anselmo Turazza (Turin: Einaudi, 1966).
O'Neill, Alexandre, *Portogallo, mio rimorso*, trans. by Joyce Lussu (Turin: Einaudi, 1966).
Plath, Sylvia, *Lady Lazarus e altre poesie*, trans. by Giovanni Giudici (Milan: Mondadori, 1976).
Poggioli, Renato, ed., *Poeti slavi: versioni da poeti bulgari e boemi* (Milan: All'insegna del pesce d'oro, 1956).
Prampolini, Giacomo, ed., *Poeti olandesi: 1946–1966* (Milan: All'insegna del pesce d'oro, 1959).

Ransom, John Crowe, *Le donne e i cavalieri*, trans. by Giovanni Giudici (Milan: Mondadori, 1971).
Riba, Carles, *Elegie di Bierville*, trans. by Giuseppe E. Sansone (Turin: Einaudi, 1977).
Roethke, Theodore, *Sequenza nordamericana e altre poesie*, trans. by Mariolina Meliadò (Milan: Mondadori, 1966).
Sansone, Giuseppe E., *Dodici liriche di Carles Riba* (Rome: De Luca, 1962).
Scheiwiller, Vanni, ed., *Poeti stranieri del Novecento tradotti da poeti italiani* (Milan: Mondadori, 1956).
Tjutčev, Fedor Ivanovič, *Poesie*, trans. by Tommaso Landolfi, preface by Angelo Maria Ripellino (Turin: Einaudi, 1964).
Valeri, Diego, *Lirici tedeschi* (Milan: Mondadori, 1959).
Valeri, Diego, *Lirici francesi* (Milan: Mondadori, 1960).

Secondary sources

Agazzi, Elena, 'Il "demonismo della forma" e il "trascendimento nel nulla": Ferruccio Masini legge Gottfried Benn', in *Ah, la terra lontana... Gottfried Benn in Italia*, ed. by Amelia Valtolina and Luca Zeboni (Pisa: Pacini Editore, 2018), pp. 57–88.
Ajello, Nello, *Intellettuali e Pci. 1944–1958* (Rome–Bari: Laterza, 1979).
Albanese, Angela, and Franco Nasi, eds, *L'artefice aggiunto. Riflessioni sulla traduzione in Italia, 1900–1975* (Ravenna: Longo Editore, 2015).
Alcini, Laura, 'Renato Poggioli traduttore e comparatista: attualità del duplice esilio di uno spirito cosmopolita nel nome della libertà di pensiero', *Forum Italicum*, 50:1 (2016), 87–128.
Alexander, Victoria D., 'Heteronomy in the Arts Field: State Funding and British Arts Organizations', *British Journal of Sociology*, 69:1 (2018), 23–43.
Andrews, Chris, 'Wordplay and the Contextual Circle in Queneau's *Petite Cosmogonie Portative*', *French Forum*, 29:1 (2004), 69–82.
Angelucci, Dario, *Tante pagine bianche. La ricezione di Samuel Beckett nella cultura italiana* (Chieti: Tabula Fati, 2018).
Aronoff, Eric, *Composing Cultures: Modernism, American Literary Studies, and the Problem of Culture* (Charlottesville: University of Virginia Press, 2013).
Asor Rosa, Alberto, *Scrittori e popolo. Il populismo nella letteratura italiana contemporanea* (Rome: Samonà e Savelli, 1966).
Bachmann-Medick, Doris, 'The Trans/National Study of Culture: A Translational Perspective', in *The Trans/National Study of Culture: A Translational Perspective*, ed. by Doris Bachmann-Medick et al. (Berlin: De Gruyter, 2014), pp. 1–22.

Baker, Mona, *Translation and Conflict: A Narrative Account* (New York and Abingdon: Routledge, 2006).

Baldini, Anna, Daria Biagi, Stefana De Lucia, Irene Fantappiè, and Michele Sisto, *La letteratura tedesca in Italia: Un'introduzione (1900–1920)* (Macerata: Quodlibet, 2018).

Bàrberi Squarotti, Giorgio, and Anna Maria Golfieri, *Dal tramonto dell'ermetismo alla neoavanguardia* (Brescia: Editrice La Scuola, 1984).

Barilli, Renato, *La neoavanguardia italiana. Dalla nascita de 'il verri' alla fine di 'Quindici'* (Lecce: Manni, 1995).

Barilli, Renato, and Angelo Guglielmi, *Gruppo 63: critica e teoria* (Milan: Feltrinelli, 1976).

Bassnett, Susan, 'From Cultural Turn to Translational Turn: A Transnational Journey', in *Literature, Geography, Translation: Studies in World Writing*, ed. by Cecilia Alvstad, Stefan Helgesson, and David Watson (Newcastle: Cambridge Scholars Publishing, 2011), pp. 67–80.

Bassnett, Susan, and Harish Trivedi, *Post-Colonial Translation: Theory and Practice* (London: Routledge, 1999).

Batchelor, Kathryn, *Translation and Paratexts* (London: Routledge, 2018).

Berman, Antoine, *L'épreuve de l'étranger* (Paris: Gallimard, 1984).

Billiani, Francesca, *Culture nazionali e narrazioni straniere. Italia, 1903–1943* (Florence: Le Lettere, 2007a).

Billiani, Francesca, 'Renewing a Literary Culture through Translation: Poetry in Post-War Italy', in *Translation as Intervention*, ed. by Jeremy Munday (London: Continuum, 2007b), pp. 138–59.

Blakesley, Jacob, *Modern Italian Poets: Translators of the Impossible* (Toronto: Toronto University Press, 2014).

Blakesley, Jacob, *A Sociological Approach to Poetry Translation: Modern European Poet-Translators* (London: Routledge, 2018a).

Blakesley, Jacob, ed., *Sociologies of Poetry Translation: Emerging Perspectives* (London: Bloomsbury, 2018b).

Boase-Beier, Jean, *Stylistic Approaches to Translation* (Manchester: St Jerome Publishing, 2006).

Bobbio, Norberto, 'Gli anni dell'impegno', in *Profilo ideologico del Novecento* (Milan: Garzanti, 1993), pp. 210–26.

Bollati, Giulio, *L'italiano: il carattere nazionale come storia e come invenzione*, 2nd edn (Turin: Einaudi, 1983).

Bond, Emma, 'Towards a Trans-National Turn in Italian Studies?', *Italian Studies*, 69:3 (2014), 415–24.

Bonsaver, Guido, '*Il Menabò*, Calvino and the "Avanguardie": Some Observations on the Literary Debate of the Sixties', *Italian Studies*, 50:1 (1995), 86–96.

Boschetti, Anna, 'La recomposition de l'espace intellectuel en Europe après 1945', in L'espace intellectuel en Europe – De la formation des Etats-nations à la mondialisation – 19ème-20ème siècle, ed. by Gisèle Sapiro (Paris: La Découverte, 2009), pp. 147–82.

Boschetti, Anna, 'Pour un comparatisme réflexif', in L'Espace culturel transnational, ed. by Anna Boschetti (Paris: Nouveau Monde, 2010), pp. 7–51.

Bosco Tedeschini Lalli, Biancamaria, 'Il "mito" americano di Agostino Lombardo', in Agostino Lombardo: la figura e l'opera, ed. by Mario Faraone (Rome: Bardi editore, 2008), pp. 27–38.

Bourdieu, Pierre, Outline of a Theory of Practice, trans. by Richard Nice (Cambridge: Cambridge University Press, 1977).

Bourdieu, Pierre, 'Field of Power, Literary Field and Habitus', in The Field of Cultural Production: Essays on Art and Literature, trans. and ed. by Randal Johnson (New York: Columbia University Press, 1993), pp. 161–75.

Bourdieu, Pierre, Distinction: A Social Critique of the Judgement of Taste, trans. by Richard Nice (Cambridge, MA: Harvard University Press, 1994).

Bourdieu, Pierre, The Rules of Art: Genesis and Structure of the Literary Field, trans. by Susan Emanuel (Cambridge: Polity, 1996).

Bricco, Elisa, André Frénaud e l'Italia (Fasano: Schena, 1999).

Bronzini, Giovanni Battista, 'L'iter del concetto crociano di poesia popolare', Lares, 52:1 (1986), 17–41.

Brooker, Jewel Spears, ed., Conversations with Denise Levertov (Jackson: University Press of Mississippi, 1998).

Bru, Sascha, 'Politics', in A Companion to Modernist Poetry, ed. by David E. Chinitz and Gail McDonald (Chichester: Wiley-Blackwell, 2014), pp. 107–18.

Buffoni, Franco, 'Wilcock traduttore e interprete', in Saggi sul nulla: studi e testimonianze su Rodolfo Wilcock, ed. by Roberto Deidier (Rome: Istituto della enciclopedia italiana, 2012), pp. 113–23.

Burdett, Charles, Nick Havely, and Loredana Polezzi, 'The Transnational/Translational in Italian Studies', Italian Studies, 75:2 (2020), 223–36.

Burns, Jennifer, Fragments of Impegno: Interpretations of Commitment in Contemporary Italian Narrative, 1980–2000 (Leeds: Northern Universities Press, 2001).

Buzelin, Hélène, 'Unexpected Allies: How Latour's Network Theory Can Complement Bourdieusian Analyses in Translation Studies', The Translator, 11:2 (2005), 193–218.

Buzelin, Hélène, 'Translations "in the making"', in Constructing a Sociology of Translation, ed. by Michaela Wolf and Alexandra Fukari (Amsterdam: John Benjamins, 2007), pp. 135–70.

Cadioli, Alberto, L'industria del romanzo: editoria letteraria in Italia dal 1945 agli anni Ottanta (Rome: Editori Riuniti, 1981).

Cadioli, Alberto, *Letterati editori. L'industria culturale come progetto*, 2nd edn (Milan: il Saggiatore, 2003 [1994]).
Cadioli, Alberto, and Andrea Kerbaker, eds, *I due Scheiwiller. Editoria e cultura nella Milano del Novecento* (Milan: Skira, 2009).
Cadioli, Alberto, and Giuliano Vigini, *Storia dell'editoria italiana dall'unità ad oggi: un profilo introduttivo* (Milan: Editrice Bibliografica, 2004).
Calvino, Italo, *Una pietra sopra. Discorsi di letteratura e società* (Turin: Einaudi, 1980).
Cantini, Catia, 'Beniamino Dal Fabbro: arte e vita di un *maudit*', in *Beniamino Dal Fabbro scrittore. Atti della giornata di studi. Belluno, 29 ottobre 2010*, ed. by Rodolfo Zucco (Florence: Olschki editore, 2011), pp. 19–38.
Capancioni, Chiara, 'Travelling and Translation: Joyce Lussu as a Feminist Cultural Mediator', in *Translating Gender*, ed. by Eleonora Federici (Bern: Peter Lang, 2011), pp. 177–87.
Capoferro, Riccardo, 'Antologie e canone letterario: poesia inglese in Italia dagli anni Trenta agli anni Sessanta', in *Traduzione e poesia nell'Europa del Novecento*, ed. by Anna Dolfi (Rome: Bulzoni, 2004), pp. 303–22.
Caproni, Giorgio, *Il mondo ha bisogno dei poeti. Interviste e autocommenti 1948–1990*, ed. by Melissa Rota (Florence: Florence University Press, 2014).
Casanova, Pascale, 'Consécration et accumulation de capital littéraire', *Actes de la recherche en sciences sociales*, 144 (2002), 7–20.
Caselli, Daniela, and Daniela La Penna, eds, *Twentieth-Century Poetic Translation: Literary Cultures in Italian and English* (London: Continuum, 2008).
Catalogo Einaudi: Le edizioni Einaudi negli anni 1933–1998 (Turin: Einaudi, 1999).
Cerchi, Luciano, 'Strumenti della poesia contemporanea: le collane letterarie Mondadori e Feltrinelli', *Poesia e critica*, 3 (1961), 84.
Ceserani, Remo, 'Sulle teorie poetiche di John Crowe Ransom', *Studi Americani*, 6 (1960), 307–37.
Chiappini, Gaetano, *Antinomie novecentesche. II. Juan Ramón Jiménez, Federico García Lorca, Rafael Alberti* (Florence: Alinea editrice, 2002).
Clavin, Patricia, 'Defining Transnationalism', *Contemporary European History*, 14:4 (2005), 421–39.
Collini, Stefan, *Absent Minds: Intellectuals in Britain* (Oxford: Oxford University Press, 2006).
Cordingley, Anthony, and Chiara Montini, 'Genetic Translation Studies: An Emerging Discipline', *Linguistica Antverpiensia*, 14 (2015), 1–18.
Crisafulli, Edoardo, 'The Quest for an Eclectic Methodology of Translation Description', in *Crosscultural Transgressions. Research Models in Translation Studies II: Historical and Ideological Issues*, ed. by Theo Hermans (Manchester: St Jerome Publishing, 2002), pp. 26–43.

Crocco, Claudia, *La poesia italiana del Novecento. Il canone e le interpretazioni* (Rome: Carrocci, 2015).

Croce, Benedetto, *Estetica come scienza dell'espressione e linguistica generale: teoria e storia* (Milan: Adelphi, 1965 [1902]).

Curi, Fausto, *La poesia italiana del Novecento* (Rome–Bari: Laterza, 1999).

Dal Fabbro, Beniamino, 'Un poeta a Praga', *Il Resto del Carlino*, 10 March 1976.

Darconza, Giuseppe, 'La poetica dell'assenza nei versi di guerra di Miguel Hernández', *Linguae. Rivista di lingue e culture moderne*, 2 (2006), 47–58.

De Cesari, Chiara, and Ann Rigney, eds, *Transnational Memory: Circulation, Articulation, Scales* (Berlin: De Gruyter, 2014).

De Lucia, Stefania, '"Giuochi di astrali coincidenze" e "rari gelidi cristalli": Leone Traverso traduttore di Gottfried Benn', in *Ah, la terra lontana... Gottfried Benn in Italia*, ed. by Amelia Valtolina and Luca Zeboni (Pisa: Pacini Editore, 2018), pp. 217–54.

de Swaan, Abraham, *Words of the World: The Global Language System* (Malden, MA: Blackwell, 2001).

Decleva, Enrico, *Arnoldo Mondadori*, 2nd edn (Turin: UTET, 2007 [1993]).

Del Zoppo, Francesca, 'Traduttrici di poesia per Mondadori: il caso dello "Specchio"', in *L'altra metà dell'editoria. Le professioniste del libro e della lettura nel Novecento*, ed by Roberta Cesana and Irene Piazzoni (Dueville: Ronzani, 2022), pp. 123–39.

Dolfi, Anna, ed., *Traduzione e poesia nell'Europa del Novecento* (Rome: Bulzoni, 2004).

Dolfi, Anna, 'Translation and the European Tradition: The Italian "Third Generation"', in *Twentieth-Century Poetic Translation: Literary Cultures in Italian and English*, ed. by Daniela Caselli and Daniela La Penna (London: Continuum, 2008), pp. 45–54.

Eco, Umberto, *Apocalittici e integrati* (Milan: Bompiani, 1964).

Einaudi, Giulio, *Frammenti di memoria* (Milan: Rizzoli, 1988).

Elena Croce e il suo mondo. Ricordi e testimonianze (Naples: CUEN, 1999).

Feltrinelli, Carlo, *Senior Service* (Milan: Feltrinelli, 1999).

Fernández, Fruela, '"The Einaudi Libel": A Battle of Translations in the Cold War', *The International Journal for Translation & Interpreting*, 12:2 (2020), 7–18.

Ferrero, Ernesto, *I migliori anni della nostra vita* (Milan: Feltrinelli, 2005).

Ferretti, Gian Carlo, *L'editore Vittorini* (Turin: Einaudi, 1992).

Ferretti, Gian Carlo, *Il mercato delle lettere. Editoria, informazione e critica libraria dagli anni Cinquanta agli anni Novanta* (Milan: il Saggiatore, 1994).

Ferretti, Gian Carlo, *Poeta e di poeti funzionario: il lavoro editoriale di Vittorio Sereni* (Milan: il Saggiatore/Fondazione Arnoldo e Alberto Mondadori, 1999).

Ferretti, Gian Carlo, *Storia dell'editoria letteraria in Italia, 1945–2003* (Turin: Einaudi, 2004).
Ferretti, Gian Carlo, *Vanni Scheiwiller: uomo, intellettuale, editore* (Milan: Libri Scheiwiller, 2009).
Ferretti, Gian Carlo, *Siamo spiacenti: controstoria dell'editoria italiana attraverso i rifiuti dal 1925 a oggi* (Milan: Bruno Mondadori, 2012).
Ferretti, Gian Carlo, *Un editore imprevedibile: Livio Garzanti* (Novara: Interlinea, 2020).
Ferretti, Gian Carlo, and Giulia Iannuzzi, *Storie di uomini e libri. L'editoria letteraria italiana attraverso le sue collane* (Milan: Minimum Fax, 2014).
Fioretti, Daniele, *Utopia and Dystopia in Postwar Italian Literature: Pasolini, Calvino, Sanguineti, Volponi* (Basingstoke: Palgrave Macmillan, 2017).
Folkart, Barbara, *Second Findings: A Poetics of Translation* (Ottawa: University of Ottawa Press, 2007).
Forgacs, David, 'The Italian Communist Party and Culture', in *Culture and Conflict in Postwar Italy: Essays on Mass and Popular Culture*, ed. by Zygmunt G. Baranski and Robert Lumley (New York: St Martin's Press, 1990), pp. 97–114.
Forti, Marco, *Le proposte della poesia e nuove proposte* (Milan: Mursia, 1971).
Fortini, Franco, *Verifica dei poteri. Scritti di critica e di istituzioni letterarie*, 2nd edn (Milan: il Saggiatore, 1974 [1965]).
Foucault, Michel, 'What is an Author?', trans. by Donald F. Bouchard and Sherry Simon, in *Language, Counter-Memory, Practice*, ed. by Donald F. Bouchard (Ithaca, NY: Cornell University Press, 1977), pp. 113–38.
Foucault, Michel, 'The Order of Discourse', trans. by Ian McLeod, in *Untying the Text: A Poststructuralist Reader*, ed. by Robert Young (London: Routledge and Kegan Paul, 1981), pp. 48–78.
Foucault, Michel, *The Archaeology of Knowledge*, trans. and ed. by A.M. Sheridan-Smith (London: Routledge, 2002 [1969]).
Franco, Teresa, 'L'ironia "romanzesca" di John Crowe Ransom nelle traduzioni di Giovanni Giudici', *Studi Novecenteschi*, 95 (2018), 121–41.
Franco, Teresa, *La lingua del padrone. Giovanni Giudici traduttore dall'inglese* (Soveria Mannelli: Rubbettino, 2020).
Ghidinelli, Stefano, 'Taccuini di poesia 1936–1953', in *I due Scheiwiller. Editoria e cultura nella Milano del Novecento*, ed. by Alberto Cadioli and Andrea Kerbaker (Milan: Skira edizioni, 2009), pp. 143–50.
Gibellini, Cecilia, ed., *Libri d'artista: le edizioni di Vanni Scheiwiller* (Rovereto: MaRT, 2007).
Ginsborg, Paul, *A History of Contemporary Italy: Society and Politics 1943–1988*, 2nd edn (London: Penguin, 2003 [1990]).
Giovannetti, Paolo, 'Un enciclopedismo poetico in 32°', in *I due Scheiwiller. Editoria e cultura nella Milano del Novecento*, ed. by Alberto Cadioli and Andrea Kerbaker (Milan: Skira edizioni, 2009), pp. 151–62.

Grata, Giulia, 'La fortuna di André Frénaud (1903–1997) in Italia. Appunti sulle corrispondenze inedite presso la Bibliothèque Littéraire Jacques Doucet di Parigi', *Aevum*, 87:3 (2013), 949–62.

Guglielmi, Giuseppe, 'Arcana Scheiwiller', in *Arcana Scheiwiller: gli archivi di un editore*, ed. by Linda Ferri and Gianfranco Tortorelli (Milan: Scheiwiller, 1986), pp. 9–17.

Guillén, Jorge, and Vanni Scheiwiller, *Un epistolario*, ed. by María Nieves Arribas Esteras (Rome: Aracne, 2012).

Gundle, Stephen, 'The Legacy of the Prison Notebooks: Gramsci, the PCI and Italian Culture in the Cold War Period', in *Italy in the Cold War: Politics, Culture and Society 1948–58*, ed. by Christopher Duggan and Christopher Wagstaff (Oxford: Berg, 1995), pp. 131–48.

Hanna, Sameh, *Bourdieu in Translation Studies: The Socio-Cultural Dynamics of Shakespeare Translation in Egypt* (London: Routledge, 2016).

Heilbron, Johan, and Gisèle Sapiro, 'La traduction littéraire, un objet sociologique', *Actes de la recherche en sciences sociales*, 144 (2002), 3–5.

Hollenberg, Donna, *A Poet's Revolution: The Life of Denise Levertov* (Los Angeles: University of California Press, 2013).

Holmes, James S., *Translated! Papers on Literary Translation and Translation Studies* (Amsterdam: Rodopi, 1988).

Iannuzzi, Giulia, 'La poesia straniera in Italia, "un dono di libertà"', *Tradurre: pratiche teorie strumenti*, 10 (2016), https://rivistatradurre.it/la-poesia-straniera-in-italia-un-dono-di-liberta/ [accessed 30 December 2019].

Inghilleri, Moira, 'The Sociology of Bourdieu and the Construction of the "Object" in Translation and Interpreting Studies', *The Translator*, 11:2 (2007), 125–45.

Jewell, Keala, *The Poiesis of History: Experimenting with Genre in Postwar Italy* (Ithaca, NY: Cornell University Press, 1992).

Jones, Francis R., *Poetry Translating as Expert Action* (Amsterdam: John Benjamins, 2011a).

Jones, Francis R., 'The Translation of Poetry', in *The Oxford Handbook of Translation Studies*, ed. by Kirsten Malmkjaer and Kevin Windle (Oxford: Oxford University Press, 2011b), Oxford Handbooks Online.

Kalczyńska, Alina, ed., *Per Vanni Scheiwiller* (Milan: Libri Scheiwiller, 2000).

Kerbaker, Andrea, 'Scheiwiller e l'editoria bancaria e aziendale', in *Vanni Scheiwiller 'editore milanese' – atti del convegno Milano, 24 ottobre 2019*, ed. by Laura Novati (Milan: All'insegna del pesce d'oro, 2020), pp. 33–54.

Kinnahan, Linda A., *Poetics of the Feminine: Authority and Literary Tradition in William Carlos Williams, Mina Loy, Denise Levertov, and Kathleen Fraser* (Cambridge: Cambridge University Press, 1994).

Kosters, Onno, '"The gantelope of sense and nonsense run": *Echo's Bones and Other Precipitates* in the 1930s', in *Beckett and Modernism*, ed. by Olga Beloborodova, Dirk Van Hulle, and Pim Verhulst (Basingstoke: Palgrave Macmillan, 2018), pp. 129–45.

La Belle, Jenijoy, *The Echoing Wood of Theodore Roethke* (Princeton, NJ: Princeton University Press, 1976).

La Penna, Daniela, 'Traduzioni e traduttori', in *Gli anni '60 e '70 in Italia. Due decenni di ricerca poetica*, ed. by Stefano Giovannuzzi (Genoa: San Marco dei Giustiniani, Fondazione Giorgio e Lilli Devoto, 2003), pp. 297–322.

Lagazzi, Paolo, *Attilio Bertolucci* (Florence: La Nuova Italia, 1981).

Lawner, Lynn, 'Tre nuovi poeti americani', *L'Approdo letterario*, 7:13 (1961), 39–57.

Leavitt, Charles L., '*Impegno nero*: Italian Intellectuals and the African-American Struggle', *California Italian Studies*, 4:2 (2013), 1–34.

Leavitt, Charles L., 'Probing the Limits of Crocean Historicism', *The Italianist*, 37:3 (2017), 387–406.

Leavitt, Charles L., *Italian Neorealism: A Cultural History* (Toronto: University of Toronto Press, 2020).

Ledesma, Eduardo, '"Lembras-Te de Quando Era Tudo Diferente?" Concrete Poetry and Revolution in Portugal in the 1960s and '70s', *Luso-Brazilian Review*, 55:1 (2018), 51–84.

Leotta, Paola Clara, *Tales of the Grotesque and Arabesque: Elio Vittorini e Giorgio Manganelli traduttori di Edgar Allan Poe, un caso traduttologico* (Acireale/Rome: Bonanno, 2007).

Levato, Vincenzina, *Lo sperimentalismo tra Pasolini e la neoavanguardia (1955–1965)* (Soveria Mannelli: Rubbettino editore, 2002).

Lombardo, Agostino, 'Thom Gunn e il Nuovo Movimento', in Thom Gunn, *I miei tristi capitani*, trans. by Camillo Pennati (Milan: Mondadori, 1968), pp. 9–25.

Lombardo, Anna, 'Joyce Lussu: le traduzioni e la storia dei popoli in lotta attraverso la voce dei loro poeti', in *Joyce Lussu. Sibilla del Novecento. Atti del Convegno del 17 novembre 2007*, ed. by Vittoria Ravagli (Sasso Marconi: Le Voce della Luna, 2008), pp. 39–45.

Lorenzini, Niva, *La poesia italiana del Novecento*, 2nd edn (Bologna: il Mulino, 2005).

Luperini, Romano, *Il Novecento. Apparati ideologici, ceto intellettuale, sistemi formali nella letteratura italiana contemporanea*, vol. II (Turin: Loescher, 1981).

Lupo, Giuseppe, *Vittorini politecnico* (Milan: FrancoAngeli, 2011).

Luti, Giorgio, and Paolo Rossi, *Le idee e le lettere. Un intervento su trent'anni di cultura italiana* (Milan: Longanesi, 1976).

Luzi, Mario, *Tutto in questione* (Florence: Vallecchi, 1965).

Lyall, Scott, 'MacDiarmid, Communism and the Poetry of Commitment', in *The Edinburgh Companion to Hugh MacDiarmid*, ed. by Scott Lyall and Margery Palmer McCulloch (Edinburgh: Edinburgh University Press, 2011), pp. 68–81.

Macrí, Oreste, 'La traduzione poetica negli anni Trenta (e seguenti) [1989]', in *La vita della parola. Da Betocchi a Tentori*, ed. by Anna Dolfi (Rome: Bulzoni, 2002), pp. 47–64.

Magris, Carlo, 'Un poeta dell'editoria', in *Per Vanni Scheiwiller*, ed. by Alina Kalczyńska (Milan: Libri Scheiwiller, 2000), pp. 186–88.

Mainardi, Angelo, ed., *Storia dell'editoria d'Europa*, 2 vols (Florence: Shakespeare & Company–Futura, 1995).

Manganelli, Giorgio, 'Poesia inglese contemporanea', *Ulisse*, 38:6 (1960), 38–44.

Manganelli, Giorgio, *Estrosità rigorose di un consulente editoriale*, ed. by Salvatore Silvano Nigro (Turin: Adelphi, 2016).

Mangoni, Luisa, *Pensare i libri. La casa editrice Einaudi dagli anni Trenta agli anni Sessanta* (Turin: Bollati Boringhieri, 1999).

Mannucci, Enrico, ed., *'Non è un libro per noi'. Oreste del Buono lettore in Mondadori* (Milan: Fondazione Alberto e Arnoldo Mondadori, 2014).

Marchetti, Mario, 'Quando si leggeva (e si pubblicava) poesia', *Tradurre: pratiche teorie strumenti*, 10 (2016), https://rivistatradurre.it/quando-si-leggeva-e-si-pubblicava-poesia/ [accessed 30 December 2019].

Masini, Ferruccio, 'Prefazione', in Gottfried Benn, *Aprèslude: poesie 1955*, trans. by Ferruccio Masini (Milan: All'insegna del pesce d'oro, 1963), pp. 15–16.

Melchiori, Giorgio, *I Funamboli* (Turin: Einaudi, 1963).

Meliadò, Mariolina, 'Theodore Roethke', *Studi Americani*, 9 (1963), 425–54.

Meschonnic, Henri, *Pour la poétique II* (Paris: Gallimard, 1973).

Miglio, Camilla, 'Gottfried Benn à l'epreuve de la traduction', in *Klassiker neu übersetzen. Zum Phänomen der Neuübersetzungen deutscher und italienischer Klassiker. Ritradurre i classici. Sul fenomeno delle ritraduzioni di classici italiani e tedeschi*, ed. by Barbara Kleiner, Michele Vangi, and Ada Vigliani (Stuttgart: Franz Steiner, 2014), pp. 77–94.

Milani, Mila, 'Publishing Contemporary Foreign Poetry in Post-War Italy: A Bourdieusian Perspective on Mondadori and Scheiwiller', *New Voices in Translation Studies*, 8 (2012), 99–114.

Milani, Mila, 'L'editoria italiana e le antologie di poesia straniera contemporanea alle soglie della globalizzazione (1960–1980): sfide metodologiche per lo studio della traduzione', *TransPostCross*, 1 (2013a), 1–15, http://www.transpostcross.it/index.php?option=com_content&view=article&id=84:l-editoria-italiana-e-le-antologie-di-poesia&catid=8:interventi&Itemid=11 [accessed 16 January 2019].

Milani, Mila, 'Il ruolo della traduzione nel campo editoriale italiano di poesia (1953–1969): note sulla poesia tedesca', in *Letteratura italiana e tedesca: campi, polisistemi, transfer*, ed. by Irene Fantappiè and Michele Sisto (Rome: Istituto di Studi Germanici, 2013b), pp. 97–108.

Milani, Mila, '*Impegno*, National and Transnational Identities in *Il Politecnico* and *Sud* (1945–1947)', *Modern Italy*, 21:2 (2016), 157–70.

Milani, Mila, 'The Role of Translation in the History of Publishing: Publishers and Contemporary Poetry Translation in 1960s Italy', *Translation Studies*, 10:3 (2017), 296–311.

Minuscoli, Mario, 'Piccoli libri per grandi poeti', *Studi Cattolici*, 190 (1976), 745–50.

Mondadori, Alberto, *Lettere di una vita, 1922–1975*, ed. by Gian Carlo Ferretti (Milan: Fondazione Arnoldo e Alberto Mondadori, 1996).

Morini, Massimiliano, *La traduzione. Teorie, strumenti, pratiche* (Milan: Sironi, 2007).

Munari, Tommaso, ed., *I verbali editoriali. Riunioni editoriali Einaudi 1943–1952* (Turin: Einaudi, 2011).

Munari, Tommaso, ed., *I verbali editoriali. Riunioni editoriali Einaudi 1953–1963* (Turin: Einaudi, 2013).

Munari, Tommaso, *L'Einaudi in Europa* (Turin: Einaudi, 2016).

Munday, Jeremy, 'Using Primary Sources to Produce a Microhistory of Translation and Translators: Theoretical and Methodological Concerns', *The Translator*, 20:1 (2014), 64–80.

Neri, Laura, *I silenziosi circuiti del ricordo. Etica, estetica e ideologia nella poesia di Giovanni Giudici* (Rome: Carocci, 2018).

Nida, Eugene, 'Principles of Correspondence' [1964], in *The Translation Studies Reader*, ed. by Lawrence Venuti (London: Routledge, 2012), pp. 141–55.

Nord, Christiane, *Translating as a Purposeful Activity: Functionalist Approaches Explained* (Manchester: St Jerome Publishing, 1997).

Novati, Laura, 'Vanni Scheiwiller "editore milanese"', in *Vanni Scheiwiller 'editore milanese' – atti del convegno Milano, 24 ottobre 2019*, ed. by Laura Novati (Milan: All'insegna del pesce d'oro, 2020), pp. 23–53.

Pala, Valeria, *Tommaso Landolfi traduttore di Gogol* (Rome: Bulzoni, 2009).

Papetti, Viola, ed., *Le foglie messaggere: scritti in onore di Giorgio Manganelli* (Rome: Editori Riuniti, 2000).

Pareschi, Luca, and Maria Lusiani, 'What Editors Talk about When they Talk about Editors? A Public Discourse Analysis of Market and Aesthetic Logics', *Poetics*, 81 (2020), 1–14.

Pasolini, Pier Paolo, *Passione e ideologia* (Milan: Garzanti, 1994 [1960]).

Pavese, Cesare, 'L'influsso degli eventi' [5 February 1946], in *La letteratura americana e altri saggi* (Turin: Einaudi, 1951), pp. 245–48.

Pennacchietti, Laura, '"Books written by the so-called colonials or half-bloods": Italian Publishers' Reception of Novels by the Windrush Writers in the 1950s and 1960s', *Modern Italy*, 23:4 (2018), 411–28.

Peterson, Thomas E., 'Pascolian Intertexts in the Lyric Poetry of Attilio Bertolucci', in *The Revolt of the Scribe in Modern Italian Literature* (Toronto: Toronto University Press, 2010a), pp. 81–96.

Peterson, Thomas E., 'Diego Valeri: A Classical Poet in the Modern Era', in *The Revolt of the Scribe in Modern Italian Literature* (Toronto: Toronto University Press, 2010b), pp. 112–28.

Piazzoni, Irene, *Il Novecento dei libri: una storia dell'editoria in Italia* (Rome: Carocci, 2021).

Piccone Stella, Simonetta, *Intellettuali e capitale nella società italiana del Dopoguerra* (Bari: De Donato, 1972).

Pontillo, Corinne, *"Il Politecnico" di Vittorini: progretto e storia di una narrazione visiva* (Rome: Carocci, 2020).

Porchera, Beatrice, 'La *Poesia del '900* di Falqui per gli "Oscar"', in *Libri e scrittori da collazione. Casi editoriali in un secolo di Mondadori*, ed. by Roberto Cicala and Maria Villano (Milan: Quaderni del Laboratorio di editoria – Università Cattolica, 2008), pp. 247–51.

Prenz, Bertina, ed., *Il plusvalore della vita. Omaggio a Vasko Popa* (Trieste: Hammerle, 2008).

Puglisi, Giovanni, 'I linguaggi di Wilcock', in *Segnali sul nulla: studi e testimonianze su Rodolfo Wilcock*, ed. by Roberto Deidier (Rome: Istituto della enciclopedia italiana, 2002), pp. 2–6.

Pulsoni, Carlo, ed., *Vanni Scheiwiller editore europeo* (Perugia: Volumnia, 2011).

Ragone, Giovanni, *Un secolo di libri. Storia dell'editoria in Italia dall'Unità al post-moderno* (Turin: Einaudi, 1999).

Reynolds, Matthew, *The Poetry of Translation: From Chaucer & Petrarch to Homer & Logue* (Oxford: Oxford University Press, 2011).

Ripellino, Angelo Maria, *Lettere e schede editoriali (1954–1977)*, ed. by Antonio Pane (Turin: Einaudi, 2018).

Robinson, Peter, *Poetry and Translation: The Art of the Impossible* (Liverpool: Liverpool University Press, 2010).

Romano, Sergio, 'Una famiglia di editori', in *Arcana Scheiwiller: gli archivi di un editore*, ed. by Linda Ferri and Gianfranco Tortorelli (Milan: Scheiwiller, 1986), pp. 19–25.

Rundle, Christopher, *Publishing Translations in Fascist Italy* (Bern: Peter Lang, 2010).

Rundle, Christopher, and Kate Sturge, eds, *Translation under Fascism* (Basingstoke: Palgrave Macmillan, 2010).

Salvioni, Amanda, 'Wilcock e la generazione poetica argentina degli anni Quaranta', in *Segnali sul nulla: studi e testimonianze su Rodolfo Wilcock*, ed. by Roberto Deidier (Rome: Istituto della enciclopedia italiana, 2002), pp. 37–65.

Santoro, Marco, *Storia del libro italiano. Libro e società in Italia dal Quattrocento al nuovo millennio*, 2nd edn (Milan: Editrice Bibliografica, 2008 [1994]).

Sapiro, Gisèle, 'Modèles d'intervention politique des intellectuels: Le cas français', *Actes de la Recherche en Sciences Sociales*, 176–77 (2009a), 8–31.

Sapiro, Gisèle, ed., *Les contradictions de la globalisation éditoriale* (Paris: Nouveau Monde, 2009b).

Sapiro, Gisèle, 'Globalization and Cultural Diversity in the Book Market: The Case of Literary Translations in the US and in France', *Poetics*, 38:4 (2010), 419–39.

Sassi, Carla, 'Hugh MacDiarmid's (Un)Making of the Modern Scottish Nation', in *The Edinburgh Companion to Hugh MacDiarmid*, ed. by Scott Lyall and Margery Palmer McCulloch (Edinburgh: Edinburgh University Press, 2011), pp. 111–24.

Scheiwiller, Vanni, 'Trent'anni di editoria "inutile"', in *Scheiwiller a Milano 1925–1983. Immagini e documenti da Wildt a Melotti da Fontana alla neovanguardia da Pound ai Novissimi: tre generazioni di editori d'arte e letteratura. Scritti di Eugenio Montale, Ezra Pound, Giuseppe Prezzolini e Cesare Zavattini*, exhibition catalogue, Biblioteca Comunale e Museo di Milano, ed. by Chiara Negri (Milan: Scheiwiller, 1983), pp. 127–31.

Schiffrin, André, *L'édition sans éditeurs* (Paris: La Fabrique éditions, 1999).

Scott, Clive, *Translating Baudelaire* (Exeter: Exeter University Press, 2000).

Scotto, Fabio, 'Maria Luisa Spaziani traduttrice di Marceline Desbordes-Valmore: tra fedeltà e modernizzazione', *Agon*, 4 (2015), 19–34.

Scuderi, Vincenza, *Il palinsesto invisibile. La poesia di Gottfried Benn in Italia* (Rome: Bonanno editore, 2006).

Sela-Sheffy, Rakefet, 'How to be a (Recognized) Translator: Rethinking Habitus, Norms, and the Field of Translation', *Target*, 17:1 (2006), 1–26.

Sela-Sheffy, Rakefet, 'Translators' Identity Work: Introducing Microsociological Theory of Identity to the Discussion of Translators' Habitus', in *Remapping Habitus in Translation Studies*, ed. by Gisella M. Vorderobermeier (Amsterdam: Rodopi, 2014), pp. 43–55.

Seruya, Teresa, Lieven D'hulst, Alexandra Assis Rosa, and Maria Lin Moniz, eds, *Translation in Anthologies and Collections (19th and 20th Centuries)* (Amsterdam: John Benjamins, 2013).

Sisto, Michele, *Traiettorie. Studi sulla letteratura tradotta in Italia* (Macerata: Quodlibet, 2019).

Spaziani, Maria Luisa, 'La revisione: istruzioni per l'uso', *Agon*, 4 (2015), 130–33.

Spina, Alessandro, 'Nell'ordine degli imperdonabili', in *Per Vanni Scheiwiller*, ed. by Alina Kalczyńska (Milan: Libri Scheiwiller, 2000), pp. 283–86.

Spivak, Gayatri Chakravorty, 'Can the Subaltern Speak?', in *Marxism and the Interpretation of Culture*, ed. by Cary Nelson and Lawrence Grossberg (Urbana, IL: University of Illinois Press, 1988), pp. 271–313.

Srivastava, Neelam, *Italian Colonialism and Resistances to Empire, 1930–1970* (Basingstoke: Palgrave Macmillan, 2018).

Sullam, Sara, 'Illuminating *Botteghe Oscure*'s British Network', *Modern Italy*, 21:2 (2016), 171–84.

Tagliaferri, Aldo, 'Introduction', in Denise Levertov, *La scala di Giobbe e altre poesie*, trans. by Mary de Rachewiltz (Milan: Mondadori, 1968), pp. 8–18.

Taronna, Annarita, 'En-Gendering Translation as a Political Project: The Subversive Power of Joyce Lussu's Activist Translation(s)', in *Feminist Translation Studies: Local and Transnational Perspectives*, ed. by Olga Castro and Emek Ergun (London: Routledge, 2017), pp. 151–66.

Tranfaglia, Nicola, and Albertina Vittoria, *Storia degli editori italiani. Dall'Unità alla fine degli anni Settanta* (Rome–Bari: Laterza, 2000).

Trenti, Federica, *Il Novecento di Joyce Salvadori Lussu* (Sasso Marconi: Le Voci della poesia, 2009).

Turconi, Sergio, *La poesia neorealista italiana* (Milan: Mursia, 1977).

Turi, Gabriele, *Casa Einaudi. Libri uomini idee oltre il fascismo* (Bologna: il Mulino, 1990).

Tymoczko, Maria, *Translation in a Postcolonial Context: Early Irish Literature in English Translation* (Manchester: St Jerome Publishing, 1999).

Underhill, Hugh, *The Problem of Consciousness in Modern Poetry* (Cambridge: Cambridge University Press, 1992).

Venuti, Lawrence, *The Translator's Invisibility: A History of Translation* (London: Routledge, 1995).

Venuti, Lawrence, *Translation Changes Everything* (London: Routledge, 2013).

Verbaro, Caterina, 'Il dibattito delle poetiche tra neorealismo e neoavanguardia', in *Dal Neorealismo alla Neoavanguardia. Il dibattito letterario in Italia negli anni della modernizzazione (1945–1969)*, ed. by Giorgio Luti and Caterina Verbaro (Florence: Le Lettere, 1995), pp. 51–113.

Vertovec, Steven, *Transnationalism* (London: Routledge, 2009).

Vertovec, Steven, and Robin Cohen, eds, *Conceiving Cosmopolitanism: Theory, Context and Practice* (Oxford: Oxford University Press, 2002).

Villano, Maria, ed., '"Così conobbi l'inarrivabile Montale". Marco Forti, gli amici poeti e il laboratorio dello "Specchio"', *QB*, 20 (2020), https://www.fondazionemondadori.it/rivista/20-qb-marco-forti/ [accessed 24 December 2020].

Vorderobermeier, Gisella M., ed., *Remapping Habitus in Translation Studies* (Amsterdam: Rodopi, 2014).

Wallerstein, Immanuel, *The Modern World-System* (Berkeley: University of California Press 2011 [1974]).

Warde, Alan, and Mike Savage, 'Il capitale culturale e l'analisi sociologica della cultura: una reinterpretazione', in *La cultura come capitale. Consumi, produzioni, politiche, identità*, ed. by Marco Santoro (Bologna: il Mulino, 2009), pp. 27–50.

Wasserman, George Russell, 'The Irony of John Crowe Ransom', in *John Crowe Ransom: Critical Essays and a Bibliography*, ed. by Thomas Daniel Young (Baton Rouge: Louisiana State University Press, 1968), pp. 143–55.

Weiner, Joshua, 'Introduction', in *At the Barriers: On the Poetry of Thom Gunn* (Chicago: University of Chicago Press, 2009), pp. 1–7.

Werner, Michael, and Bénédicte Zimmermann, 'Beyond Comparison: *Histoire croisée* and the Challenge of Reflexivity', *History and Theory*, 45:1 (2006), 30–50.

Wilkinson, James D., *The Intellectual Resistance in Europe* (Cambridge, MA: Harvard University Press, 1981).

Wolf, Michaela, and Alexandra Fukari, eds, *Constructing a Sociology of Translation* (Amsterdam: John Benjamins, 2007).

Woods, Michelle, 'Reassessing Willa Muir: Her Role and Influence in the Kafka Translations', *Translation Studies*, 4 (2011), 58–71.

Wright, Chantal, *Literary Translation* (London: Routledge, 2016).

Zancan, Marina, *Il progetto Politecnico: cronaca e strutture di una rivista* (Venice: Marsilio, 1984).

Zucco, Rodolfo, 'Fonti metriche della tradizione nella poesia di Giovanni Giudici', *Studi novecenteschi*, 45–46:2 (1993), 171–208.

Index

Accrocca, Elio Filippo 18, 35, 45n, 68
actor network theory 7
AIE, Associazione Italiana Editori 206
Aiken, Conrad 64, 86
Alberti, Rafael 20, 59, 67, 77, 82, 83n, 164, 176
Aldrovandi, Renata 16
Aleixandre, Vicente 63
Aletti, Adelina 79–80
Alighieri, Dante 107–08, 110
Allen, Donald 90
Almanacco dello Specchio (book series) 98, 209
Altichieri, Gilberto 15, 150
Anceschi, Luciano 20, 60
antifascism 4, 15–16, 20, 22, 27, 33, 59, 64, 134, 136, 165–66, 179
anti-fascist *see* antifascism
Antonini, Gianni 14n
Apollinaire, Guillaume 29, 151n, 172
Approdo letterario, L' (literary journal) 43, 160, 178
Auden, W.H. 64, 98, 148, 172
Auden group 100, 102, 150
Avanti, L' (journal) 59

Baldacci, Luigi 178
Balestrini, Nanni 38, 130
Banti, Anna 152
Baretti, Il (journal) 15
Barilli, Renato 87
Barral, Carlos 199
Bassani, Giorgio 38
Baudelaire, Charles 161, 172
Beckett, Samuel 122, 126, 127–28, 130

Bellini, Giuseppe 191
Benjamin, Walter 110
Benn, Gottfried 63, 73–74, 83–84
    Aprèslude 63, 73–74
Berman, Antoine 73, 105
Berti, Luigi 15, 20, 60, 84, 85n
Bertolucci, Attilio 15, 22, 36–37, 45, 52, 162, 171–74, 176–81
    Poesia straniera del Novecento 169, 171–74, 178–80
Betocchi, Carlo 24–25
Bianciardi, Luciano 38
Bigongiari, Piero 14n, 41–43, 92–93, 162–64
Bishop, Elisabeth 147
Black Mountain Group 88, 90
Blake, Nicholas *see* Day Lewis, Cecil
Blake, William 109
Blakesley, Jacob 4, 116
Blok, Alexander 15
Bo, Carlo 15, 30, 155, 185
Bodini, Vittorio 33, 45, 77–78, 94n, 136n
Bollati, Giulio 38
Bonetti, Umberto 195–98
Bonnefoy, Yves 92–93
Borges, Jorge Luis 126, 178
Borghese, Il (journal) 57
Botteghe oscure (journal) 26, 175
Bourdieu, Pierre 5–6, 12, 23, 33, 48, 56–57, 171, 212, 214
Bourdieusian *see* Bourdieu, Pierre
Brecht, Bertolt 20, 32, 122, 130, 200–02
Bréton, André 146
Browning, Robert 148
Buffoni, Franco 128

Cadou, Guy René 172
Calvino, Italo 22, 35, 38, 119n, 125–26, 129, 135, 138n, 140n, 144, 146, 177–83, 195, 209
Campo, Cristina 34, 89
Cannarozzo, Franco 196
canon 26–32, 34, 58, 81–83, 87–90, 96, 123, 138, 157–58, 175
Cantini, Raffaele 43
Capoferro, Riccardo 157–58, 164, 175–79
Caproni, Giorgio 15n, 37, 45
Cardarelli, Vincenzo 40
Carena, Carlo 140n, 196n, 213n
Carrieri, Raffaele 41
Cases, Cesare 38, 118n, 119, 120n, 200, 209
Castellet, Josep Maria 93, 194, 199
Cavafy, Constantine 45, 63, 91, 94–95, 121n, 139, 178
Cederna, Enrico 14n
Cederna (book series) 73
Celaya, Gabriel 93–96, 154
Céline, Louis-Ferdinand 57
Cendrars, Blaise 145
censorship 3, 11, 14
Cerchi, Luciano 42
Ceserani, Remo 112
Char, René 43, 92, 163
Chiusano, Alighiero 74
Cicognani, Mario 41, 101–03, 149
Ciliberti, Aurora 147
Cocteau, Jean 64, 67, 145
Cold War 49, 194
Collezione di poesia (book series) 11, 47, 50, 91, 118–26, 139–45, 150–52, 162, 180, 187–90, 194, 208–10, 213
Collini, Stefan 23
Collins, Armand (publishing house) 31
Condini, Nereo 148, 190
Confindustria (General Confederation of Italian Industry) 206
Conquest, Robert 106
Coralli (book series) 33, 209
Corso, Gregory 189
cosmopolitan 2, 7–8, 55, 59, 64, 72, 80, 166, 200
Crane, Hart 164

Craveri, Raimondo 175
Creeley, Robert 88, 90
crepuscular 25, 37, 140–41
Croce, Benedetto 42, 161, 164, 175, 177, 179, 183, 200
Croce, Elena 174–83, 187, 190, 196
   Poeti del Novecento italiani e stranieri 174–83
Croce Craveri, Elena *see* Croce, Elena
crocean *see* Croce, Benedetto
croceanism *see* Croce, Benedetto
Crovi, Raffaele 38, 42n, 43, 97n, 105n
cultural capital 5, 19, 21, 23n, 24, 33, 40, 82–83, 98, 109, 117, 119, 129, 160, 162, 165, 174, 178, 191, 194, 201, 207, 209
cultural production 2–3, 5, 7, 9, 13, 33, 47n, 49, 55, 81, 177, 212, 215
cummings, e.e. 63–64, 183

Dal Fabbro, Beniamino 24–25, 140–41
Dalmati, Margherita 139
Davico Bonino, Guido 120n, 123, 125–26, 127n, 128n, 130n, 135n, 136, 137n, 142, 145n, 148n, 149n, 150n, 151–52, 159, 189–91, 193n, 194n, 195–99, 210n
Davie, Donald 146
Day Lewis, Cecil 100–02, 149
De Angelis, Milo 211
de Libero, Libero 21, 40, 70n
De Luca (publishing house) 136
De Michelis, Cesare G. 187
De Michelis, Eurialo 151n
De Nardis, Luigi 180
de Rachewiltz, Mary 45–46, 71, 106–07
de Sponde, Jean 32, 151
Decleva, Enrico 40, 44
del Buono, Oreste 88
Desbordes-Valmore, Marceline 126
Dickinson, Emily 46, 110, 151–52, 189
Die Brücke movement 84
distinction (sociological term) 48, 56, 61–62, 66–69, 72–73, 79–80, 125, 129, 153, 163, 186, 206
Donne, John 110
Douglas, Keith 147

Index

economic capital 12, 25, 30, 69, 81, 207
Editori Riuniti (publishing house) 95–97
Edizioni dell'Avanti (publishing house) 96–97, 167
Edizioni della Meridiana 20–21, 87, 155n
Einaudi, Giulio 4, 10, 31, 33, 58, 94, 120–22, 123n, 124–25, 128n, 130, 132n, 134, 139n, 162, 181n, 199, 209
Einaudi, Giulio (publishing house) 4–5, 8, 11, 13, 19, 21–26, 30–34, 38, 47, 50, 55, 58, 64, 91–98, 105n, 110, 117–54, 156, 160, 162, 174, 177–82, 187–200, 205–06, 208–11, 213
Eliot, T.S. 15, 22, 42, 60, 64, 69, 83, 109, 100n, 172–73, 176
Éluard, Paul 22, 32, 34, 42, 123, 145, 163
Emmanuel, Pierre 172
entangled history *see histoire croisée*
Erba, Luigi 20, 45, 87
Errante, Guido 46
Europa letteraria (journal) 96
Everyday Library (publishing house) 31
Evola, Julius 57, 74

Falqui, Enrico 35, 99n
fascism 3, 11, 13–14, 16–18, 58–59, 67, 100, 140, 177
fascist *see* fascism
Feltrinelli, Giangiacomo 37–38, 70, 94, 129, 133, 206
Feltrinelli Giangiacomo (publishing house) 34, 37–38, 47, 52, 130–34, 142, 144, 155, 187–88, 194
Fenice, La (book series) 1, 11, 15, 211
Ferlinghetti, Lawrence 189
Ferretti, Gian Carlo 53, 72, 88
Fertonani, Roberto 199–202
field (sociological term) 1–9, 11–13, 17–53, 55–61, 65–66, 70, 73, 81–82, 84–88, 91–93, 95n, 103, 117–19, 124, 126, 129, 131, 133–34, 137, 140, 143, 144–45, 153, 157, 159, 160, 165, 168, 169, 174, 176–77, 179, 183, 187, 195, 198–99, 205–15
Fiera letteraria, La 107, 127n, 146
Firpo, Edoardo 22
Folkart, Barbara 170

Formentor International Prize (prize) 199
Forte, Luigi 189, 193
Forti, Marco 35, 42, 48, 92n, 94n, 95n, 97n, 98–99, 105n, 106–07, 111n, 122–13, 115–16, 147n, 166–68, 187n, 207n, 208n
Fortini, Franco 22, 25, 26n, 32, 33n, 38, 47, 59, 104, 123, 130, 134, 163–64, 209–10
Fossati, Paolo 138n, 139n, 147n, 150n, 188–92
Foucault, Michel 5n
  author function 129
Franco, Francisco 93
Frénaud, André 92, 134
Frost, Robert 99
Fruttero, Carlo 105, 130n, 179

Gadda, Carlo Emilio 37, 57
Gallimard (publishing house) 120, 209
Gallo, Niccolò 44
Garzanti, Aldo 37
Garzanti, Livio 37, 171
Garzanti (publishing house) 37, 45, 47, 52, 171, 173, 186, 211
Gatto, Alfonso 41, 45
Gettoni, I (book series) 39
Ginsberg, Allen 85n, 189
Ginzburg, Natalia 25, 26n
Giorno, John 197
Giudici, Giovanni 65, 87, 111–17, 140n, 182, 187
Giuliani, Alfredo 36, 127
globalisation 2, 9, 159, 203, 205, 212, 214–15
Glück, Louise 197
Gobetti, Piero 15
Goytisolo, José Augustin 93
Gozzano, Guido 141
Graham, W.S. 147
Gramsci, Antonio 177
Grande, Adriano 24–25
Gruppo 63 36–38, 47, 51, 87, 103, 141–46, 201–02
Guanda (publishing house) 2, 11, 14–15, 21, 29–30, 60, 68, 83, 89, 96–97,

99–100, 103, 126, 150, 155, 167, 176, 185, 190–92, 196, 209–11
Guandalini, Ugo 21, 29, 61, 211
Guevara, Ernesto 'Che' 195
Guglielmi, Giuseppe 53
Guidacci, Margherita 65, 76, 78, 127
Guillén, Jorge 63–66, 72n, 78–80, 163, 176
Gunn, Thom 97, 104–06

habitus (sociological term) 5–8, 55, 57, 79, 88, 112, 131, 144, 151, 157, 162, 167, 171, 174, 179, 183, 184
Hamm, Peter 200
Hardy, Thomas 149, 172
hermeticism 11–21, 25–26, 30, 34, 36–37, 39, 41–45, 54, 55, 57, 60, 73–74, 77, 83–84, 92, 99–100, 102, 104, 117, 123, 131, 140, 141, 151, 155, 157, 160–65, 168–71, 173–74, 176–77, 180, 183, 185–86, 190–91, 193, 202
Hernández, Miguel 33
Hier et Aujourd'hui (publishing house) 31
Hikmet, Nazim 20
histoire croisée 2, 3, 215
Hodder & Stoughton (publishing house) 31
Hölderlin, Johann Christian Friedrich 15, 123, 161
Huber, Max 120
Huidobro, Vicente 135–36
Hungarian revolution 35, 129, 184

Illyés, Gyula 64
impegno 17, 19, 34–35, 131, 143, 193, 195
insegna del pesce d'oro, All' (book series) 11, 66
Inventario (journal) 15, 110n
Italian Communist Party (PCI) 17, 22, 38, 131
Izzo, Carlo 138, 149, 155, 176, 182–83
   Poesia inglese contemporanea: da Thomas Hardy agli apocalittici 138, 155

Jacob, Max 145
Jahier, Piero 22
Jarrell, Randal 190
Jiménez, Juan 83, 176
Joyce, James 14n, 57, 63, 64, 127, 146
Jung, Carl Gustav 106

Kästner, Erich 179
Kingsley, Amis 146

Landolfi, Tommaso 130n, 131
Larkin, Philip 98, 146–47
Latour, Bruno 7
Lee Masters, Edgar 20
Leonetti, Francesco 138n
Lerici, Roberto 27
Lerici (publishing house) 27, 96–97
letterati editori [literati publishers] 5–6, 18, 205
Levertov, Denise 90–91, 106–08, 147n, 189
Libri Scheiwiller (book series) 2, 206, 212
Linder, Erich 21, 39, 60
Linea lombarda 20, 65, 87
Lombardo, Agostino 89–91, 98n, 100–03, 105–06, 109, 115, 117, 149
   Realismo e simbolismo 89, 115
Lorca, Federico García 15, 20, 30, 35, 176
Lucentini, Franco 105
Luraghi, Giuseppe Eugenio 20
Lussu, Joyce 8, 96, 97n, 136, 137n, 156, 165–68, 187
   Tradurre poesia 164–68
Luzi, Mario 24–25, 34, 41, 72, 121, 207

MacDiarmid, Hugh 138–39
Machado, Antonio 27, 176
MacNeice, Louis 102–03
Macrí, Oreste 14n, 15, 43, 63n, 77–79, 102, 155, 171, 186, 193
Magris, Claudio 52, 202
Manacorda, Giorgio 201–02
Mandelbaum, Allen 69
Mansfield, Katherine 15, 150
   Poemetti 15, 150
Mansour, Joyce 145–46
Manzini, Gianna 20
Marianni, Ariodante 32, 189
Martini, Fritz 74
Marxism 17, 22n, 112, 131, 148, 195
Masini, Ferruccio 74–75
Matacotta, Franco 15n, 18
Mayakovsky, Vladimir 35
Mazzucchetti, Lavinia 84

Index

Melchiori, Giorgio 106, 124–25, 128n, 148, 180–81
Meliadò, Mariolina 8, 97, 108–11
Menarini, Gianni 190n, 196–98
Mendes, Murilo 63
Mentor Books (publishing house) 31
Mercurio (journal) 18
Michaux, Henri 145
microhistory 5
modernism 13–15, 20–21, 24, 27, 33, 54, 57, 60, 75, 78, 80, 96, 138, 164
Momenti (journal) 18
Mondadori, Alberto 40, 69, 82, 85, 94, 99n, 163n
Mondadori, Arnoldo 18, 44, 87, 104, 205–06
Mondadori (publishing house) 5, 11, 13, 18, 21, 25, 26, 27, 29, 35, 37, 39–46, 47–48, 50–51, 55, 58, 64, 69, 81–117, 119–22, 127, 129, 130, 134, 139, 147, 149, 153, 154, 156, 160, 162, 164, 167, 186, 187, 189, 199, 205, 207–09
Montale, Eugenio 22, 28–29, 37, 41, 63, 66, 78, 120, 155n, 174, 207
Moore, Marianne 64, 89, 147, 149
Morgenstern, Christian 123
Mounin, George 110
Movimento Arte Concreta 67
Munari, Bruno 67, 120
Munday, Jeremy 5
Muscetta, Carlo 22

Nabokov, Vladimir 15
narrative (sociological term) 5, 43, 58, 59, 69, 71, 72, 73, 79, 81, 82, 88, 120, 165–66, 197
Narratori stranieri tradotti (book series)
Neoavanguardia 21, 36, 46–47, 51, 87, 138–54, 193–95, 199–200, 202, 206
neorealism 12, 13, 16, 18–20, 22, 26, 33–35, 45n, 54, 176
neorealist *see* neorealism
Neri, Guido 144–46, 151
Neruda, Pablo 22, 29, 32–33, 35
New Criticism movement 112
New Movement 98, 106

Nida, Eugene 101
Nobel prize 22, 63, 83, 98, 197, 208
nouveau roman 36
Nouvelle Revue Française, La (NRF) 20, 92
Noventa, Giacomo 45
Novissimi, I 36, 65, 72, 102, 103, 142–43
NUE [Nuova Universale Economica] (book series) 125
Nuova Accademia (publishing house) 145
Nuova Corrente (journal) 61

O'Hara, Frank 189
O'Neill Alexandre 136–37, 144
Ocampo, Victoria 127
Officina (journal) 35
Oliva, Renato 98n
Olson, Charles 99, 189–90
Omnibus (book series) 39
Orelli, Giorgio 78
Orten, Jiří 140–41
Oscar (book series) 48, 99, 129, 187, 208
Oxford University Press (publishing house) 31

Paci, Francesca Romana 103
Panetta, Ester 196
Panzieri, Raniero 130
Paragone (journal) 35, 37, 107, 110, 178
paratexts 7, 55, 58, 66, 73, 81, 105, 116, 119, 120, 123, 152, 160, 164, 165, 167, 172, 175, 187, 188, 196, 197
paratextual *see* paratexts
Pascoli, Giovanni 36, 113
Pasolini, Pier Paolo 21, 35–37, 45, 47, 87
Pasternak, Boris 34, 37, 133
Paulhan, Jean 20–21
Pavese, Cesare 19, 22, 23n, 24n, 25
Pelican Books (publishing house) 31
Penna, Sandro 37, 45
Pennati, Camillo 91, 98n, 104–06
Perosa, Sergio 213
Pintor, Giaime 22–25, 120
Pivano, Fernanda 85, 109
Pizzuto, Antonio 57
Plath, Sylvia 114, 117
Poeti stranieri tradotti da poeti italiani (book series) 22, 31–35, 94, 118

poet-translator 125, 153, 160–62, 168–70, 184–85, 188, 196, 198, 202
Poggioli, Renato 15, 33, 70, 131, 184
Polillo, Sergio 206, 207n, 208n
Politecnico, Il (journal) 16–17, 134
Ponchiroli, Daniele 38
Ponge, Francis 43, 92–93, 163
Pontani, Filippo Maria 53, 63n, 64, 65n, 71n, 95, 139, 140n, 196
Popa, Vasko 96–97
Porta, Antonio 72, 142, 145, 193n, 194
postmodernism 99, 172
Pound, Ezra 27, 28n, 29, 45, 57–65, 69, 70n, 71, 75–77, 83–86, 98, 107, 109, 150, 153, 172, 173, 177
Prampolini, Giacomo 14, 185
Praz, Mario 60, 124–25, 128–29
Premio Città di Alghero (prize) 43
Premio Etna-Taormina (prize) 134
Premio Monselice (prize) 95n, 114
Prévert, Jacques 30, 99
Prezzolini, Giuseppe 57
Primato (journal) 40
Pulitzer prize 109, 147

Quaderni della Fenice (book series), 211
quaderno di traduzioni 86, 125, 155n, 156, 159–64, 165, 168, 169, 171, 173–75, 177, 183–86, 188, 190–91, 196, 202, 210
Quasimodo, Salvatore 19, 22, 26, 28, 32, 33, 37, 40, 45, 86–87, 104, 123, 207
Que Sais-je? Presses universitaires de France (publishing house) 31
Queneau, Raymond 146
Questo e altro (journal) 87, 189

Raboni, Giovanni 41, 87, 210–11
Raimondi, Giuseppe 43–44
Ransom, John Crowe 111–17, 182
Ravegnani, Giuseppe 39, 40, 44
Rebora, Clemente 37, 65
Recam (publishing house) 31
Resistance movement 33, 35, 79, 93, 134
Resto del Carlino, Il (journal) 140, 196
Reverdy, Pierre 145, 163, 172

Rexroth, Kenneth 90
Riba, Carles 135–36
Rilke, Rainer Maria 14n, 15, 22, 83, 123, 161
Rimbaud, Arthur 125, 161
Rinaldi, Antonio 43
Ripellino, Angelo Maria 15n, 34, 131–33, 135, 155n
Risi, Nelo 20, 65, 91
Ritsos, Yiannis 64, 94–96, 139–40
Rivista IB (journal), 113
Rizzoli (publishing house) 92–93, 97, 129, 207
Roethke, Theodore 97, 109–11
Rosselli, Aldo 27
Rossi, Alberto 127
Rossi, Aldo 110
Rossi, Rosa 199, 210n
Różewicz, Tadeusz 186

Saba, Umberto 22, 24, 36, 40, 45, 86–87, 207
Saggiatore, Il (publishing house) 90, 126, 134, 205
Salinas, Pedro 15, 64, 70
Sanesi, Roberto 187–88
Sangiglio, Crescenzio 196
Sanguineti, Edoardo 127, 130n, 141
Sansone, Giuseppe 136
Sansoni (publishing house) 37
Saroyan, Aram 197
Sbarbaro, Camillo 25, 28–29, 37, 65
Scarfoglio, Carlo 75–77
Scheiwiller, Giovanni 4, 14–15, 25, 50, 57–58
Scheiwiller, Vanni 4, 11, 27, 28–29, 37, 50–53, 56–82, 84, 127, 148, 169–71, 173, 206, 212
Scheiwiller (publishing house) 2, 4, 5, 8, 13, 27, 30, 34, 37, 47, 50, 53, 55–82, 96, 100, 119–22, 134, 140, 145, 153, 156, 205, 211
Schwarz (publishing house) 27
Scotellaro, Rocco 18, 22
Seferis, Giorgos 64, 94–95, 208
Sela-Sheffy, Rakefet 171
Serao, Matilde 75

Index

Sereni, Vittorio 20, 21, 24–25, 28–29, 34, 39, 43–48, 58, 65, 72, 78, 82, 86–99, 105n, 106n, 107n, 109n, 111n, 112–13, 115n, 116n, 117, 160, 162, 163n, 164, 166–168, 186, 187n, 207, 208n, 210–11
Sigma Books (publishing house) 31
Sinisgalli, Leonardo 21, 24–25, 40, 87
Skey, Malcom 213
social capital 59, 70, 78, 86, 128
social network analysis (SNA) 6–7
Sollazzo, Lucia 119n, 151, 152n
Solmi, Renato 32n
Solmi, Sergio 24, 61, 87, 120, 122, 125, 146, 170–71, 191
Spaziani, Maria Luisa 126, 145, 183
Specchio, Lo 11, 21, 25–26, 29, 39–46, 48, 50–51, 81–99, 117, 122, 139, 160, 162–64, 168, 186, 207–09
Spettatore italiano, Lo (journal) 175
Spivak, Gayatri 165, 167
Stagione (journal) 61
Stevens, Wallace 33
Strada, La (journal) 18
Strada, Vittorio 130
Supercoralli (book series) 122, 125–26, 147, 174, 209
Sur (journal) 127
Surrealism 36, 39, 92, 96, 145, 163
symbolic capital 5, 7, 12, 23–24, 27, 32, 44, 49–50, 53, 55, 59, 61,66, 68–69, 119–20, 123–24, 134–35, 144–45, 169, 176, 186, 202, 210

Tanassi, Mario 138
Tel Quel (journal) 142, 156
Tentori, Francesco *see* Tentori Montalto, Francesco
Tentori Montalto, Francesco 30, 68, 185, 188n, 191–93, 211n
Thomas, Dylan 29, 147
Thomas, Edward 147
Tofanelli, Arturo 40
Togliatti, Palmiro 17
Tomasi di Lampedusa, Giuseppe 37
Tornasole, il (book series) 87, 207
Toulet, Paul-Jean 126, 172, 183

Trakl, Georg 14n
translation notebook *see* quaderno di traduzioni
Traverso, Leone 15, 63n, 73–74, 83, 155n, 174, 178, 180–81
Turazza, Anselmo 123n
Tynyanov, Yury 113
Tyutchev, Fyodor 122, 130–31, 133

Ungaretti, Giuseppe 14, 28–29, 37, 40, 43, 45, 61, 66, 69, 78, 84, 86, 87, 92–93, 155n, 164, 174, 207
Urania (book series) 39, 105n

Valduga, Patrizia 211
Valeri, Diego 15, 41, 61, 87, 125, 156, 160–62, 191
Valéry, Paul 63
Vallecchi (publishing house) 14n, 45, 64n, 73
Venturi, Franco 131
Venuti, Lawrence 101n, 102, 105n
verri, il (journal) 20, 36–37, 51
Vigolo, Giorgio 21, 24–25
Vittorini, Elio 16–17, 19, 22, 39, 43, 83, 84, 120, 125, 134, 186
Volpini, Valerio 35
von Hoffmannsthal, Hugo 14n

Wain, John 146
Whitman, Walt 20, 35, 110
Wilcock, Rodolfo 8, 126–28
Williams, William Carlos 34, 63, 87–88, 90–91, 99, 106, 109, 189
Winkler, Eugen Gottlob 123
Wordsworth, William 110, 172
Wright, David 146
Wright, Judith 213

Yeats, W.B. 14n, 15, 109, 124, 125, 172, 176, 180
Yesenin, Sergei 14, 15n

Zanzotto, Andrea 21, 78, 87, 207, 208n
Zignani, Franci 149
Zveteremich, Pietro 131–32

www.ingramcontent.com/pod-product-compliance
Lightning Source LLC
Chambersburg PA
CBHW071406300426
44114CB00016B/2196